Philippe de Montebello

and

The Metropolitan Museum of Art

1977–2008

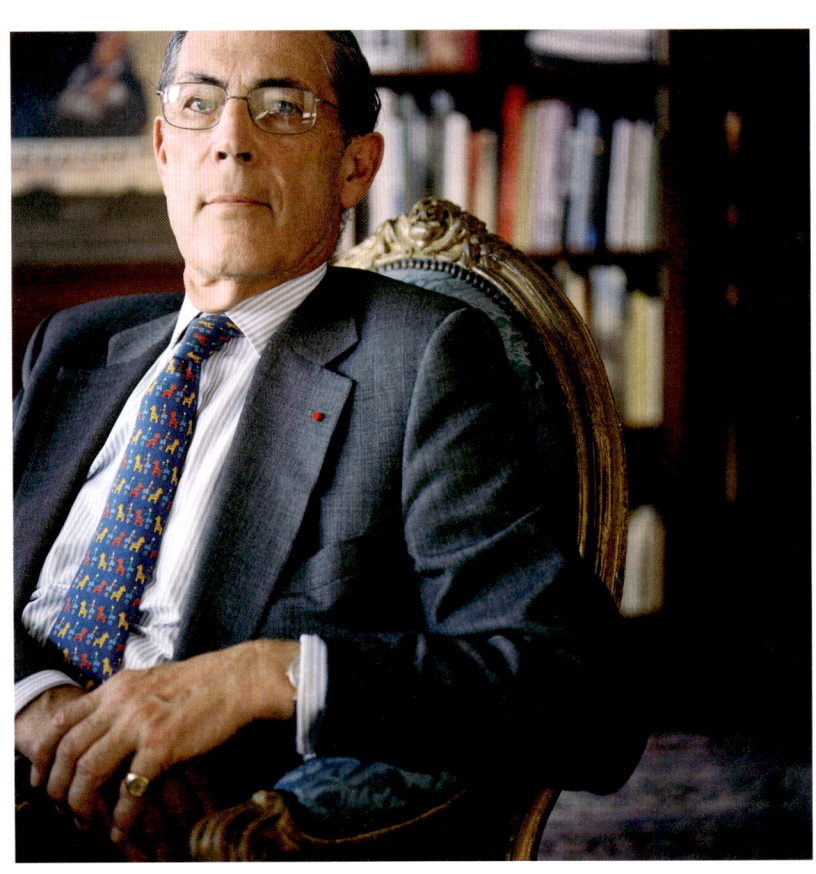

Philippe de Montebello

and

The Metropolitan Museum of Art

1977–2008

James R. Houghton

and Members of the Staff

The Metropolitan Museum of Art, New York

Yale University Press, New Haven and London

Published by The Metropolitan Museum of Art, New York

Conceived by Mahrukh Tarapor, Katharine Baetjer, and John P. O'Neill

John P. O'Neill, Publisher and Editor in Chief
Gwen Roginsky, General Manager of Publications
Margaret Chace, Managing Editor
Ruth Lurie Kozodoy, Senior Editor, with Margaret Donovan
Bruce Campbell, Designer
Christopher Zichello, Production Manager
Robert Weisberg, Assistant Managing Editor

Copyright © 2009 by The Metropolitan Museum of Art, New York

All rights reserved. No part of this publication may be reproduced or transmitted in any form or by any means, electronic or mechanical, including photocopying, recording, or any information storage and retrieval system, without permission in writing from the publisher.

Unless otherwise noted, photography is by The Photograph Studio, The Metropolitan Museum of Art. Additional photograph credits appear on p. 169.

Typeset in Adobe Garamond Pro
Printed on GardaPat Kiara 170gsm
Separations by Professional Graphics, Inc., Rockford, Illinois
Printed by Brizzolis Arte en Gráficas, Madrid
Bound by Encuadernación Ramos, S.A., Madrid
Printing and binding coordinated by Ediciones El Viso, S.A., Madrid

Cover: Philippe de Montebello in the Leon Levy and Shelby White Court, Metropolitan Museum, April 2007; *frontispiece*: Philippe de Montebello in his office, April 2007 (photographs by Damon Winter/ The New York Times/Redux)

Cataloging-in-Publication data is available from the Library of Congress.

ISBN 978-1-58839-340-1 (hc: The Metropolitan Museum of Art)
ISBN 978-0-300-15424-5 (hc: Yale University Press)

CONTENTS

Foreword
James R. Houghton / vii

Authors / viii

Introduction
Katharine Baetjer / x

Note to the Reader / xiv

ANTIQUITY
Dorothea Arnold / 3
Joan Aruz / 10
Carlos A. Picón / 16

MEDIEVAL EUROPE
Peter Barnet / 23

EUROPE FROM THE RENAISSANCE
Everett Fahy / 31
Keith Christiansen / 34
Walter Liedtke / 38
Colta Ives / 42
George R. Goldner / 45
Ian Wardropper / 48
Thomas P. Campbell / 56
Dita Amory / 61
Laurence B. Kanter / 65

AMERICAN ART
Morrison H. Heckscher / 69

MUSICAL INSTRUMENTS
J. Kenneth Moore / 75

MUSIC AT THE MUSEUM
Hilde Limondjian / 83

ARMS AND ARMOR
Stuart W. Pyhrr / 89
Donald J. La Rocca / 92

ASIAN ART
Maxwell K. Hearn / 97
James C. Y. Watt / 101

ISLAMIC ART
Stefano Carboni / 105

AFRICA, OCEANIA, AND THE AMERICAS
Julie Jones / 113
Alisa LaGamma / 115
Eric Kjellgren / 119
Virginia-Lee Webb / 122

THE MODERN ERA
Gary Tinterow / 127

PHOTOGRAPHS
Malcolm Daniel / 135

COSTUME
Harold Koda / 143

PUBLICATIONS
John P. O'Neill / 151

Index / 155

Photograph Credits / 169

FOREWORD

More than forty-five years ago—much as I hate to admit that passage of time—a French-born, Harvard-educated art historian arrived at The Metropolitan Museum of Art in search of employment as a curator. What he found here was not only his first job, but his lifelong professional home. And what the Met found in him was not only an employee, but a future leader—indeed, a future legend. His name is Philippe de Montebello.

What a gift he proved to be to his adopted country, and to the institution! Fate somehow brought us together many years later to serve at the very same time—he as its longest-serving director, and I as the chairman who was privileged to lead the Board of Trustees during the final decade of his tenure.

It would be an understatement to say that Philippe refined and remodeled the Museum. Under his stewardship the Met more than doubled in size, vastly increased its collections, reinstalled its galleries, and mounted some of the most acclaimed and widely attended exhibitions in its history. Just consider the staggering beauty of the Museum's new Greek and Roman galleries, the galleries for Byzantine art, the expanded galleries for nineteenth- and twentieth-century European paintings and sculpture, and the newly renovated American Wing. Then, consider how these spaces looked before Philippe put his hand to their refinement. Only after such a comparison can one begin to appreciate the enormous impact he had on the nation's finest art museum, as well as on the standards that visitors and museum professionals alike now routinely expect.

Today the Met's galleries sparkle as never before, animated with new life, beauty, and meaning. Its publications programs provide a priceless and permanent art library to millions, while the ever-expanding website affords to students the world over an even wider access to art and its history. The Museum's on-site programs have made available—and continue to offer—enlightenment and instruction for generations of students, teachers, and day-to-day visitors. There is no accurate way to measure how many tens of millions of people have enjoyed their most dramatic, enriching, and indelible experiences of art as a direct result of Philippe de Montebello's enormous influence, powerful leadership, and, of course, distinctive, mellifluous recorded voice as their particular guide.

Today, cultural institutions across America face especially challenging times. Economic downturn has exacted a particularly severe toll on museums, and many gird for even more daunting challenges to come. Although Philippe retired from the Met in 2008, his impact and example remain crucially important to its future. That is because his standards and spirit continue to guide those who worked with him and walk in his footsteps.

The Met's special farewell tribute came with the 2008 exhibition "The Philippe de Montebello Years: Curators Celebrate Three Decades of Acquisitions," which highlighted many of the director's triumphs in his effort to build the Museum's collections. For the show, curators selected works of art from among the numerous objects whose acquisition their director so passionately supported. Very much like the man himself, as this publication attests, the exhibitions demonstrated his dazzling array of interests, his lifetime of support for his professional staff, his exquisite and diverse taste, and his indomitable determination—qualities that resonate in this book, as they endure in the Museum he blessed for so long with his leadership.

James R. Houghton
Chairman, Board of Trustees
The Metropolitan Museum of Art

AUTHORS

Dita Amory
Acting Associate Curator in Charge and Administrator
Robert Lehman Collection

Dorothea Arnold
Lila Acheson Wallace Chairman
Department of Egyptian Art

Joan Aruz
Curator in Charge
Department of Ancient Near Eastern Art

Katharine Baetjer
Curator
Department of European Paintings

Peter Barnet
Michel David-Weill Curator in Charge
Department of Medieval Art and The Cloisters

Thomas P. Campbell
Director and Chief Executive Officer
Former Curator, Department of European Sculpture and
Decorative Arts, and former Supervising Curator,
Antonio Ratti Textile Center

Stefano Carboni
Former Curator and Administrator, Department of Islamic Art
Director, Art Gallery of Western Australia

Keith Christiansen
Jayne Wrightsman Curator
Department of European Paintings

Malcolm Daniel
Curator in Charge
Department of Photographs

Everett Fahy
John Pope-Hennessy Chairman
Department of European Paintings

George R. Goldner
Drue Heinz Chairman
Department of Drawings and Prints

Maxwell K. Hearn
Douglas Dillon Curator
Department of Asian Art

Morrison H. Heckscher
Lawrence A. Fleischman Chairman
Departments of American Art

Colta Ives
Curator
Department of Drawings and Prints

Julie Jones
Andrall E. Pearson Curator in Charge
Department of the Arts of Africa, Oceania, and the Americas

Laurence B. Kanter
Senior Consultant and former Curator in Charge, Robert Lehman
Collection
Lionel Goldfrank III Curator of Early European Art, Yale University
Art Gallery

Eric Kjellgren
Evelyn A. J. Hall and John A. Friede Associate Curator
Department of the Arts of Africa, Oceania, and the Americas

Harold Koda
Curator in Charge
The Costume Institute

Alisa LaGamma
Curator
Department of the Arts of Africa, Oceania, and the Americas

Donald J. La Rocca
Curator
Department of Arms and Armor

Walter Liedtke
Curator
Department of European Paintings

Hilde Limondjian
General Manager
Concerts & Lectures

J. Kenneth Moore
Frederick P. Rose Curator in Charge
Department of Musical Instruments

John P. O'Neill
Publisher and Editor in Chief
Editorial Department

Carlos A. Picón
Curator in Charge
Department of Greek and Roman Art

Stuart W. Pyhrr
Arthur Ochs Sulzberger Curator in Charge
Department of Arms and Armor

Gary Tinterow
Engelhard Chairman
Department of Nineteenth-Century, Modern, and Contemporary Art

Ian Wardropper
Iris and B. Gerald Cantor Chairman
Department of European Sculpture and Decorative Arts

James C. Y. Watt
Brooke Russell Astor Chairman
Department of Asian Art

Virginia-Lee Webb
Research Curator, Photograph Study Collection
Department of the Arts of Africa, Oceania, and the Americas

INTRODUCTION

Born in Paris in 1936 and educated there through the baccalaureate, Philippe de Montebello came to New York with his family in 1950. He was graduated magna cum laude from Harvard College in 1958 with a B.A. in art history—he wrote his thesis on Eugène Delacroix—and in 1961 entered New York University's Institute of Fine Arts, where he presented an M.A. paper on the sixteenth-century French artist Jean Cousin the Elder. He abandoned academic studies in favor of a museum career on February 1, 1963, when he joined the staff of The Metropolitan Museum of Art as a curatorial assistant in the Department of European Paintings, doubtless on the recommendation of curator Theodore Rousseau Jr. Rousseau found the average American graduate student of art history woefully unsophisticated, and one imagines that he took the name de Montebello and the slight accent as evidence that their owner's worldview was wider than that of most students matriculated at the Institute. Certainly this is what he would have been looking for, together with the language skills the new curatorial assistant brought to his post.

It is often remarked that the Metropolitan Museum raises its own curators and directors, and such was the case with P. de M., who was appointed assistant curator in European Paintings in 1967 and promoted to associate curator in 1968. Even so, in the sixties salaries were very low. He resigned effective June 30, 1969, to become director of the Museum of Fine Arts, Houston; there he gained the practical experience required of an administrator of a sizable American museum. In 1974 he left Houston and returned to the Metropolitan Museum as vice director for curatorial and educational affairs under Ted Rousseau, who by then was chief curator, and Director Thomas Hoving.

The Metropolitan had embarked upon a new chapter in P. de M.'s absence. It first welcomed over five million visitors in 1969, and, celebrating its centennial on April 13, 1970, began a second century amid changes of every kind. After the death of Robert Lehman in 1969, ownership of his splendid collection was transferred from the Robert Lehman Foundation to the Metropolitan, which assumed the obligation to construct a suitable building. Arthur Houghton succeeded Lehman as chairman of the Board, while Douglas Dillon was elected its president. The firm of Kevin Roche John Dinkeloo and Associates had been engaged to develop a master plan that included enclosing the Temple of Dendur, providing new quarters for The Michael C. Rockefeller Memorial Collection of Primitive Art, and increasing the size of The American Wing; additionally, centennial activities stimulated a renewal of interest in the arts of the twentieth century; and thus the Museum began a series of massive building projects.

October 15, 1976, would mark the completion of Phase One of the Egyptian reinstallation, which comprised thirteen galleries housing the earliest and latest works—from the Paleolithic period through Dynasty 11 and from Dynasty 30 through the Coptic era. The aim was to put forty-five thousand objects on view, using primary galleries and parallel study spaces, in an arrangement both contextual and chronological. The installation, funded entirely by Lila Acheson Wallace, was a critical and popular success. In time there would be ten additional rooms and in their midst the Temple of Dendur in The Sackler Wing—overlooking, and overlooked by, Central Park, through a curtain wall at the Museum's north end designed by Roche Dinkeloo. Simultaneously, The American Wing was expanded and The Michael C. Rockefeller Wing constructed at the south end.

The plan accompanying all this building was to refine rather than enlarge the collections and to introduce a discretionary admission charge that would assure financial stability. However, an ambitious exhibition program, devised for the Museum's anniversary year, had raised expectations on the part of the public that would not be put to rest. It would perhaps be reasonable to yoke the birth of the so-called blockbuster exhibition with the program of exhibitions staged, principally in 1970, to mark the centennial year: "New York Painting and Sculpture: 1940–1970," "The Year 1200," "19th-Century America," "Before Cortes," and "Masterpieces of Fifty Centuries." The last-named consisted of works of art from the permanent collection, but all the others were loan shows whose successes were predicated upon borrowing works of art in the hundreds from public and private collections in the United States, Central America, and Western Europe. Ultimately of greater importance to P. de M. was a 1972 agreement to organize exhibitions of mutual interest with the Musées de France, which first bore fruit in 1974 with "Masterpieces of

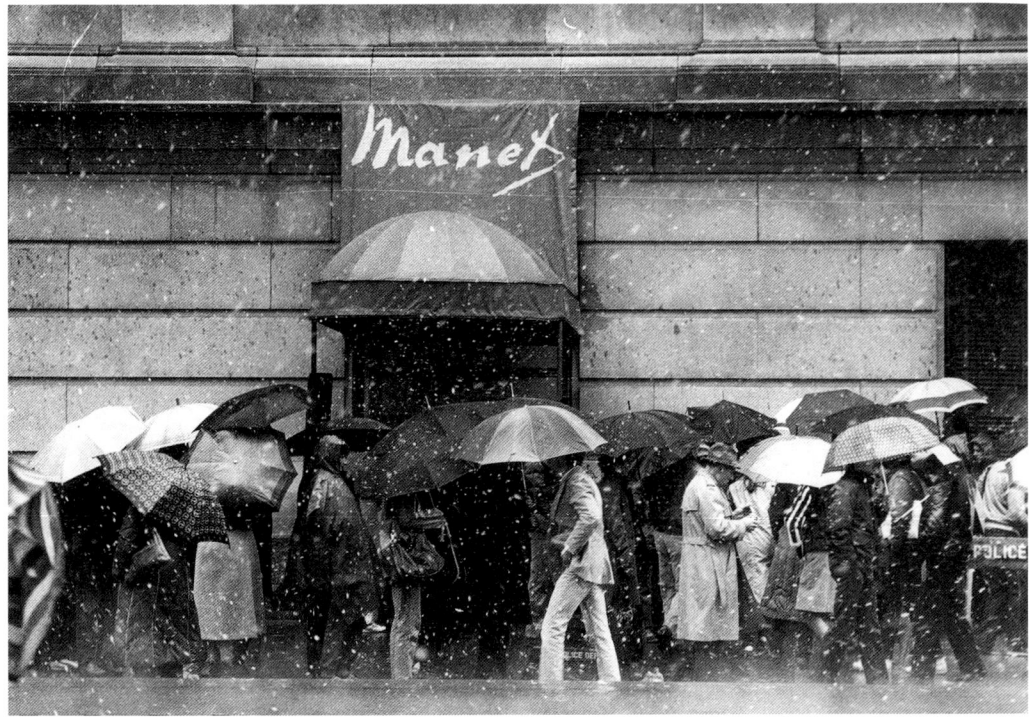

1. Outside the Museum's south entrance, visitors wait for admission to "Manet," November 1983.

Tapestry" and "The Impressionist Epoch." Also in 1974 a similar understanding was reached with the Soviet Union (as it then was), and in 1975 "From the Lands of the Scythians: Ancient Art from the Museums of the U.S.S.R." was staged here while a reciprocal show of European and American paintings went to Leningrad and Moscow. The Hoving era closed in 1976 with "Two Worlds of Andrew Wyeth: Kuerners and Olsons," organized by the outgoing director himself, and "Age of Spirituality: Late Antique and Early Christian Art, Third to Seventh Century," one of the most beautiful and instructive of our exhibitions.

Tom Hoving had bought Claude Monet's *Garden at Sainte-Adresse* in 1967, and both Diego Velázquez's *Juan de Pareja* and the Euphronios Krater (which before P. de M.'s watch ended would be returned to Italy) in 1971. He also was instrumental in securing the Michael C. Rockefeller and Robert Lehman collections. However, he will be remembered not so much for the works of art that were acquired (and disposed of) as for his rapid pace and expansionist ambitions. Early in 1977 Hoving announced his intention to leave the Museum, and a search committee of five trustees led by Richard S. Perkins was appointed and given its first brief: to determine whether the institution would be best served by the addition of a paid president who would also be chief executive officer and have overall administrative responsibility, leaving the director free to devote himself exclusively to curatorial and educational affairs. The decision would be in the affirmative.

P. de M., who became the acting director on July 1, 1977, would eventually become the Museum's longest-serving director as well as its chief executive officer—a symbol of stability, civility, and steady governance in the art world, with titles suiting him so well that we tend to forget he assumed one of them relatively recently. On April 18, 1978, the Board of Trustees elected the Museum's first paid president and chief executive officer, William B. Macomber, former United States ambassador to Turkey, whose background was as an administrator at the State Department. The search committee then chose P. de M. as director, a decision affirmed by the Board on May 25. Mr. Macomber presided over an internal reorganization, effectively bifurcating what had been a unitary management structure and separating those responsible for the collection from a much larger administrative and support staff. In the autumn of 1983 Mr. Dillon retired from his position as chairman of the Board, and he and his fellow trustees elected J. Richardson Dilworth, a trustee since 1961 who was greatly admired by colleagues and staff alike. Sadly, his tenure would be short. When Mr. Macomber retired, his successor, chosen in 1986, was William H. Luers, a career diplomat who was serving as ambassador to Czechoslovakia. In 1987 Arthur Ochs Sulzberger, publisher of the *New York Times*, was unanimously elected chairman in succession to Mr. Dilworth. An adjustment ensued leading to a new parity in the relationship of president and director, whose joint statements reflected, in their words, "the strength of their partnership." After seismic changes of various kinds, the Museum entered upon a period of greater stability.

Early in his career as director, P. de M. presided over the enormously successful run of the exhibition "Treasures of Tutankhamun" as well as openings of the Temple of Dendur in The Sackler Wing; The American Wing and the newly enclosed Charles Engelhard Court (whose most recent rebirth we witness as I write); the Douglas Dillon Galleries and The Astor Court; and The Michael C. Rockefeller Wing (also retransformed in very recent times). Projects initiated in the early 1980s included the reinstallation of paintings by Giovanni Battista Tiepolo at the top of the Great Hall staircase and of the Assyrian reliefs in a gallery adjoining the Great Hall balcony. New paintings conservation and education facilities were completed. The Museum secured the promised gift of Muriel Kallis Steinberg Newman's collection, especially strong in postwar American pictures; acquired, installed, and published Jack and Belle Linsky's European old master paintings and decorative arts; and continued to receive magnificent gifts from Jayne and Charles Wrightsman. With colleagues foreign and domestic, we organized, among many other splendid exhibitions, "The Great Bronze Age of China," "The Vatican Collections: The Papacy and Art," and, notably, "Manet" (fig. 1), "Van Gogh in Arles," and "Degas."

The energies of the Museum's Board and senior management and of P. de M. personally during his first full decade as director were taken up chiefly with envisioning and financing the southwest wing, the last major component of the Eighty-second Street building. The new structure, built in partnership with the city of New York, would be dedicated in great part to the arts of the twentieth century, and now of course of the twenty-first. In the initial stages a very significant grant to underwrite the construction was given in memory of Lila Acheson Wallace by the Wallace Funds. The 110,000-square-foot Lila Acheson Wallace Wing, inaugurated in 1987, would be joined to the old building by the Henry R. Kravis Wing for European sculpture and decorative arts, given by that valued trustee and dedicated in 1990. The new construction also embraced the Tisch Galleries and the Iris and B. Gerald Cantor Exhibition Hall, both on the second floor; the much-visited Iris and B. Gerald Cantor Roof Garden, home in the summer months to temporary displays of contemporary sculpture; and the courtyard underwritten by Carroll and Milton Petrie, which houses monumental European sculptures from the permanent collection. I well remember that I was standing by P. de M.'s desk in his old office overlooking Fifth Avenue when he received a telephone call confirming Mr. Petrie's gift.

Areas of collecting that received P. de M.'s closest attention at the time were those judged to be in greatest need of expansion: that is, in addition to twentieth-century art, the arts of Japan, Southeast Asia, and Korea, and photography. To this end the Far Eastern Art Department, as it grew to embrace the Japanese and ancient Chinese galleries, became the vastly enlarged Department of Asian Art, while in 1992 P. de M. brought into being an independent Department of Photographs, with corresponding conservation functions. To close out the decade, the 1989–90 season offered an exceptional program of exhibitions accompanied by characteristically lavish and exacting publications: "The New Vision: Photography Between the World Wars, Ford Motor Company Collection at The Metropolitan Museum of Art"; "Velázquez," in cooperation with the Museo del Prado; "Canaletto," with exceptional loans from Her Majesty Queen Elizabeth II; "Twentieth-Century Modern Masters: The Jacques and Natasha Gelman Collection"; and "From Poussin to Matisse: The Russian Taste for French Painting," from the U.S.S.R.

In furtherance of interests on this continent, "Mexico: Splendors of Thirty Centuries," a traveling exhibition from the Americas of epic scale and, as may be judged from its title, complexity, was organized by the Museum under P. de M.'s leadership and started its historic U.S. tour in New York in the autumn of 1990. Nine months later we celebrated one of the great moments in the Museum's history: the announcement by Walter H. Annenberg of his decision to bequeath to the Metropolitan his Impressionist and Post-Impressionist masterpieces. "Strength going to strength" was the phrase Ambassador Annenberg used to explain his choice of the Metropolitan as the ultimate repository of his collection, which would be exhibited with the storied works given and bequeathed by Mr. and Mrs. H. O. Havemeyer some sixty years earlier.

A great source of pride to P. de M. must certainly be the recent reinstallations, all of which (unlike projects dating to the beginning of his tenure) lie within the Museum's footprint: the Florence and Herbert Irving Galleries in the Florence and Herbert Irving Asian Wing, renamed to honor the Irvings in 2004; the Mary and Michael Jaharis Galleries for Byzantine and medieval art; and the Greek and Roman Galleries, the centerpiece of which is the Leon Levy and Shelby White Court. Indeed, it was a visionary leadership gift from Leon Levy and Shelby White that allowed Philippe to develop his ambitious Greek and Roman Master Plan, some fifteen years in the making.

In 1978, not long after he was appointed director, P. de M. accepted an Alumni Achievement Award from New York University. His honors include but are not limited to that of Knight Commander of the Pontifical Order of Saint Gregory the Great in 1984, Chevalier de la Légion d'Honneur in 1991, and recipient of the Orden de Isabel la Católica in 1992. In a certain sense, these awards followed upon the most successful of our special exhibitions and permanent installations and were marks of the Museum's role as a cultural ambassador in New York and abroad. It is a testimony to the increasing breadth and depth of P. de M.'s interests and the Museum's commitment to the arts of Asia as well as Europe that in 2007 the government of Japan honored him with the Order of the Rising Sun, Silver and Gold Star.

Curatorial department heads and senior curators, together with John P. O'Neill and Hilde Limondjian, have written in the following pages of P. de M.'s leadership and of the enhancement of their programs and collections. I close with the retirement in 1998 of our much esteemed chairman of the Board, Punch Sulzberger, and the election of our current chairman, James R. Houghton. In the following year Bill Luers stepped down and was succeeded as president by former IBM executive David E. McKinney. From this time until his retirement at the end of 2008, P. de M. served not only as director but also as the Museum's chief executive officer. As noted above, the leaders of this Museum have by tradition been trained in its ranks, and such is the case today, as we are guided through a difficult period under the leadership of Emily K. Rafferty, president since 2005, who joined the staff of the Development Office in 1976, and our new director and chief executive officer, Thomas P. Campbell, who has con-

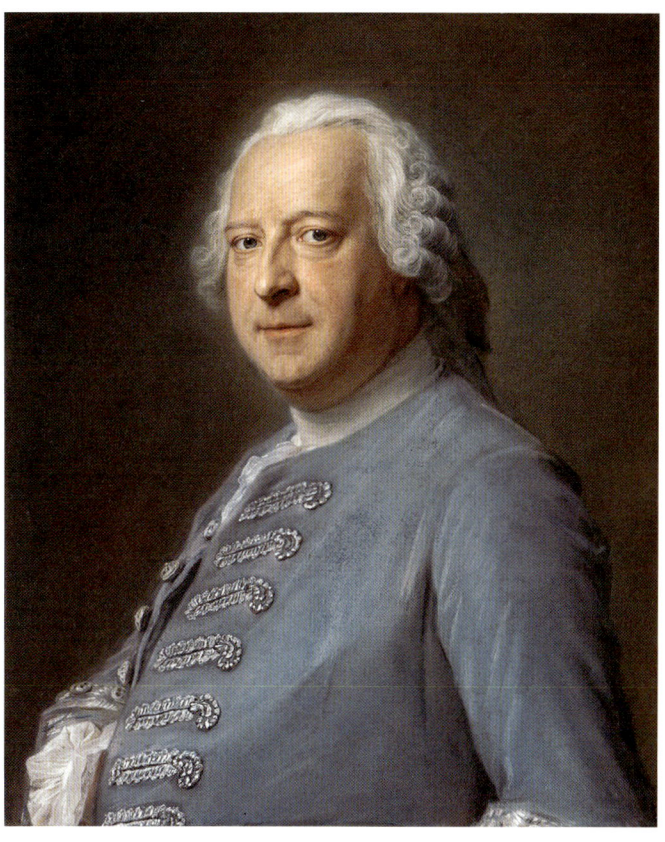

2. Maurice Quentin de La Tour, *Jean Charles Garnier d'Isle*, ca. 1750. Pastel and gouache on paper, laid down on canvas, 25⅜ × 21¼ in. (64.5 × 54 cm). Purchase, Walter and Leonore Annenberg and The Annenberg Foundation Gift, 2002 (2002.439)

tributed to this volume as a tapestry expert and former curator in the Department of European Sculpture and Decorative Arts.

While I do not remember meeting P. de M. for the first time, I can say that I am the only curator here who ever worked for him when he was a curatorial department head (in 1975–76 he was briefly in charge of the Department of European Paintings). He contributed to my growing interest in a variety of eighteenth-century subjects, especially Canaletto, and in recent years indulged my taste for pastels and my desire to acquire them for the Museum. Thus I close with a pastel by Maurice Quentin de La Tour (fig. 2) portraying a Frenchman of impeccable taste and style who in the eighteenth century occupied a position of influence in the cultural realm perhaps roughly equivalent to that of our director emeritus.

Katharine Baetjer

NOTE TO THE READER

All works illustrated are in the collection of The Metropolitan Museum of Art, unless otherwise identified.

Accession numbers, in parentheses, are provided where appropriate to aid in identification of works.

Actual titles are in italic type; assigned names are in roman type.

Unless otherwise noted, dimensions given are in this order: height, width, depth.

Philippe de Montebello

and

The Metropolitan Museum of Art

1977–2008

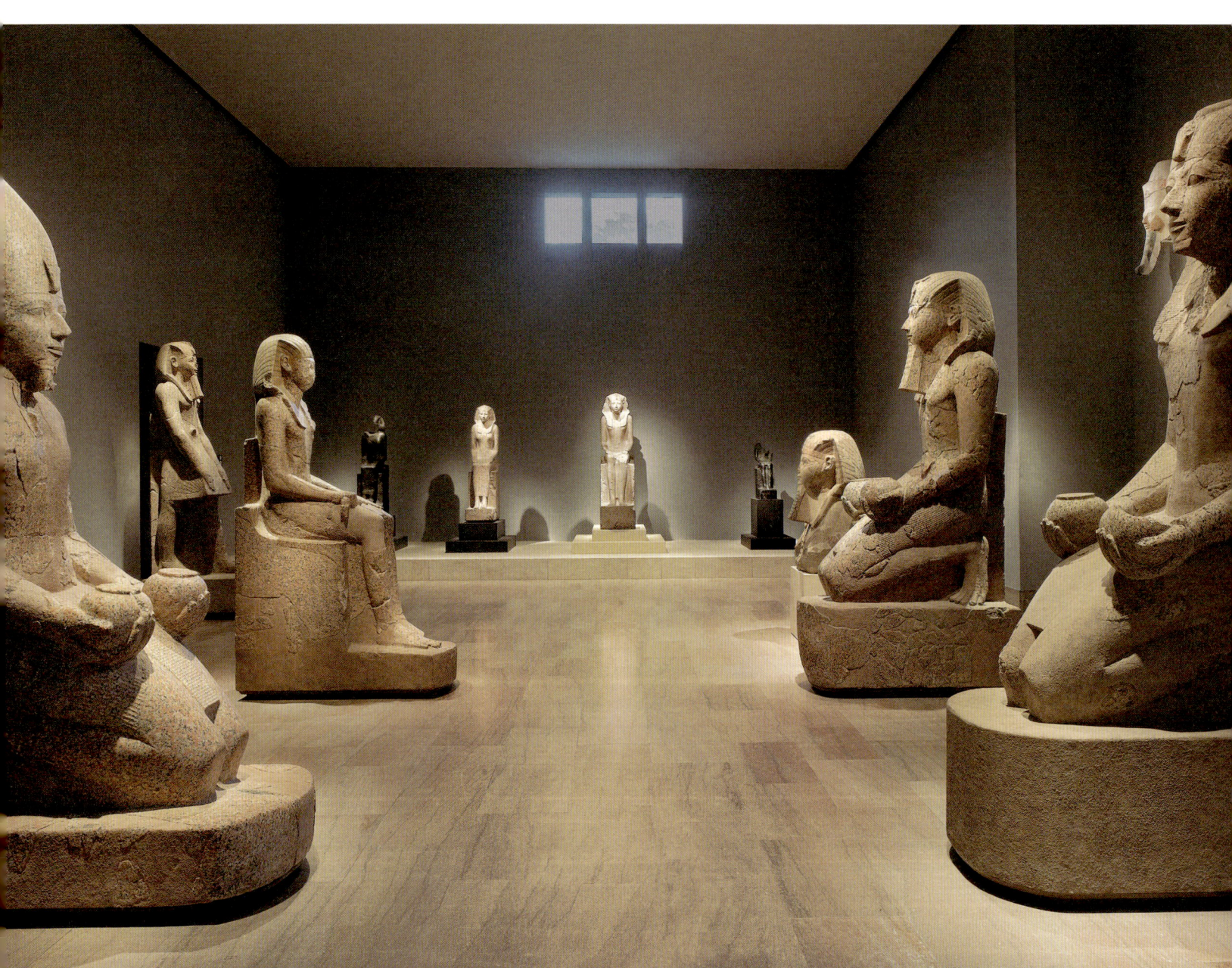

ANTIQUITY

EGYPTIAN ART AT THE METROPOLITAN: INSTALLING THE COLLECTION

Philippe de Montebello's involvement with Egyptian art is best understood in the context of our department's development, and therefore I begin with a thumbnail history of the collection. When the Egyptian department was established in 1906, its holdings consisted most significantly of a few 19th-Dynasty tomb objects. But the fledgling department soon undertook major excavation activities at several sites, which were overseen by the first curator of Egyptian art, Albert M. Lythgoe, and were carried out under the direction of outstanding excavators, chief among them Arthur C. Mace and Herbert E. Winlock. By the time Winlock became director of the Metropolitan in 1932, the collection included well over ten thousand excavated objects; these represented about half the total number of finds from the excavations and had been allotted to the Museum by the Egyptian antiquities authorities following the practice called partage. Most famous among these finds are perhaps the miniature ships and workshop models from the 12th-Dynasty tomb (ca. 1981–1975 B.C.) of the chancellor Meketra and statues (ca. 1470–1453 B.C.) from the 18th-Dynasty temple of the female pharaoh Hatshepsut. Over the years, a number of complete private collections and single pieces were also added to the Museum's holdings.

In what might be thought of as a second period, from the 1940s through the 1960s, the department's principal achievements were the scholarly appraisal and consolidation of this collection carried out by two outstanding scholar-curators, William C. Hayes and Henry George Fischer. Fischer became curator of Egyptian art in 1964, and in that decade, under Museum director James R. Rorimer, a new, third phase began: planning for a definitive display of the entire collection. Not the least of Fischer's achievements was securing sponsorship of the new installation from Lila Acheson Wallace, cofounder of Reader's Digest. A great admirer not only of ancient Egypt but of Fischer and his scholarship, she subsequently also established for him the position of research curator in Egyptology, which he assumed in 1970. The

Opposite: 3. The new Hatshepsut gallery, opened in 2008

young and gifted Christine Lilyquist then became both head of the department and leader of a formidable project—the first post–World War II installation anywhere in the world of a major collection of Egyptian art. A whole generation of young American Egyptologists contributed to this extended effort.

The new installation was accomplished in three stages. The first, of galleries for Predynastic, Old Kingdom, and early Middle Kingdom art and also objects made from the fourth century B.C. to Roman/Coptic times, completed while Mr. de Montebello was vice director for curatorial and educational affairs, opened in 1976. Galleries for works from the later New Kingdom through the Late Period were opened in November 1978, and those dedicated to art of most of the Middle Kingdom and the early New Kingdom were completed in June 1983. In September 1978 the Roman-period Temple of Dendur had also opened to the public in The Sackler Wing. A gift from Egypt to the United States in recognition of financial support for the safeguarding of monuments that otherwise faced submersion behind the new dam at Aswan, the temple had been dismantled at its original site and reerected in its own hall in the Museum. And on December 15, 1978, doors were thrown open to the groundbreaking exhibition "Treasures of Tutankhamun." During these significant events of 1978 and after, Philippe was already director.

The Museum's approach to installing its Egyptian collection is worth examining. In the 1950s in *The Scepter of Egypt*, William C. Hayes had explicated a "historical" treatment of the material: "Armed with a knowledge of the background and purpose of the objects, the visitor or reader will inevitably discover for himself the true, the good, and the beautiful in what he sees. This is . . . the only honest and enduring basis for the enjoyment of a collection" containing, "in addition to pieces instantly recognizable as works of art, many others of a preponderantly utilitarian or ritual nature." It was this philosophy that, two decades later, guided the planners of the Metropolitan installation. The display not only was arranged in chronological order but—its most innovative feature—was set forth as an exhibition of the

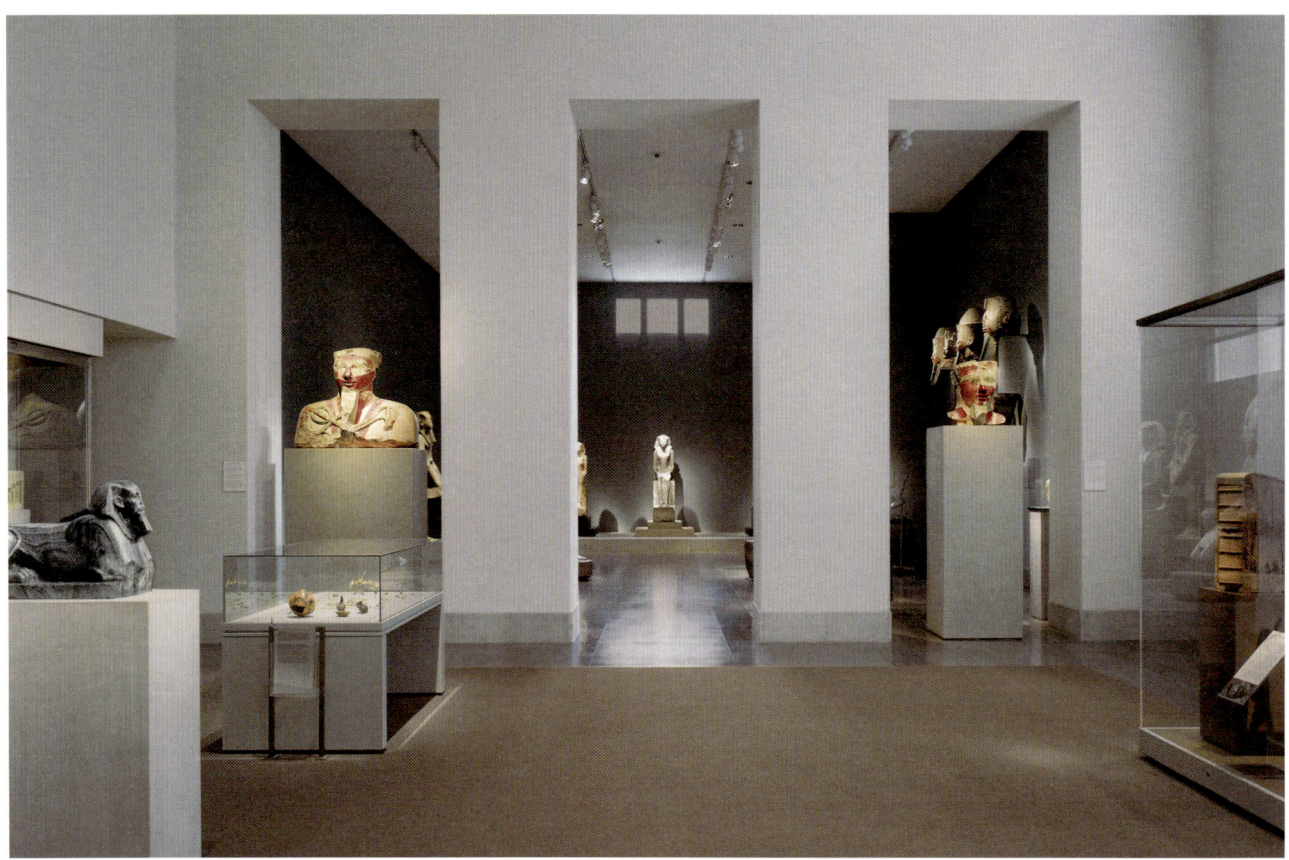

4. View toward the new Hatshepsut gallery from the main Middle Kingdom room, both reinstalled in 2008

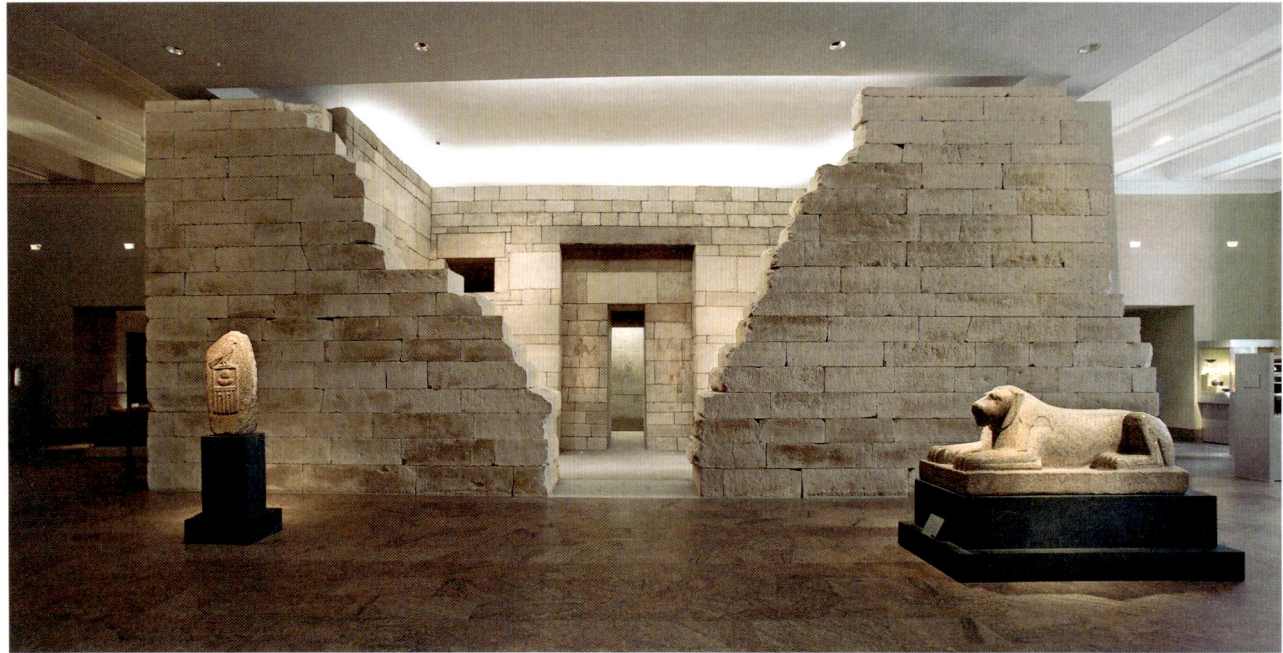

5. The tomb of Perneb in its new architectural setting, completed in 2004. Egyptian, from Saqqara, Old Kingdom (ca. 2381–2323 B.C.). Gift of Edward S. Harkness, 1913 (13.183.3). At right, the statue of a recumbent lion, Old Kingdom, ca. 2575–2450 B.C. Granite, L. 79⅛ in. (201 cm). Purchase, Anonymous Gift, in honor of Annette de la Renta; Annette de la Renta Gift; and Anne and John V. Hansen Egyptian Purchase Fund, 2000 (2000.485)

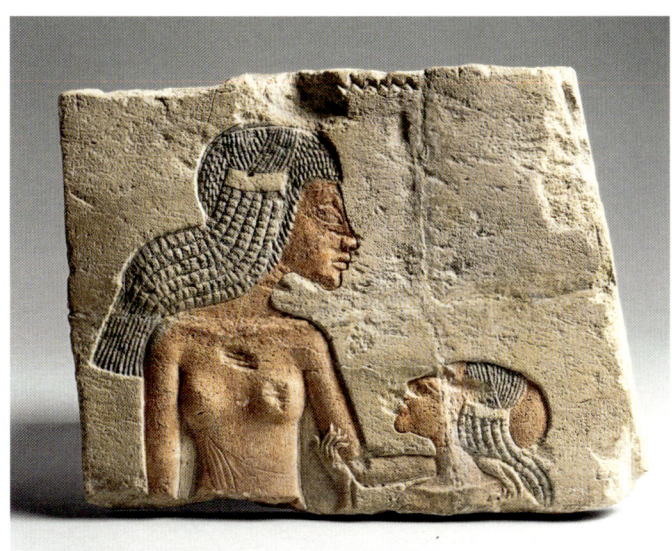

6. *Talatat* (relief block) with depiction of two princesses. Egyptian, New Kingdom, Amarna Period, ca. 1353–1336 B.C. Limestone with paint, 8¾ × 11½ in. (21.2 × 29.2 cm). Gift of Norbert Schimmel, 1985 (1985.328.6)

entire collection. In order to exhibit all the small objects such as beads, pots, baskets, and figurines in the groups in which they had been found during excavation, a two-tiered system was established: major objects were installed in the main rooms, while archaeological finds and pieces of more specialized interest were arranged in tight order on the shelves of secondary study galleries—"open storage."

Compare to this comprehensive display principle the 1978 installation of masterpieces in Egypt's Luxor Museum, as described by its creator, Bernard V. Bothmer: the museum "has display areas on two levels spanned by a free-floating ceiling. . . . All illumination is artificial, which, with walls and ceiling painted gray-black, permits a visual concentration on the works of art on display." Fascinating to this day, Bothmer's Luxor Museum was an early example of the "black style" in Egyptian art installation that continues to entrance visitors in the twenty-first century (although nobody has yet determined what concept of ancient Egyptian culture induces us to enjoy in impenetrable darkness objects from one of the most sun-drenched countries in the world).

The authors of the Metropolitan's postwar installation did not subscribe to the "black style." Windows were (and are) screened only by blinds or scrims, permitting subdued, natural ambient lighting in the galleries, with additional spotlights enhancing the three-dimensionality of the sculptures. To assure an awareness of cultural and historical context, assemblages of pieces displayed in large glass cases predominated over isolated individual works. Atmospheric environments were created by means of beige walls and dark green carpets intended to evoke the Egyptian landscape, both desert sands and lush agricultural land. The six miniature ships from the Meketra find were placed in a row on a watery green glass shelf suggesting the river Nile; the brightly painted Third Intermediate Period coffins from Winlock's excavations at Deir el-Bahri were installed upright in a large space, tomblike but not black-walled. Last but not least, Kevin Roche John Dinkeloo and Associates' airy hall sheltering the Temple of Dendur on its artificial riverbank is flooded with light by day and magically illuminated at night. The great glass wall of this temple space is an early example of the use of design to connect a museum's interior display with the city and park that surround it.

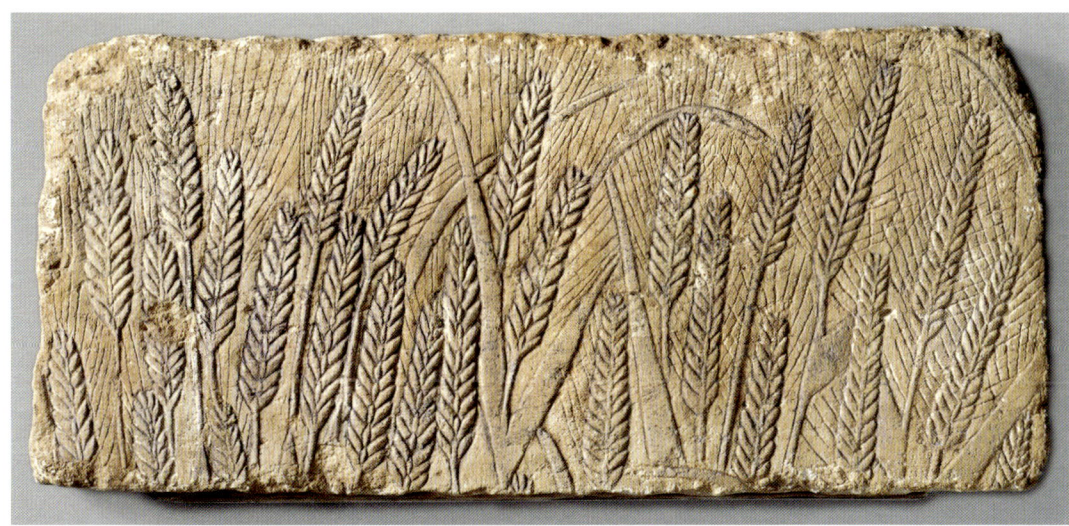

7. *Talatat* (relief block) with depiction of ripe barley. Egyptian, New Kingdom, Amarna Period, ca. 1353–1336 B.C. Limestone with paint, 9¹⁄₁₆ × 20½ in. (23 × 52 cm). Gift of Norbert Schimmel, 1985 (1985.328.24)

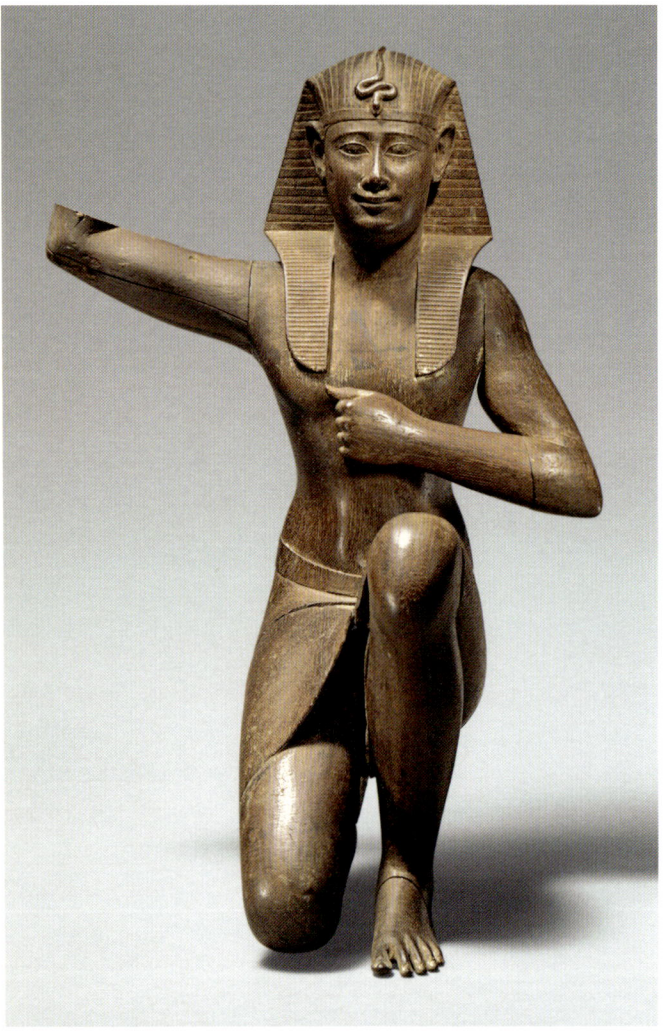

8. Ritual figure. Egyptian, 4th century B.C.–early Ptolemaic Period, 380–246 B.C. Wood, formerly clad with lead sheet, H. 8¼ in. (21 cm). Purchase, Anne and John V. Hansen Egyptian Purchase Fund, and Magda Saleh and Jack Josephson Gift, 2003 (2003.154)

Having joined the Museum staff only in 1985 I have no direct recollections of Philippe's creative participation in the planning and execution of these installations. However, notes and memoranda in the departmental files provide glimpses of his substantial input not only concerning general approach and organization but also on issues of conservation and—above all—aesthetics. I know that to this day Philippe is especially attracted by parts of the original display in which exquisite small objects are grouped together, and he still expresses wonder about the depth of the collection on view in the study rooms. In 1983 he wrote, "The profusion of objects in the study galleries permits the alert visitor to be his own archaeologist and 'discover' in the rows upon rows of amulets, shawabtis, or canopic jars that object that might yet be included in the primary galleries, for this is a living collection that will be ever reassessed and studied." The words are entirely characteristic of this director's approach to the collections in his care. He believes that refining, adapting, and refreshing even the most successful displays is a never-ending process. Since becoming head of the department twenty years ago I have been privileged to experience directly Philippe's method of guiding the care and presentation of the collection—through general directives, a continuing yes-or-no interchange with the curators, and the acute awareness he maintained of everything going on. One felt challenged and supported at the same time.

Displays were reinstalled in the galleries for Amarna art (New Kingdom, fourteenth century B.C.) in 1995 and in the Middle Kingdom and early New Kingdom galleries in 2008. Reconstruction of the front galleries directly adjacent to the Egyptian Wing entrance included creating a new architectural setting for the tomb of Perneb (Old Kingdom, ca. 2381–2323 B.C.), a New York landmark (fig. 5). I will certainly never forget the invigorating back-and-forth of planning sessions with Philippe, architect Kevin Roche, and designer Jeff Daly. Deeply appreciated sponsorship for both the Amarna gallery renewal and the renovation of the entrance spaces came from Judith and Russell Carson, generous benefactors of the Department of Egyptian Art.

Looking back over the refinements in our display of the Egyptian collection during the last twenty years, I believe that the primary goal was to sharpen the focus on individual works of art not by spotlighting them in a dark environment but by careful positioning, so that objects enhance each other and vistas through the rooms create expectation and excitement. A good example is the new arrangement of the Middle Kingdom galleries and the Hatshepsut sculptures. Philippe's interest in this project was especially vivid and persistent; I heard "When will you redo the Hatshepsut gallery?" more than once.

In the 1983 installation, the gallery with our famous royal heads of the Middle Kingdom (ca. 1850–1750 B.C.) and the room of large sculptures from the temple of Hatshepsut at Deir el-Bahri (ca. 1470–1458 B.C.) had been separated by a freestanding display case. On its Middle Kingdom side the jewelry of Princess Sithathoryunet from Lahun (ca. 1850 B.C.) was exhibited, while the side facing the Hatshepsut gallery contained jewelry from tombs of the Hyksos elite (ca. 1640–1550 B.C.). The display thus ingeniously suggested the gallery transition between the Middle and New Kingdom periods, but it also blocked the long view of one of the Museum's great masterpieces, a majestic limestone statue of the seated Hatshepsut (29.3.2). One day as Philippe and I stood before the jewelry case he said, "Why don't you take that away?" It was a truly liberating moment.

In our new display configuration, the enthroned Hatshepsut, of polished, honey-colored stone, can be seen from three galleries away (fig. 4). After taking in the distant view, visitors pass through rooms of works, predominantly small, from the Middle Kingdom; when they finally enter the Hatshepsut gallery, both the beauty of the seated image and the overwhelming size and grandeur of the other sculptures from the temple become apparent (fig. 3). And this gradual approach does not appear to distract visitors from enjoying works in the first two galleries. On the contrary, there are always groups of people looking attentively at the portrait heads, statues, reliefs, and works of minor arts in those rooms. It is true that the clear-cut differentiation between the Middle Kingdom and New Kingdom–18th Dynasty periods is now somewhat less apparent. Rather, the viewer experiences the range of qualities of Egyptian art, encompassing everything from delicate small items and representations of individuals' faces to sculptures of superhuman subjects on a grand scale. A visitor is thus more likely to leave with memories of great artistic expressions of the human condition than with intellectual insight into a historical development; nevertheless, the chronological ordering principle underlying the display is, for those interested, easily discerned.

Of course the period of Philippe's leadership reflects his particular viewpoint not only on how to display the works but on how best to enrich an already extremely rich collection of Egyptian art. The difficulty of finding any type of work not already represented in the collection, together with the appropriate constraints of strict provenance controls, meant the number of acquisitions would be minimal, but we were still able to add about one or two pieces each year. The director's unequaled eye for artistic quality and his common sense about financial possibilities played a decisive role, and so too, naturally, did the willingness of patrons to support purchases. I would like to mention above all Annette de la Renta and the anonymous donor who made possible our acquisition of the large early Old Kingdom lion sculpture (at right in fig. 5), and also Mr. and Mrs. Jonathan P. Rosen, Liana Weindling, Beatrice T. Cooper, Anne W. and David T. Mininberg, Anne and John V. Hansen, and Magda Saleh and Jack Josephson.

I will cite here just two instances in which new acquisitions broadened the scope of the collection. The first concerns the

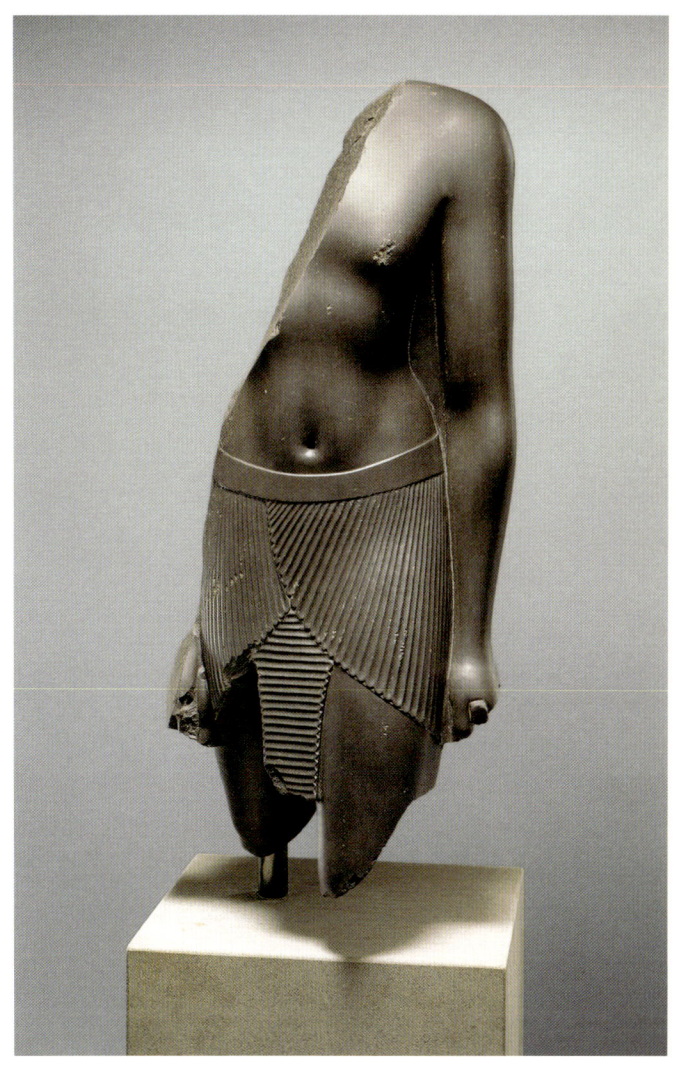

9. Torso of a general. Egyptian, Late Period, 4th century B.C. Schist, H. 24½ in. (62.2 cm). Purchase, Lila Acheson Wallace Gift, Gift of Henry Walters, by exchange, Asher B. Edelman Gift, Judith and Russell Carson Gift, Ernest L. Folk III Bequest, Ludlow Bull Fund, and funds from various donors, 1996 (1996.91)

Metropolitan's collection of works from the Amarna Period (ca. 1353–1336 B.C.). During this era, which was in many respects revolutionary, King Akhenaten directed religious worship to a single, supreme deity, the sun, and artists responded to that innovative call by creating refined works of a hitherto unknown naturalism. In 1992 Sherman E. Lee, former director of the Cleveland Museum of Art, and his wife, Ruth Lee, gave the Museum the fragment of a stone head of Akhenaten that precisely fitted with two other fragments in the Museum since 1957 (1992.227; 57.180.79, 80); they had been recovered in William Flinders Petrie's 1891–92 excavations at the main temple of the king's residence at Amarna. In 2005 we were able to acquire the head of a

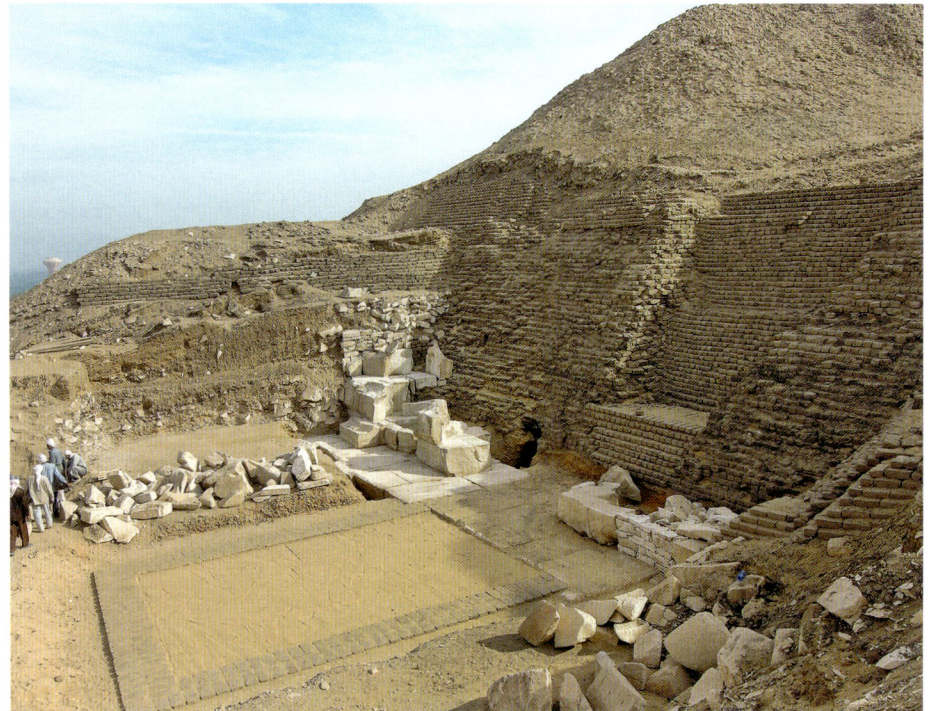

10. The Metropolitan Museum of Art's excavations at Dahshur, Egypt, here showing the north side of the pyramid of King Senwosret III (r. ca. 1878–1840 B.C.). To the right is the brick core of the pyramid with remains of the lowest courses of the limestone casing; in the foreground is the outline of the north chapel; in the back are layers of debris, the lowest layer containing fragments of the wall decoration.

daughter of Akhenaten that comes from a quartzite group of two or several princesses (2005.363), and in 2007 the fragmentary statue of a vizier was added (2007.363). Images of nonroyal individuals such as this one are rare for the period.

Among the very interesting Amarna works are reliefs on limestone blocks, so-called *talatat*, of a standard size of about 21 by 9 inches. They probably came from one of the large temples at Amarna and were transported after Akhenaten's demise and the destruction of his buildings to nearby Hermopolis, where they were reused in later New Kingdom building projects. *Talatat* have found their way into various European and American collections beginning at least as far back as the 1960s, and Norbert Schimmel, one of the twentieth century's most important collectors of ancient art, gave twenty-four extremely beautiful and expressive reliefs of this type to the Museum in 1985 (figs. 6, 7). In 1991 we purchased another eighteen *talatat* from Mr. and Mrs. Jonathan P. Rosen, who then gave eighty-seven others as a gift (1991.240.1–.18; 1991.237.1–.87). Now the largest collection of relief blocks from Amarna temples outside Egypt, the Museum's group will undoubtedly continue to play an important role in studies of that period.

Egyptian works of art from the fourth century B.C. constitute my second example. Although this late period might be thought an unimportant appendix to a glorious earlier history, that is far from the case. During the second half of the fourth century Egypt experienced the all-encompassing changes of conquest by Alexander the Great and the beginnings of a new age under the Macedonian Greek Ptolemies; but before that, in the first half of the century, it had reached yet another cultural peak under the last indigenous pharaohs, especially Nectanebo I and II (r. 380–362 B.C. and 360–343 B.C.) of the 30th Dynasty. Then newly freed from Persian domination and the heavy taxation that went with it, the country regained self-confidence and wealth. Large structures were built and decorated with fine relief carvings in hard stone. Statues of high-quality workmanship commissioned by the rulers and their officials ensured that their likenesses could be seen in temples all across Egypt.

Beginning in 1911 the Metropolitan has acquired a number of outstanding fourth-century-B.C. works, establishing our collection of Egyptian art from this period as one of the most important worldwide. Three further works were added under Philippe's directorship. Most important are a magnificent torso of a general (fig. 9) and a wooden ritual figure of a royal ancestral soul (fig. 8). Both are of strikingly skillful and precise execution, defying any suggestion that Egyptian art deteriorated during this late phase; and both delight the viewer by their sensitive—indeed, sensuous—surface modeling. Without abandoning any of the age-old conventions of Egyptian art, these beautiful works easily hold their own beside famous Greek sculptures

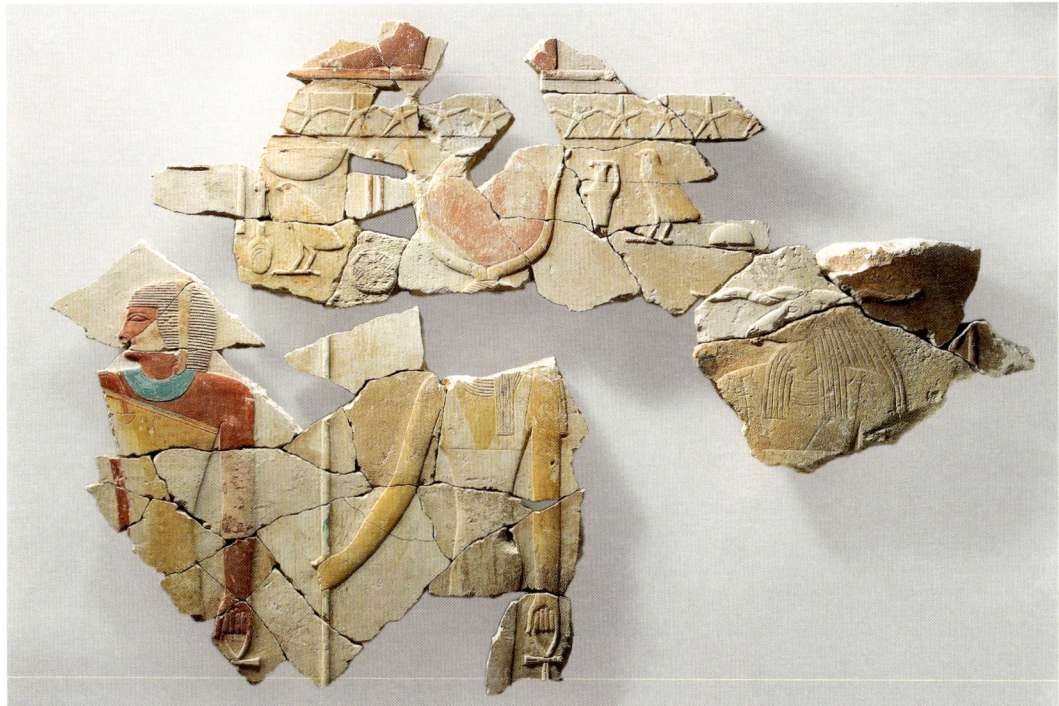

11. Part of the painted limestone relief that decorated a wall of the pyramid temple of Senwosret III. Reconstructed from fragments by Adela Oppenheim

that are contemporaneous. Those of the sculptor Praxiteles first come to mind.

Ten exhibitions, since the 1978 Tutankhamun show, were organized by the Egyptian department during Philippe's directorship. As well, eight volumes on our excavations in Egypt and objects in the collection from these excavations have been published, sponsored largely by the Adelaide Milton de Groot Fund, in memory of the de Groot and Hawley Families, Malcolm H. Wiener, Mrs. Henry A. Grunwald, Mr. and Mrs. James M. Vaughn Jr., and Prof. William Kelly Simpson. And, with the support of the de Groot Fund; the Institute for Bioarchaeology and Dr. Roxie Walker; and Mrs. Henry A. Grunwald, since 1984 a crew of curators and archaeologists has been excavating in Egypt every season. One might ask why a museum department continues to undertake archaeological fieldwork at a time when the division of finds has ceased to be practiced. That objection was never raised by Director de Montebello. He knew that, as the Greek giant Antaios had to touch the earth in order to keep his strength in battle, historians and curators of Egyptian art need constantly to renew their connection with the soil and monuments of Egypt. This refreshing of contact with the ancient culture and its environment opens their eyes to new understandings of the objects under their care, keeps them on their toes in competition with other Egyptologists, and enlivens their discourse with colleagues from institutions here and abroad who also work in the field. Finally, it strengthens relationships with Egyptian scholars and excavators, without whose cooperation neither excavations nor museum exhibitions will take place in the future.

I end this brief overview with two images from the Museum's excavations in Egypt. The first (fig. 10) shows the north side of the pyramid of the pharaoh Senwosret III (r. ca. 1878–1840 B.C.) at Dahshur. No stone still stands of the chapel that was once built against the pyramid's north face. All that remains, embedded in the stratigraphy, is a deposit of limestone fragments, easily recognized by their whiteness. Many of them still carry areas of brightly colored relief. The fragments are what were discarded when New Kingdom quarrymen destroyed the Middle Kingdom buildings and hacked relief decoration off the limestone blocks to make them fit for reuse. However, by carefully gathering these fragments and piecing them together, the department's archaeologists have succeeded in reassembling large parts of the original reliefs (fig. 11). Thus, section by section, destroyed buildings are to some degree reconstructed. "I have made firm what was ruined. I have raised up what was dismembered," reads Hatshepsut's inscription at the Speos Artemidos temple. "Damage will not happen again." It is a good motto for archaeologists and museums alike.

Dorothea Arnold

THE "UNIVERSAL MUSEUM" AND THE ART OF EXCHANGE

The year 2003, a memorable one for the Department of Ancient Near Eastern Art, saw the launching of the special exhibition "Art of the First Cities: The Third Millennium B.C. from the Mediterranean to the Indus," which had been in preparation for five years. Mounted in what may be the world's most intensely urban environment, the show opened at the start of the third millennium of our own era. It is not easy to foster a connection with the remote ancient past, but we hoped that this exhibition, with its focus on the earliest instances in which cultures coalesced into cities and then states, would bring to visitors' attention the foundations on which all societies were built, including our own. The rich and varied artistic traditions presented in "Art of the First Cities" display many common elements but also a great diversity of approach to basic questions about the nature of man and his vision of the world. Such issues have been at the heart of philosophies of history, as was well expressed by Karl Jaspers when he wrote, "The unity of mankind is impressively evident in the fact that similar basic traits of religion, forms of thought, implements, and social forms recur all over the earth," while speaking as well of individual qualities, the "unique creations, breakthroughs and realizations" that "lay the foundations of the humanity that comes after." These thoughts became all the more poignant just a few weeks before our opening, when the Iraq Museum was effectively destroyed and many great works of art from Mesopotamia, often called the cradle of civilization, were tragically lost.

One goal of "Art of the First Cities" was to emphasize the advances achieved during this seminal period for the development of civilizations. But another aspect of the exhibition, articulated in its subtitle—"from the Mediterranean to the Indus"—truly made it unique, as these phenomena were explored not only in the Mesopotamian heartland but also across the vast expanse of Asia. It was this aspect of the show that led Philippe to ask me to speak, along with curators from the British Museum, the Louvre, the Hermitage, and the Staatliche Museen zu Berlin, at the annual meeting of museum directors from Europe and the United States in 2003, which had as its theme the Enlightenment concepts of "understanding the world" and the "universal museum." I spoke about the Indus Valley civilization from the perspective of a curator of ancient Near Eastern art and of "Art of the First Cities," in which we demonstrated that examining cultural interaction is vital to understanding the great advances represented by Mesopotamian civilization. Such ideas were very much in the mind of the great archaeologist Sir John Marshall, who noted in 1924, after announcing the discovery of Mohenjodaro and Harappa, that "India must henceforth be recognized along with Persia, Mesopotamia and Egypt, as one of the most important areas where the civilizing processes of society were initiated and developed . . . long before the heroic age of Priam and Agamemnon and the time of the Vedas." Marshall had begun his career working at Knossos on Crete under Sir Arthur Evans; his finds came in the wake of the great nineteenth-century discoveries by Heinrich Schliemann at Troy and Mycenae, and about the same time as those of Sir Leonard Woolley and Ernst Mackay at Ur and Kish. He was thus well prepared not only for exploring the extraordinary finds emerging far to the east but also for comprehending their relationship to civilizations west of them.

The museum directors delivered papers, published in the *British Museum Magazine* in 2004, each of which provided a different perspective on the "universal museum." Peter-Klaus Schuster suggested that the idea of universal art in literature as expressed by Goethe has become a guiding principle for the Berlin museums as a center for arts and cultures from all over the world, all treated equally and accessible to all. Neil MacGregor pointed out that when Parliament established the British Museum, "the idea of bringing objects together was not that they should simply be seen as objects, but that the contact between them, and the contrasts between them, would generate knowledge. Out of material juxtaposition would come ideas to have a special benefit . . . to generate tolerance." Our director, in distinguishing the Metropolitan Museum from other institutions, emphasized its encyclopedic breadth, which allows the curator to point out interconnections and the visitor to "traverse one gallery to another to see the distinctions as well as the similarities." The broad characters of civilizations can indeed be powerfully experienced in a universal museum such as ours. Still, exploring interconnections has been a challenge, whether creating displays in our permanent installations or crafting temporary exhibitions. It is our experience that some essential keys to understanding works in their wider cultural contexts would be lost without direct, side-by-side comparison.

"Contact and Exchange in the Ancient World" was the subject of a conference held in 2001 for which the historian Jerry H. Bentley

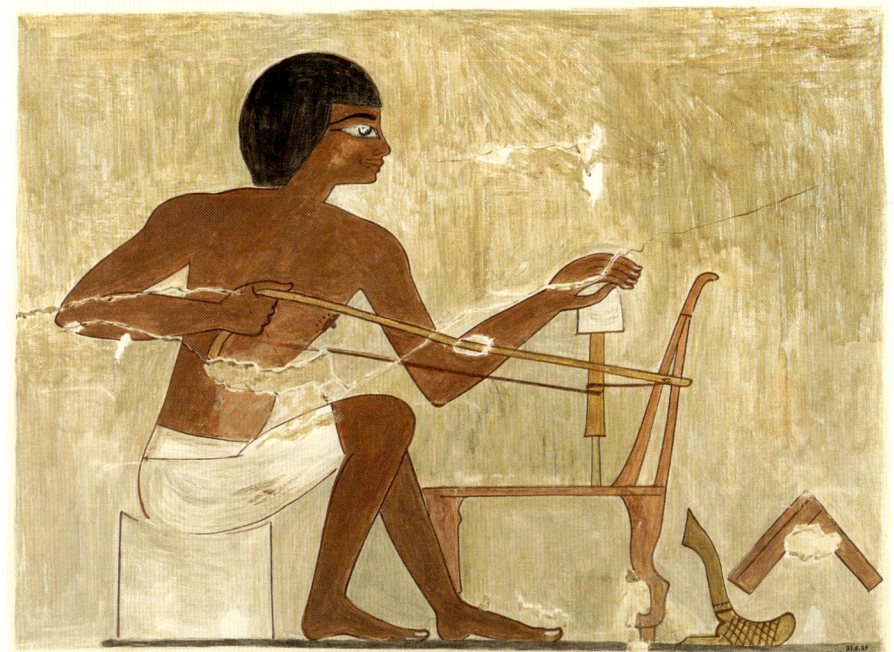

12. Facsimile painting from the tomb of Rekhmire: Craftsman making a chair with a bow drill. Egyptian, Thebes, New Kingdom, ca. 1479 B.C. Rogers Fund, 1931 (31.6.29)

Below: 13. Furniture supports. Anatolia, Middle Bronze Age, 18th century B.C. Ivory, H. 5⅝ in. (14.2 cm); 5½ in. (13.9 cm). Gift of Mrs. George D. Pratt, in memory of George D. Pratt, 1936 (36.70.7, 36.152.1). The Anatolian supports in the form of lion's legs are very similar in type to Egyptian ones.

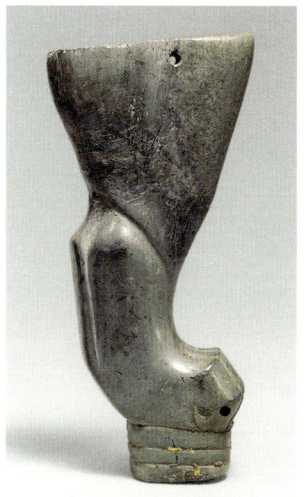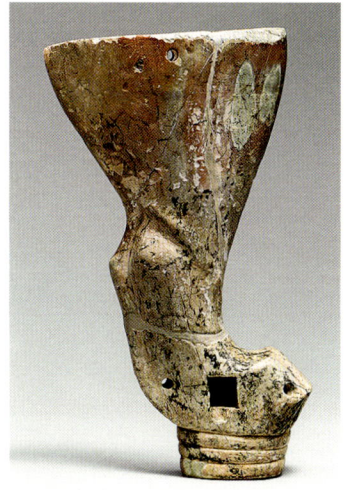

wrote, "Networks of cross-cultural interaction, communication, and exchange are defining contexts of human historical experience just as surely as are the myriad ostensibly distinct societies. . . . Thus attention to processes of cross-cultural interaction is . . . indispensable for . . . understanding the trajectories of individual societies and the development of the larger world as a whole." The relationships among contemporaneous cultures in some instances actively shaped their developments. But illuminating them with visual displays carries enormous challenges, even in an encyclopedic museum, since the internal geography may place considerable distances or obstacles such as staircases and hallways between related civilizations. Without the objects themselves juxtaposed, how can one fully appreciate the relationship between the brilliant jewels adorning individuals buried in the royal cemetery at Ur and the exquisite carnelian beads from the resource-rich Indus Valley civilization—vivid testimony to the extensive trade that traversed Asia in the third millennium B.C.? How can one reveal the transfer of technology and traditions that stand behind significant developments in the arts of the eastern Mediterranean world (figs. 12, 13) and are often reflected in texts of the Late Bronze Age? In the Metropolitan's Ancient Near Eastern galleries, opportunities to address such challenges, although still limited, have been important, thanks to loans from the departments of Egyptian, Greek and Roman, and Islamic art and to our long-term loan program (fig. 14). Despite the difficulties involved, this is an approach that, with Philippe's unwavering support, informed not only "Art of the First Cities" but also our 2008–9 exhibition "Beyond Babylon: Art, Trade, and Diplomacy in the Second Millennium B.C." In both cases we explored cultural manifestations across a vast geographic spectrum during one historical phase, rather than adopting the more conventional approach of examining in isolation works from a specific ancient region or modern country over time.

The complexities involved in mounting both exhibitions were immense, since loans were sought from countries as diverse as

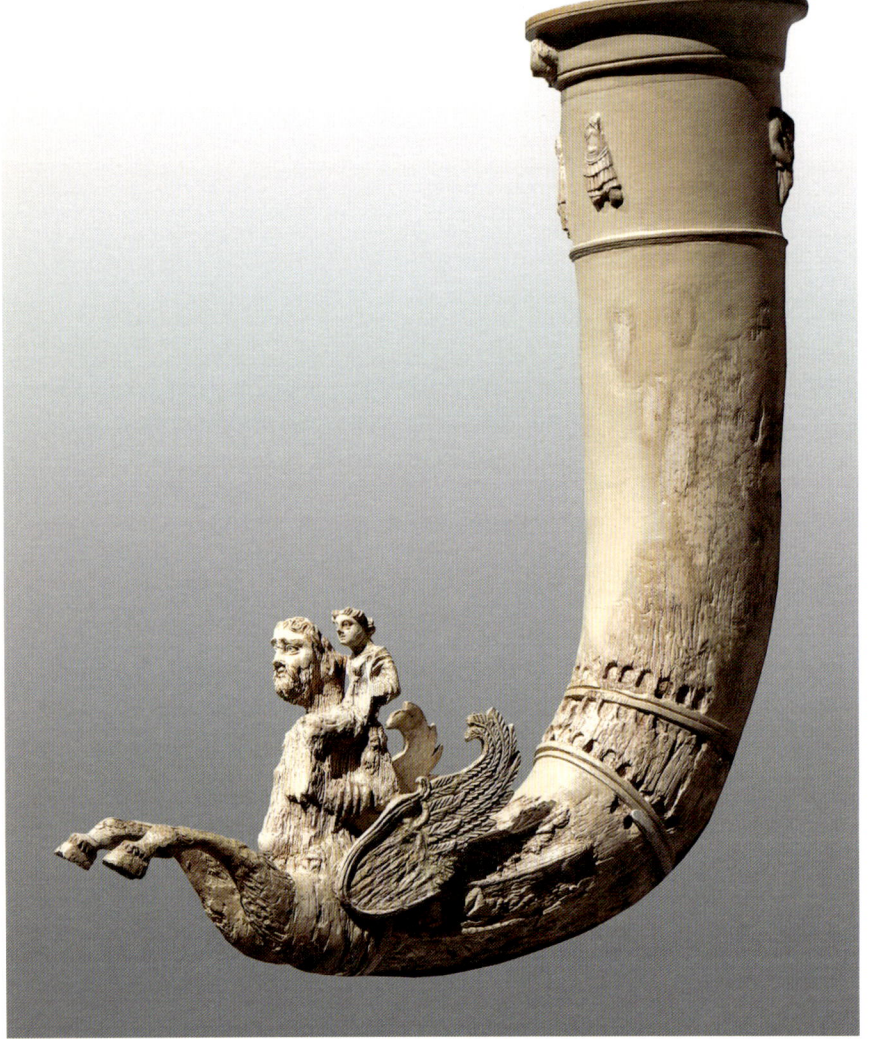

14. Rhyton. Central Asia, Turkmenistan, Nysa, 3rd–2nd century B.C. Ivory, H. 11⅞ in. (30 cm). Lent by the State Museum of Oriental Art, Moscow

Pakistan, Saudi Arabia, Egypt, Greece, Turkey, Lebanon, and Syria—and Philippe will remember at firsthand our travels from Aleppo to Damascus in October 2005—lands rich in resources but often also rich in restrictions and requirements. But perhaps more formidable than logistical challenges was another that came at the very beginning, the need to create conceptual frameworks in which the interrelations among cultures, and the advances in art and thought that ensued, would be epitomized by the displays of works of art. I would like to review a few such challenges that lay behind aspects of the recent exhibition.

"Beyond Babylon" began with the Middle Bronze Age (ca. 2000–1600 B.C.). During this period the ancient Near East experienced a drastic shift from a Mesopotamia-centric world to one with new centers that had arisen or gained prominence along major trading corridors—on the central Anatolian plateau and along the Euphrates River and the eastern Mediterranean coast. The quest for metals, particularly copper and tin for making bronze weapons and tools and also precious gold and silver, was the driving force in this age of intensive exchange. Raw materials and manufactured goods were carried over long distances, and travelers shared new discoveries and innovative technologies. Their interaction fostered a brilliant period in the arts in which international styles were created that combined elements from a variety of cultures.

Thousands of cuneiform tablets divulge information about individual transactions and legal disputes and provide glimpses into the complex personal lives of merchants and their families, offering a vivid picture of the era (fig. 15). Our task was to select compelling works of art that manifest visually the many facets of

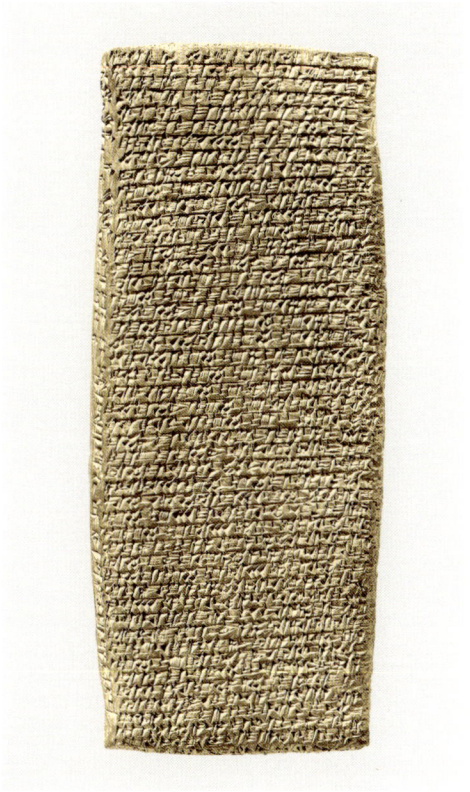
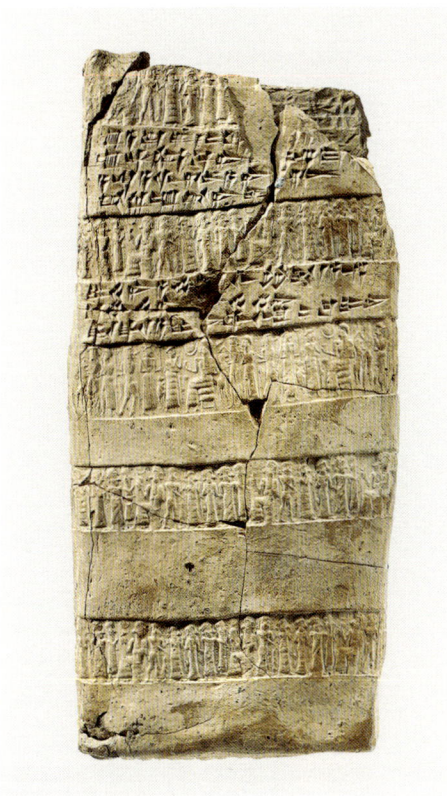

15. Cuneiform tablet and case. Anatolia, *karum* Kanesh II, ca. 1950–1836 B.C. Clay, H. of tablet 6⅝ in. (16.9 cm), H. of case 7¼ in. (18.5 cm). Gift of Mr. and Mrs. J. J. Klejman, 1966 (66.245.5)

this intense interaction. Among the various phenomena are the spread of Egyptian royal and ritual motifs throughout the Mediterranean (fig. 16); an extraordinary openness to foreign imagery— even for royal depictions—that occurred at this time of transition between the Egyptian Middle and New Kingdoms and is observable on spectacular ceremonial weapons (fig. 18); and shared practices such as bull leaping (fig. 17), which perhaps was spread by acrobats who traveled—as did other specialists mentioned on cuneiform tablets, such as musicians, doctors, priests, and craftsmen. In texts celebrating their expertise, kings demand skilled foreign artisans capable of transforming a piece of metal or wood into lifelike images. With the recent groundbreaking discoveries of frescoes in Minoan Cretan style that adorned the walls of elite residences around the Mediterranean littoral, such as one found in Egypt that depicts characteristically Minoan bull leapers— reproduced in the exhibition—our understanding of these cultural exchanges has truly been transformed.

Another transformative discovery became the centerpiece of "Beyond Babylon": extraordinary finds from the wreckage of the oldest known seagoing ship. Found off the Grand Promontory, or

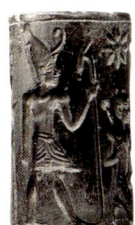 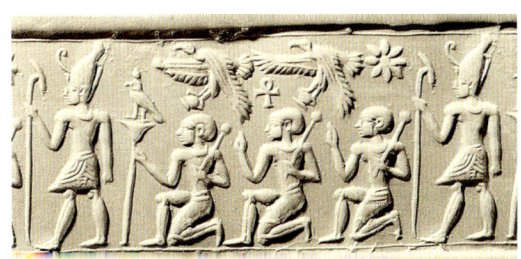

16. Cylinder seal and modern impression: Pharaoh and kneeling figures below vultures and Egyptian symbols. Old Syrian, early 2nd millennium B.C. Hematite, H. ¾ in. (1.85 cm). Gift of The Right Reverend Paul Moore Jr., 1985 (1985.357.16)

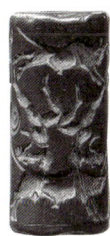 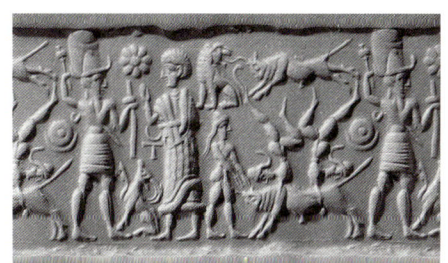

17. Cylinder seal and modern impression: Bull-vaulting scene, lion and bull, weather god and worshiper. Old Syrian, early 2nd millennium B.C. Hematite, H. ⅞ in. (2.1 cm). Anonymous loan (ex-Erlenmeyer Collection)

Uluburun, on Turkey's southern shore, the ship carried the precious cargo that fed the complex diplomatic and commercial enterprises developing among the great powers of the era—forecasting the explosion of Mediterranean trade in later Phoenician times. While very little survives of the vessel's cedar planks, it is thought to have been about forty-nine feet long (about the size of the ship reconstructed in the galleries) and probably was formed like Syrian ships depicted in Egyptian tomb paintings. Archaeologists, who worked for eleven years to recover the remains, came upon stacks of copper and tin ingots, in the proper ratio to make eleven tons of bronze, and more than 170 ingots of colored raw glass. There were also exotic raw materials such as elephant and hippopotamus ivory and ebony. This is just what we would expect from depictions of Nubians bringing ebony and ivory to the Egyptian court, and from a letter found at Amarna describing the greeting gift of ebony beds, chairs, and footrests overlaid with ivory and gold given by the king of Egypt to the king of Babylonia, who had sent his daughter to become the pharaoh's bride. These were the materials coveted to make luxury furniture, many examples of which survived in the tomb of Tutankhamun. Elaborate objects were also on board, among them duck-shaped cosmetic boxes made of ivory, which the excavation director, Cemal Pulak, thinks were diplomatic gifts. A very similar example is depicted among other New Year's gifts, including foreign treasures, in paintings in the tomb of the Egyptian official Kenamun. Gold was also on the ship: the unique gold scarab bearing the name of Nefertiti, queen of Egypt, a golden chalice weighing more than seven ounces, and large, impressive pendants (fig. 20). In addition to finished pieces there was scrap, pieces cut up perhaps for use as bullion during the trip. But it is personal belongings that have allowed the excavators to bring the ship even further to life, with its Canaanite captain and merchants, Mycenaean Greek envoys, and perhaps a Balkan mercenary accompanying the voyage toward a destination that may have been on the Greek mainland.

This fateful journey is thought to have taken place about 1300 B.C., just over a generation after correspondence between the great kings of Egypt, the Near East, and Cyprus that was discovered at Amarna. These texts, some of the most impressive on display in the exhibition, offer us a glimpse into the system of diplomatic exchange among the principal royal courts of the time, enumerating goods given as greeting gifts, dowries for foreign princesses, and elaborate wedding presents from one ruler to another. Such lavish works made in precious materials, some reflecting a fusion of stylistic traditions, were represented in an area of the show devoted to the "art of exchange." They came from Mesopotamia, Syria, Egypt, Cyprus, and the Aegean world. The funerary adornment of a foreign bride of the great pharaoh Thutmose III—presented in an extraordinary display prepared

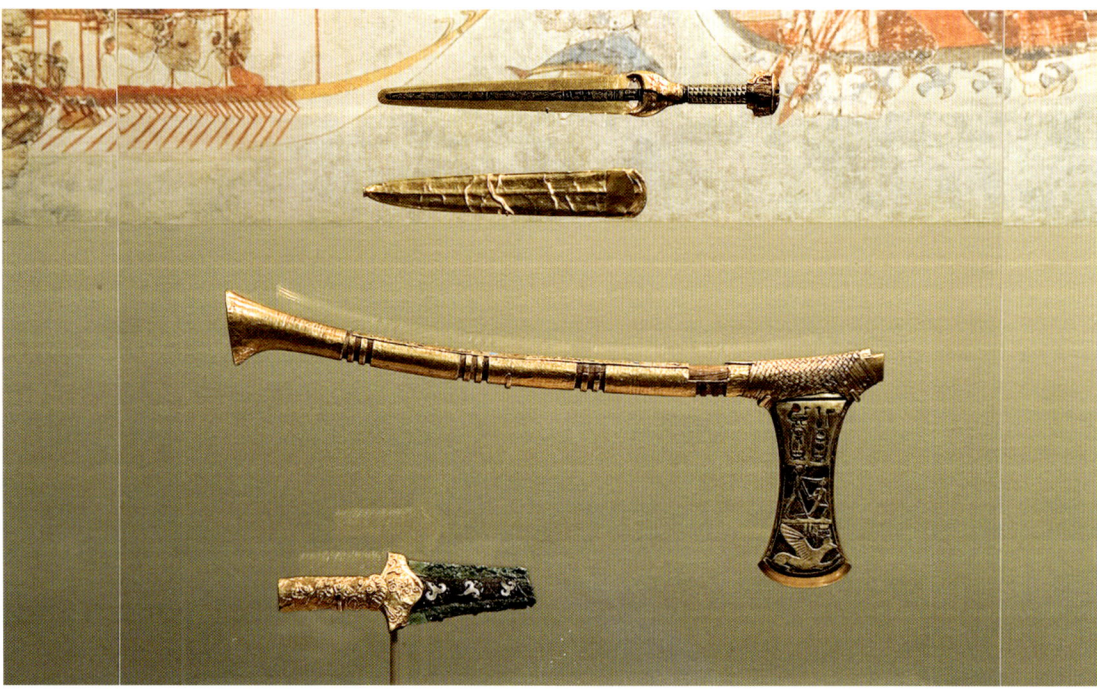

18. "Beyond Babylon" exhibit: Inlaid dagger with sheath and axe from Ahhotep burial, Thebes, Egypt; dagger from tholos tomb, Rutsi, Greece. Late Bronze Age, 16th century B.C. Gold and other materials. Luxor Museum (JE 4666, JE 4673); National Archaeological Museum, Athens (8340)

by the Department of Egyptian Art under the supervision of Dorothea Arnold—highlighted the tradition of diplomatic marriage between royal families of the Levant and Egypt (fig. 19).

The Uluburun ship sailed on its last voyage just twenty-five years or so before the occurrence of one of the greatest battles of antiquity, waged at the Syrian provincial capital of Qadesh, between Egypt (under the recently crowned Ramesses II) and its Hittite rivals. This battle and others fought by Egyptian pharaohs are depicted in graphic detail and with inscribed accounts on the walls of many temples in the Nile Valley. Such encounters, however, and other wars alluded to in the texts and later epics—the most famous of all being the Trojan War—are invisible in the artistic record of the Near East and only generally reflected in renderings of battle and hunt. Some of the most evocative of these images were displayed in the last gallery of the exhibition, where one case was devoted to the Homeric world. Homeric-type boar's-tusk helmets are depicted in the frescoes of ancient Thera and actually survive at sites such as Mycenae; the helmet type also appears in the representation of a foreign warrior incised on a bowl from the Hittite capital of Hattusa. Such tangible parallels bring us closer to the realities of this era of intense interaction in times of both war and peace.

It has frequently been remarked that exhibitions such as "Art of the First Cities" and "Beyond Babylon" could have been mounted only at the Metropolitan. As Philippe concluded in his talk at the British Museum, "The great value of the universal museum is that it is ultimately the greatest of family trees on which every culture finds its branch and is hung in harmony with the others." These shows have allowed us to illuminate connections between some of the branches and to explore ideas—universal from the Nile to the Tigris, and even to the Indus—that lie at the very roots of our shared human past.

Joan Aruz

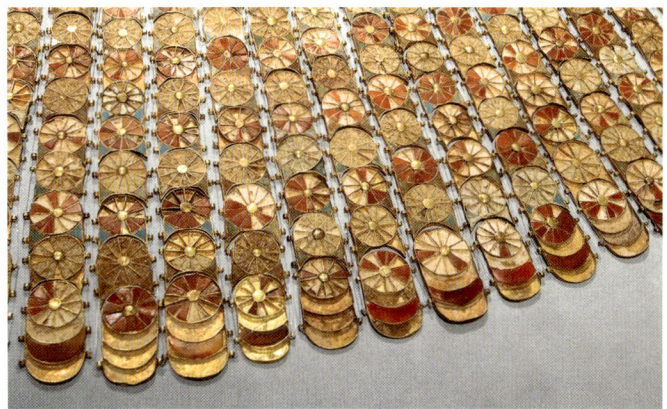

19. "Beyond Babylon" exhibit: Jewelry elements from the tomb of the three foreign wives of Thutmose III. Thebes, Egypt, New Kingdom, ca. 1458 B.C. Gold, carnelian, jasper, and glass. Purchase, Henry Walters and Edward S. Harkness Gifts, 1920 (26.8.117a)

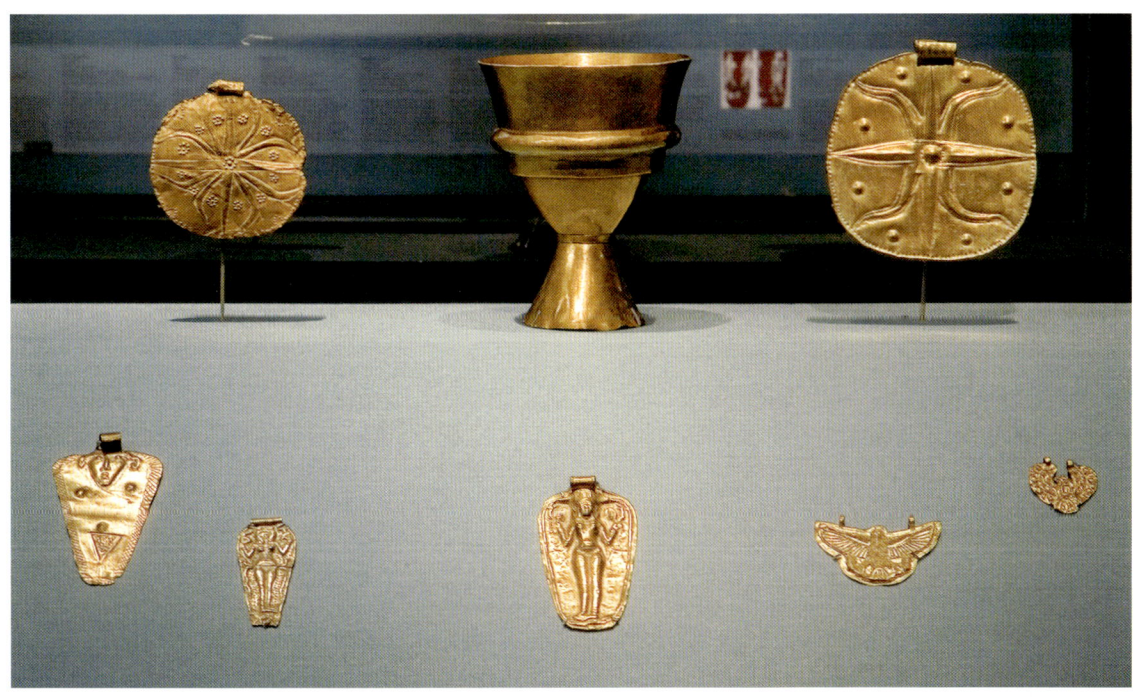

20. "Beyond Babylon" exhibit: Pendants and chalice from the Uluburun shipwreck, shown with Levantine pendants and earring depicting similar themes: rayed stars, female nude, and falcon. Late Bronze Age, 15th–14th century B.C. Gold. Bodrum Museum of Underwater Archaeology, Turkey (KW138, KW99, KW1672, KW703, KW94); Musée du Louvre, Paris (AO14714); The Trustees of the British Museum, London (130761, 130764)

GLASS AND GOLD OF THE HELLENISTIC AND EARLY ROMAN WORLD

In April 1926 the Metropolitan Museum's original Roman Court and surrounding galleries opened to the public, to great acclaim (fig. 21). Meticulously conceived by Museum director Edward Robinson—a classical archaeologist by training—and curator Gisela M. A. Richter, and realized by the architectural firm McKim, Mead and White, the handsome design stood for less than a quarter century. Francis Henry Taylor, Robinson's successor and a medievalist with little interest in the art of classical antiquity, decided in 1949 to convert the court and galleries into a public restaurant and administrative offices. In the dining room designed by society decorator Dorothy Draper that subsequently opened, the court's central atrium was given over to a pool adorned with bronzes by the Swedish sculptor Carl Milles. Over ensuing decades the restaurant underwent several further transformations, none for the better.

When the Department of Greek and Roman Art lost half its exhibition space in that 1949 takeover, thousands of works of art—entire categories of objects—were consigned to out-of-view storerooms. Most of our Greek jewelry, glass, gems, and terracottas vanished to the basements, as did all the Roman decorative arts and countless other antiquities. We owe the rebirth of the court to Leon Levy and Shelby White as well as to the clear vision and heroic endurance of Philippe de Montebello, under whose leadership the fifteen-year Greek and Roman Master Plan was conceived and brought to fruition. One of the glories of the reinstallation has been the unveiling of a vast quantity of material that had been off view for more than two generations; it is further enriched by many works acquired in recent years. For this celebratory volume I would like to present some particularly notable examples of Hellenistic and early Roman decorative arts, especially cast glass and gold jewelry, that are now on permanent display.

The Metropolitan houses the largest and most comprehensive selection of Greek and Roman glass in America—indeed, one of the finest in the world—much of it collected early in the Museum's history. A vast assortment of Cypriot antiquities purchased in the 1870s from General Luigi Palma di Cesnola contained more than 1,700 pieces of ancient glass. Shortly thereafter, trustee Henry G. Marquand secured for the Museum the finest

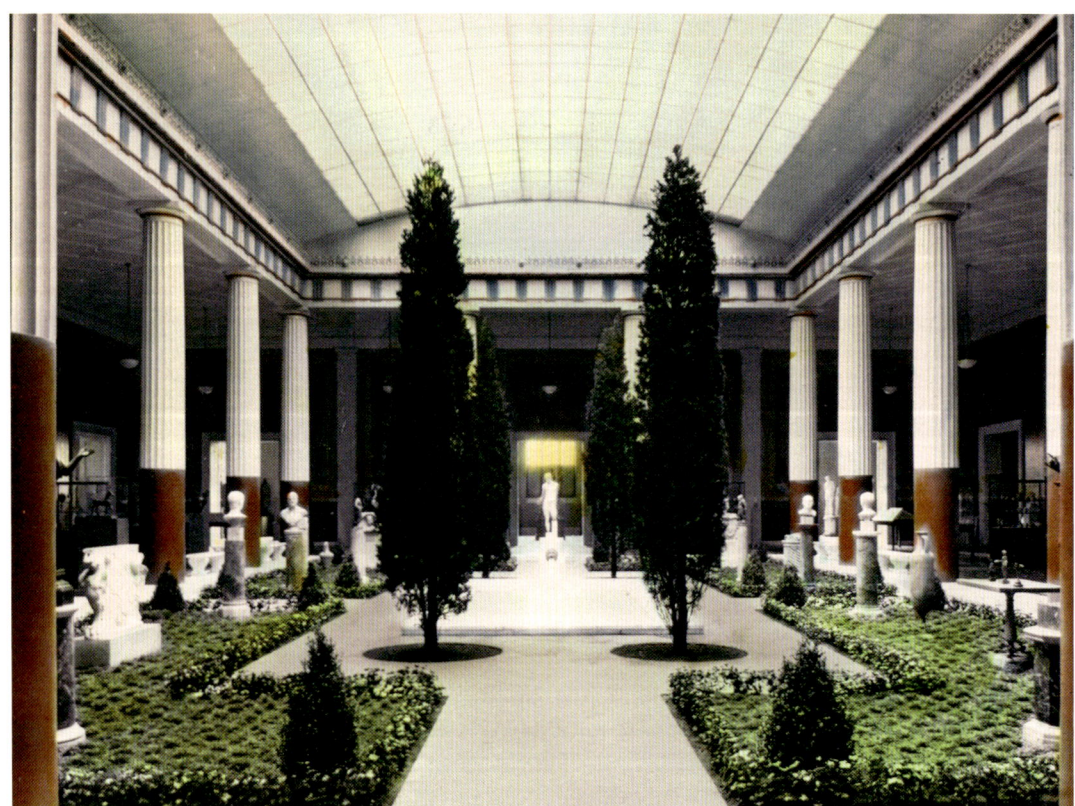

21. The Roman Court (Wing K, Gallery K2), as it was in 1926

assemblage of ancient glass available in France at the time; it had been formed by the collector Jules Charvet and consisted of about 350 outstanding pieces. There followed an important bequest from Edward C. Moore in 1891, and magnificent holdings from the collection of J. Pierpont Morgan were presented to the Museum in his name by his son in 1917. Morgan had purchased the entire collection of about five thousand pieces assembled by the French connoisseur Julien Gréau and published by Wilhelm Froehner in 1903.

Among these early acquisitions are many of our best mosaic glasses, objects that reflect the opulence and sophistication of the Hellenistic age. Long before the invention of glassblowing in the first century B.C., cast glass was formed in molds. To create a complex "mosaic" design, long canes of glass with circular, star, or spiral polychrome designs were first produced; these were sliced into sections, which, along with contrasting patches of translucent or opaque glass, were placed over the mold and fused together. Once cool, the vessel was ground and polished. This painstaking glassmaking was a luxury industry, and the finest products were very highly prized.

Our most remarkable example, a large jar, is a tour de force of Hellenistic glassmaking (fig. 22). Few vessels of comparable scale or technique have been preserved intact. There is no doubt that the jar was cast in a mold, but precisely how remains uncertain, since a container with this ovoid profile and flaring rim and base would be no easy matter to produce by draping glass over a mold or by lining the mold's interior. The pattern of curving ribbons in amber-brown and opaque white imitates semiprecious stones, such as onyx and banded agate, of which some luxury vessels were carved. Very few such coveted hardstone vessels survive intact from antiquity; one is a little Roman amphora of banded agate recently acquired by the Museum (2001.253) that represents the very highest level of craftsmanship and refinement.

Two other mosaic glasses, both gifts of Henry G. Marquand, have the relatively simple profiles more characteristic of the Hellenistic repertoire. Hemispherical mosaic bowls (81.10.35) were especially popular, not least because light can filter through the tall walls, heightening the polychrome effects. We do not know where these bowls were manufactured; they have been found in many locations including Greece, Italy, Egypt, and Syria. Prominent yellow squares on a decorative dish (81.10.43) are meant to

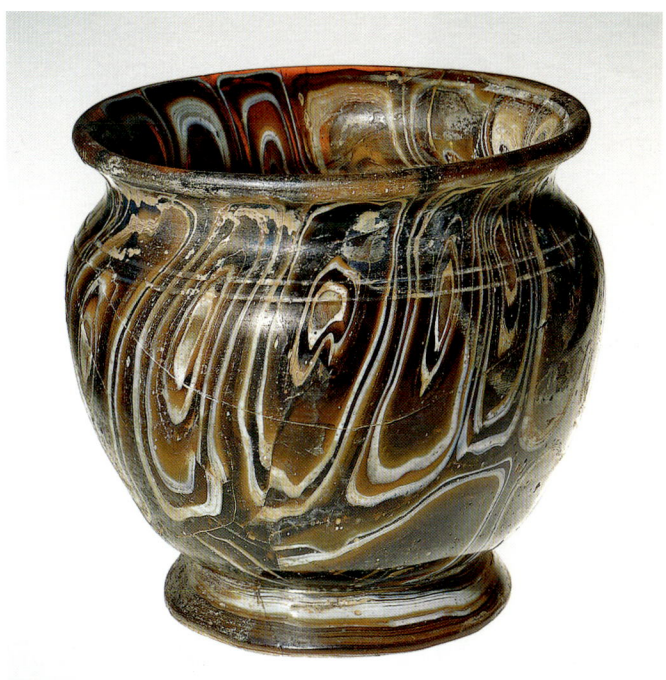

22. Jar. Greek, Hellenistic, 2nd–early 1st century B.C. Mosaic cast glass, H. 5⁷⁄₁₆ in. (13.8 cm). Edward C. Moore Collection, Bequest of Edward C. Moore, 1891 (91.1.1303)

suggest gold. This work imitates an even more luxurious product of the Hellenistic glassmaker, known as gold-band glass. In this technique, introduced in the first century B.C., swirling colored bands are combined with strips of gold foil sandwiched between ribbons of colorless glass. The dazzling effect is very evident in an alabastron, or perfume bottle, on view in the Hellenistic Treasury (fig. 23).

Experimentation with new shapes and decorative techniques led to the invention of glassblowing in late Hellenistic workshops on the eastern Mediterranean (the Syro-Palestinian region) in about 50 B.C. The most important glassmaking development since the discovery of glass itself thousands of years before, this innovation allowed glass to be mass-produced. But while blown vessels proliferated, some workshops continued to craft luxury glasses of great technical complexity, and new production centers of fine wares were established in Rome and elsewhere in the West, probably during the reign of Augustus (27 B.C.–A.D. 14).

Whether a very rare conical bowl (17.194.2535), probably of the first century B.C., was manufactured in the East or the West is

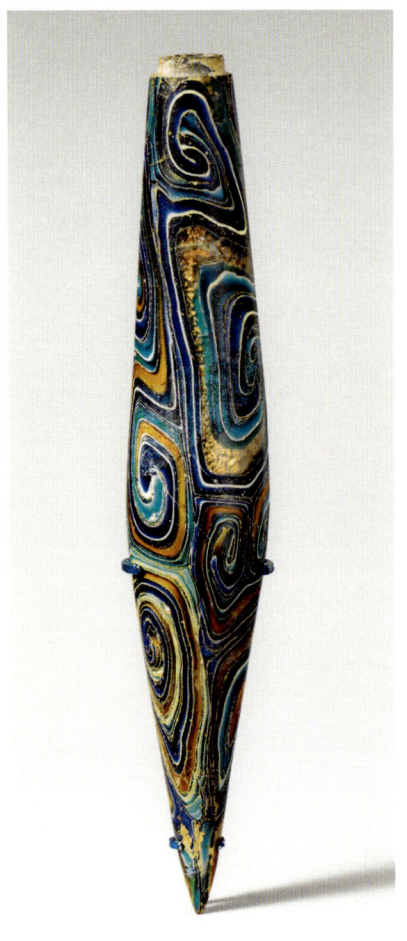
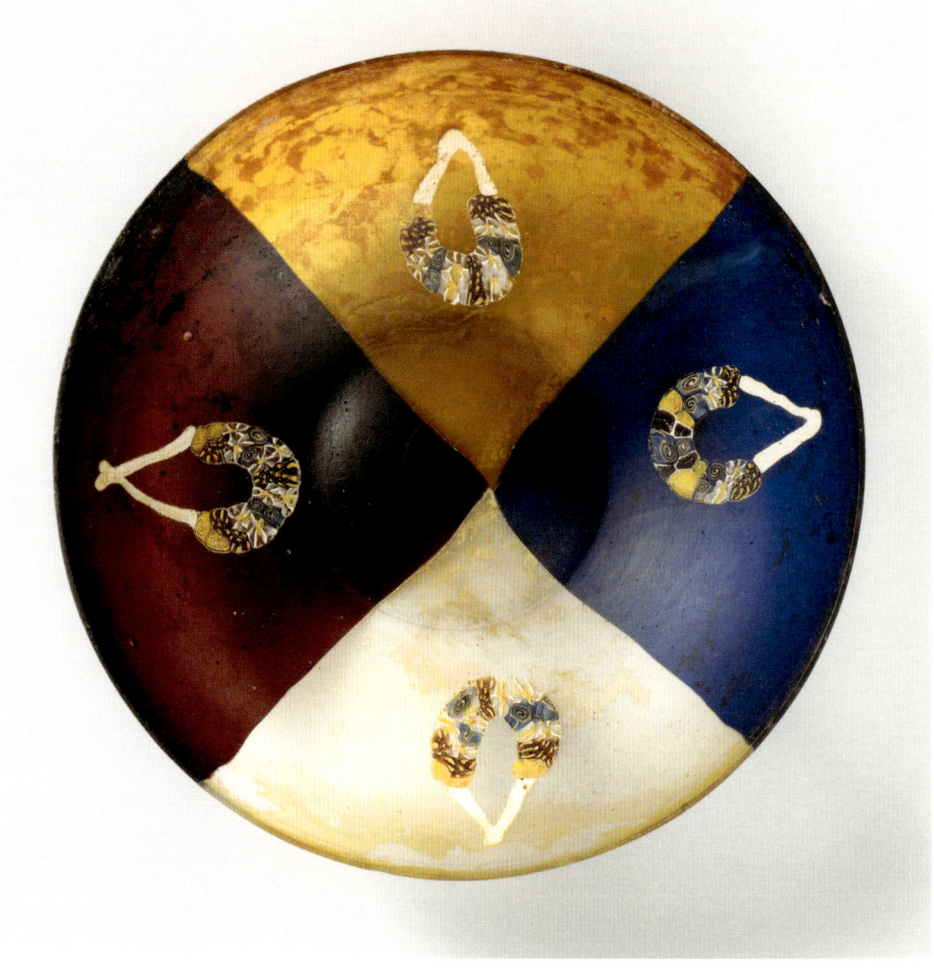

23. Alabastron (perfume bottle). Greek, Hellenistic, 1st century B.C. Gold-band mosaic glass, cast (probably around a rod), H. 8⅜ in. (21.3 cm). Gift of J. Pierpont Morgan, 1917 (17.194.285)

24. Garland bowl. Roman, Augustan, late 1st century B.C. Cast glass, H. 1½ in. (3.8 cm), Diam. 7⅛ in. (18.1 cm). Edward C. Moore Collection, Bequest of Edward C. Moore, 1891 (91.1.1402)

difficult to ascertain. Its deep cone shape, the thinness of its walls, and the concentric grooves placed below the rim on the inside are all indications that the piece imitates silver vessels. However, a strip of clear colorless glass bisecting the translucent dark blue owes nothing to metal prototypes. Only a few other bicolored vessels survive; most likely they were all made in the same workshop.

Our exceptional garland bowl (fig. 24) was made by first pressing four slices of translucent glass, purple, yellow, blue, and colorless, side by side in a casting mold. Each segment was then decorated with fused-on millefiori glass arranged to represent a garland hanging from an opaque white cord. Ours seems to be the only intact example that combines these two rare techniques. Another outstanding work is our elegant opaque glass oinochoe, or handled jug (fig. 25), whose shape imitates that of a metal vessel. It represents a transitional phase in glassmaking: the handle was cold-carved and the base was cut on a lathe, but the body seems to have been blown. The light blue color is quite unusual.

The rarest and most elaborate luxury vessels of the early Roman Empire are those made of cameo glass. Only sixteen reasonably complete cameo vessels have been recorded, plus an estimated two hundred fragments; they were found principally in Italy and were made in the period about 25 B.C. to A.D. 50. Of our sixteen cameo fragments, the most evocative and tantalizing comes from an oval platter or tabletop that must have measured more than three feet across. Over a translucent, deep purple background the glassmaker applied patches of opaque white glass that were carved by the lapidary to represent various sea animals, including a crab and a squid (fig. 26). This astonishing object,

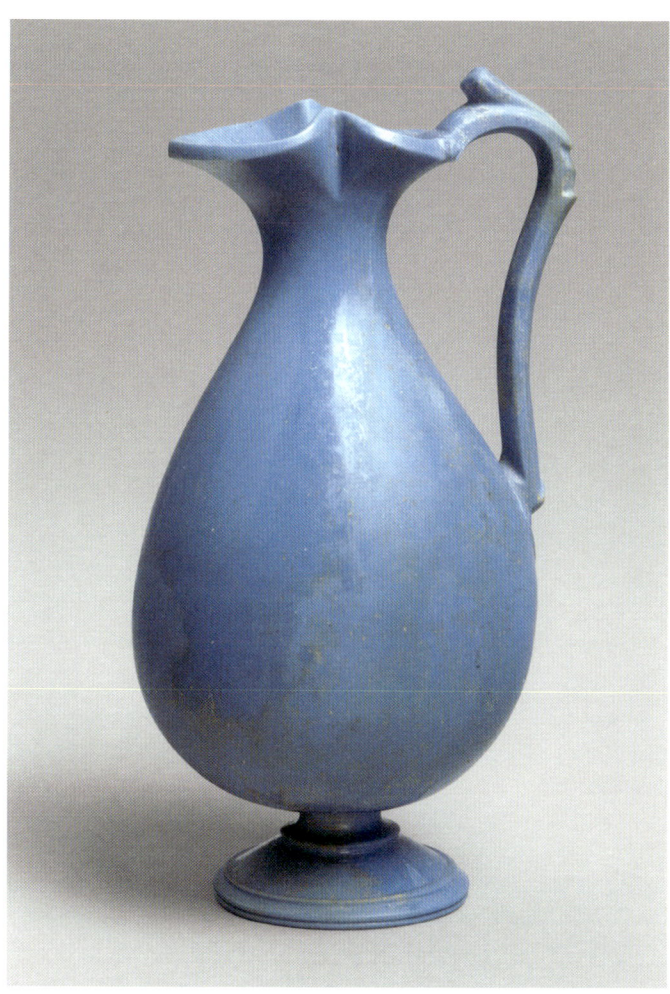

25. Oinochoe (jug). Roman, late 1st century B.C.–early 1st century A.D. Opaque blue glass, cast and blown, H. 7⅛ in. (18.1 cm). Gift of J. Pierpont Morgan, 1917 (17.194.170)

said to have been found in 1888 on Capri near the villa of Emperor Tiberius, attests to the wealth and refined taste of occupants of the island's sumptuous villas.

Of all the decorative arts from classical antiquity, gold jewelry usually evokes the strongest response. Our visitors first discovered the depth and quality of the Metropolitan's holdings in this field in the mid-1990s, when we presented "Greek Gold: Jewelry of the Classical World" in conjunction with the British Museum and the Hermitage. Now, virtually all of our material is back on permanent view, with the Gold Room of the original McKim, Mead and White plan reborn as the Hellenistic Treasury. The Hellenistic age saw the zenith of Greek goldwork. The Met's collection is especially strong in jewelry of this era, with works that come from many parts of the ancient world.

One important early Hellenistic assemblage, the so-called Ganymede group, takes its name from a superb pair of earrings on which a tiny figure of the Trojan prince Ganymede is seen in the clutches of Zeus, who has assumed the guise of an eagle (fig. 30). Zeus coveted Ganymede for his beauty and carried him off to Mount Olympus to be a cupbearer for the gods. These goldwork pendants, sculptural masterpieces in miniature, probably reflect the composition of a famous large-scale bronze group made by Leochares in the first half of the fourth century B.C. The parure (37.11.8–.17) also includes a strap-necklace with pendants in the shape of beechnuts, a pair of rock-crystal hoop bracelets with gold ram's heads, four fibulae of Macedonian type,

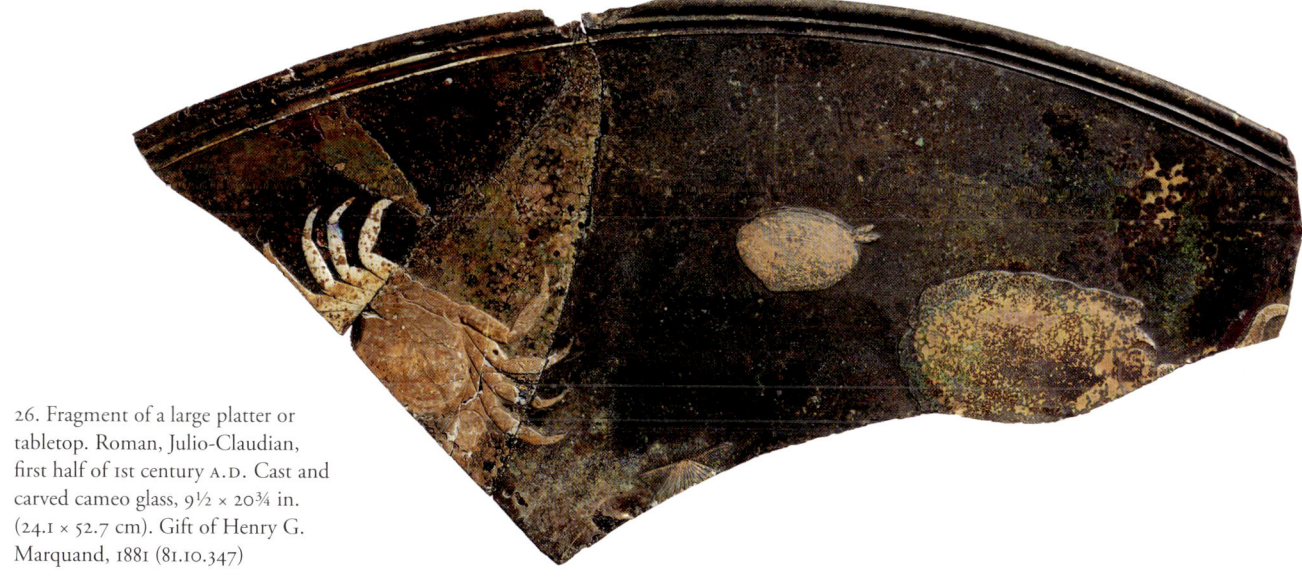

26. Fragment of a large platter or tabletop. Roman, Julio-Claudian, first half of 1st century A.D. Cast and carved cameo glass, 9½ × 20¾ in. (24.1 × 52.7 cm). Gift of Henry G. Marquand, 1881 (81.10.347)

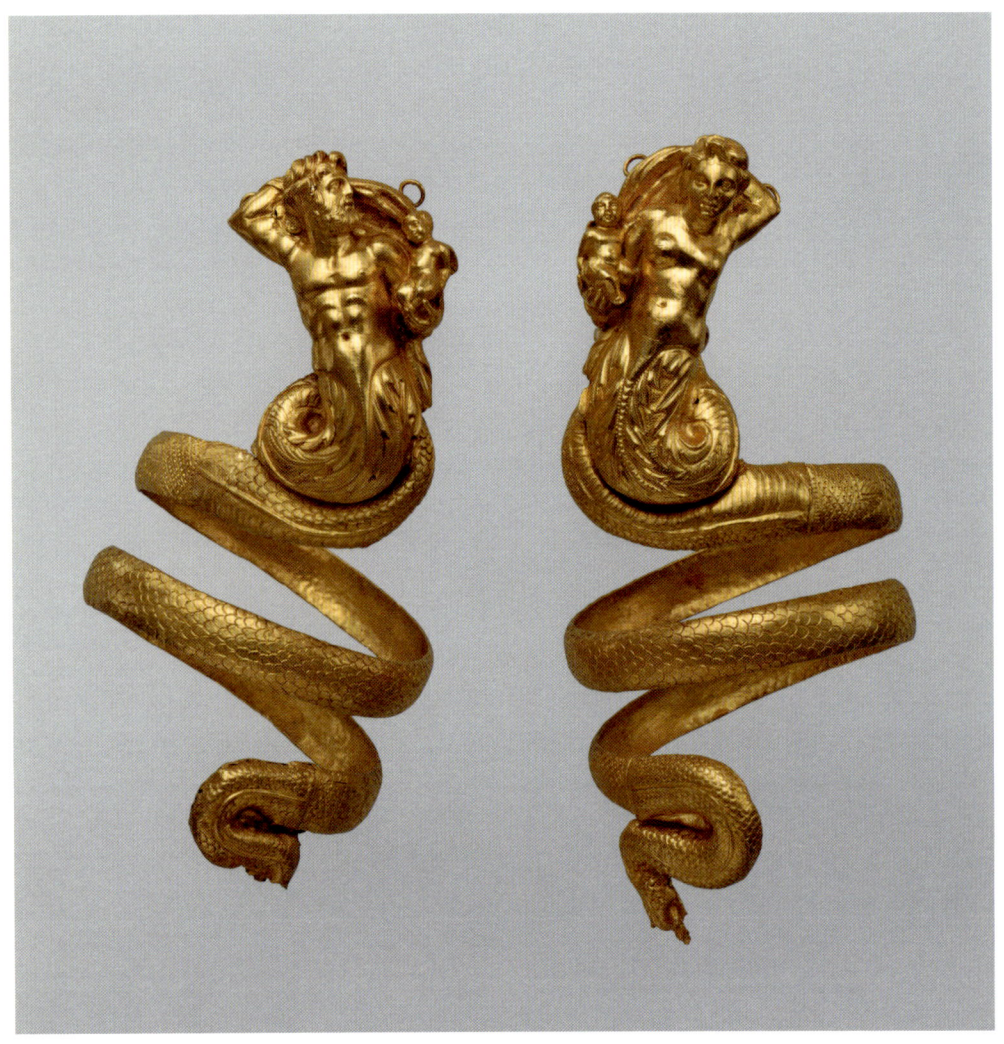

27. Pair of armbands with tritoness and triton holding Erotes. Greek, Hellenistic, ca. 200 B.C. Gold; tritoness: H. 6¼ in. (15.9 cm), triton: H. 5¾ in. (14.6 cm). Rogers Fund, 1956 (56.11.5, .6)

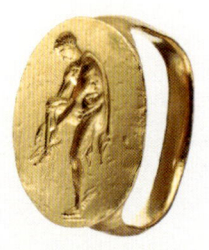

28. Ring. Greek, South Italian, late 4th century B.C. Gold, ¹³⁄₁₆ × ⁷⁄₁₆ in. (2 × 1.1 cm). Purchase, The Bothmer Purchase Fund and Lila Acheson Wallace Gift, 1994 (1994.230.3)

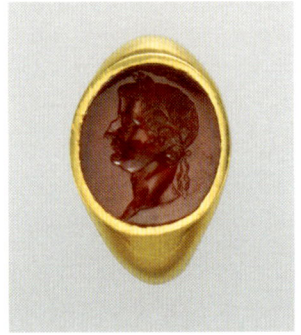

29. Ring with intaglio portrait of Tiberius. Roman, A.D. 14–37. Gold and carnelian, 1 × 1¹⁄₁₆ in. (2.5 × 2.7 cm). Purchase, The Bothmer Purchase Fund and Lila Acheson Wallace Gift, 1994 (1994.230.7)

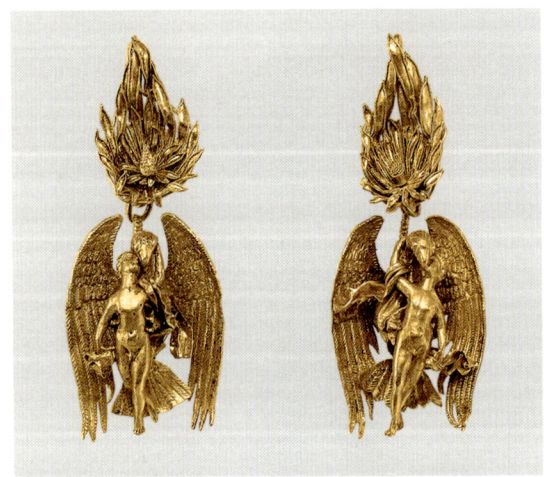

30. Pair of earrings from the Ganymede group. Greek, ca. 330–300 B.C. Gold, H. 2⅜ in. (6 cm). Harris Brisbane Dick Fund, 1937 (37.11.9–.10)

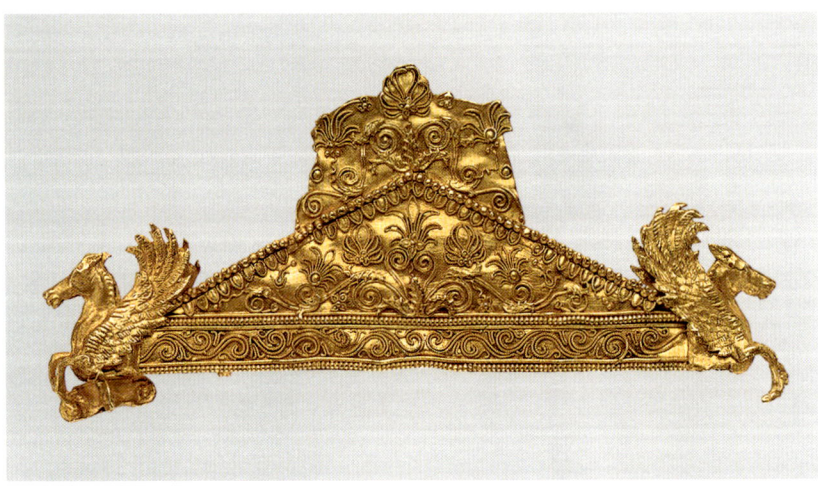

31. Pediment-shaped brooch. Greek, ca. 340–320 B.C. Gold, L. 3¹⁄₁₆ in. (7.8 cm). Rogers Fund, 1906 (06.1159)

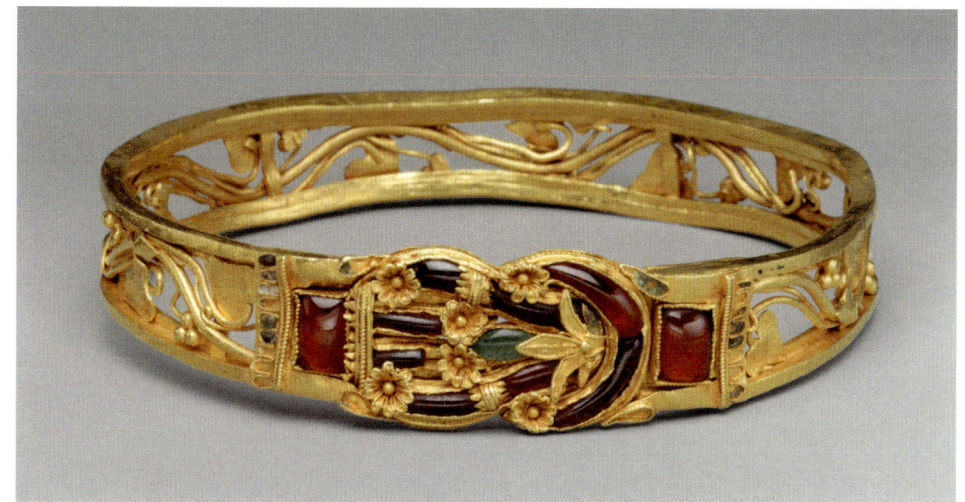

32. Armband with Herakles knot. Greek, Hellenistic, 3rd–2nd century B.C. Gold, emerald, garnet, and enamel, W. 3½ in. (8.9 cm). Purchase, Mr. and Mrs. Christos G. Bastis Gift, 1999 (1999.209)

and a ring set with a cabochon emerald (emeralds first appeared in Greek jewelry at this time). The pieces are said to have been found together in Macedonia near Thessaloníki, but they do not show a clear uniformity of style and perhaps did not originally belong together.

An unusual pediment-shaped brooch (fig. 31), reportedly found in Patras in the northern Peloponnese, features the forepart of a winged horse at each corner. An Ionic volute capital under the Pegasus at the left suggests that originally an entire facade was represented. Probably from Tarentum in southern Italy comes a ring (fig. 28) that can be grouped stylistically with a handful of other early Hellenistic gold rings from Magna Graecia. Engraved in intaglio on its oval bezel is the youthful messenger-god Hermes, balancing on his left leg as he fastens a wing to his raised right foot. The ultimate source of the composition is a monumental Greek sculpture of the Sandal-Binder Hermes traditionally ascribed to the fourth-century-B.C. sculptor Lysippos.

Several works donated in the 1990s by Christos G. Bastis take us into the third or early second century B.C. A finely crafted fillet with a central Herakles knot (1995.539.7) is an outstanding example of this well-known Hellenistic jewelry type. The lion's-head terminals and the women's heads joining the chains to the knot are tiny, delicate sculptures. The Herakles-knot motif gets an entirely different treatment as a massive, richly designed armband (fig. 32). This knot is composed of inlaid garnets and set between two large rectangular garnet cabochons. A flowering plant bearing six gold blossoms spreads over the knot; at its base is a whorl of leaves, with an emerald above its large center leaf. Green and white enamel, of which only traces remain, were also used to great effect.

Colorful inlays again combine with gold in an extravagant, beautifully composed pair of earrings whose upper portions represent the Egyptian Atef crown, with its sun disk and feathers (1995.539.11a, b). The semiprecious stones and mosaic glass of this later Hellenistic work are in a remarkably well-preserved state. Also from Egypt but of totally different style is an openwork hairnet made to be worn at the back of the head over a bun (1987.220). In its central medallion, skillfully worked in repoussé, is the head of a maenad, or follower of Dionysus, wearing the god's signature panther-skin over her right shoulder.

A pair of armbands (fig. 27) presents one male and one female triton, each holding a small winged Eros. Behind the heads of these fish-tailed demigods are loops used to fasten the armbands to the sleeves of a garment; otherwise the heavy adornments (each weighing more than 6½ ounces) would have slipped down the wearer's arms. Finally, a necklace and earrings that form a matching set (1994.230.4–.6) have thick-corded chains and cabochon garnets in hinged box settings. The unusual chain loops on the earrings must have passed behind the ear so that the garnet and gold decoration would hang over the front of the ear.

I end my brief discussion with one example of Roman goldwork, an exceptional Julio-Claudian finger ring with a carnelian bearing an intaglio portrait of the emperor Tiberius (fig. 29). Of icy purity and elegance, the intaglio is a courtly production from the period when Roman gem cutting was at its height. This gives me an opportunity to mention another branch of Greek and Roman decorative arts very richly represented at the Museum, our collection of engraved gems, the catalogue of which was reissued not long ago.

Carlos A. Picón

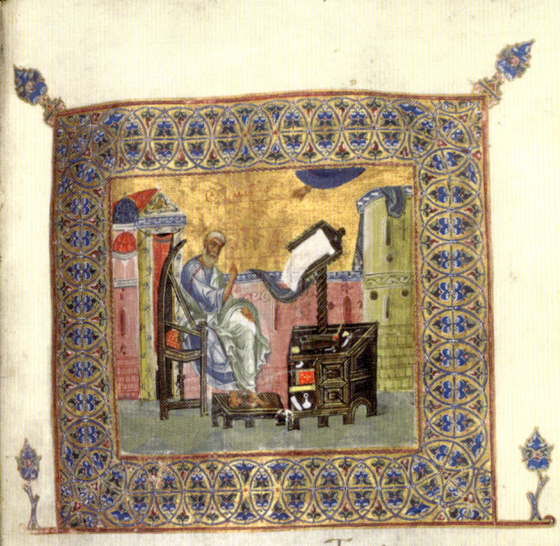

ΕΚ ΤΟΥ ΚΑΤΑ ΜΑΤΘΑΙΟΝ

MEDIEVAL EUROPE

MEDIEVAL ART IN THE MUSEUM COLLECTION, 1977–2008

When Philippe de Montebello became director of the Metropolitan Museum there were two curators in charge of medieval art, one at the main building on Fifth Avenue and the other at The Cloisters in northern Manhattan. Philippe hired William D. Wixom, a distinguished medievalist then at the Cleveland Museum of Art, to serve as chairman of a new comprehensive department, a position held by Wixom until he retired in 1998 and I succeeded him. The department has thrived for the past three decades, thanks in significant part to the director's foresight. The Michel David-Weill chair, which I am honored to occupy, was endowed in 1993, and the Mary and Michael Jaharis Curatorship of Byzantine Art, held by Helen C. Evans, in 2007.

Major acquisitions were a priority for Wixom when he joined the Museum in 1979, and many of them came to The Cloisters Treasury. The Cloisters had opened in 1938 principally for the display of western European monumental arts of the Romanesque and Gothic periods, about 1100–1500. The core of the collection then consisted of the cloister arcades collected by the American sculptor George Grey Barnard, supplemented by the famed Hunt of the Unicorn tapestry series donated by John D. Rockefeller Jr., whose vision and generosity stood behind The Cloisters' creation. With Rockefeller's gift of an endowment in the 1950s it became possible to expand the collection in new directions, and the acquisition of precious small-scale works—"Treasury objects"—accelerated. A few, chosen to suggest the variety and high quality of these acquisitions, are described below.

Soon after coming to the Museum, Wixom was able to purchase an exquisite English ivory statuette of the Virgin and Child (1979.402) with funds from the Rockefeller endowment. Large for an ivory (more than 10 inches tall) and dating about 1300, the work is a rare example of English carving at a time when Parisian style was dominant. The Virgin was immediately regarded as one of the Treasury's masterpieces. A second superb ivory, a richly carved segment from the shaft of a crozier dating from the late twelfth century (1981.1), was added to the Treasury in 1981.

In 1983 a pack of fifty-two playing cards from the late fifteenth century (1983.515.1–.52)—the only painted set of this era to survive complete—was acquired for The Cloisters. The oblong cards have rounded corners and are decorated in ink and tempera, with each suit of thirteen distinguished by the type of hunting equipment depicted: gaming nooses, dog collars, tethers, or horns. The kings, queens, and knaves wear the extravagant costumes of the court of the Burgundian Lowlands in about 1470–80. Five years later, a masterpiece of Sienese goldsmith work, the silver-gilt and enamel chalice of Peter of Sassoferrato (1988.67), came to The Cloisters collection. The decoration on its knop and base in the fragile medium of translucent enamel is of very fine quality and extraordinarily well preserved. Latin inscriptions on the chalice naming Brother Peter and the Franciscan church at Sassoferrato make it possible for us to date the work to about 1341–42.

The emergence on the art market of major works from the collection of Victor Martin Le Roy provided an opportunity for further key acquisitions. While a small group of illuminated manuscripts of the Gothic period, including the precious *Hours of Jeanne d'Évreux* and *Belles Heures of Jean, Duc de Berry* (54.1.2, 54.1.1), have been at The Cloisters since their acquisition in the 1950s, major illuminations of the Romanesque period had long been sought for the collection. This important lacuna was filled in 1991 when we purchased for The Cloisters fourteen leaves from a late twelfth-century Spanish manuscript of the commentary on the Apocalypse by an Asturian monk of the eighth century, Beatus of Liébana (fig. 34). This visionary text has a long history of vivid illustration. The brightly colored, rhythmic, masterfully drawn illuminations of our Beatus pages depict the Book of Revelation with imagery that is often strikingly literal. Two years later an early tenth-century ivory panel depicting the Three Women at the Tomb (1993.19), also from the Martin Le Roy

Opposite: 33. Jaharis Byzantine Lectionary. Byzantine, Constantinople, ca. 1100. Tempera, ink, and gold leaf on parchment; leather binding, overall 14½ × 11⅝ × 4⅞ in. (36.8 × 29.6 × 12.4 cm). Purchase, Mary and Michael Jaharis Gift and Lila Acheson Wallace Gift, 2007 (2007.286)

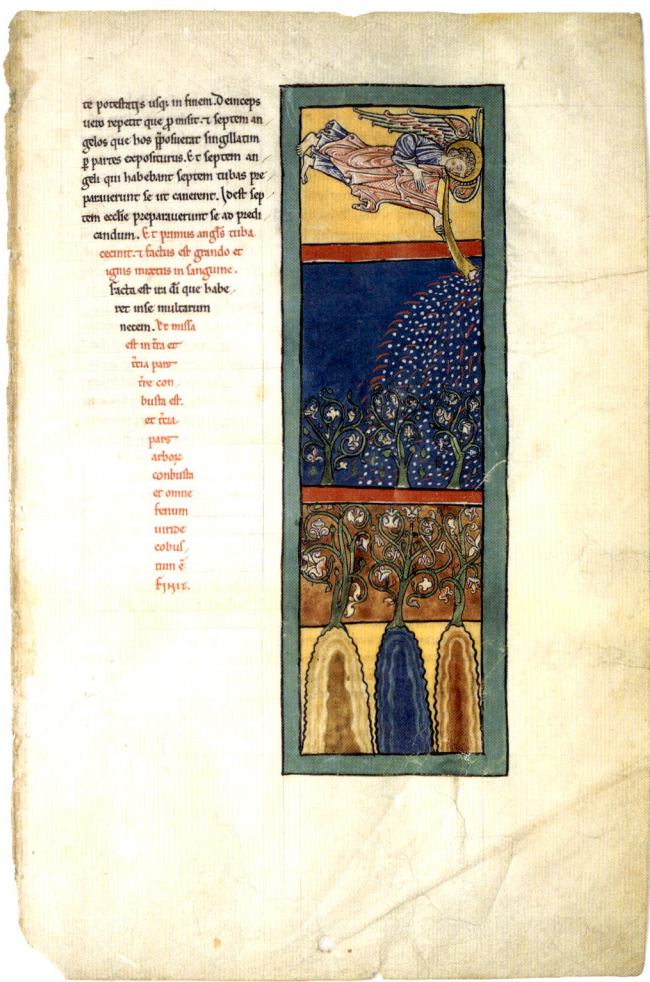

34. Leaf from a Beatus manuscript illustrating *The First Angel Sounds the Trumpet; Fire, Hail-stones, and Blood Are Cast upon the Earth* (Rev. 8: 6–7). Spanish, Castile, ca. 1180. Tempera, gold, and ink on parchment, 17½ × 11¹³⁄₁₆ in. (44.4 × 30 cm). Purchase, The Cloisters Collection, Rogers and Harris Brisbane Dick Funds, and Joseph Pulitzer Bequest, 1991 (1991.232.8r)

collection, was acquired for The Cloisters Treasury. An aquamanile in the form of a lion (1994.244) was added in 1994 to our preeminent collection of medieval aquamanilia—vessels for hand washing cast in animal or human form. Standing erect, teeth bared and tongue extended, our lion, which dates from about 1400, has an energy and boldness that make it a favorite work of visitors to The Cloisters. This aquamanile, I might add, has particular meaning for me personally, since before joining the Metropolitan I had tried to obtain it for another institution.

All the medieval works acquired between 1978 and 1998, when Wixom retired, were fully published in the catalogue of the 1999 exhibition prepared in his honor, "Mirror of the Medieval World." Since then many other outstanding objects have entered the collection. A monumental marble relief from a Milanese tomb (2001.221), carved by Giovanni di Balduccio about 1340, was a major addition to our holdings in medieval Italian sculpture. A powerful, bearded male head carved in the late thirteenth century from the red sandstone characteristic of Strasbourg and the Upper Rhine (2004.453) joins the Gothic architectural sculptures at The Cloisters, which include a figure of the Virgin from the choir screen at Strasbourg Cathedral carved a generation earlier.

Since 1917 the main building has housed an important group of medieval Limoges enamels from the J. Pierpont Morgan collection, but The Cloisters lacked a major work of this type until 2001, when a large, late twelfth-century plaque depicting two mournful angels swinging censers (2001.634) was acquired. Also from the Morgan collection is a group of four enamel corner plaques bearing symbols of the evangelists; they surrounded a void until 2007, when, thanks to the generosity of Michel David-Weill, we acquired an extremely rare enamel roundel representing the Crucifixion that is undoubtedly the missing centerpiece (fig. 35). The ensemble of enamels, probably created to decorate a book cover, must have been made about 1100 for the Abbey of Saint Foy in Conques.

Secular ivory carvings of the Gothic period—among the most appealing works of the Middle Ages—until recently were not represented in The Cloisters Treasury, but in 2003 the Museum bought a group of four such carvings, all dating to the fourteenth century, from the princely Oettingen-Wallerstein collection. It includes a large relief plaque showing a stag hunt (fig. 39), which originally formed the back of a casket, and another relief in the form of a disk, probably a mirror back, that depicts an allegorical Attack on the Castle of Love (2003.131.1).

In the years preceding the 2005 exhibition "Prague, The Crown of Bohemia, 1347–1437," the Museum was extraordinarily fortunate to acquire three masterworks attributed to the workshops of Prague during that fertile period: an elegant jasper cup with silver-gilt mounts of the third quarter of the fourteenth century (fig. 36) came to the main building in 2000 thanks to the generosity of Jayne Wrightsman; and a fine limestone Pietà (2001.78) as well as the only known terracotta sculpture from Prague, a bust of the Virgin (2005.393)—both works in the so-called Beautiful Style that emerged in Prague just before 1400—entered The Cloisters collection.

While the Western medieval works discussed above are mostly on view at The Cloisters, the years since 1978 have also seen splendid additions to the holdings of Byzantine art exhibited in the Museum's main building. Among the most important is an extraordinary group of silver liturgical objects of the sixth or seventh century known as the Attarouthi Treasure (1986.3.1–.16). These ten chalices, three censers, wine strainer, and dove representing the Holy Spirit were acquired in 1986. In 1993 a large processional cross in silver and silver gilt (1993.163) came to the Museum. A monumental mosaic fragment of the early sixth century depicting a wide-eyed woman identified as Ktisis, personification of the act of foundation (1998.69), was acquired in 1998; a rare Byzantine marble relief sculpture of a griffin dating from the thirteenth century (2000.81) arrived in 2000. Exceptionally fine Byzantine works recently donated to the Museum by John Weber include a fine agate cameo of the eleventh century carved with an image of the Virgin in prayer, her arms outstretched in the posture of an orant (2007.445). The elaborate gold frame that

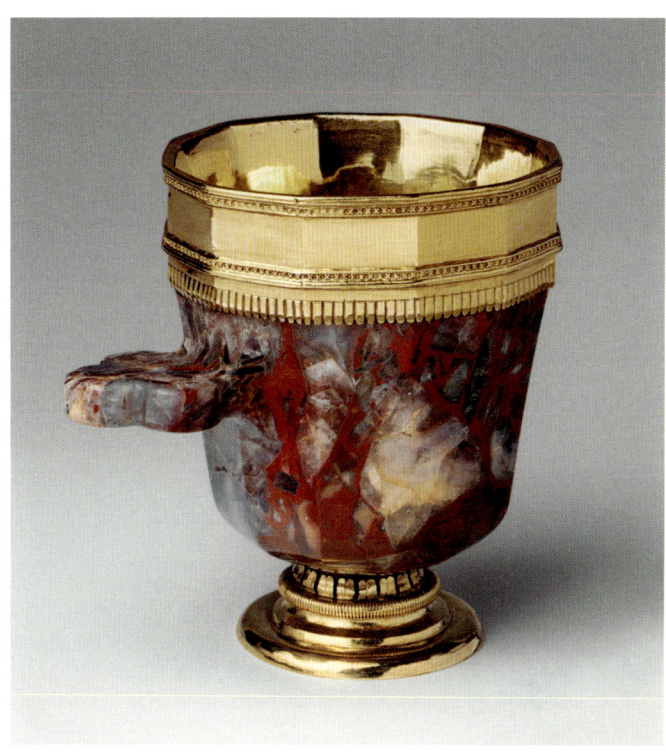

36. Cup with gilded silver mounts. Bohemian, Prague, third quarter of the 14th century. Jasper, gilded silver mount and foot, 4⅛ × 4½ × 3⁷⁄₁₆ in. (10.5 × 11.5 × 8.8 cm). Purchase, Mrs. Charles Wrightsman Gift, in honor of Annette de la Renta, 2000 (2000.504)

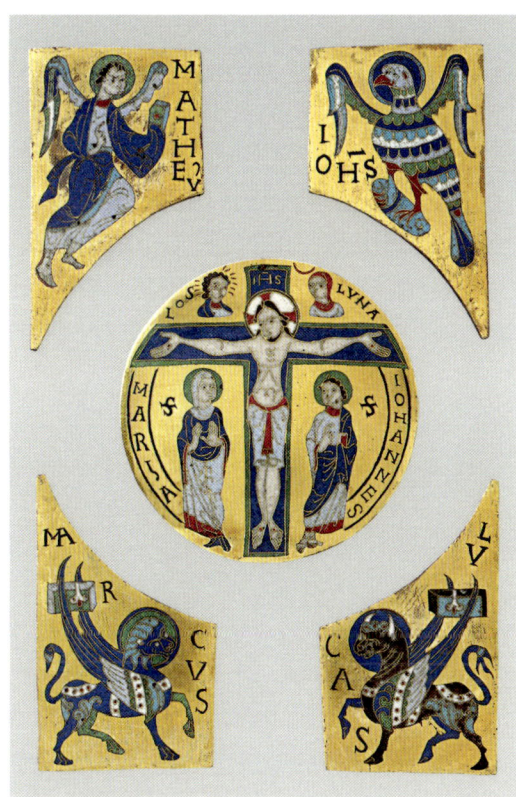

35. *The Crucifixion with Symbols of the Evangelists.* French, Conques, ca. 1100. Champlevé and cloisonné enamel on gilded copper, corner plaques each approx. 4 × 2⅜ × ⅛ in. (10.1 × 6.2 × .3 cm), central roundel 4¹⁄₁₆ × ⅛ in. (10.3 × .3 cm). Corner plaques, Gift of J. Pierpont Morgan, 1917; roundel, Purchase, Michel David-Weill Gift and 2006 Benefit Fund, 2007 (17.190.426–.429; 2007.189)

houses the cameo was made in Paris about 1800 and testifies to an appreciation for Byzantine art during the age of Napoleon. Finally and most extraordinarily, thanks to the generosity of Mary and Michael Jaharis the Museum acquired in 2007 a magnificent Byzantine gospel lectionary that was produced in Constantinople about 1100 (fig. 33). The manuscript is richly illuminated with large portraits of the four evangelists as well as ornamented headings and initials throughout. It is a distinguished Eastern counterpart to the small group of masterworks of illumination at The Cloisters.

In addition to the acquisitions, this period was rich in temporary exhibitions, gallery renovations, and other projects. Among exhibitions, a trio of large shows devoted to the art and culture of late antiquity and Byzantium stand out. "Age of Spirituality: Late Antique and Early Christian Art, Third to Seventh Century" opened in 1977, while Philippe de Montebello was acting director of the Museum. Organized by curator Margaret Frazer with Kurt Weitzmann of Princeton University, this expansive reappraisal presented 594 objects and included loans from 115 institutions. Twenty years later, in 1997, "The Glory of Byzantium: Art and

[25]

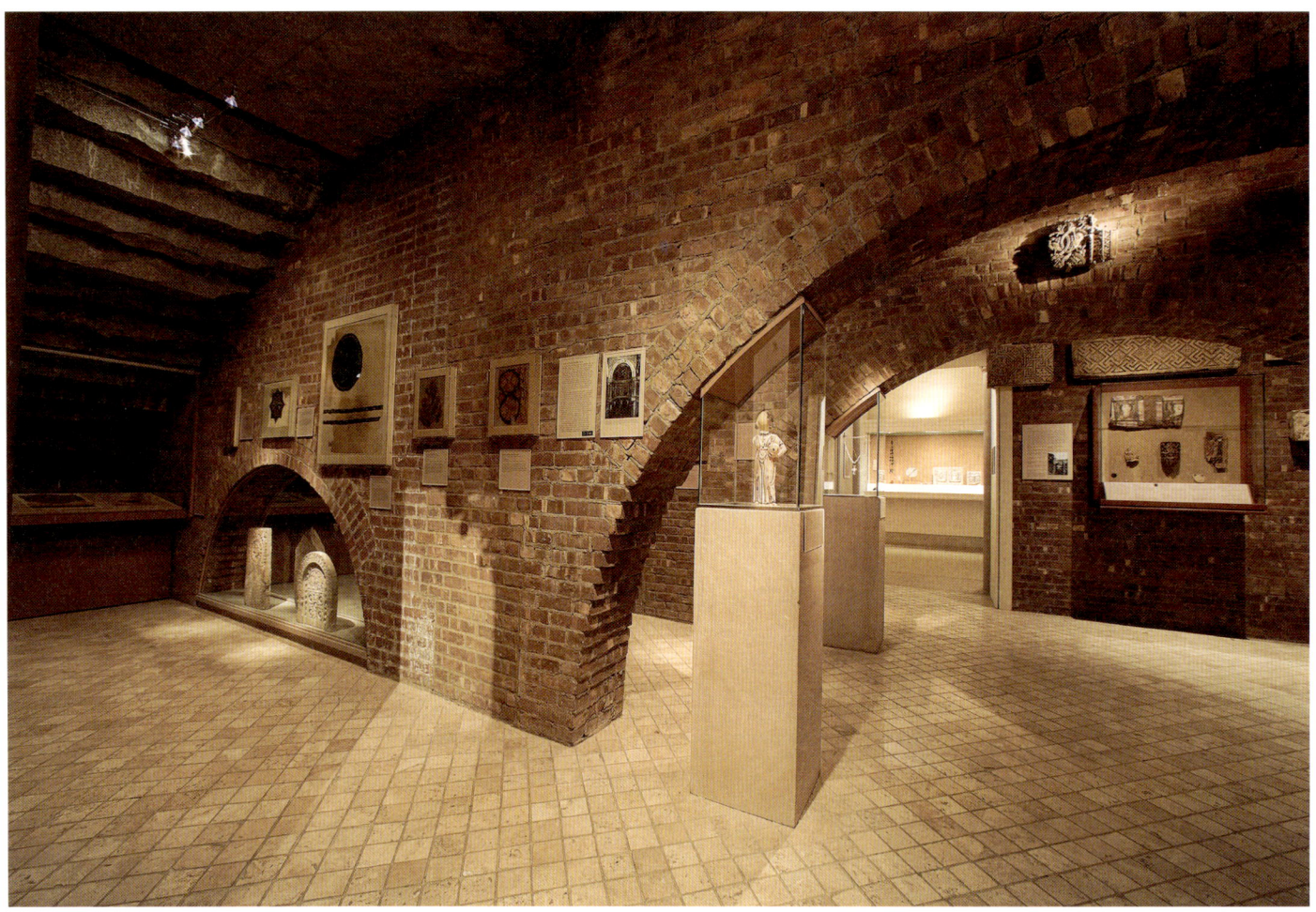

37. In the Mary and Michael Jaharis Galleries for Byzantine Art

Culture of the Middle Byzantine Era, A.D. 843–1261" was organized by Helen C. Evans and William D. Wixom. Works from nearly one hundred institutions, including ten unprecedented loans from the Holy Monastery of Saint Catherine at Sinai, made "The Glory of Byzantium" not only dazzling but of sufficient depth to support an important reappraisal of the era. This exhibition was followed in 2004 by "Byzantium: Faith and Power (1261–1557)," organized by Helen C. Evans, which examined the less-familiar late Byzantine era. "Faith and Power" featured more than forty works from the Monastery of Saint Catherine and 355 loans altogether from more than one hundred institutions. Both Byzantium shows were recognized by *Apollo* magazine as among the top five exhibitions in the world for their respective years, and the catalogue for "The Glory of Byzantium" received the Alfred Barr Award from the College Art Association and the Wittenborn Award from the Art Libraries Society of North America.

Art of the medieval West too was the subject of major exhibitions. In 1986 the Metropolitan collaborated with the Germanisches Nationalmuseum, Nuremberg, to present "Gothic and Renaissance Art in Nuremberg, 1300–1500," an exhibition of nearly three hundred works in all media that explored the art of that imperial city from the late Gothic period through the era of the great Northern Renaissance master Albrecht Dürer. The exhibition was curated by William Wixom and Rainer Kahsnitz of the Germanisches Nationalmuseum. Some of its themes were picked up twenty years later in an exhibition already mentioned, "Prague, The Crown of Bohemia, 1347– 1437," organized by curator Barbara Drake Boehm together with Jiří Fajt of the University of Leipzig and the Technical University of Berlin, which opened in New York in 2005 and traveled to Prague Castle the next year. It introduced audiences to the little-known era when Holy Roman Emperor Charles IV made Prague his capital and sought to rival there the achievements of Paris and other great artistic centers. "Tilman Riemenschneider: Master Sculptor of the Late Middle Ages," organized by curator Julien Chapuis with the National Gallery of Art in Washington, D.C., was shown in New York in 2000. The exhibition presented to an American public the innovative late Gothic work of Riemenschneider, one of the great sculptors in the Western tradition. Notable among the thirty lenders was the Skulpturensammlung of the Staatliche Museen zu Berlin, which, thanks to the renovation of Berlin's Bode-Museum at that time, agreed to send a number of the master's finest works.

Four important exhibitions each focused on a specific medium. In 1995 "The Luminous Image: Painted Glass Roundels in the Lowlands, 1480–1560," curated by Timothy Husband, examined an important area of late medieval stained glass. The 1996 "Enamels of Limoges: 1100–1350," curated by Barbara Boehm and Elisabeth Taburet-Delahaye, brought together the collections of medieval Limoges enamels of the Metropolitan Museum and the Musée du Louvre and offered a major reexamination of this material. "Lions, Dragons and Other Beasts: Aquamanilia of the Middle Ages, Vessels for Church and Table," drawn principally from the Museum's collection but held at the Bard Graduate Center for Studies in the Decorative Arts, Design, and Culture (New York) in 2006, I organized with conservator Pete Dandridge. And in 2009 the Museum presented Melanie

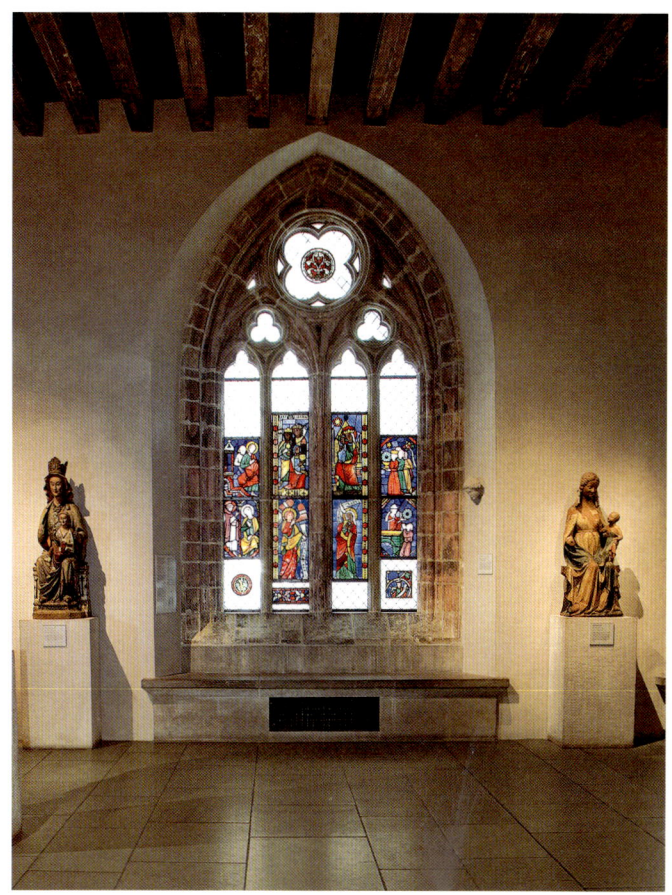

38. Medieval stained glass in the Early Gothic Hall, The Cloisters

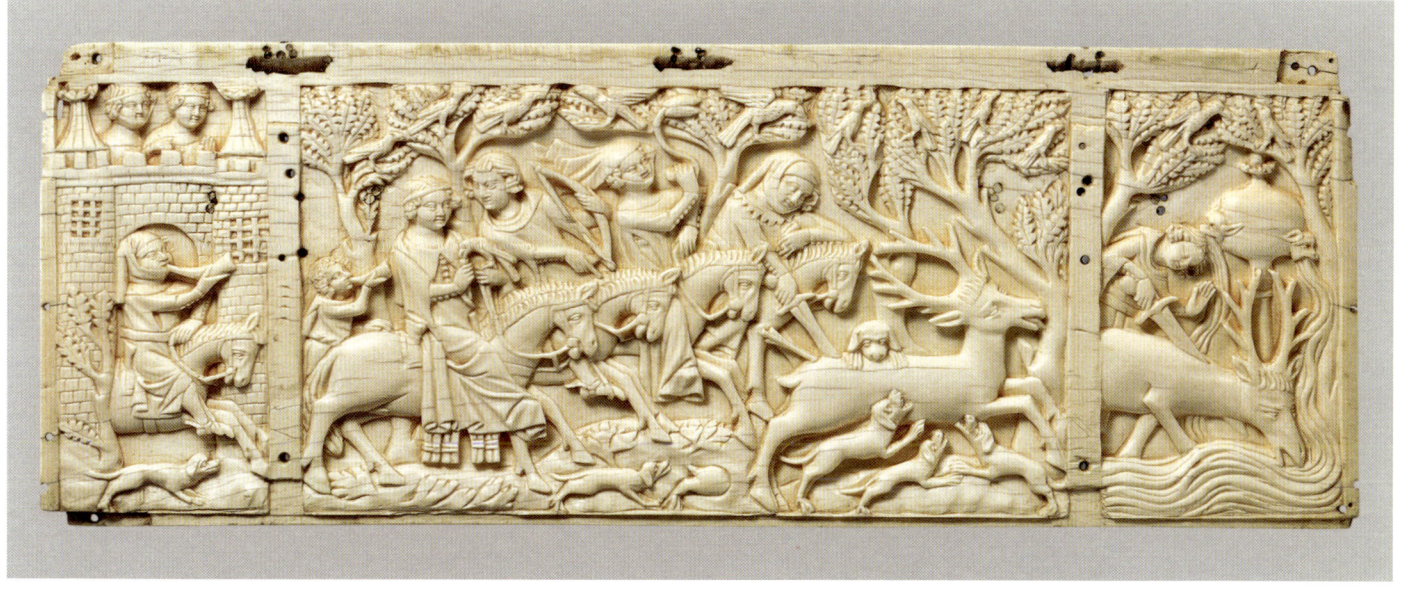

39. Panel with hunting scenes. French, Paris, ca. 1350. Ivory, 4⁵⁄₁₆ × 12⅛ × ³⁄₁₆ in. (11 × 30.8 × .5 cm). The Cloisters Collection, 2003 (2003.131.2)

Holcomb's "Pen and Parchment: Drawing in the Middle Ages," the first exhibition devoted to this essential subject.

The Department of Medieval Art and The Cloisters takes pride in the many important scholarly publications of the collection. The exhibitions described above were all accompanied by major catalogues, and in many cases symposia held during the exhibitions were subsequently published. Other notable volumes include Adolph Cavallo's catalogue *Medieval Tapestries in The Metropolitan Museum of Art* (1993) and *English and French Medieval Stained Glass in the Collection of The Metropolitan Museum of Art* (2003) by Jane Hayward (after her death, overseen by Mary B. Shepherd). A comprehensive catalogue of the medieval Italian sculpture collection by Lisbeth Castelnuovo-Tedesco and Jack Soultanian is forthcoming. *From Attila to Charlemagne* (2000), edited by Katharine R. Brown, Dafydd Kidd, and Charles T. Little, is the first major publication of the Museum's extensive collection of art of the so-called Migration period. *The Art of Medieval Spain: A.D. 500–1200* (1993), edited by Charles T. Little, serves as an important introduction to the period even though, sadly, the exhibition itself was canceled. *The Cloisters: Studies in Honor of the Fiftieth Anniversary* (1988) includes twenty-two essays by an international group of distinguished scholars. Also issued were Barbara Boehm's monograph *The Hours of Jeanne d'Évreux* (1999) and Timothy Husband's *Art of Illumination: The Limbourg Brothers and the Belles Heures of Jean de France, Duc de Berry* (2008).

Gallery renovations and the presentation of the collection have increasingly been understood as integral to the development of the department. In 1988, the fiftieth-anniversary year of the opening of The Cloisters, its Treasury was expanded and renovated. These improvements, made possible by the generosity of Michel David-Weill, permitted many small-scale works added to the collection with funds from the Rockefeller endowment to be properly accommodated. It was also at this half-century point that it became clear the Cloisters building required significant attention, and in recent years time and funds have been devoted to upgrading roofs, windows, and storerooms, as well as galleries. Of the many generous donors who deserve thanks for contributions to these building projects, the City of New York and The Alice Tully Foundation are preeminent. The galleries housing the Hunt of the Unicorn and Nine Heroes tapestries were reroofed and refurbished. Perhaps most notably, the track lighting was eliminated and the original louvered lighting system restored. The original, leaky skylight over the Saint Guilhem Cloister was replaced in 2003 with a new skylight that provides much improved lighting for the fine medieval carvings. In all the gallery renovations, great care was taken to install unobtrusive lighting systems and to restore the original stucco wall colors, which were intended to harmonize with the stonework. (Over the years many of the walls at The Cloisters had been painted white, with the effect of visually flattening the sculptures.)

Most of the main-floor galleries at The Cloisters have now been renovated. Notable among them is the Early Gothic Hall, with its dramatic view of the Hudson River. In addition to new lighting and refurbishing, protective glazing on the hall's thirteenth-century windows has permitted many marvelous stained-glass panels of that century to be installed in exterior windows as intended (fig. 38). The Sherman Fairchild Foundation provided funds in 2002 for the creation at The Cloisters of a state-of-the-art conservation laboratory that has greatly enhanced care and preservation of the collection. Since 2006 a new HVAC system, funded mostly by New York City, has been providing a stable climate in the galleries, something never before achieved at The Cloisters. The remarkably successful system was installed with little visible alteration of the building.

Like The Cloisters, the medieval galleries in the main building on Fifth Avenue had seen little change over the years until 2000, when Mary and Michael Jaharis provided funds for the renovation of the Byzantine galleries that flank the Museum's central staircase. The collection was reorganized and the two corridors were united by opening an intriguing cryptlike space beneath the stairs that is devoted to Egyptian art of the Byzantine period (fig. 37). The Museum's holdings in this area are extensive, and some of our finest pieces are well-preserved textiles; for these, the crypt, far from any natural light, is an ideal setting. Elsewhere in the Jaharis galleries, well-sealed cases and outstanding lighting display the Museum's significant Byzantine collection to maximum effect. The extraordinary Jaharis gifts provided an impetus for continuing renovations of the Byzantine and Western medieval galleries, and in 2008 the space to the west of the staircase became a Byzantine apse housing the new lectionary and other ecclesiastical masterworks of the middle and late Byzantine periods. The gallery to the west of the Byzantine galleries, long known as the Tapestry Hall, has now been completely renovated for the display of Western medieval art from 1050 to 1300 (fig. 40) and includes small-scale works formerly exhibited in the medieval treasury. New, state-of-the-art cases follow the

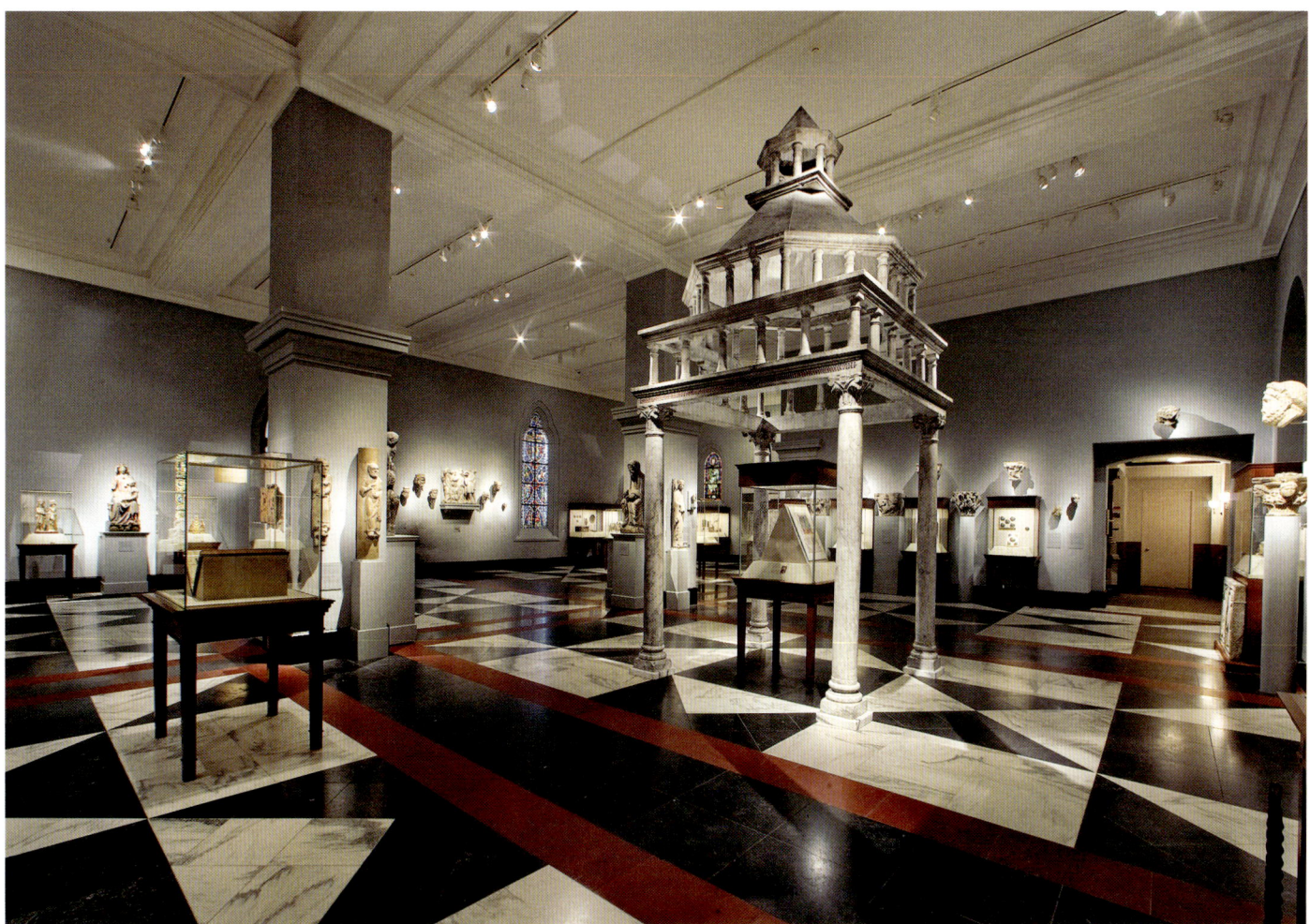

40. The new Medieval Europe Gallery

design of antique wood cases that housed the J. Pierpont Morgan collection. Oculus windows into side stairwells that had been part of the 1880 Victorian Gothic building designed by Calvert Vaux—long since covered over as the Museum grew—were restored and are now a feature of the gallery. Also from the original structure was the hall's marble floor with its geometric design in black, white, and red. Since this was considerably damaged, we replaced it with a new floor that reproduces the old design. But obtaining marble in the original colors was a challenge, and Philippe proved a great stickler for finding the perfect match. He sent back many samples—especially an assortment of not-quite-right whites—until the proper stone had at last been found.

At the center of our new Medieval Europe Gallery and dominating the space stands a marble ciborium eighteen feet tall. Dating from the middle of the twelfth century, it originally sheltered the altar of the church of Santo Stefano in Fiano Romano, near Rome. Although this monument entered the Museum collection in 1909 it had long been displayed at The Cloisters, where it occupied the apse of the Langon Chapel. The idea of moving it to the Fifth Avenue building generated excitement and was strongly supported by Philippe; the undertaking itself was a formidable logistical effort, but in 2008 the ciborium took its place as the focal point of the new gallery. Now for the first time, a Museum visitor walking west from the Great Hall can move past late antique works such as the Ktisis mosaic into a tour through early, middle, and late Byzantium that continues as a chronological overview of Western medieval art.

Peter Barnet

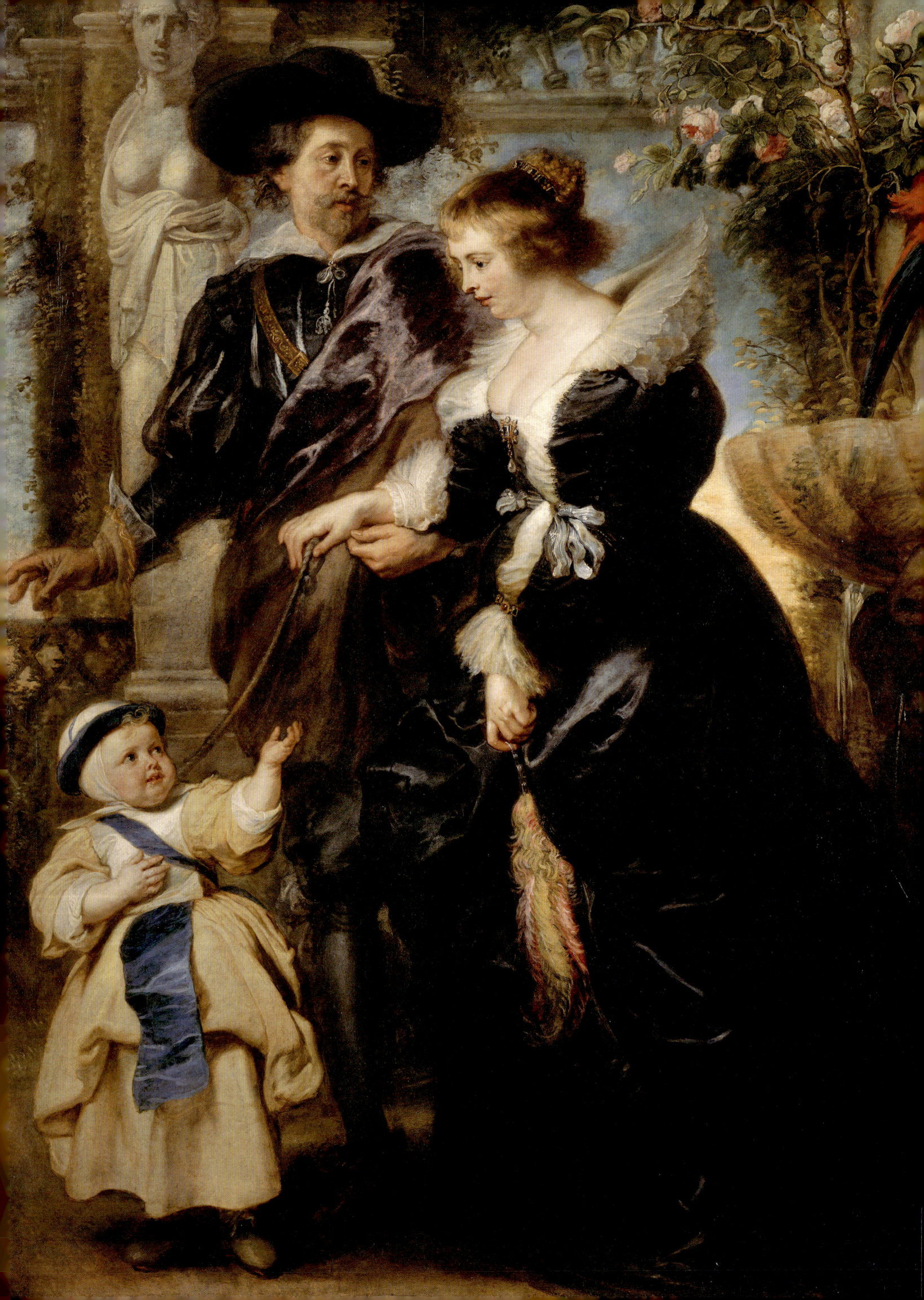

EUROPE FROM THE RENAISSANCE

JAYNE WRIGHTSMAN, INSPIRED COLLECTOR

Back in 1968, when Philippe was an associate curator of European paintings, his duties included organizing "New York Collects," a then-annual showing of paintings from private collections. The precocious curator introduced the exhibition with a verbal flair instantly recognizable forty-one years later: "When the summer approaches and the exodus from the hot, humid city begins, many paintings which decorate favored spots over sofas and sideboards in New York houses, are removed and trucked to the Museum where they are placed on exhibition until Labor Day. . . . One would have to be hopelessly blasé to leaf through the present checklist without wonderment at the inexhaustible riches and surprises of New York." He concluded by expressing gratification that "New York collectors continue to show extraordinary public spirit in their willingness, often at considerable sacrifice, to share their treasures with us." The statement is signed "Guy-Philippe de Montebello." Nine years later, as the new director of the Met, Philippe was blessed to have just such public-spirited benefactors in Jayne and Charles Wrightsman, whose gifts never cease to astonish visitors to the Museum.

In the 1950s the couple began to form a legendary collection, primarily of French furniture and the occasional French Impressionist picture. They bought their first old master, Johannes Vermeer's *Study of a Young Woman*, in 1955. A decade later their apartment in Manhattan and their house in Palm Beach,

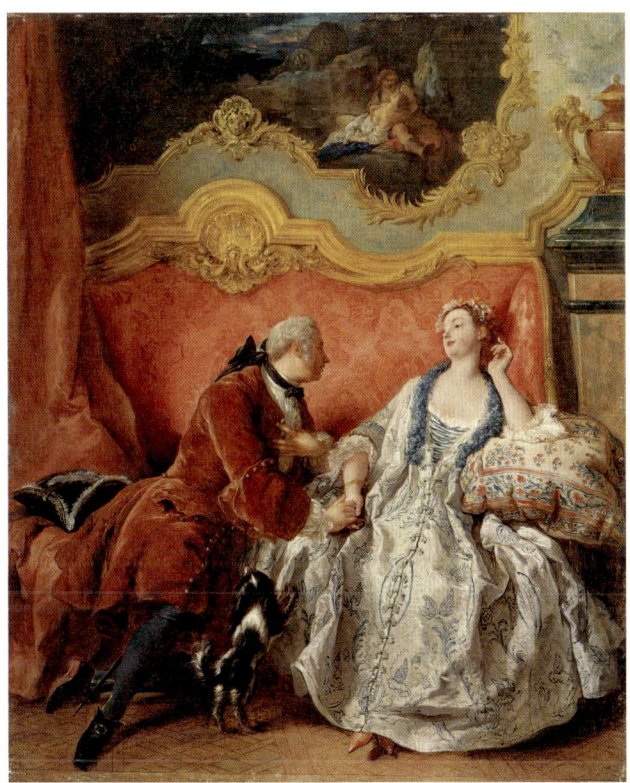 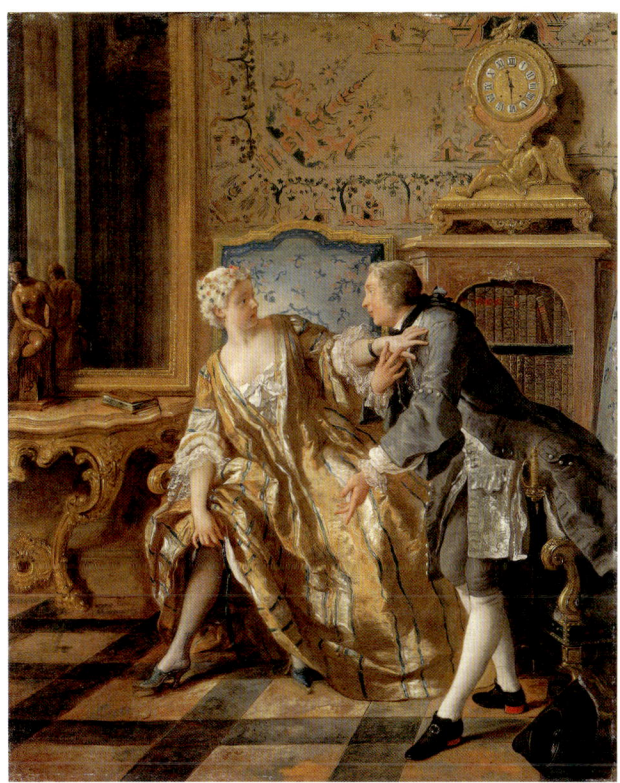

41. Jean François de Troy, *The Declaration of Love* and *The Garter*, 1724. Oil on canvas, each ca. 25½ × 21 in. (64.8 × 53.3 cm). Mrs. Charles Wrightsman, New York

Opposite: 42. Peter Paul Rubens, *Rubens, His Wife Helena Fourment, and Their Daughter Clara Joanna*, ca. 1633. Oil on wood, 80¼ × 62¼ in. (203.8 × 158.1 cm). Gift of Mr. and Mrs. Charles Wrightsman, in honor of Sir John Pope-Hennessy, 1981 (1981.238)

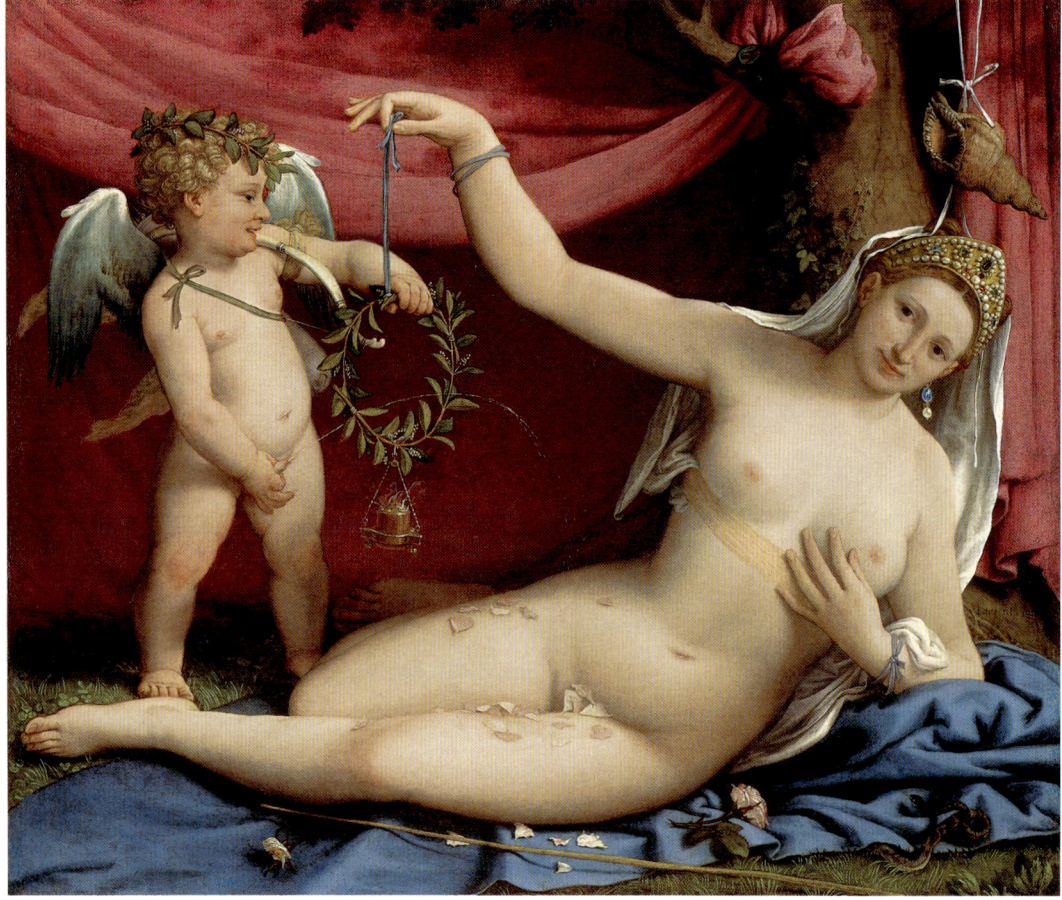

43. Lorenzo Lotto, *Venus and Cupid*, ca. 1523–26. Oil on canvas, 36⅜ × 43⅞ in. (92.4 × 111.4 cm). Purchase, Mrs. Charles Wrightsman Gift, in honor of Marietta Tree, 1986 (1986.138)

Florida, were filled with a marvelous group of eighteenth-century Venetian pictures as well as masterpieces by Anthony van Dyck, El Greco, and Jean François de Troy (fig. 41), to name a few. Their taste has ranged widely within the roomy category of decorative arts, but always to European objects, predominantly of the eighteenth and nineteenth centuries.

In 1963 Jayne Wrightsman first bought a work on her own; it was a book of *placets*, or petitions, addressed to Marie Antoinette and Louis XVI by an army officer requesting promotion. Illustrated with detailed ink drawings by Gabriel Jacques de Saint-Aubin portraying the monarchs and their court, each page elaborately penned and bordered in colors, the whole bound in red leather stamped with gold, it was irresistible to Mrs. Wrightsman, who besides being a great art collector is also an insatiable bibliophile. She saw the book at Rosenberg & Stiebel, bought it, and walked out with it under her arm.

When Charles retired as a trustee of the Metropolitan in 1975, Jayne took his place on the Board. For decades the two had given money to make it possible for the Museum to acquire works of European art, but only after Philippe became director did they begin to donate paintings from their own collection on a regular basis; among them, Georges de La Tour's *The Penitent Magdalen* (in 1978) (fig. 44), the Vermeer *Study of a Young Woman* (in 1979) (fig. 52), and Giovanni Domenico Tiepolo's *A Dance in the Country* (in 1980). They also purchased for the Museum paintings that they had never lived with, such as Nicolas Poussin's poetic canvas *The Companions of Rinaldo* (in 1977); Rubens's lifesize self-portrait with his young second wife, Helena Fourment, and their daughter, Clara Joanna (in 1981) (fig. 42); and Guercino's important early work *Samson Captured by the Philistines* (in 1984).

Jayne performed an enormous service as chairman of the Acquisitions Committee from 1985 to 1997 and was instrumental in bringing innumerable treasures to the Museum. (Ironically, the year she took over the committee was the year Philippe changed the title of the Museum's annual publication from *Notable Acquisitions* to *Recent Acquisitions*.) One major area of contribution grew from her observation that it was difficult to acquire desirable works in the middle range of price. Either they were too expensive to be bought with curators' ordinary discretionary funds, or they were lost to other buyers before approval and funding could be arranged. So Jayne set up a fund, which she has replenished every year, for the purchase of works below a certain price. Careful readers of credit lines will note that many extraordinarily beautiful works of art—not just European paintings but sculpture, drawings, furniture, silver, and china—have come to the Museum thanks to the Wrightsman Fund. Among the European paintings of note acquired through the fund are Pierre-Paul Prud'hon's full-length portrait of Talleyrand (in 1994) and, by a stroke of good fortune eight years later, Baron Gérard's matching portrait of Talleyrand's wife (in 2002).

The stipulations for the Wrightsman Fund were challenged when, in 1986, the rare opportunity arose to acquire a Renaissance masterpiece, Lorenzo Lotto's *Venus and Cupid*. As Calvin Tomkins relates in *Merchants and Masterpieces: The Story of the Metropolitan Museum of Art*, the price, for the time, was steep—$3 million—and Philippe appealed to Jayne for special permission

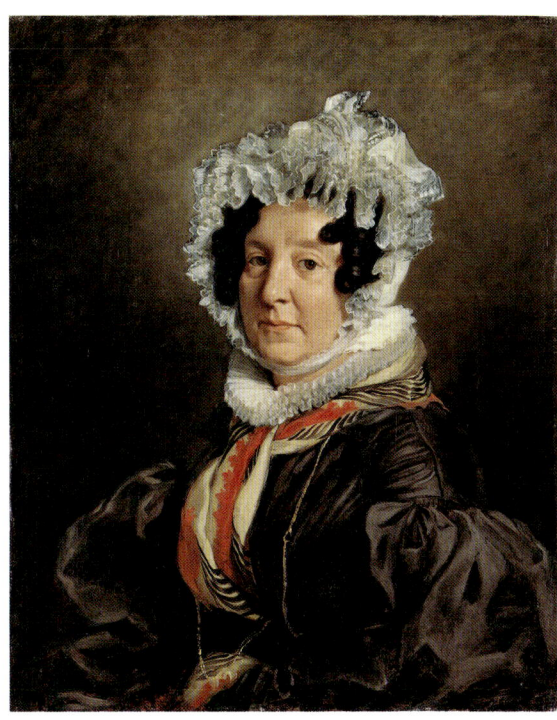

45. Eugène Delacroix, *Madame Henri François Riesener*, 1835. Oil on canvas, 29¼ × 23¾ in. (74.3 × 60.3 cm). Gift of Mrs. Charles Wrightsman, 1994 (1994.430)

to use a large lump sum from her fund. At first she did not consent, pointing out that this was the exact opposite of the fund's intention. However, in a few days she had a new idea; she gave the Museum a further $3 million, and thus the painting was secured. In this beguiling marriage allegory (fig. 43), the goddess of love is surrounded by symbols of fertility and conjugal fidelity to confer good fortune on a wedding couple. Compared to idealized images by Titian or Giorgione, the directly gazing Venus and roguish Cupid have the vivid immediacy of living people. A joyous mood and lush coloring contribute to the delight afforded viewers by this painting—our most important acquisition since Velázquez's *Juan de Pareja* in 1971.

Jayne continues to be an extremely generous benefactor—not only through purchases from her fund but also with gifts of works of art with which she has lived for many years, notably Eugène Delacroix's portrait of his aunt, *Madame Henri François Riesener* (in 1994) (fig. 45), and, during Philippe's last year as director, 2008, Jean-Léon Gérôme's unforgettable portrait *Bashi-Bazouk*. Indeed, most of the paintings the Wrightsmans collected over the years now belong to the Museum. On every level we must count ourselves indebted to these peerless friends of the Metropolitan, and enormously fortunate.

Everett Fahy

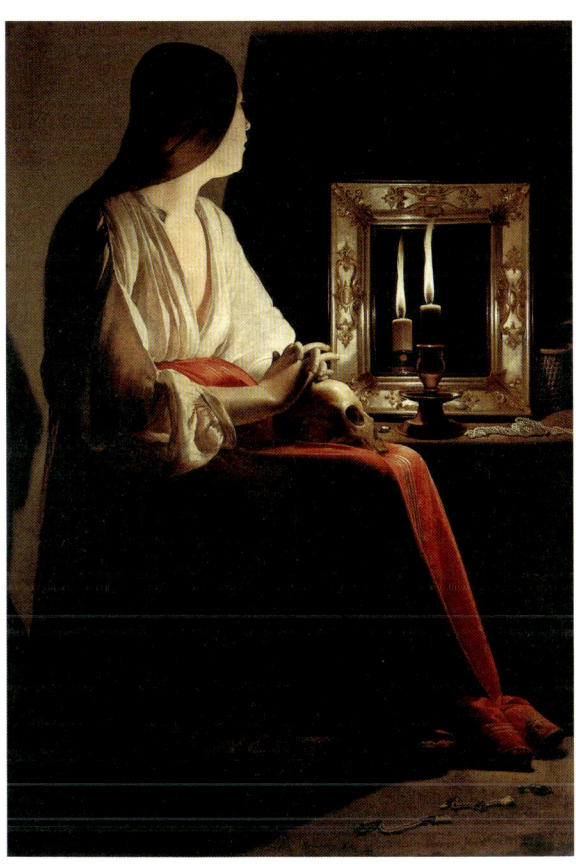

44. Georges de La Tour, *The Penitent Magdalen*, ca. 1640. Oil on canvas, 52½ × 40¼ in. (133.4 × 102.2 cm). Gift of Mr. and Mrs. Charles Wrightsman, 1978 (1978.517)

BUILDING THE COLLECTION

On July 7, 2008, I received an email from my colleague George Goldner of the Department of Drawings and Prints. He had been contacted by a New York dealer asking if he had any idea who might be interested in a work by the seventeenth-century French artist Valentin de Boulogne. Attached to the message was a jpeg of the painting, which represents a seated young man wearing a plumed hat and playing the lute, while to one side an open part book lies on a cloth-covered table. This haunting image is the work of a painter who has been on my short list of desiderata for as long as I can remember. Indeed, over the past twenty-five years, when a dealer occasionally asked me what artists I was especially keen to see in the Metropolitan's collection, I always put Valentin near the top. In my opinion, he and Jusepe de Ribera were the most individual and accomplished of Caravaggio's followers. Valentin could paint with the virtuosity of the young Velázquez, and his works have a compelling psychological as well as physical presence. The effect is one of lyricism, combined with an edgy naturalism. For some reason the comparison with Velázquez does not receive much attention in the art-historical literature, but I am convinced that when Velázquez visited Rome in 1630, the painter for whose works he felt the greatest affinity was Valentin, then at the apex of his brief career (he died two years later).

After replying to George so that I could be in direct touch with the dealer I called Michael Gallagher, who is in charge of our Department of Paintings Conservation, to get his reaction, and the chairman of my department, Everett Fahy. Their enthusiasm further filling my sails, I put in a call to the director. "Philippe, I have an image of a work by Valentin on offer to us. Shall I come to you?" "No, I'll be right over," he responded, with that note of excitement that, over the years, I have come to associate with release from the doldrums of endless appointments by expectation of an unscheduled pleasure. Five minutes later we sat down together in front of my computer screen and I opened the file. We examined it with mounting excitement—mine in anticipation of his response, his from viewing the image. We zoomed in to scrutinize various passages, making observations on the work's strengths and noting possible issues of conservation that would have to be checked out. Philippe was decisive: "See what you can do about the price and get it over here for examination—and see if it can be done before I go on vacation in a couple of weeks. This is something I've wanted for thirty years."

Against all odds, an export license was obtained and the picture shipped to the Museum within that brief time frame. The director was therefore able to see it and pronounce, "This is a 'must have,'" before he left for his annual retreat in Quebec. I got to work, contacting people who might contribute toward the painting's acquisition and conducting research on its provenance: in the seventeenth century it formed part of the famous collection of Cardinal Mazarin, minister to Louis XIV, and for the last century and a half it had been owned by successive members of a single French family. Presented for acquisition in October and purchased with the help of generous contributions from many funders including several trustees, *The Lute Player* (fig. 46) became the last old master painting acquired during the de Montebello directorship.

In my experience, acquisitions rarely move along so smoothly. There are the inevitable disappointments: the price may be beyond the reach of the Museum at the time; or something proposed by another department takes priority; or the curator's enthusiasm simply is not shared by the director and acquisition committee. But it is gratifying to record that over the last three decades, the director's commitment to expanding our collections to embrace all cultures has not meant neglecting the great achievements of European painting, which for many still constitute the high point of a visit to the Metropolitan. During the thirty-one years of Philippe's directorship, no fewer than nine significant works by seventeenth-century French painters have entered the collection—some by gift, some by acquisition. These include the sublime *Penitent Magdalen* by Georges de La Tour (fig. 44), the refined *Annunciation* painted by Philippe de Champaigne for Anne of Austria's private chapel in the Palais Royale in Paris, Eustache Le Sueur's elegantly choreographed *Rape of Tamar*, the astonishingly fresh *View of La Crescenza* by Claude Lorrain, and, now, Valentin's *Lute Player*. These works have vastly enriched the visitor's experience of French painting in its golden age. Remarkably, we still lack a major work by either Simon Vouet or Charles Le Brun—the two artists who represent official painting in Paris—but I trust that when the opportunity to rectify these omissions arises, it will be seized by Philippe's successor with ardor and excitement.

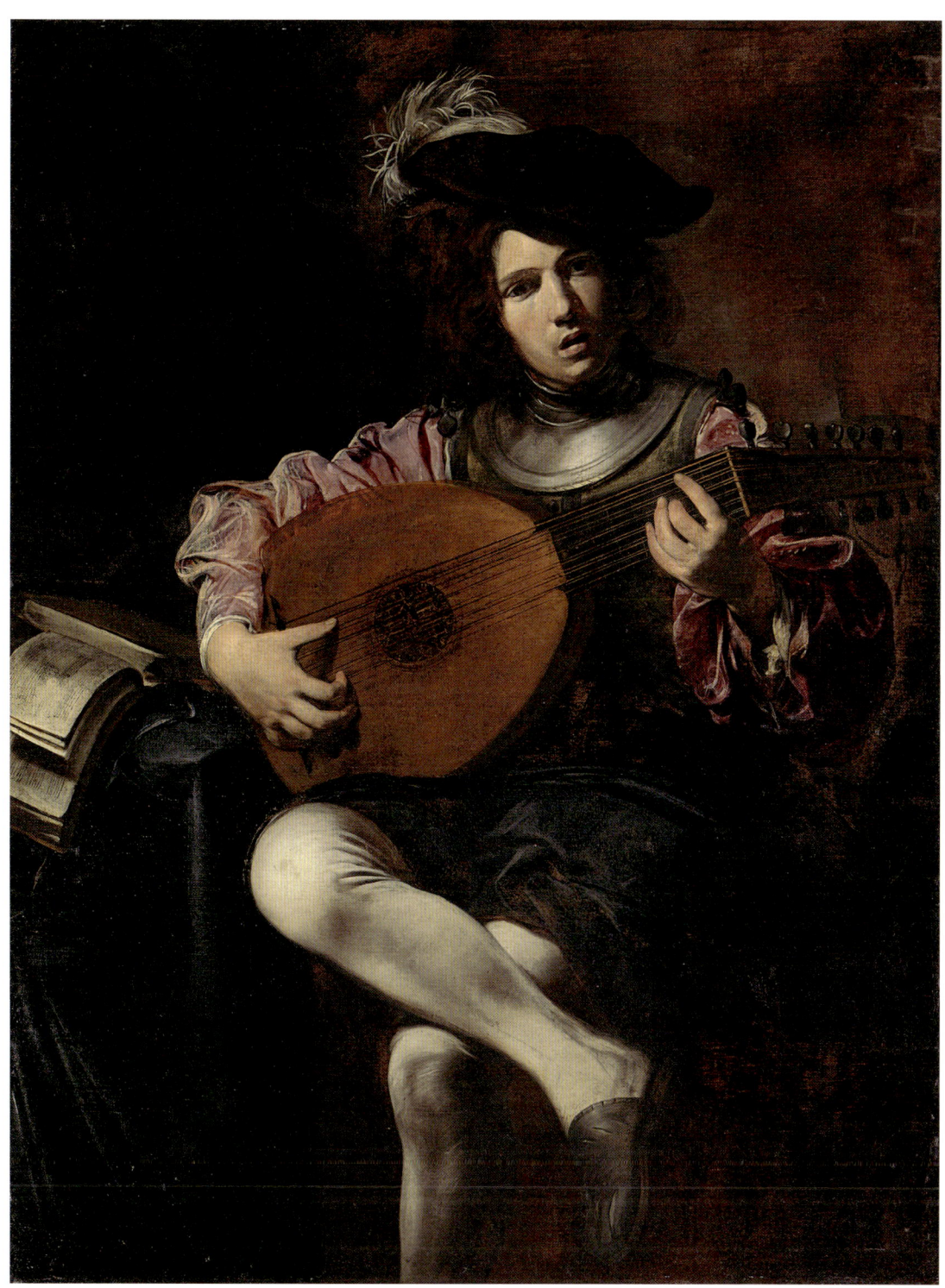

46. Valentin de Boulogne, *The Lute Player*, ca. 1626. Oil on canvas, 50½ × 39 in. (128.3 × 99.1 cm). Purchase, Walter and Leonore Annenberg Acquisitions Endowment Fund; funds from various donors; Acquisitions Fund; James and Diane Burke and Mr. and Mrs. Mark Fisch Gifts; Louis V. Bell, Harris Brisbane Dick, Fletcher, and Rogers Funds and Joseph Pulitzer Bequest, 2008 (2008.459)

To gain a broader view of the ways the collection of European paintings has been transformed during the last thirty-odd years, under the departmental leadership first of Sir John Pope-Hennessy and then of Everett Fahy, it is enough to list the following pictures that should be on every informed visitor's must-see list: Peter Paul Rubens's grand yet touching portrait of himself with his adored wife Helena Fourment and their child (fig. 42), and his *Forest at Dawn with a Deer Hunt*—a modestly scaled but

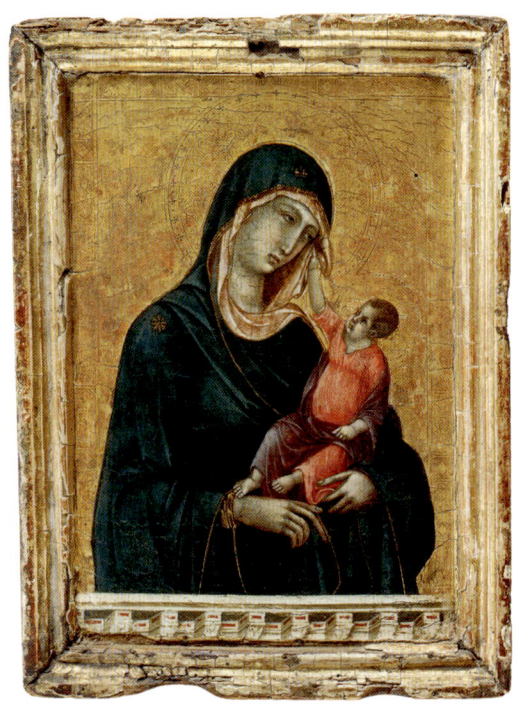

47. Duccio di Buoninsegna, *Madonna and Child*, ca. 1300. Tempera and gold on wood, 11 × 8¼ in. (27.9 × 21 cm). Purchase, Rogers Fund, Walter and Leonore Annenberg and The Annenberg Foundation Gift, Lila Acheson Wallace Gift, Annette de la Renta Gift, Harris Brisbane Dick, Fletcher, Louis V. Bell, and Dodge Funds, Joseph Pulitzer Bequest, several members of The Chairman's Council Gifts, Elaine L. Rosenberg and Stephenson Family Foundation Gifts, 2003 Benefit Fund, and other gifts and funds from various donors, 2004 (2004.442)

astonishing work that, in its evocation of sunlight breaking through the gnarled branches of a tree, looks ahead to Romanticism (fig. 51); Lorenzo Lotto's enchantingly cheeky and blithely poetic *Venus and Cupid*, painted to celebrate a marriage (fig. 43); Johannes Vermeer's entrancing *Study of a Young Woman* (fig. 52); Michiel Sweerts's affecting *Clothing the Naked*; Caravaggio's dark psychodrama *The Denial of Saint Peter*, one of the last works carried out before the artist's untimely death (fig. 48); Guercino's *Samson Captured by the Philistines*, a tragic story of deceit and betrayed love told with cinematic bravura; Giovanni Battista Tiepolo's light-filled oil sketch for his most important project, the frescoed ceiling over the staircase of the Residenz in Würzburg, which shows Apollo driving his chariot across the sky with figures along the edges that personify the four continents; Juan de Flandes's exquisitely domestic *Marriage Feast at Cana*; Hans Baldung Grien's *Saint John on Patmos*; and two masterpieces of fourteenth-century Sienese painting, Pietro Lorenzetti's dramatically pitched *Crucifixion* and Duccio's tender *Madonna and Child* (fig. 47). It is difficult to imagine our collection without these

pictures, which have become as closely associated with the Metropolitan as Rembrandt's *Aristotle with a Bust of Homer*, Velázquez's *Juan de Pareja*, and El Greco's *View of Toledo*. As they remind us, the Metropolitan is a museum that redefines itself through its acquisitions and remakes with equal vigor its visitors' experience of the great achievements of the past. No less significantly, we are reminded that this magnificent expansion of the collection is enormously indebted to the support and generosity of our trustees, and above all to Jayne Wrightsman, the guardian angel of the Department of European Paintings.

As I pass through the galleries on the way to my office each day, I am constantly made aware of this transforming impact, wrought by acquisitions of the last three decades. And nowhere so conspicuously as in the two galleries dedicated to Italian Baroque painting, where we see not merely the addition of a masterpiece or the filling of a perceived gap but the representation of an entire period neglected by previous generations. While New Yorkers have always felt an affinity for Dutch merchants of the seventeenth century and have avidly collected the work of Rembrandt and his contemporaries, they have been less comfortable with the Grand Manner of Italian and French Baroque painters, with their large, gestural compositions illustrating stories taken from classical history and mythology or the Bible. Consider this: had you visited the Metropolitan Museum in 1950, you would have found only two of the pictures currently displayed in the Baroque galleries, both by Salvator Rosa: *Self-Portrait* (as a Cynic philosopher) and *Bandits on a Rocky Coast*. A playwright and poet as well as a painter and printmaker, Salvator Rosa was seen throughout the nineteenth century as a proto-Romantic painter, and this surely is the reason the *Self-Portrait* appealed to Mary L. Harrison, who bequeathed it to the Museum in 1921.

During the 1950s a number of groundbreaking exhibitions devoted to the great figures of Baroque painting were mounted in Europe, and by 1970 the signs of a changing taste could be discerned at the Metropolitan. Six more paintings had been added to the collection, most significantly Caravaggio's *Musicians* and Guido Reni's *Immaculate Conception*. The Caravaggio was purchased a year after the landmark exhibition in Milan that firmly asserted his position as one of the great revolutionaries of European painting; the Guido Reni was acquired five years after an exhibition in Bologna had reaffirmed this refined master as one of the presiding geniuses of seventeenth-century painting. These developments remind us that American museums tend to be

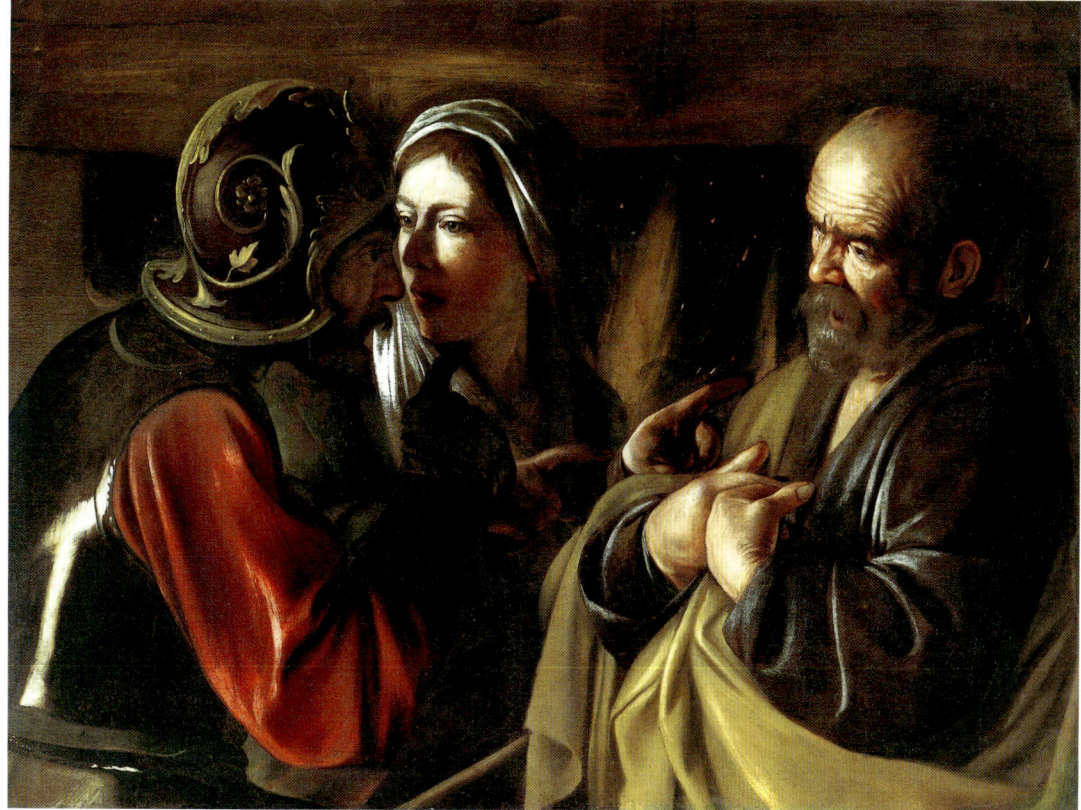

48. Caravaggio (Michelangelo Merisi), *The Denial of Saint Peter*, 1610. Oil on canvas, 37 × 49⅜ in. (94 × 125.4 cm). Gift of Herman and Lila Shickman, and Purchase, Lila Acheson Wallace Gift, 1997 (1997.167)

conservative in their approach to collecting, often running a generation behind European institutions and private collectors in their responses to shifts of taste.

Given the late date that the Metropolitan began collecting seventeenth-century Italian painting, what we have achieved is remarkable. Of the thirty-nine paintings that normally hang in the two galleries devoted to Baroque painting today, six are loans from private collections—evidence of the popularity this period now enjoys among collectors—while eighteen, or almost half, entered the collection in the last thirty-five years. The masterpieces by Caravaggio and Guercino that I mentioned are joined by, among others: two marvelous paintings by Ludovico Carracci, one of the founders of Baroque painting; a rare and engaging early genre painting, *Two Children Teasing a Cat*, by Annibale Carracci; Guido Reni's beautiful allegory *Charity*, painted for the Prince of Liechtenstein; Andrea Sacchi's stunning and unique full-length portrait of Rome's celebrated male soprano Marcantonio Pasqualini; Mattia Preti's *Pilate Washing His Hands*; and two ravishing, small-scale works by Domenichino, the great promoter of Raphaelesque classicism. While there is still a long way to go before we achieve the depth and variety that are the glory of the Dutch collection, it is now possible for visitors to gain some understanding of why Italian Baroque painting enjoyed broad and sustained prestige throughout Europe. Last fall, a professor of art history teaching a class on Baroque art commented to me on the astounding transformation that has taken place since she was a student at NYU's Institute of Fine Arts. Then there were a handful of works to look at, and classes were taught mainly from books and slides. Now a trip to the Met is an indispensable part of any course. Surely this is what the Metropolitan Museum is all about.

Philippe played an active role in this transformation, not only by enthusiastically supporting the acquisitions during his tenure as director but by actively helping set the process in motion earlier as a young member of the department. When Salvator Rosa's deeply poetic *Dream of Aeneas* was purchased in 1965, Philippe was a curatorial assistant (and in the department's archive files for the painting is his typewritten draft of an essay on Rosa that was never published). But, as he knows from personal experience, curators propose, directors dispose. For this reason Philippe can take enormous satisfaction in what has been achieved in the Department of European Paintings during his directorship.

Keith Christiansen

DE MONTEBELLO'S ALCHEMY: TURNING GOLD INTO GOLD

There is a story I enjoy retelling when I'm asked to compare teaching with a curatorial career, or when the question is simply, "What is it like to work at the Metropolitan Museum?" On a Thursday afternoon in 1984 I was summoned to the office of the chairman of my department, Sir John Pope-Hennessy, who said without prefatory remarks, "Come to Liechtenstein on Tuesday." Only those who knew Sir John will successfully imagine the tone of this command (it was not quite an invitation), which was like the contralto whine of a rocket falling on a distant London street. The effect on my immediate plans could be similarly described. A week later, Pope-Hennessy and I, representing European Paintings, were with Olga Raggio (European Sculpture and Decorative Arts), Stuart Pyhrr (Arms and Armor), and the director in Schloss Vaduz, the seat of His Serene Highness the Prince of Liechtenstein, surveying hundreds of treasures dating from the fourteenth through the nineteenth century. From the castle's galleries, private quarters, and great storerooms emerged masterworks that became one of the Museum's largest and most impressive exhibitions, "Liechtenstein: The Princely Collections" (1985–86).

As most readers will know, Philippe de Montebello's tenure as director of the Metropolitan coincided with an age of "blockbuster" exhibitions, intended to be not enormous bombs (the original meaning of the term) but magnets for visitors and revenue. Furthering knowledge was not always the main concern of every museum (although one did learn that a hundred Renoirs are half as appealing as fifty). Nor were the more bombastic titles always true to the matter at hand; for example, the period covered in "The Search for Alexander," seen in Washington and elsewhere in 1980–81, was about fifteen times longer than the king of Macedon's reign. But with very few, if any, exceptions, the exhibitions mounted at the Metropolitan under Philippe's leadership have been noteworthy for their art-historical significance. Curators will have their own preferences; in this context, what is important is not the individual fruits but the cornucopia itself.

Among my favorites are exhibitions of Italian paintings organized by my colleagues Keith Christiansen and Andrea Bayer, such as "The Age of Caravaggio" in 1985 and "Art and Love in Renaissance Italy" in 2008. Of my own exhibitions the most memorable for me was "Vermeer and the Delft School" (2001) (fig. 49), not so much for its sixteen paintings by Vermeer but for the 143 other objects that came from sixteen countries. They included great tapestries from London and Stockholm, paintings from as far east as Saint Petersburg (by Pieter de Hooch) and as far west as Los Angeles (by Emanuel de Witte), silver-gilt objects from a church in Utrecht, and nearly unknown but revealing items from a range of far-flung places. When the best possible (in my opinion) peasant scene by the Delft painter Egbert van der Poel proved to be in the museum at Riga, it was sent to New York in the care of a rather dazzled Latvian courier. And when a catalogue promised at about 250 pages expanded to well over 600, the director encouraged the editorial staff with the observation, "It's not about the money." That is how the Museum came to publish the only comprehensive survey on the arts in Delft, and 555,000 visitors discovered one of the most important schools of Dutch painting and the fact that genius does not come out of nowhere.

An unspoken (to my knowledge) tenet is that popular exhibitions make more recherché endeavors possible. The Metropolitan's emphasis on substance in exhibitions is also exemplified by its willingness to present the unfamiliar or even the obscure. I recall telling Keith on several occasions that the Donato Creti exhibition (which in fact just fell into our laps) was a stroke of genius on his part, because when Andrea's exhibition of Dosso Dossi opened not long thereafter it would seem like something on the order of Raphael. Another exhibition that lacked a household name, Maryan Ainsworth's 1994 gathering of paintings by Petrus Christus, was a revelation to specialists as well as laymen (when that fact was lamented by *New York Times* art critic Michael Kimmelman, his review became the last by him that this writer ever read).

Perhaps the most remarkable aspect of our program of exhibitions during the de Montebello decades has been the sequence of "in-house" shows, those focused on the permanent collections. Who first had the idea for "Rembrandt/Not Rembrandt in The Metropolitan Museum of Art" is not clear, but there is no forgetting the day in early January 1995 when the director suddenly set the project in motion—with an opening scheduled for nine months later and a catalogue deadline in May. Although the rush

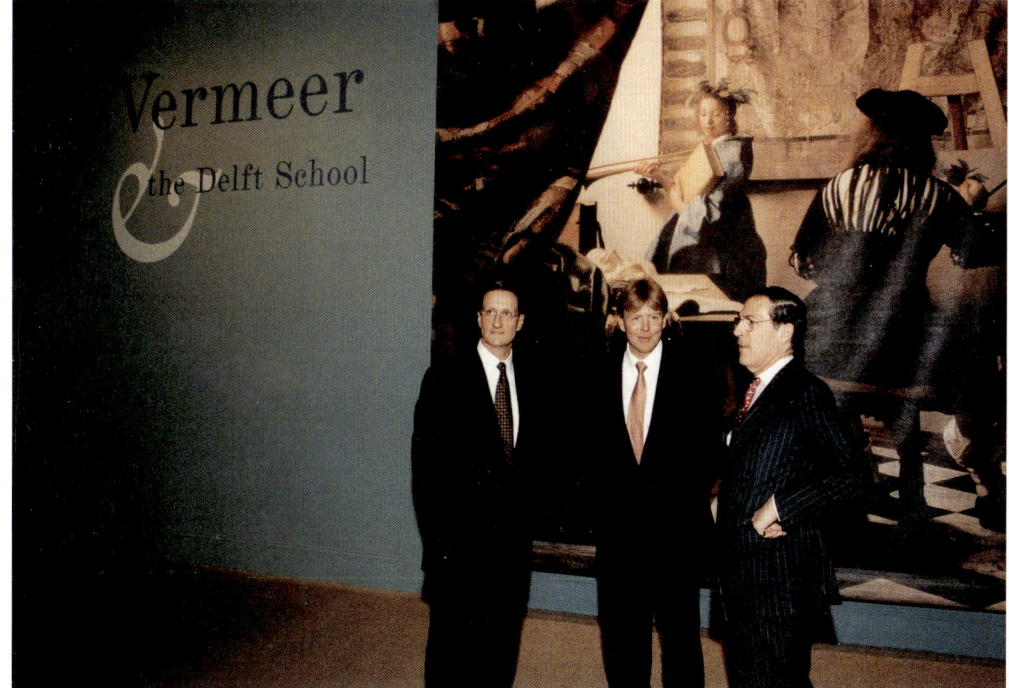

49. Walter Liedtke; His Royal Highness The Prince of Orange, the Netherlands; and Philippe de Montebello at the opening of "Vermeer and the Delft School," 2001

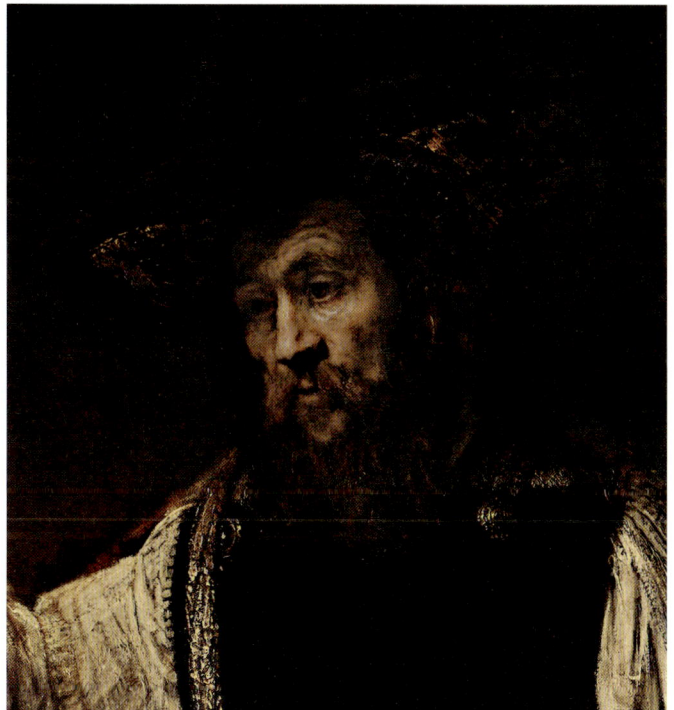 

50. Details of two paintings that were juxtaposed in the exhibition "Rembrandt/Not Rembrandt" (1995). *Left*: Rembrandt van Rijn, *Aristotle with a Bust of Homer*, 1653. Oil on canvas, 56½ × 53¾ in. (143.5 × 136.5 cm). Purchase, special contributions and funds given or bequeathed by friends of the Museum, 1961 (61.198). *Right*: Follower of Rembrandt, *Portrait of a Man ("The Auctioneer")*, third quarter of the 17th century. Oil on canvas, 42¾ × 34 in. (108.6 × 86.4 cm). Bequest of Benjamin Altman, 1913 (14.40.624)

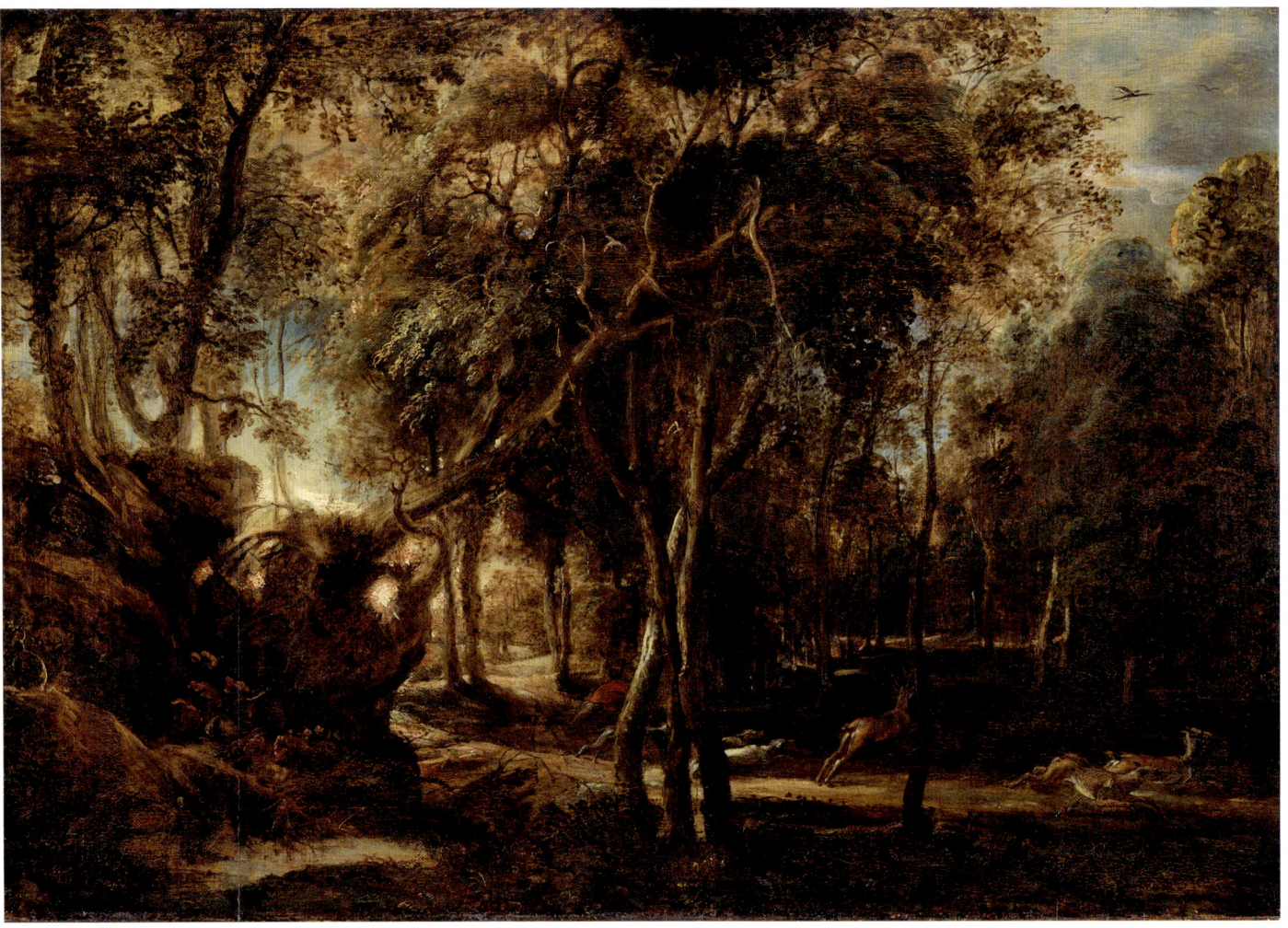

51. Peter Paul Rubens, *A Forest at Dawn with a Deer Hunt*, ca. 1635. Oil on wood, 24¼ × 35½ in. (61.5 × 90.2 cm). Purchase, The Annenberg Foundation, Mrs. Charles Wrightsman, Michel David-Weill, The Dillon Fund, Henry J. and Drue Heinz Foundation, Lola Kramarsky, Annette de la Renta, Mr. and Mrs. Arthur Ochs Sulzberger, The Vincent Astor Foundation, and Peter J. Sharp Gifts; special funds, gifts, and other gifts and bequests, by exchange, 1990 (1990.196)

was caused by the sudden collapse of a show from Spain, this exhibition of about twenty paintings by Rembrandt and an equal number once considered to be by him (fig. 50) became a major step toward the intended cataloguing of the Museum's great collection of seventeenth-century Dutch pictures. In retrospect, I can think of no other project undertaken during my twenty-eight years as curator of the Museum's Dutch and Flemish paintings that was so valuable a learning experience. It was a great opportunity for the public to learn as well—not only about Rembrandt and his many pupils and followers but also about the nature of museum work, art history, and connoisseurship. The dueling labels (in about six instances my colleague Hubert von Sonnenburg and I could not agree about attributions) were somewhat sensational, but they were only the most difficult of the generally challenging texts throughout the exhibition, which also included sections on drawings and prints. A positive response from the public is often a source of pride, but in this case it was the curator who was proud of the public: for rising to the occasion and, after hard looking and thinking, gaining some sense of what makes the whole world of Rembrandt connoisseurship so complicated.

A very different exhibition also drawn (principally) from the Museum's holdings was "Splendid Legacy: The Havemeyer Collection" of 1993. About 450 of the 4,500 objects given to the Museum by Louisine and Henry Osborne Havemeyer— European paintings above all, but also American, ancient, Asian, Egyptian, Islamic, and medieval works of quite diverse kinds—were here seen together for the first time since 1930. Curators from throughout the Museum collaborated in this enterprise, which gave visitors a spectacular view of how the collections of the greatest American art museums were formed.

Several other undertakings represent the scholarly mission of the Museum as carried out in our department. In 1998–99 all the Museum's early Netherlandish paintings were placed on view in the exhibition "From Van Eyck to Bruegel," which was accompanied by a substantial catalogue by Maryan Ainsworth and seven other members of the staff. The depth and breadth of the collection surprised even insiders; the paintings came from not only the main galleries but also the Lehman and Linsky collections, The Cloisters, and storage. There is no other collection of comparable type and scope on this side of the Atlantic, even though major works hang in Philadelphia, Washington, and other American cities. More formal catalogues of the Netherlandish paintings are to come, following one for the Museum's fifteenth- and sixteenth-century German pictures (in preparation).

Our most recent in-house exhibition of European paintings was something quite unusual in the history of art museums, a presentation to the public of an entire collection. All 228 of the Museum's Dutch paintings dating from 1600 to 1800 were hung, to accompany the publication of the collection catalogue *Dutch Paintings in The Metropolitan Museum of Art* (2008) by the present writer. This was an inversion of the usual state of affairs: catalogues generally accompany shows, not vice versa. It was appropriate, however, because the Dutch collection (composed almost entirely of works painted during Rembrandt's lifetime) is so rich not only in masterworks by the most famous artists—Rembrandt, Hals, Vermeer (fig. 52), Ruisdael, and so on—but also in paintings of almost every type by about a hundred other artists, with exceptional strengths in landscapes, portraits, and genre scenes. Dutch pictures formed a large part of the Museum's founding 1871 purchase and from 1887 through 2005 have figured importantly in major donations—the Marquand, Huntington, Altman, Morgan, Havemeyer, Friedsam, Bache, Lehman, Markus, and other gifts and bequests. Consequently, this installation of "The Age of Rembrandt" by approximate date

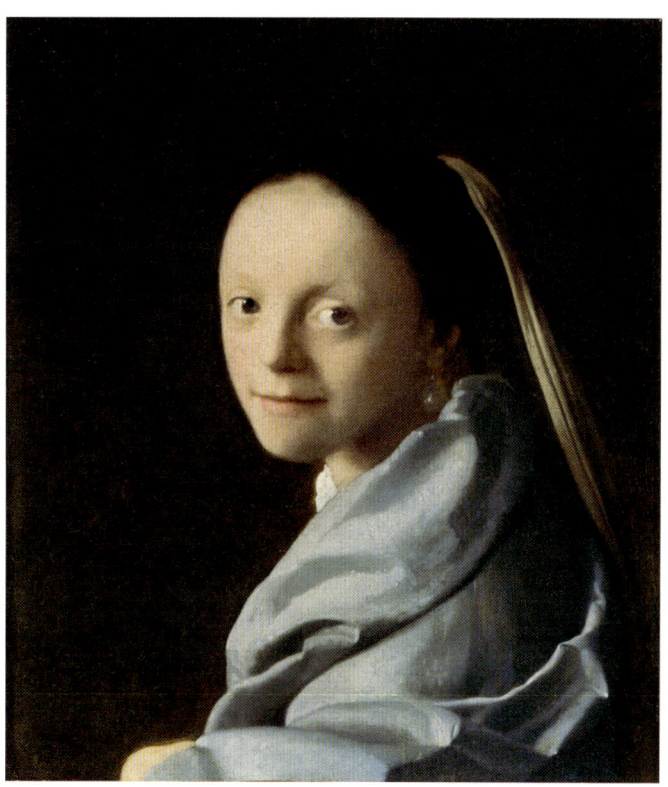

52. Johannes Vermeer, *Study of a Young Woman*, ca. 1665–67. Oil on canvas, 17½ × 15¾ in. (44.5 × 40 cm). Gift of Mr. and Mrs. Charles Wrightsman, in memory of Theodore Rousseau Jr., 1979 (1979.396.1)

of acquisition produced an illuminating overview of a great collection's gradual formation and illustrated a long epoch in American taste.

In all these publications and exhibitions the director took more than a passing interest. His brusque queries as to the progress of the Dutch catalogue over the years always had the effect of encouragement, quite as his complaint about the hefty weight of the two volumes could be taken as a compliment. Everyone who has worked for Philippe, even at a certain distance, knows how to read such subtle or not so subtle signs because we understand his vision of what the Museum should be, we share his convictions, and we are extremely grateful for them.

Walter Liedtke

PRINTS, PHOTOGRAPHS, AND DRAWINGS, 1978–1993

During the first half of Philippe de Montebello's term as director, from 1977 to 1993, I was curator in charge of what was then the Department of Prints and Photographs. Development and expansion of the collection were continual, and in 1980 the department's new suite of three galleries devoted to changing exhibitions of works on paper opened. Two of the galleries were later named after collector-patrons Karen B. Cohen and Charles Z. Offin. While the practice of exhibiting selections from the department's long-established treasury of old master prints was maintained, curators were also encouraged to explore relatively uncharted areas of the collections. The result was a succession of exhibitions and catalogues on a wide range of subjects, such as architectural and ornament drawings and prints, lesser-known Italian engravings, nineteenth-century French and American prints, and selected photographs.

Among the special exhibitions held during this period were "The Collection of Alfred Stieglitz: Fifty Pioneers of Modern Photography" (1978, catalogue by Weston J. Naef), "The Painterly Print: Monotypes from the Seventeenth to the Twentieth Century" (1980, catalogue by Colta Ives, David W. Kiehl, et al.), "Renaissance Ornament Prints and Drawings" (1981–82, catalogue by Janet S. Byrne), "Counterparts: Form and Emotion in Photographs" (1982, catalogue by Weston J. Naef), "The Engravings of Giorgio Ghisi (1520–1582)" (1985, catalogue by Suzanne Boorsch, Michal Lewis, and R. E. Lewis), "The American Art Poster of the 1890s: The Gift of Leonard A. Lauder" (1987–88, catalogue by David W. Kiehl), "The New Vision: Photography Between the World Wars, Ford Motor Company Collection at The Metropolitan Museum of Art" (1989, catalogue by Maria Morris Hambourg and Christopher Phillips), "Pierre Bonnard: The Graphic Art" (1989–90, catalogue by Colta Ives, Helen Giambruni, and Sasha M. Newman), "French Architectural and Ornament Drawings of the Eighteenth Century" (1991–92, catalogue by Mary L. Myers), and "The Waking Dream: Photography's First Century. Selections from the Gilman Paper Company Collection" (1993, catalogue by Maria Morris Hambourg, Pierre Apraxine, et al.).

Other publications authored by members of the department included issues of the Museum's *Bulletin* on aspects of the permanent collection, especially recent acquisitions, published in 1978, 1982–83, and 1988. The curators edited two publications occasioned by the death in 1980 of A. Hyatt Mayor, curator emeritus: *A. Hyatt Mayor: Selected Writings and a Bibliography* (1983) and *Artists and Anatomists* (based on his previously unpublished manuscript, 1984).

Long recognized as the repository of one of the world's largest and most encyclopedic print collections, the department employed acquisition funds to purchase rarities that had somehow escaped an earlier grasp. Most notable among these was the purchase in 1986 of the monumental late fifteenth-century engraving *Bacchanal with a Wine Vat* by Andrea Mantegna in the finest impression known, from the collection of the Dukes of Devonshire, Chatsworth (fig. 54). We also acquired singular prints by Jacques Bellange, Gabriel de Saint-Aubin, Francisco Goya (fig. 53), Eugène Delacroix, Édouard Manet, and Edgar Degas (fig. 55), often with the financial support of the department's Visiting Committee chair, Janet Ruttenberg.

Among the extraordinary gifts made by devoted print collectors were superb engravings and woodcuts by Albrecht Dürer from George and Marianne Khuner, seventeenth- and eighteenth-century Italian prints from Robert L. and Bertina Suida Manning, lithographs by James McNeill Whistler from Paul W. Walter,

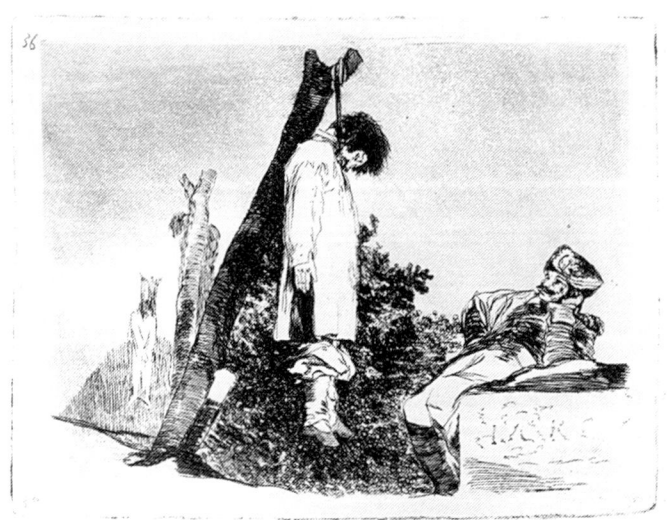

53. Francisco de Goya y Lucientes, *Not This Time Either (Tampoco)*, working proof for pl. 36 of *The Disasters of War*, 1810–14. Etching, burnished aquatint, drypoint, burin, and burnisher on laid paper, image 7⅜ × 5½ in. (18.7 × 13.9 cm). Purchase, Derald H. and Janet Ruttenberg, Dr. and Mrs. Goodwin M. Breinin, Arthur Ross Foundation, and Peter H. B. Frelinghuysen Gifts, and The Elisha Whittelsey Collection, The Elisha Whittelsey Fund, 1987 (1987.1014)

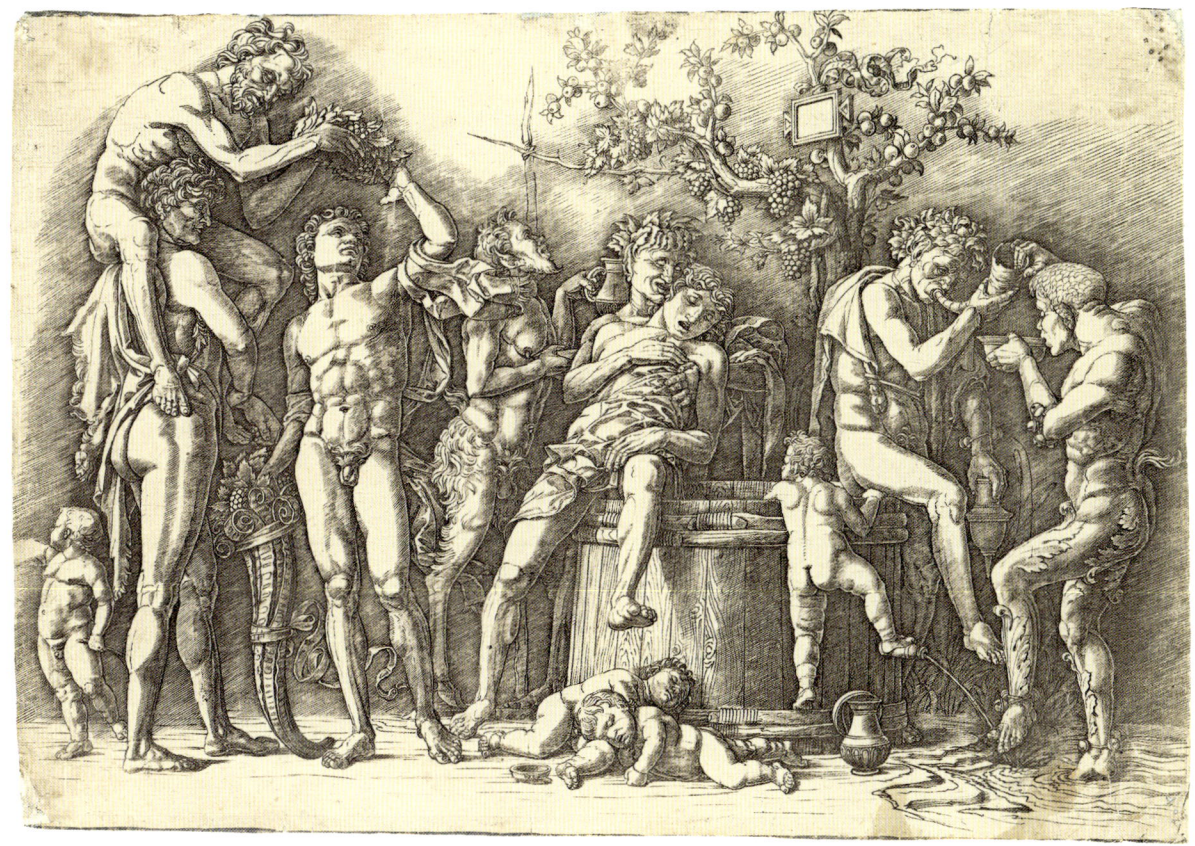

54. Andrea Mantegna, *Bacchanal with a Wine Vat*, ca. 1470–90. Engraving and drypoint, 11¾ × 17¼ in. (29.8 × 43.8 cm). Purchase, Rogers Fund, The Charles Engelhard Foundation Gift, and The Elisha Whittelsey Collection, The Elisha Whittelsey Fund, 1986 (1986.1159)

American posters from Leonard and Evelyn Lauder, modern European prints from the estate of Scofield Thayer, linoleum cuts by Pablo Picasso from Mr. and Mrs. Charles Kramer, and contemporary lithographs published by Universal Limited Art Editions (ULAE) from Dr. Joseph I. Singer.

One of the department's priorities was the expansion of the photography collection, an effort for which purchase funds were generously provided by, among others, Warner Communications, Inc., the Ford Motor Company, The Howard Gilman Foundation, and Joyce and Robert Menschel. In response to growing interest in the art of photography and the rise of a unique constituency devoted to the medium, an independent Department of Photographs was established in 1992, with Maria Morris Hambourg as curator in charge.

The separate Department of Drawings was, during the period 1977–93, under the leadership of Jacob Bean, who had been appointed the Museum's first curator of drawings in 1960. The

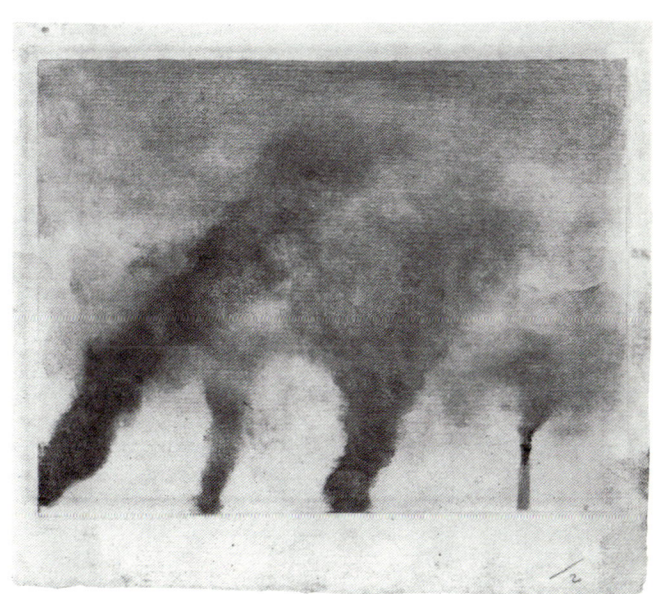

55. Hilaire-Germain-Edgar Degas, *Factory Smoke*, 1877–79. Black ink on laid paper (monotype), sheet 5¹³⁄₁₆ × 6¹³⁄₁₆ in. (14.7 × 17.3 cm). The Elisha Whittelsey Collection, The Elisha Whittelsey Fund, 1982 (1982.1025)

[43]

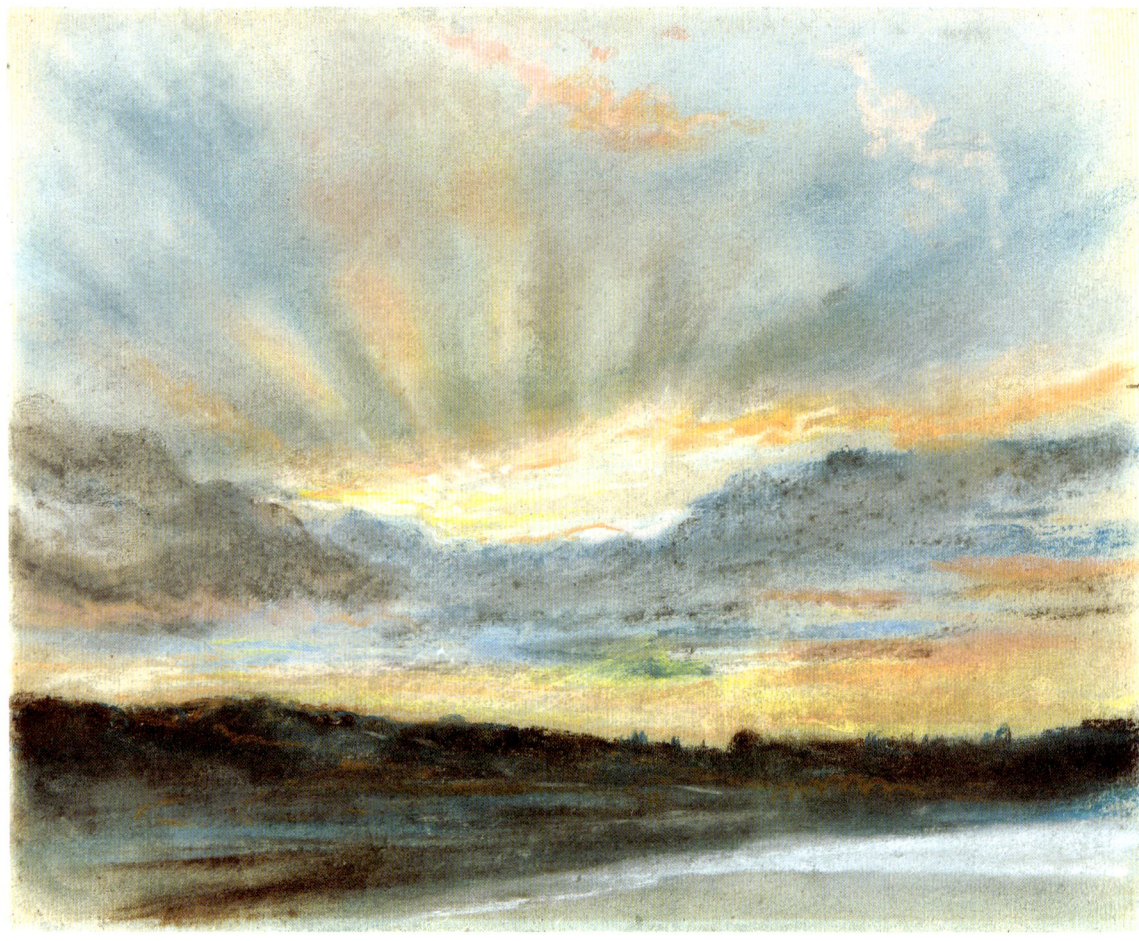

56. Eugène Delacroix, *Sunset*, ca. 1850. Pastel on blue laid paper, 8¼ × 10¼ in. (21 × 26.2 cm). Promised Gift from the Karen B. Cohen Collection of Eugène Delacroix, in honor of Philippe de Montebello

department concentrated its efforts on the publication of illustrated collection catalogues, which included *17th Century Italian Drawings in The Metropolitan Museum of Art* (1979, by Jacob Bean), *15th and 16th Century Italian Drawings in The Metropolitan Museum of Art* (1982, by Jacob Bean with the assistance of Lawrence Turčić), *15th–18th Century French Drawings in The Metropolitan Museum of Art* (1986, by Jacob Bean with the assistance of Lawrence Turčić), and *18th Century Italian Drawings in The Metropolitan Museum of Art* (1990, by Jacob Bean and William Griswold). Two issues of the *Bulletin* written by the department's junior curators were published in 1985 and 1991.

Drawings were displayed on a rotating basis in the galleries for works on paper, often in thematic collaborations with the Department of Prints and Photographs. Special loan exhibitions of drawings from noted public and private collections were also mounted, among them "Leonardo da Vinci: Nature Studies from the Royal Library at Windsor Castle" (1981), "Leonardo da Vinci: Anatomical Drawings from the Royal Library, Windsor Castle" (1984), "Master Drawings from the Woodner Collection" (1990), "Drawings from the J. Paul Getty Museum" (1993), and "Daumier Drawings" (1993, catalogue by Colta Ives, Margret Stuffmann, and Martin Sonnabend). Staff of several departments collaborated on an exhibition to highlight the Museum's collection of works by Eugène Delacroix, which was shown in 1991 and accompanied by the catalogue *Eugène Delacroix (1798–1863): Paintings, Drawings, and Prints from North American Collections* (fig. 56).

With the generosity of patrons Karen B. Cohen, David Schiff, Mrs. Carl Selden, Alice F. Steiner, and Alexander and Grégoire Tarnopol, combined with support provided by the Harry G. Sperling Fund, the Museum's drawings collection continued to grow. Among the outstanding acquisitions were particularly fine examples of French and Italian draftsmanship from the sixteenth to the eighteenth century, including works by Perino del Vaga, the Carracci, Gianlorenzo Bernini, Guido Reni, Charles de La Fosse, and François Boucher.

Colta Ives

DRAWINGS AND PRINTS, 1993–2009

After the death in 1992 of Jacob Bean, Drue Heinz Curator in the Department of Drawings and from March 1992 curator emeritus, the Department of Drawings and the Department of Prints were united into a single department, of which I became chairman. A major effort was embarked upon to develop the drawings collection and expand the exhibitions program. The Museum acquired Italian drawings by Perugino, Vittore Carpaccio, Leonardo da Vinci, Raphael, Pontormo, Titian, Agnolo Bronzino, Domenichino, Giovanni Battista Piranesi, and many other figures both major and minor. In the field of French drawings a small but important group of sixteenth- and seventeenth-century works were purchased, including important examples by Jacques Bellange and Jacques Callot. And strength was added to strength with the department's acquisition of notable sheets by Nicolas Poussin, Claude Lorrain, Jean-Honoré Fragonard (fig. 59), Jean-Auguste-Dominique Ingres, Théodore Gericault, Paul Gauguin (fig. 60), and many other artists of all periods.

However, the greatest emphasis has been on building collections of Netherlandish and German drawings, areas that had been largely neglected in previous decades. Several hundred such

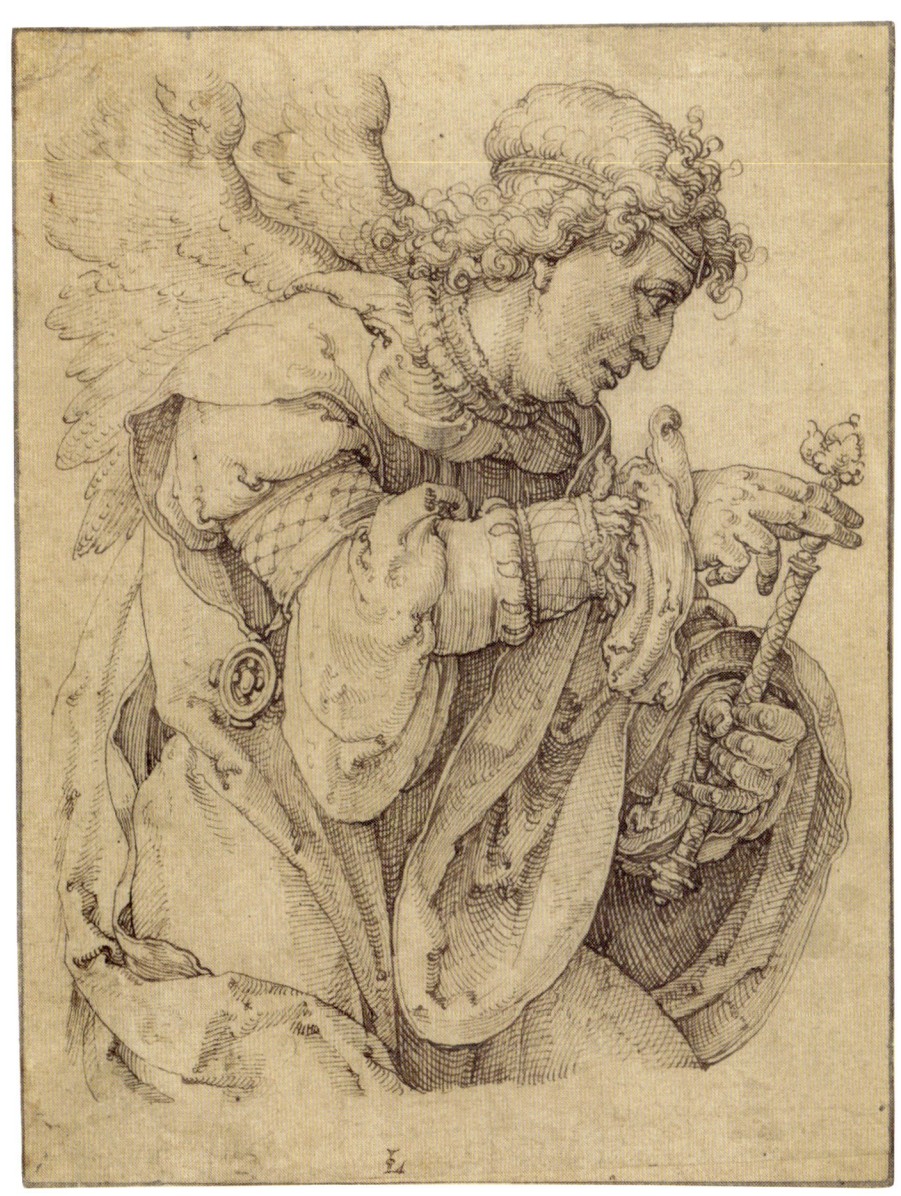

57. Lucas van Leyden, *The Archangel Gabriel Announcing the Birth of Christ*, 1520s. Pen and brown ink, traces of black chalk, 8 5/16 × 6 1/2 in. (21.1 × 16.5 cm). Promised Gift of Leon D. and Debra R. Black, and Purchase, Lila Acheson Wallace Gift and 2007 Benefit Fund, 2008 (2008.253)

[45]

drawings have been acquired; the Museum collections are now reasonably balanced, offering both historical continuity and individual high points. Among the major Netherlandish additions are drawings by Lucas van Leyden (fig. 57), Maarten van Heemskerck, Bartholomeus Spranger, Hendrick Goltzius, Jacques de Gheyn II, Peter Paul Rubens, Anthony van Dyck, Rembrandt van Rijn, Aelbert Cuyp, and Jacob van Ruisdael. Within the German/Swiss sphere there have been notable additions by Urs Graf, Hans Hoffmann (fig. 58), Joseph Heintz the Elder, Henry Fuseli, Caspar David Friedrich, and Adolph Menzel, as well as a great many fine drawings by second-tier artists. Lastly, the Museum has established the beginnings of a small collection of Scandinavian drawings and expanded its holdings of British watercolors and drawings.

This growth of the collection has been made possible in part through the generosity of several new donors to the department, notably Leon and Debra Black, the late Frits and Rita Markus, David and Julie Tobey, Jean Bonna, and Jessie and Charles Price. The overall result is that the Museum now has the most widely representative collection of drawings in the United States, in parallel with its long-standing leadership in the field of prints. In that area fewer new acquisitions were called for, but some important additions have been made in the last decade and a half, including an engraving by the Master of the Playing Cards and outstanding series of prints by Israhel van Meckenem and Ferdinand Olivier, as well as a splendid etching by Edgar Degas. We have also been much more active than formerly in acquiring prints by contemporary American artists.

The exhibition program too has been vastly expanded. A series of mainly monographic loan exhibitions on major artists who had not been seen in comprehensive exhibitions in recent decades (or in some cases at all) has included "Poussin: Works on Paper. Drawings from the Collection of Her Majesty Queen Elizabeth II" (1996), "The Print in the North: The Age of Albrecht Dürer and Lucas van Leyden" (1997), "The Drawings of Filippino Lippi and His Circle" (1997–98, catalogue by George R. Goldner and Carmen C. Bambach), "Eighteenth-Century French Drawings in New York Collections" (1999, catalogue by Perrin Stein and Mary Tavener Holmes), "Correggio and Parmigianino: Master Draftsmen of the Renaissance" (2001, catalogue by Carmen Bambach, George R. Goldner, et al.), "William Blake" (2001), "The Prints of Vija Celmins" (2002, catalogue by Samantha Rippner), "Leonardo da Vinci: Master Draftsman" (2003, catalogue by Carmen C. Bambach et al.), "Hendrick Goltzius, Dutch Master (1558–1617): Drawings, Prints, and Paintings" (2003), "Vincent van Gogh: The Drawings" (2005, catalogue by Colta Ives, Susan Alyson Stein, et al.), and "Clouet to Seurat: French Drawings from the British Museum" (2005–6, catalogue by Perrin Stein). Members of the department authored *Bulletin*s that were published in 1997, 2000, 2004, and 2006.

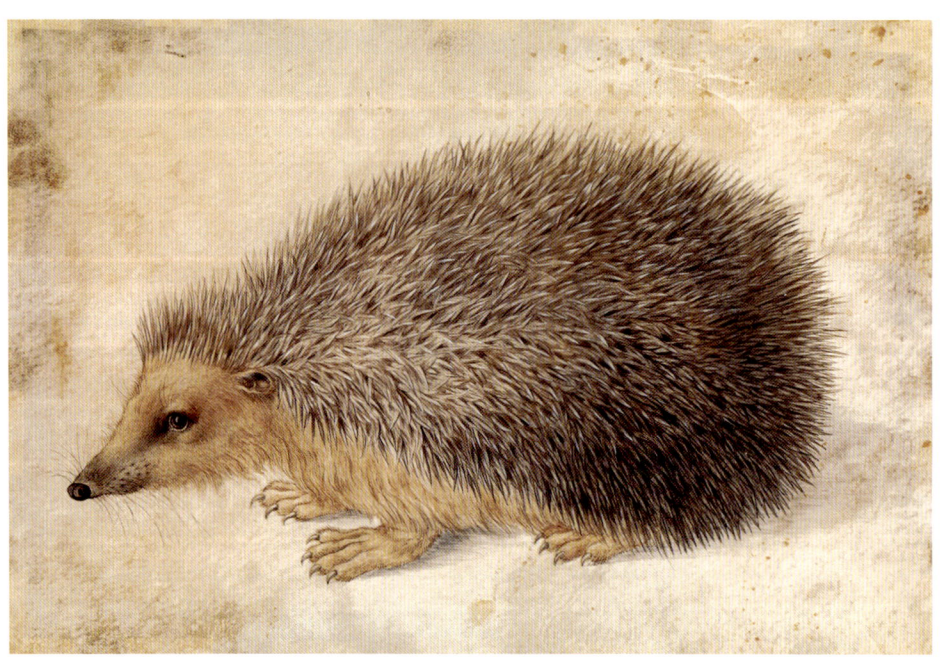

58. Hans Hoffmann, *A Hedgehog*, before 1584. Watercolor and gouache on parchment, 7⅞ × 11¾ in. (20 × 29.8 cm). Purchase, Annette de la Renta Gift, 2005 (2005.347)

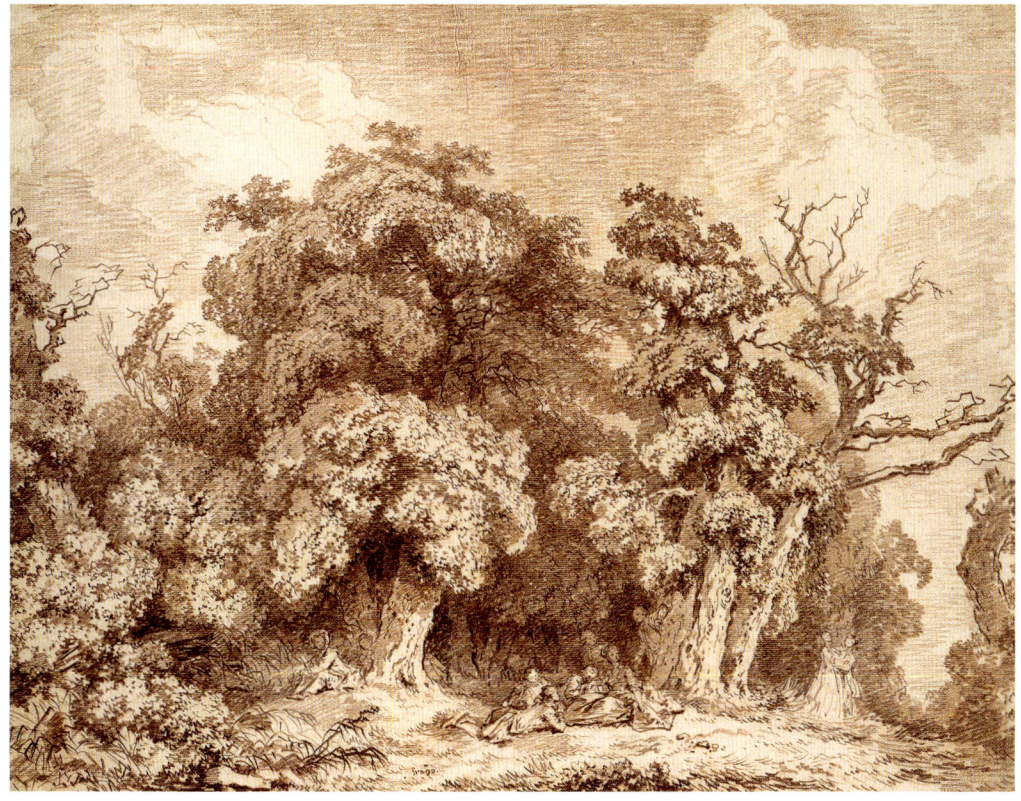

59. Jean-Honoré Fragonard, *A Gathering at Woods' Edge*, 1761–73. Red chalk, 14¾ × 19⅜ in. (37.5 × 49.2 cm). Purchase, Lila Acheson Wallace Gift, 1995 (1995.101)

60. Paul Gauguin, *Tahitian Faces*, ca. 1899. Charcoal on laid paper, 16⅛ × 12¼ in. (41 × 31.1 cm). Purchase, The Annenberg Foundation Gift, 1996 (1996.418)

Other departmental developments include the opening of the Robert Wood Johnson Jr. Gallery, established in 1992, designated by the director as a space for continuing rotations of drawings, prints, and photographs from the permanent collection. This innovation has made it possible for us to give visitors a taste of the range and quality of our collections and to highlight new acquisitions. We have also made computerized records of the entire collection of drawings and have begun to do so for prints, with the eventual hope of having them available to the public. Lastly, we have maintained a particularly active educational program, bringing a great many visiting scholars and interns into association with the department over the years.

George R. Goldner

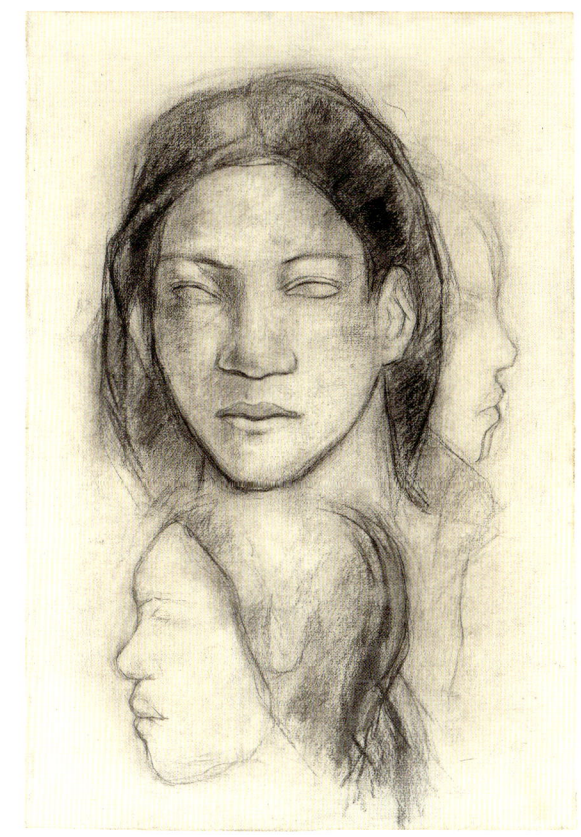

ESDA IN THE PHILIPPE DE MONTEBELLO YEARS

In 1977 Philippe de Montebello was appointed acting director and the department formerly known as Western European Arts acquired a new name, European Sculpture and Decorative Arts. From simpler beginnings in 1907 (when it was called the Department of Decorative Arts) it has now become a vast assemblage of some sixty thousand objects—sculpture in all media, woodwork and furniture, metalwork, ceramics, glass, textiles, clocks, and scientific instruments—representing every part of Europe and dating from the Renaissance to about 1900. Ten curators oversee the collections, which are divided among some sixty galleries, period rooms, and storage areas.

Much of this transformation came in the past thirty years, which witnessed an extraordinary expansion and refinement of the department's permanent displays, changes in the character of its temporary exhibitions, and rethinking of goals for acquisition. Doubling the entire Museum's gallery space, one of Philippe's most impressive legacies, paved the way for a dramatic redeployment of our department's holdings. In the decade from the mid-1980s to the mid-1990s, a new ESDA gallery opened virtually every year. This expansion allowed then-chairman Olga Raggio to reorganize the presentations with an eye to departmental strengths and recent gifts.

To display the rich collection given to the Museum by Jack and Belle Linsky, a new suite of galleries was designed to complement its specialized concentrations of objects and suggest the intimate spaces of a private home. Opened in 1984, these small rooms showcase the Linskys' important eighteenth-century German porcelain, French Rococo and Neoclassical furniture, and Italian and Northern European bronzes. By terms of the bequest the entire collection remains together—a tradition that dates from the earliest days of the Museum but is seldom observed today. On the walls hang European paintings also from the Linskys' collection.

Three years later the department opened the last of the Wrightsman Galleries for French decorative arts, completing a two-decade project that had been overseen by curator James Parker. The focal point of one room is a series of four embroideries of about 1685 depicting the seasons and elements and made for Madame de Montespan, mistress of Louis XIV (46.43.1–.4). They are the backdrop for a state bed hung with canopies given by Irwin Untermyer. This is not an actual period room, since there are no wall panels from a specific building, but it suggests a royal bedroom and contains a parapet copied from one at Versailles. The gallery became the chronological starting point for a series of French period rooms presenting high points of the decorative arts from the late seventeenth to the late eighteenth century. Period rooms are magnets for collecting, and, with the support and discernment of Mr. and Mrs. Charles Wrightsman, our collection of French decorative arts has become one of the finest.

In 1989 an additional Wrightsman gallery extended our reach to the arts of Central Europe—for which, despite its strong holdings in Meissen porcelain and furniture, the department had lacked a unified space. In this new gallery of German and Austrian decorative arts of the seventeenth and eighteenth centuries, a central display of porcelain is circled by vignettes of furnishings, while vitrines hold brilliant silver, glass, and ceramics from courts and urban centers of Prussia, Saxony, and other regions. The displays are anchored by magnificent objects that the department was able to acquire through the generosity, once again, of the Wrightsmans.

Construction of The Henry R. Kravis Wing provided additional gallery space. First, in 1990, came the Carroll and Milton Petrie European Sculpture Court. Threaded between the exterior wall of the Museum's original brick building and a new limestone facade, this tall court with a dramatic skylight roof at long last provided space for large-scale stone statues, principally French eighteenth-century works, conceived for the outdoors (fig. 61). Many of them were placed within boxwood hedges to suggest garden parterres, while busts lined an arcade wall as they might a palace corridor. In 2003 the parterres were removed to permit a freer arrangement of the sculptures, whose range has been broadened to take in examples from 1600 to 1900 and works from Italy and Northern Europe.

New rooms were added adjacent to the Petrie Court beginning in 1991. The Iris and B. Gerald Cantor Galleries were the first to be devoted to nineteenth-century European works and the culmination of an intense effort, led by James David Draper with Clare LeCorbeiller, to collect objects from a century that had previously been neglected. The Florence Gould Galleries established a location for exhibiting individual masterpieces from

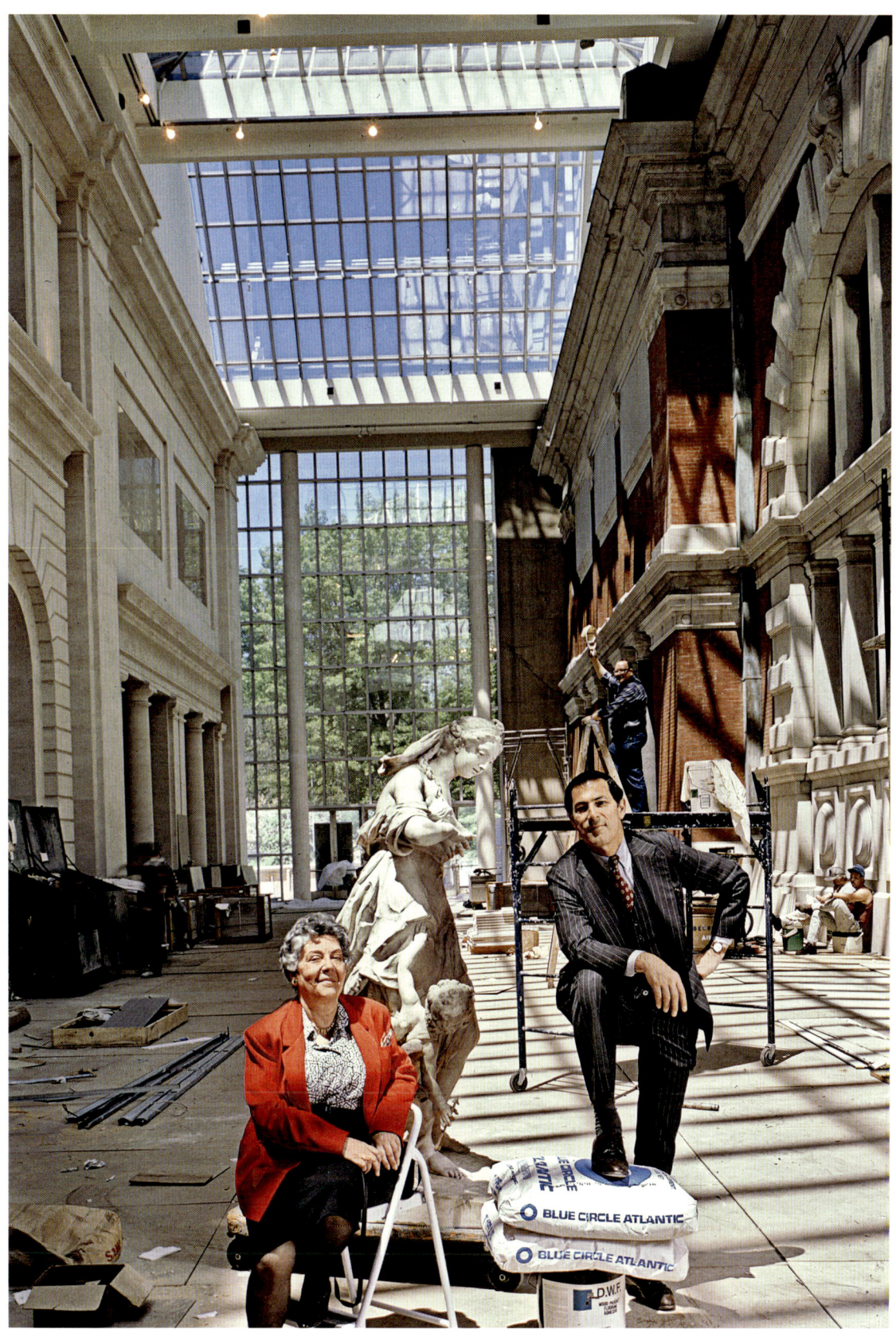
61. Olga Raggio and Philippe de Montebello in the Petrie Court as it neared completion, 1990. Photograph by Hans Namuth

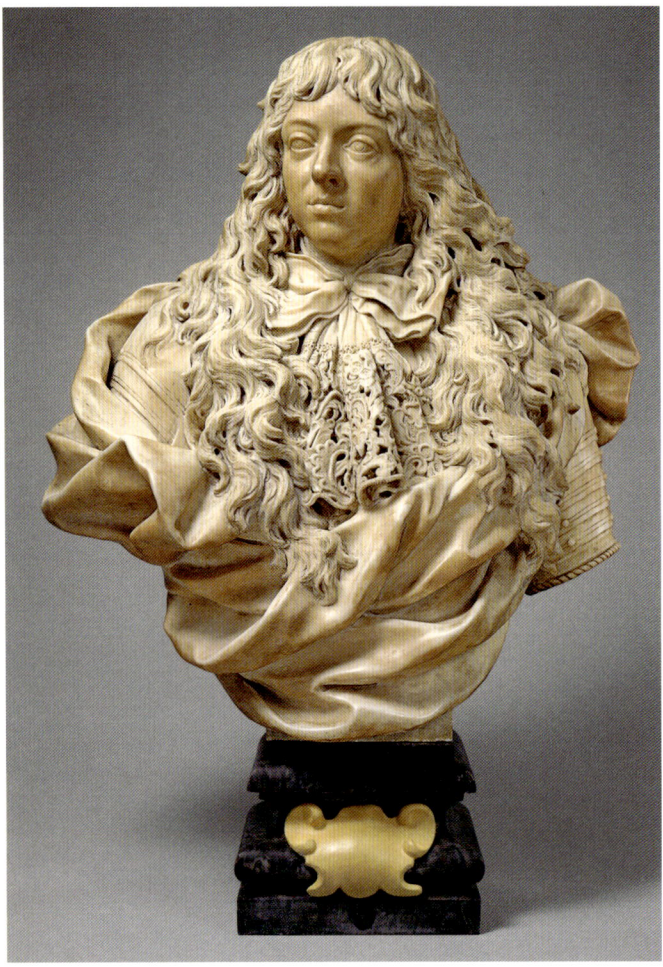

62. *Grand Prince Ferdinando de' Medici*. Italy, by Giovanni Battista Foggini, ca. 1683–85. Marble, overall H. 39 in. (99.1 cm). Purchase, The Annenberg Foundation Gift, 1993 (1993.332.2)

various countries. Magnificent acquisitions made by Olga Raggio, such as the pair of busts of Cosimo III and Ferdinando de' Medici by Giovanni Battista Foggini (fig. 62) purchased with funds from the Annenberg Foundation, were displayed before a great Baroque tapestry (92.1.15) and grand bookcases (1969.292.1, 2) of about 1715 from the Palazzo Rospigliosi, conjuring up the sumptuous interior of an Italian Baroque palace. The international breadth of the Neoclassical style is suggested by the sympathetic juxtaposition of the colossal malachite vase made for the Russian Demidoff family (44.152) with a French medals cabinet designed by Charles Percier (26.168.77) and an armchair made in Germany after designs by Karl Friedrich Schinkel (1996.30).

The English rooms and galleries reopened in 1995 as the Annie Laurie Aitken Galleries of English Decorative Arts and include important eighteenth-century period rooms from Kirtlington Park, Croome Court, and Landsdowne House, refurbished under the direction of William Rieder, as well as new galleries fitted out to display silver, ceramics, textiles, and enamels, many from the great collection of Judge Irwin Untermyer. In 1996 the fifteenth-century intarsia Studiolo from Federico da Montefeltro's palace in Gubbio reopened after extensive conservation; the two-volume work by Olga Raggio and Antoine Wilmering on the history and conservation of the room is a model of curatorial and scientific study.

Many of the objects in these new installations had formerly been housed on the ground floor; the spaces vacated became the new Antonio Ratti Textile Center. Our seventeen thousand textiles as well as those from other departments were transferred to the Ratti Center, which opened on December 14, 1995. Thomas Campbell, then a curator of European Sculpture and Decorative Arts, was named its supervising curator.

During the last eight years, under my chairmanship, ESDA has paid particular attention to renovating older installations. In 2003 the Italian Renaissance bronze gallery adjacent to the Vélez Blanco Patio was reinstalled with support from Alexis Gregory; the first comprehensive catalogue of this collection is being written by Jim Draper and several colleagues. A major effort of the 2006–7 years was the renovation of the Wrightsman Galleries after the close of the "Dangerous Liaisons" exhibition. With the full support of Jayne Wrightsman and aided by many curators and conservators, Daniëlle Kisluk-Grosheide and I reexamined lighting and window treatments and the conservation and upholstery of furniture, chandeliers, and wall sconces. A major goal was to create a more sympathetic and varied lighting ambience consonant with the lower levels customary before electrification (fig. 63). Some rooms were entirely transformed. Much work necessary for the preservation of the entire collection—new air-conditioning, security systems, fire prevention—was hidden in the infrastructure. Following this major campaign, a more modest redesign of the Aitken Galleries and the Josephine Mercy Heathcote Gallery refreshed our presentation of English decorative arts.

Study of our period rooms and their furnishings engendered several publications. The first in the series, *European Furniture in The Metropolitan Museum of Art: Highlights of the Collection*, by Daniëlle Kisluk-Grosheide, Wolfram Koeppe, and William Rieder, appeared in 2006. Jeffrey Munger is completing a second, on Continental porcelain, and a new handbook of the Wrightsman Galleries is also in progress.

ESDA exhibitions have changed enormously over the past thirty years. While many special exhibitions from the period 1975–2000 were of collections that had been given to the Museum ("The Lesley and Emma Shaefer Collection: A Selective Presentation," 1975; "Highlights of the Irwin Untermyer Collection," 1977–78; and "Rodin: The B. Gerald Cantor Collection," 1986), most prominent were shows for which Philippe played a major role as negotiator and Olga Raggio brought her erudition, range, and linguistic skills to bear as principal organizer. The works came from princely or papal collections not easily accessible to visitors. These large exhibitions of spectacular objects unfamiliar to an American audience proved to be brilliantly successful. Philippe's diplomacy and adroit sense of timing were critical for their accomplishment.

"The Splendor of Dresden: Five Centuries of Art Collecting" (1977–78) gathered paintings, tapestries, sculptures, ceramics, and arms and armor from collections formed by the rulers of Saxony. Isolated by the Iron Curtain and still recovering from the devastation of World War II, Dresden was rarely visited in those years, and its treasures were largely unknown in this country. The astute patronage of the electors of Saxony had found a response in inventive forms produced by the first European porcelain manufactory

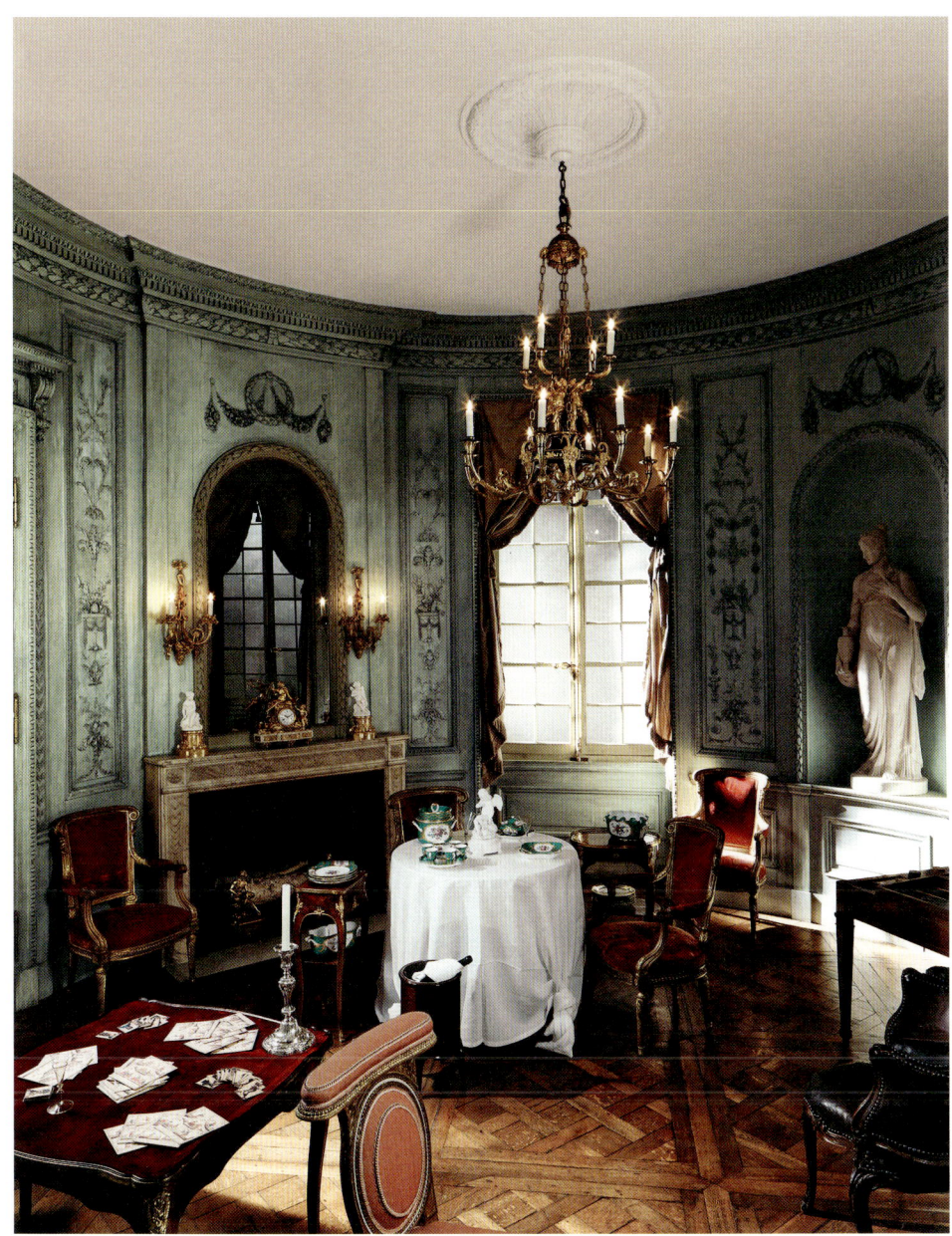

63. Period room from an *hôtel* in the Cours d'Albret, Bordeaux, France, ca. 1785. Carving attributed to Barthélemy Cabirol and workshop. Gift of Mrs. Herbert N. Straus, 1943 (43.158.1). Photographed after the 2006–7 renovation of the Wrightsman Galleries

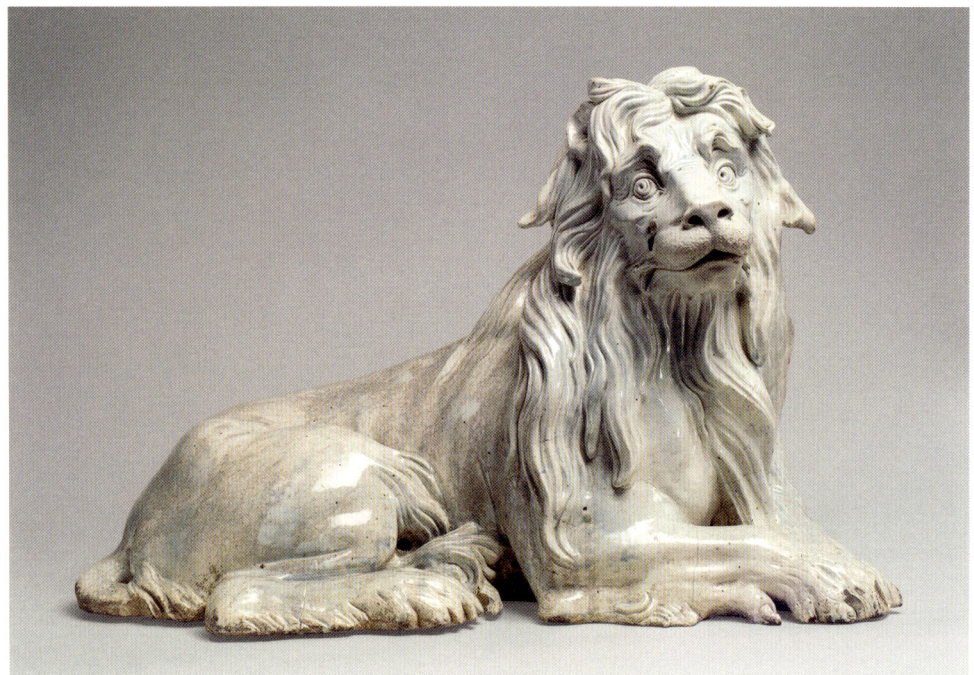

64. *Lion.* Meissen, Germany, after a model by Johann Gottlieb Kirchner, ca. 1732. Hard-paste porcelain, 21 3/16 × 32 7/8 × 15 3/8 in. (53.8 × 83.5 × 39.1 cm). Wrightsman Fund, 1988 (1988.294.1)

at Meissen, and their brilliant connoisseurship of European paintings was also a revelation. The following year the department mounted "Treasures from the Kremlin: An Exhibition from the State Museums of the Moscow Kremlin." Of even greater consequence was "The Vatican Collections: The Papacy and Art" (1981–82). The first major exhibition of works lent by the Vatican, it presented masterpieces, such as the Roman *Apollo Belvedere* and a tapestry designed by Raphael, *The Miraculous Draft of Fishes*, that until then were undreamt of as loans. Reflecting the history of collecting by the popes and the formation of the Vatican Museums, the exhibition included treasures as varied as sculpture from ancient Greece and paintings by modern European artists. This milestone in international exhibitions even became a spur to modernization of the Vatican Museums.

Two exhibitions of works from the collections of European royalty were organized with other departments. "Liechtenstein: The Princely Collections" (1985–86) brought to the Museum great bronze sculptures by masters such as Adriaen de Vries and Massimiliano Soldani, paintings and oil sketches by Peter Paul Rubens, and superb suits of armor—all vividly conveying the taste and history of the princes of Liechtenstein. (The collection has since been moved from the principality of Liechtenstein to Vienna, where it is more accessible.) Another collaborative project was "Resplendence of the Spanish Monarchy: Renaissance Tapestries and Armor" (1991).

The pace has picked up dramatically in recent years, and the shows have changed in nature as well. Rather than presenting objects assembled by collectors, our large-scale international loan shows have generally focused on works of a specific medium and period; a series of smaller exhibitions have been drawn from our own vast holdings; and unusual collaborative exhibitions have been mounted.

Two distinguished and groundbreaking exhibitions in an unusual field were organized by Tom Campbell: "Tapestry in the Renaissance: Art and Magnificence" (2002), which along with its exemplary scholarly catalogue received distinguished awards; and a continuation of the survey, "Tapestry in the Baroque: Threads of Splendor" (2007). Another first-of-its-kind exhibition was "The Colonial Andes: Tapestries and Silverwork, 1530–1830." Organized in 2004 by Johanna Hecht of ESDA and Elena Phipps of the Department of Textile Conservation, this rare survey of Spanish colonial art underscored interrelated achievements in these two media, which reflect the indigenous arts of Peru and Chile as well as the influence of Spain. Its catalogue too won awards, both here and in England. Also in 2004 the department presented "Princely Splendor: The Dresden Court, 1580–1620," which focused on one brief but brilliant period and consisted of treasures from the Staatliche Kunstsammlungen's famed Green Vault—a rich array of turned ivories, silver presentation vessels, bronze statuettes, arms and armor, and fine

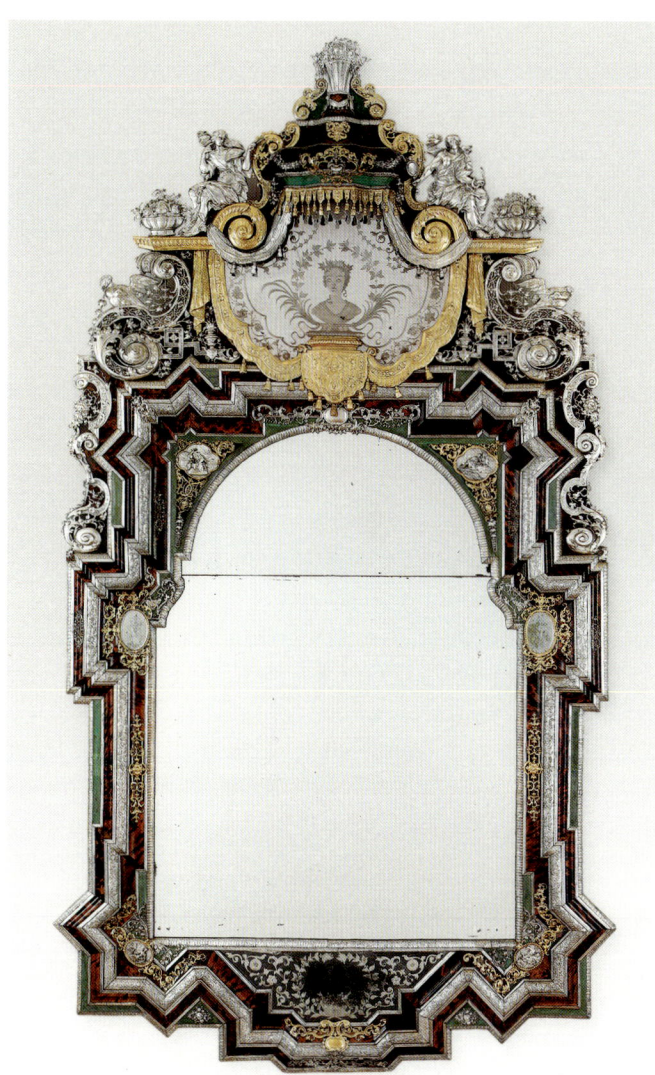

65. Mirror. Augsburg, Germany, by Johann Valentin Gevers and Johann Andreas Thelot, ca. 1710. Oak and pine veneered with tortoiseshell, silver, silver gilt, and green-stained ivory, mirror glass, 78⅞ × 39¾ in. (200.3 × 101 cm). Wrightsman Fund, 1989 (1989.20)

tools, all displaying the virtuosic craftsmanship prized for *Kunstkammer* objects.

Major collaborative exhibitions were mounted in 2008 and 2009. "Art of the Royal Court: Splendors of Pietre Dure from the Palaces of Europe" followed the development of mosaic and carving in semiprecious stone from its revival in late Renaissance Italy through its dissemination to artistic centers such as Prague, Paris, Augsburg, Madrid, and Saint Petersburg. Working with the Opificio delle Pietre Dure in Florence, the institutional inheritor of the workshops established by the Medici in the 1580s, Wolfram Koeppe and I assembled the most comprehensive review of the subject ever exhibited. "Cast in Bronze: French Sculpture from Renaissance to Revolution," the first major traveling exhibition devoted to the subject, was organized by Jim Draper and me at the Met together with curators at the Louvre.

Exhibitions drawing on stored objects in our own collection (the department is able to display only a fraction of its enormous holdings) are mounted in a gallery renovated for that purpose in 2004, with Philippe's agreement. Since it opened, seven exhibitions have examined topics ranging from collecting and patronage ("Celebrating Saint Petersburg") to materials ("Cameo Appearances," "All That Glitters Is Not Gold," "Incisive Images: Ivories and Boxwoods from the Collection") to function ("Chocolate, Coffee, Tea"; "The Art of Time: Clocks and Watches from the Collection"). The gallery is also used to host traveling exhibitions, such as "Medieval and Renaissance Treasures from the Victoria and Albert" (2008), which brought to the Met a superb group of objects offering instructive comparisons with medieval ivories, Renaissance bronzes, and ceramics on permanent display nearby. Jayne Wrightsman endowed this space as the Wrightsman Exhibition Gallery in 2007 and has established a fund to support future shows there.

Finally, the department has engaged in productive partnerships. In 2004 the Wrightsman Galleries became the setting for a showing of The Costume Institute's superb eighteenth-century French costumes, "Dangerous Liaisons: Fashion and Furniture in the Eighteenth Century." Imaginatively staged as a series of tableaux enacted by mannequins in period dress and dramatically lit, the exhibition gave new life to the rooms. Its leitmotif of seduction helped bring in the largest attendance of any show in the Museum that year, while its attention to the interaction of etiquette and the decorative arts shed new light on the design of furnishings during the ancien régime. A further, unanticipated consequence was a rethinking of the galleries' presentation and lighting, leading to a total renovation several years later. In the second exhibition, the 2006 "AngloMania: Tradition and Transgression in British Fashion," contemporary couture was displayed in eighteenth-century English period rooms, effectively spelling out the complex interaction between today's fashion and past precedent.

Another collaborative series, proposed by the Bard Graduate Center in New York, has as one goal the education of future art historians and curators: students taught by Bard professors and by Metropolitan Museum curators analyze objects in our collection and subsequently organize an exhibition held in Bard's galleries. The first in this series, "Vasemania: Neoclassical

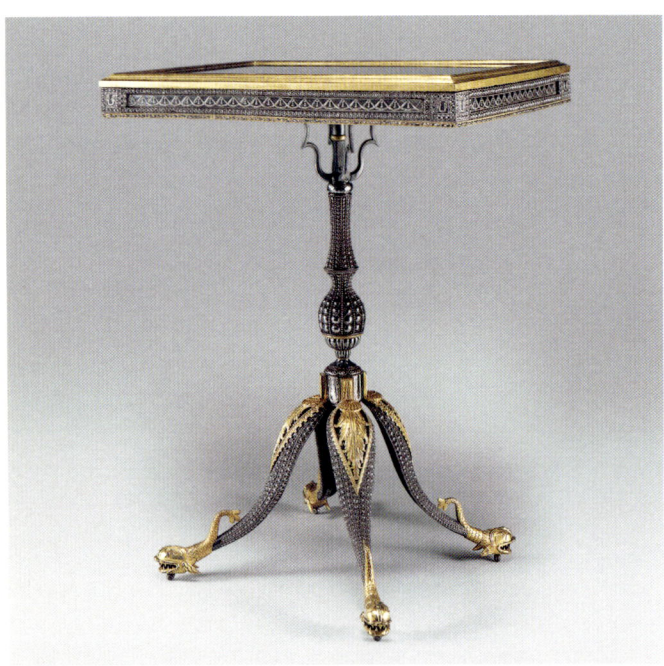

66. Center table. Imperial Armory, Tula, Russia, ca. 1780–85. Steel, silver, gilded copper, gilded brass, basswood, (replaced) mirror glass, H. 27½ in. (70 cm). Purchase, The Annenberg Foundation Gift, 2002 (2002.115)

Form and Ornament in Europe, Selections from The Metropolitan Museum of Art," took place in 2004, and the second, "English Embroidery from The Metropolitan Museum of Art, 1580–1700: 'Twixt Art and Nature," opened in December 2008.

It is hardly surprising that Philippe's influence was felt throughout the acquisitions process. Before he became director our department had already experienced tremendous growth as, with the support of the Wrightsmans, one masterpiece after another entered the collections. Their largesse continued during the de Montebello years. For the new room reflecting the period of Louis XIV they gave two important pieces of furniture: a fruitwood, tortoiseshell, and ivory table of about 1660 attributed to the foremost French cabinetmaker of his time, Pierre Gole (1986.38.1); and a *bureau brisé* of 1685 by Alexandre-Jean Oppenordt (1986.365.3), an early example of the combination of brass and tortoiseshell that appealed to Louis XIV and a piece that actually belonged to the monarch. Similarly splendid gifts were made to augment our Central European collection, including a pair of large Meissen porcelain lions (fig. 64) modeled by Johann Gottlieb Kirchner for the Japanese Pavilion of Augustus the Strong in Dresden, and a lavish and colorful mirror of about 1710 from Augsburg by Johann Andreas Thelot and Johann Valentin Gevers (fig. 65). With Jayne Wrightsman's support we have in recent years added several works of types previously unrepresented in the collection: a lusciously painted porcelain table made about 1833 by the Königliche Porzellan-Manufactur in Berlin (2000.189), a pair of wall lights composed of porcelain flowers bound by ormolu mounts made in Berlin about 1765 in the playful manner of the Frederician Rococo (2002.437.1, .2), and a Moldavian silver-gilt ewer and basin of about 1680 that exotically combine Oriental with German Baroque motifs (2005.62.1, .2a, b).

Generally neglected and even scorned in the earlier part of the twentieth century, the field of nineteenth-century decorative arts was poorly represented in the Museum until the 1980s. Excellent pieces in ceramics, glass, and metalwork have since been assembled—ranging from exquisite Sèvres services painted with the expected precision but in nineteenth-century style to modern, minimally decorated glass and earthenware designed by the Englishman Christopher Dresser. Of major furniture acquisitions, the theatrical cabinet evoking France's Merovingian past designed by Jean Brandely and made in 1867 by Charles-Guillaume Diehl with mounts by Emmanuel Frémiet (1989.197), a purchase made possible by Frank R. Richardson, is the kind of ambitious piece that was showcased in Paris's international expositions. An ebony and ivory bookstand (2006.518) made for the oldest son of King Louis-Philippe in 1839 clearly follows in the tradition of the great eighteenth-century *ebenistes*, even while it exemplifies its own century's historical revival.

In the twenty-first century, increasing attention has been paid to expanding our holdings from centers of design not broadly represented, such as Germany and Russia. Spectacular craftsmanship distinguishes a center table from Tula of about 1780–85 (fig. 66) laboriously composed of faceted "diamonds" of steel, which belonged to Czarina Maria Feodorovna and stood in her villa at Pavlovsk. The first piece of Russian furniture to be acquired by the Museum, it was purchased through the generosity of the Annenberg Foundation. Another Imperial Russian addition is a carved and gilded settee designed by Andrei Nikiforovich Voronikhin for Grand Duchess Maria Pavlovna in 1803 (2007.368). From the Baltic region comes our first important amber furnishing, a Baroque casket of about 1680 by Michel Redlin (2006.452a–c), again acquired with funds from the Annenberg Foundation. A pair of wine coolers made by Ignaz Josef Würth in 1781 for a service of Duke Albert Casimir of Sachsen-Teschen and Archduchess Maria Christina of Austria (2002.265.1a, b; .2a, b) and clad with

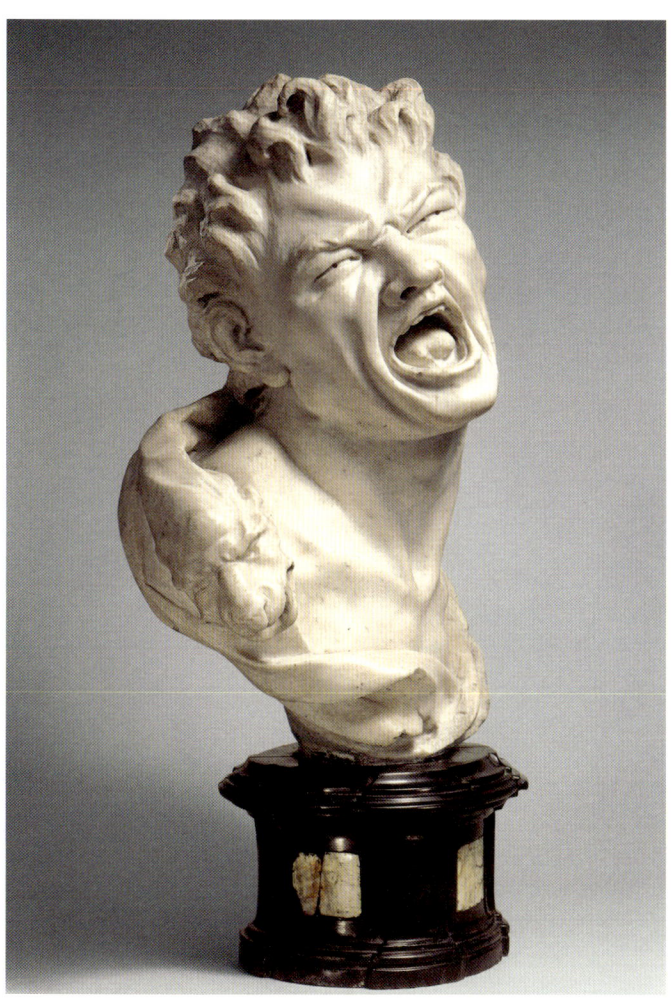

67. *Marsyas*. Germany, by Balthasar Permoser, ca. 1680–85. Marble, overall H. 27¾ in. (70.5 cm). Rogers Fund and Harris Brisbane Dick Fund, 2002 (2002.468)

lion skins and grape leaves are emphatically sculptural statements. Our most important acquisition of German Rococo silver was a forty-eight-piece toilet service with leather case from Augsburg made about 1743–45 and belonging to the Schenk von Stauffenberg family (2005.364.1–.48). An elaborate showpiece set of this type was a traditional gift from husband to bride in the marriages that linked great German families. Both of these outstanding objects were acquired with funds from the Anna-Maria and Stephen Kellen Foundation, following Philippe's suggestion of addressing the Kellens' interest in works from Germanic lands.

The department's acquisitions of tapestries have been few but notable. Most significant are a Brussels work of ca. 1502–4 purchased by the Spanish monarchy (1998.205) and a wonderfully conserved *Liberation of Oriane* (2006.36) woven about 1590–95 in the Delft workshop of Frans Spiering after designs by Karel van Mander the Elder, a splendid example of late sixteenth-century Dutch production.

In the Met's strong area of sculpture, a superbly vigorous gilt bronze *Winged Boy* from the circle of Donatello is the most important quattrocento bronze to enter the collection during Philippe's tenure (1983.356). The director's own adventurous taste is exemplified by the wooden bust purchased at his urging and later recognized to be a portrait of Alexander Menshikov, made in Russia but most likely by an Austrian sculptor—one of the most intriguing carvings we have ever acquired (1996.7).

Recent acquisitions include a marble relief of about 1470, *Saint Jerome in the Wilderness* by Benedetto da Maiano (2001.593), which added our first narrative to a collection of reliefs rich in Madonna and Child compositions, and the previously unknown terracotta bust *Bearded Elder* by Augustin Pajou (2003.25), a vivid character study from this brilliant French eighteenth-century sculptor. Our first major work by the German Balthasar Permoser is a marble bust of the satyr Marsyas suffering the torture inflicted on him by Apollo (fig. 67)—a startling, powerful work that resonates with the full impact of Gianlorenzo Bernini's reshaping of the Italian Baroque (Permoser helped spread the new, intensely dramatic style in his native Dresden). At the other extreme, the Museum's already significant representation of the preeminent Neoclassical sculptor Antonio Canova was fortified in 2003 by the bequest of two works by him and his workshop from the estate of Lillian Rojtman Berkman. No major piece by his great Danish rival Bertel Thorvaldsen was to be found in the collection until the purchase a few years ago of the striking marble relief *Nessus Abducting Deianaira* of 1814 (2004.174). Recent acquisitions of nineteenth-century sculpture include a pair of ethnographically inspired busts by Charles Cordier, *La Capresse des colonies* and *La Juive d'Alger* of 1861 and 1862 (2006.112a–d, 2006.113a–d)—mixed-media, polychrome works of onyx-marble and enameled bronze that are dramatic expressions of France's fascination with Orientalism during that epoch. And of a number of cameos and hardstone carvings, none is more riveting than Benedetto Pistrucci's *Head of the Medusa* of about 1840 (2003.431), which was purchased, along with other small-scale masterpieces, through the generosity of the family of Ignazio Peluso. With the sympathetic support of Philippe de Montebello, European Sculpture and Decorative Arts flourished during his thirty-one-year tenure. As a new era begins with a director drawn from its ranks, the department looks forward to building on the strong traditions it has established.

Ian Wardropper

TEXTILES AND TAPESTRIES

A few months after joining the Metropolitan Museum staff in early 1995 I was appointed supervising curator of the soon-to-be-completed Antonio Ratti Textile Center. For many years there had been a felt need for such an expanded center, as the field of textile conservation became more sophisticated and better defined—partly through the leadership and expertise of Nobuko Kajitani, then conservator in charge of the Department of Textile Conservation. Much of the Museum's extremely comprehensive collection had long been stored in a textile study room behind the Grace Rainey Rogers Auditorium (a space now occupied by the Asian art conservation studio). Storage practices were far from ideal: some textiles were attached to linen scrims set in wooden frames, while larger ones sat folded up in boxes. The Museum needed to do more to look after its holdings, and eventually, with Philippe's energetic participation, the Antonio Ratti Foundation had been approached for support. The center then coming into existence was a twelve-million-dollar, state-of-the-art complex that had been designed by Textile Conservation in consultation with curatorial department heads. With construction almost finished, Elena Phipps and Barbara Boehm were supervising the moving in of the collection. No one had yet devised an overall access system or decided how the new image database should be configured. And the database itself was still in an early stage of development. Still a neophyte, I was hitting the ground running.

With this project, as generally, Philippe's leadership was impressive. In April of that year, he, Emily Rafferty, Harold Holzer, Jennifer Russell, and I traveled to Como to meet with the principal funder of the center, Antonio Ratti, a prominent silk manufacturer and an honorary trustee of the Museum, and the staff of his foundation. Philippe had been busy elsewhere in Europe; I met him in Milan and we drove to Como together. At the foundation he would be delivering a lecture on the new center that he very likely had had no time to think about. But as we sped through the landscape he rapidly studied the notes and slides I had prepared for him, prepping himself with complete ease and assurance; and, a master of presentation, delivered an eloquent lecture later that day with the same finesse. Both in Como and subsequently in Paris, where our group next traveled, the discipline and focus were balanced by fun. There was a camaraderie and playfulness in which Philippe fully participated. It was my introduction to the Met's inner circle.

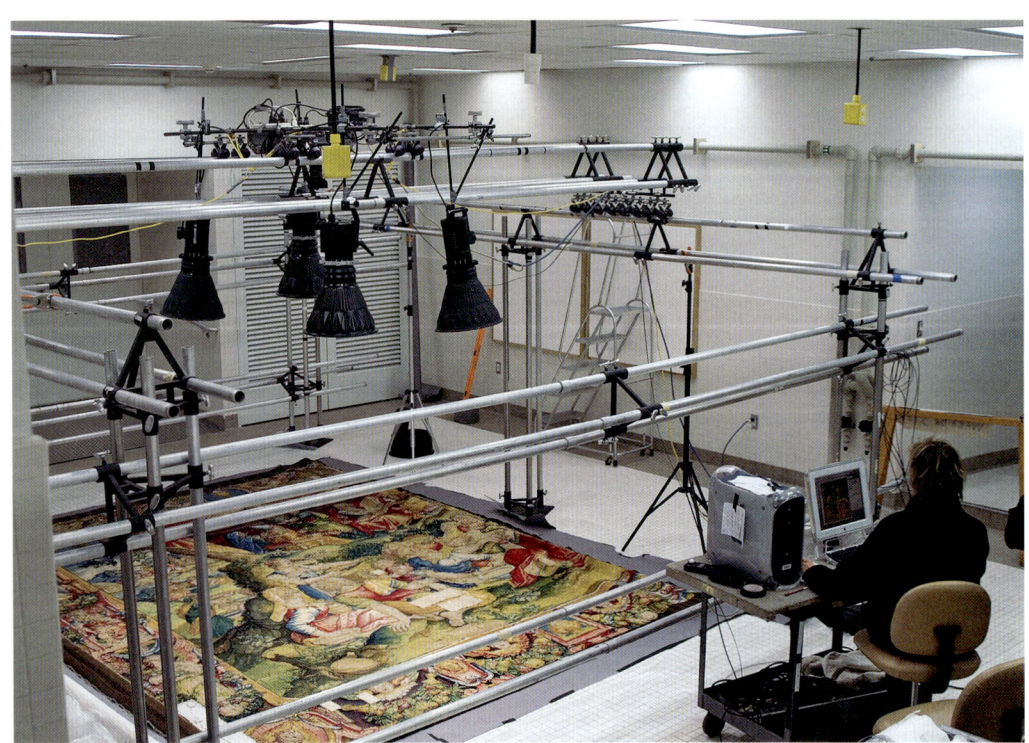

68. A tapestry is examined at the Antonio Ratti Textile Center

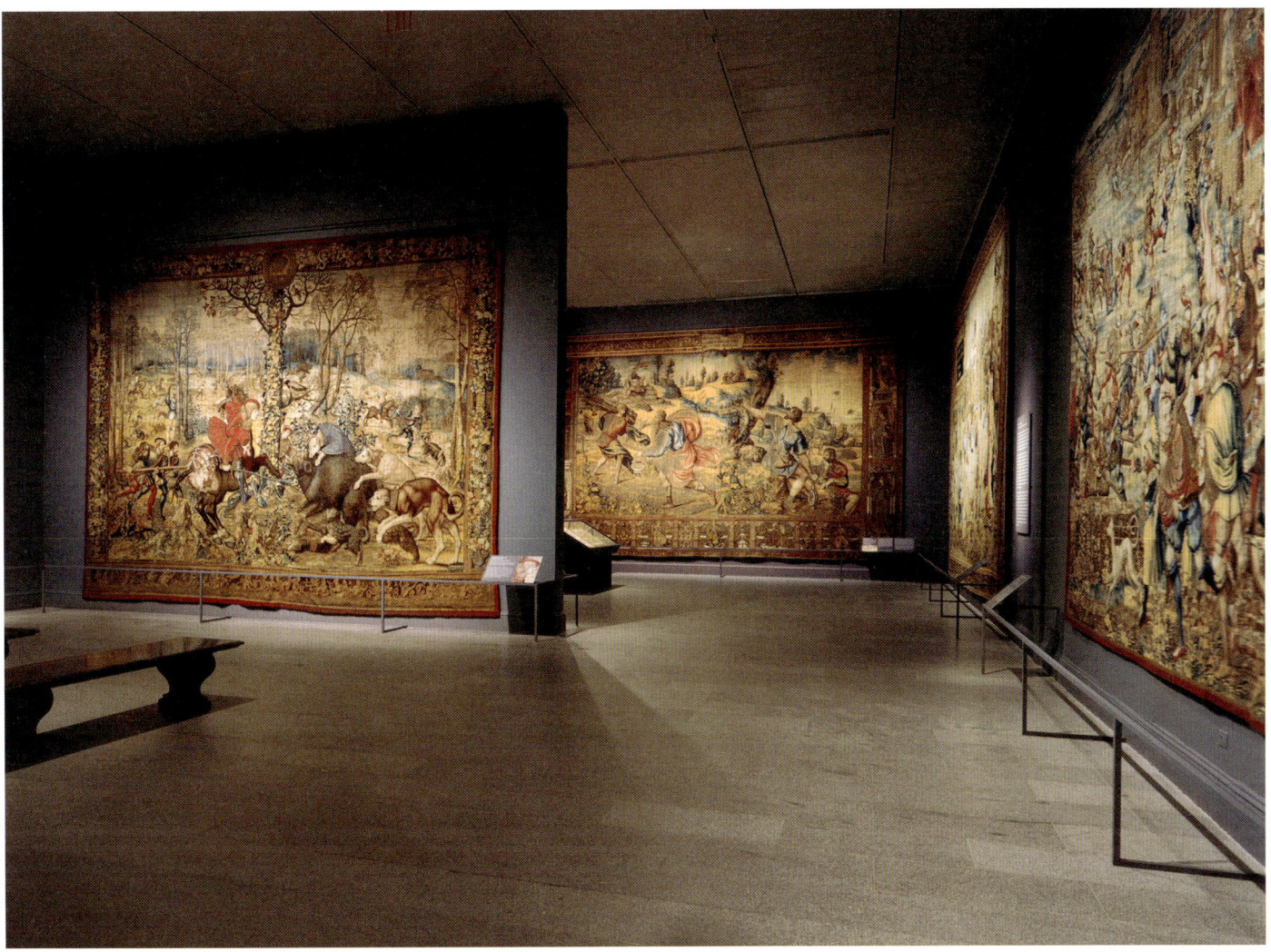

69. A gallery of the exhibition "Tapestry in the Renaissance," 2002

The Ratti Center, which opened in December 1995, houses textiles of nine or ten different departments of the Museum—silks from Asia, tapestries from Europe, rugs from the Middle East, weavings from Africa—some 36,000 individual examples, not including the textiles in The Costume Institute. It is one of the leading textile storage and study centers in the world (fig. 68). The center serves the storage and conservation needs of the Metropolitan's departments, and in addition its two study rooms welcome a constant flow of users: visiting scholars, who can find here an example of virtually anything they seek; classes of students; lay specialists; and many others. Daily operations of the storage and study areas now proceed smoothly under the management of Giovanna Fiorino-Iannace. Fragile treasures that embody an entire history of world art are preserved here with enormous care, in close proximity to the Textile Conservation Studio, constructed as part of the same development, which is now run by Florica Zaharia, Nobuko's successor.

It was not (or not principally, at any rate) to head the Ratti Center that I had been hired by the Metropolitan, but rather to join the Department of European Sculpture and Decorative Arts as an assistant curator in the field of European textiles and tapestries. In pursuing this specialty I had been inspired by one of the great scholars in the field, Edith Standen. She was curator in charge of the Met's Textile Study Room for many years and a prolific scholar revered for her high standards and dedication. Edith's regular visits to Europe had given me the opportunity to learn from her, and with her support I came to the United States for one month in 1990 and then another three months in 1991. During the second trip I spent the days working in the stacks of the Watson Library with a team of student assistants; together we culled through vast numbers of auction catalogues and books, searching for references to European tapestries. And I got to know the Metropolitan Museum. This institution on the American model and under Philippe's leadership was enormously impressive, even dazzling. Partly enabled by the abundance of available funding, it could boast a level of scholarship and a depth to its exhibitions and catalogues rarely possible in Europe, as well as a sophisticated audience responsive to these strengths.

Several years later, again with Edith Standen's support, I applied for the newly vacant position of curator of European textiles at the Met. First came a very direct dialogue with Olga Raggio, then in charge of the Department of European Sculpture and Decorative Arts, who immediately responded to my interest in the uses of tapestries in European courts and recognized the subject's value. Next she brought me to the director, in his old mezzanine office. Philippe's principal question was: "If you came here, what would you really like to do?" I spoke about organizing an exhibition of European tapestries made during the Renaissance—a period that art historians, focusing on medieval works in the medium, had undeservedly neglected. In fact, tapestries reached a high point in the Renaissance, when these works of consummate art were also possessions carrying political significance. Philippe expressed a somewhat noncommittal interest in the future of my suggested endeavor, but he hired me. His willingness to do so even though I had not yet completed my Ph.D. suggests that he did not feel particularly constrained by the niceties of hierarchical procedure.

In fact, Philippe has always been very supportive of textile studies and of exhibitions of textiles mounted by The American Wing, the Department of Asian Art, and several other departments. His own chosen field of study had been the Northern Renaissance, and he had written his master's thesis on Jean Cousin the Elder, a sixteenth-century French artist who was the designer of a set of tapestries made for Diane de Poitiers—two of which now belong to the Met. So he was sympathetic and quite well informed when, some three years later, I again raised the subject of an exhibition of Renaissance tapestries. Once the directorial go-ahead had been given I spent much of the next four years traveling, researching, and negotiating loans, on the Met's behalf, with representatives of the institutions that owned key works, especially the Kunsthistorisches Museum, Vienna, the royal collection of Spain, and the Vatican. We were able to assemble sixty-three exemplary tapestries of the fifteenth and sixteenth centuries, in excellent condition, from the great centers of production in France, Italy, and Northern Europe—particularly the Netherlands and the city that emerged as capital of the industry, Brussels. It was an ambitious undertaking, and the result was an exhibition on a scale not formerly attempted anywhere. This little-regarded category of works, we were able to demonstrate, had in an earlier age held undisputed artistic primacy: monarchs, popes, and other wealthy patrons valued tapestries more than paintings or any other works of art, and were willing to spend enormous sums to own them. At the highest level of production, tapestries were critical to creating the settings for royal displays of power. The subjects and imagery of these woven paintings as well as their refined execution offer a wealth of insights into the rapidly developing Europe that created them.

The challenges in presenting such a show were many, and at one point threateningly dramatic. I had initially set out to write the large, ever-expanding catalogue almost entirely myself—partly in order to clarify certain important issues of attribution, a complex matter in the field of tapestries. The exhibition date grew closer, the catalogue was still unfinished. There were difficult meetings, and at one point the entire enterprise seemed in jeopardy. But Philippe once again brought his support to the project; a new working schedule was hammered out; and the exhibition opened as planned, with a complete, very freshly printed catalogue.

Opening day was in March 2002 (fig. 69). This was the Metropolitan's first big show after the overturning events of the previous September 11, and in the upper reaches of the Museum, anxiety had been considerable over whether at this crucial time an audience would materialize for a large exhibition on an unfamiliar subject. But excellent reviews and word-of-mouth reports brought in substantial numbers of viewers, and they were attentive, even enthusiastic. Unexpectedly to some, "Tapestry in the Renaissance" was a success.

Soon thereafter, Philippe approved the proposal for a "sequel" exhibition, "Tapestry in the Baroque," which progressed far more smoothly and came to fruition in 2007 (fig. 71). And in January 2008, just about the time that he announced his

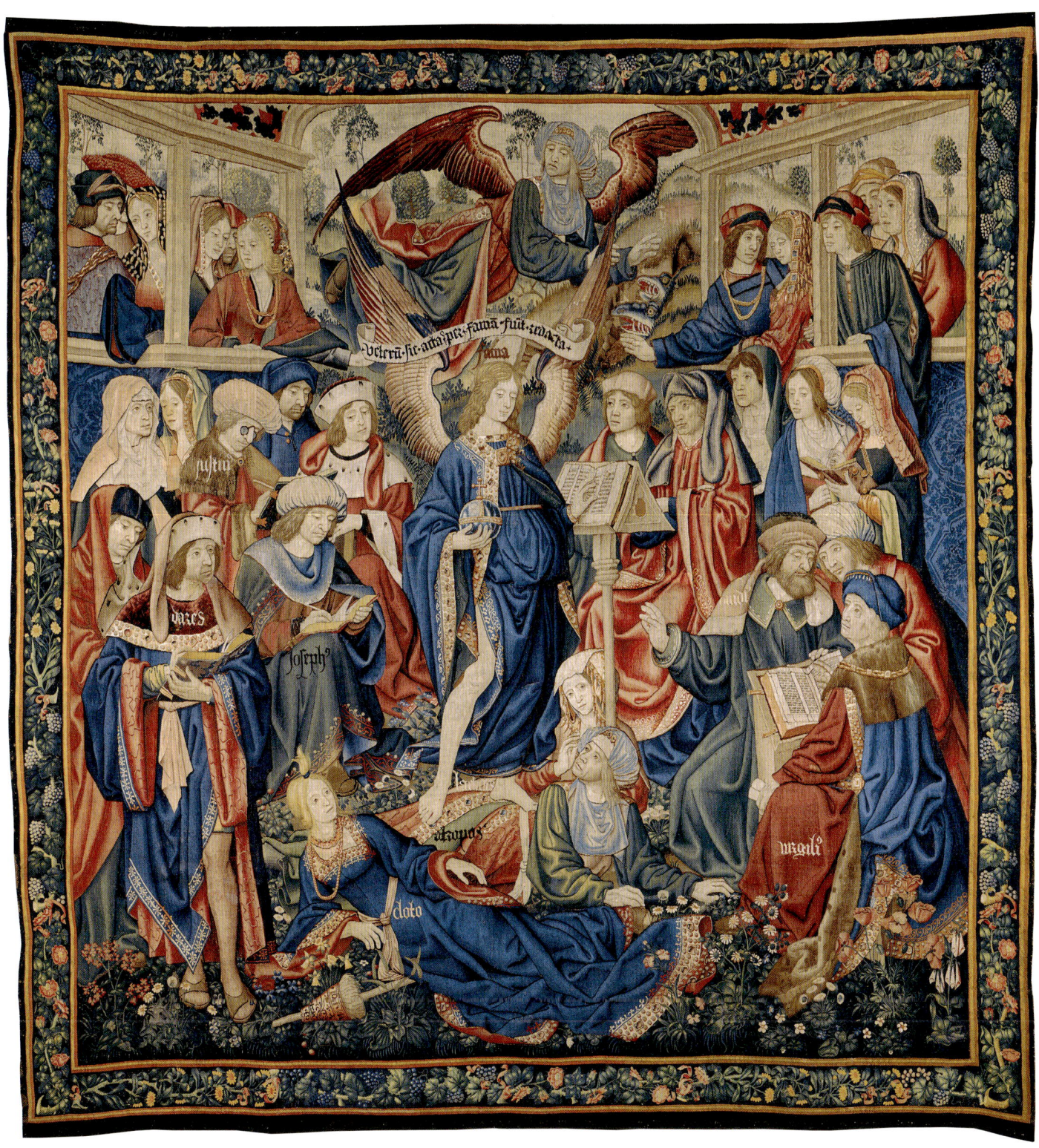

70. *The Triumph of Fame*, Flemish, ca. 1502–4. Silk and wool, 141½ × 132 in. (359.4 × 335.3 cm). Purchase, The Annenberg Foundation Gift, 1998 (1998.205)

[59]

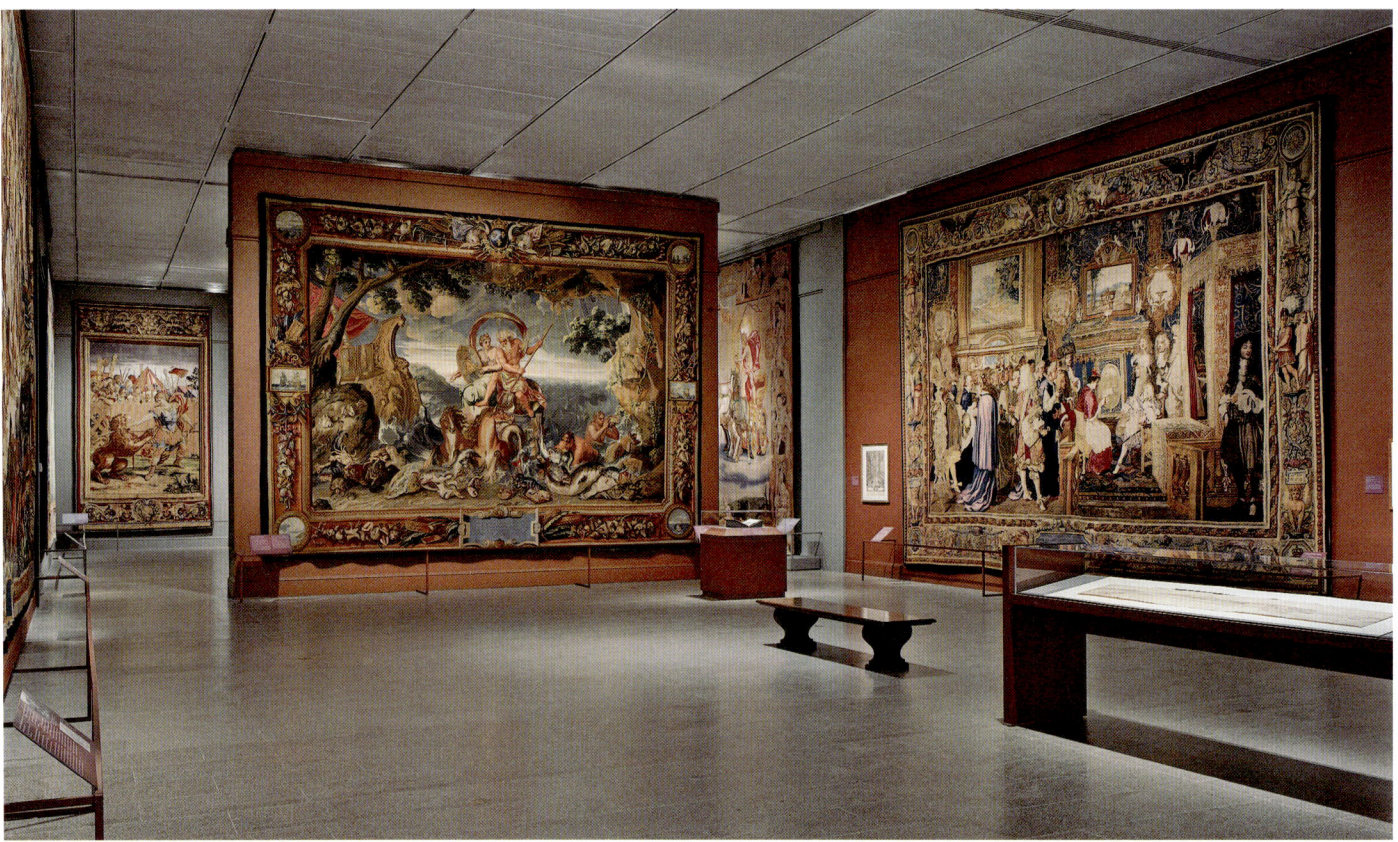

71. A gallery of the exhibition "Tapestry in the Baroque," 2007

impending retirement, the director gave his approval for a further project, slated for 2013, that would concentrate on the accomplishments of a major sixteenth-century tapestry designer in Antwerp, Pieter Coecke van Aelst. In light of my new appointment this show may be postponed somewhat, but I trust that it will still occur, collaboratively organized at the Metropolitan by several curators.

Until recently the Met's tapestry collection consisted largely of gifts made between the 1930s and the 1960s. While it included several notable examples, there were significant gaps. Working with Olga Raggio and subsequently with Ian Wardropper, I was able to make a number of key acquisitions in the late 1990s and early 2000s. These are big, expensive objects; going after them was made possible not only by Philippe's wholehearted support but also by his success in obtaining funding from generous donors, especially Lee Annenberg. Our most important acquisition, *The Triumph of Fame,* a fine Flemish tapestry of about 1500, is from a set of six representing the Triumphs of Petrarch and very possibly was made for Isabella, queen of Castile and Aragon (fig. 70). It is with Philippe's staunch support throughout that the Metropolitan has made a significant contribution to both the study of European tapestries and the heightening of public awareness about this magnificent body of works.

Thomas P. Campbell

THE ROBERT LEHMAN COLLECTION, A MAGNIFICENT BEQUEST

For centuries, the museums of Europe built their collections largely through the benefaction of royal patronage, or through plunder. The Habsburg riches form the basis of the Kunsthistorisches Museum in Vienna, while the Bavarian treasury of King Ludwig I filled the galleries of Munich's splendid *Pinakotheks*. In our country, the accumulation of great fortunes in the nineteenth and early twentieth centuries led to the assembling of splendid art collections, which over time, through gift and bequest, became the foundation of America's preeminent museums. Were it not for the patronage of John D. Rockefeller Jr., J. Pierpont Morgan, and Harry and Louisine Havemeyer, to name but a few, the holdings of the Metropolitan Museum would lack the breadth and magnificence that make it our nation's most important public art collection.

Robert Lehman's bequest added untold riches in many areas, among them Italian Renaissance gold-ground paintings, old master drawings, Italian majolica, and antique frames. Some 2,600 objects reside in the Lehman Wing of the Metropolitan Museum. Impressive as it is to have assembled this many works of remarkable quality, the energetic Robert Lehman, who gave generously to various American museums throughout his lifetime, actually amassed twice that number. As noted by Laurence Kanter, curator of the Robert Lehman Collection for nearly twenty years, this approximates the purchase of two works of art for every week of the collector's life! If we consider his parallel activity—forty-eight years of investment banking at Lehman Brothers—as well as his astute connoisseurship (he had no private curator until 1962) and trusteeships at the Metropolitan Museum and the Institute of Fine Arts, New York University, we have some notion of Lehman's extraordinary vigor. He always planned to return his art collection to the public domain and later in life said it plainly: "Great works of art should reach beyond one's own private enjoyment . . . the public at large should be afforded some means of seeing them."

The gift of Lehman's treasures to the Metropolitan Museum was most definitely not a foregone conclusion. It took the persuasive powers of former director Tom Hoving, a lasting collegiality with European paintings curator Ted Rousseau, and some political and circumstantial good fortune. To understand the machinations that led to the bequest, one must look back to the days when the collection was displayed salon-style in Lehman's family town house. A Beaux-Arts limestone residence on West Fifty-fourth Street built by Robert's parents, Philip and Carrie Lehman, the six-story structure became an opulent showcase for Lehman purchases, many acquired abroad on family holidays. When Robert, fresh from Yale and well grounded in Italian art history thanks to his study of the Yale University Art Gallery's Jarves Collection, assembled a scholarly catalogue of his family's European paintings in 1928, they already numbered some two hundred. To his father and mother's impressive legacy Robert added old master drawings, Impressionist and modern paintings, manuscript illuminations, and a small but superb selection of old master paintings—for example, Ingres's *Princesse de Broglie*, one of the artist's finest

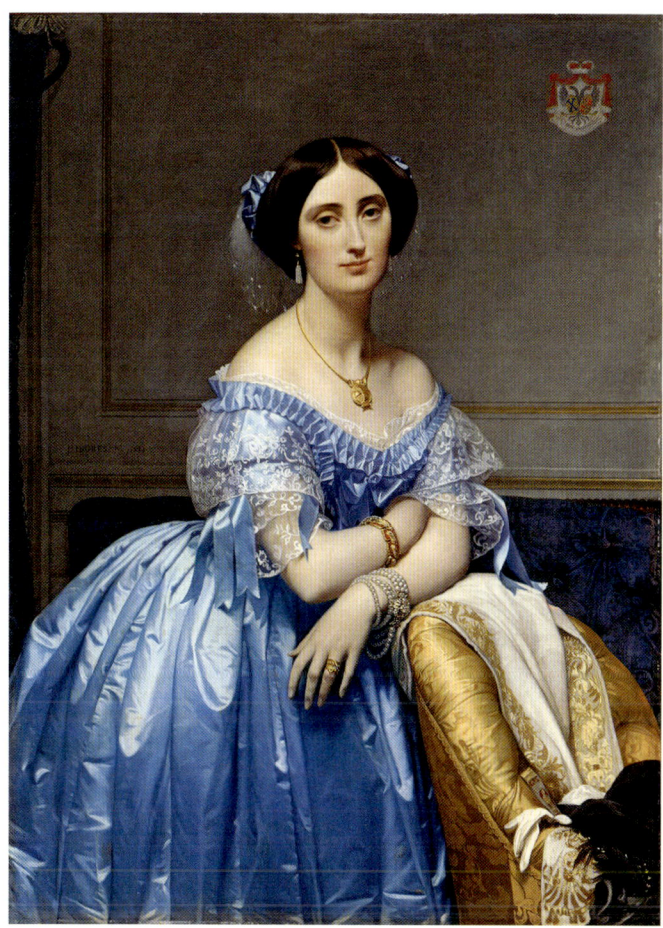

72. Jean-Auguste-Dominique Ingres, *Princesse de Broglie*, 1851–53. Oil on canvas, 47¾ × 35¾ in. (121.3 × 90.8 cm). Robert Lehman Collection, 1975 (1975.1.186)

[61]

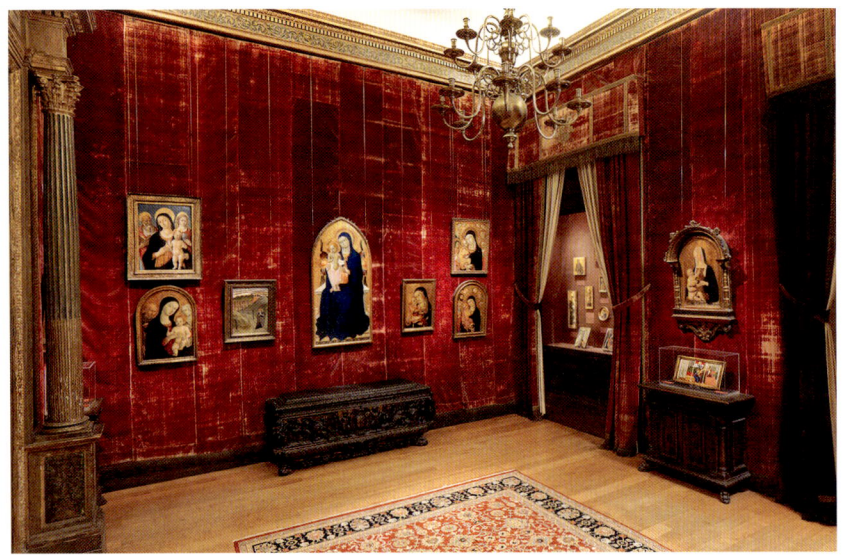

73. A gallery in the Robert Lehman Wing evoking a room of the Lehman family house

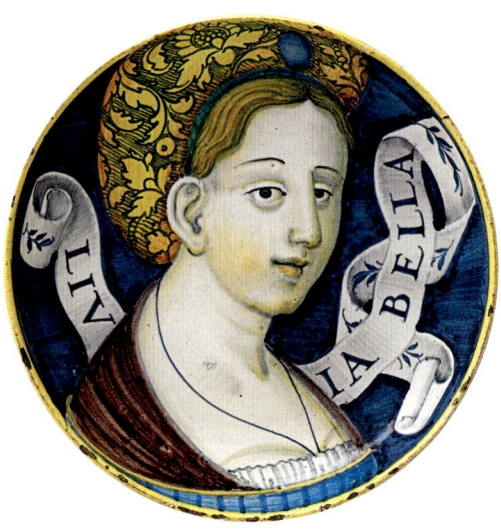

74. Majolica dish (*coppa amatoria*). Italy, probably by the "In Castel Durante" Painter, ca. 1530. Tin-glazed earthenware, Diam. 8 7/16 in. (21.5 cm). Robert Lehman Collection, 1975 (1975.1.1084)

portraits (fig. 72). The sumptuous interiors of the Lehman town house were also home to Italian Renaissance majolica—a collection of such depth and quality that it ranks among the finest of its kind anywhere (figs. 74, 80).

During the Korean War, Lehman sent his paintings to the Colorado Springs Fine Arts Center for safekeeping. After their return, ninety pictures were loaned to the Metropolitan Museum and hung in galleries refurbished for their display. Two years later, in 1957, he loaned three hundred works of art to the Louvre, sending them off by steamship for an exhibition at L'Orangerie. The Lehman collection exhibition was the talk of Paris. "We would like the purchases of our museums to be inspired by a taste as rigorous as that of which M. Robert Lehman today gives us such dazzling evidence," pronounced a critic writing in the

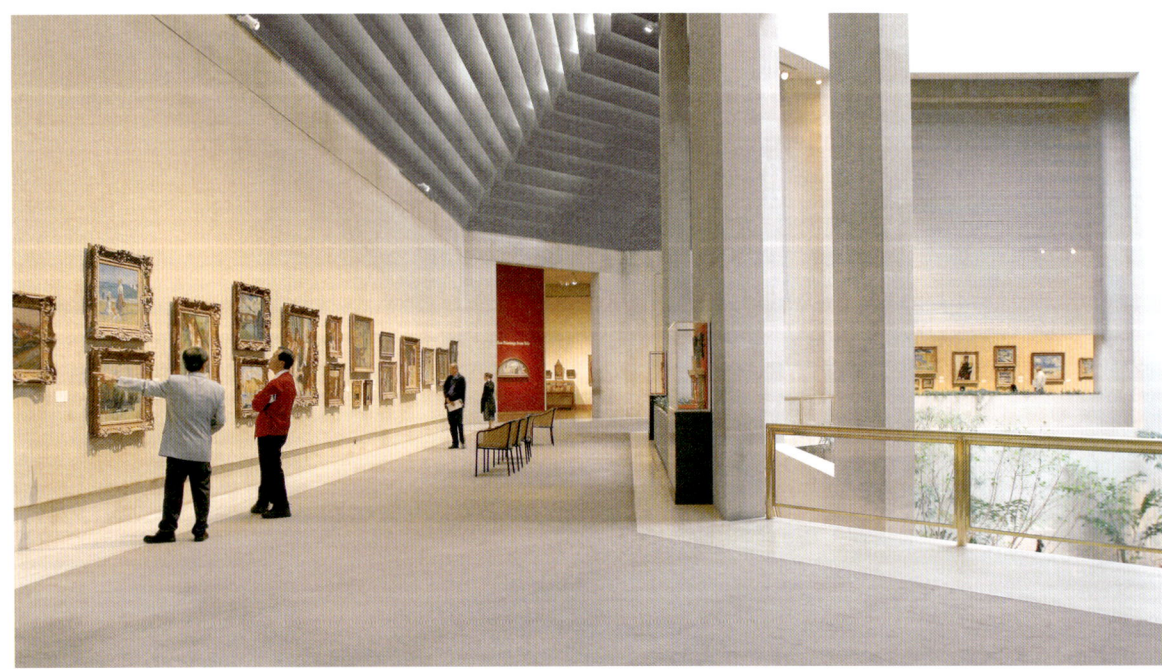

75. A view in the central gallery of the Robert Lehman Wing

[62]

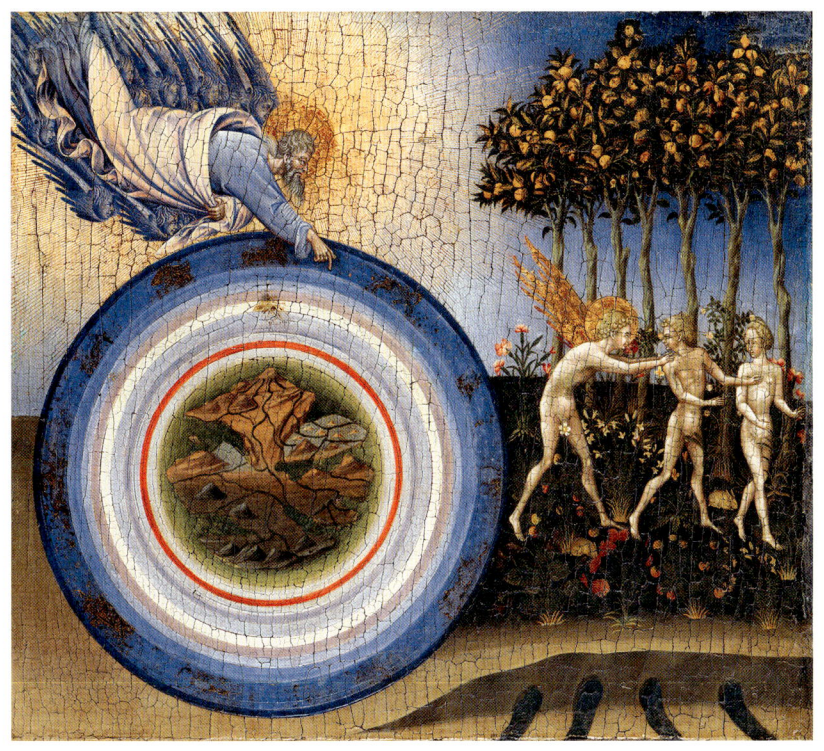

76. Giovanni di Paolo, *The Creation of the World and the Expulsion from Paradise*, 1445. Tempera and gold on wood, 18¼ × 20½ in. (46.4 × 52.1 cm). Robert Lehman Collection, 1975 (1975.1.31)

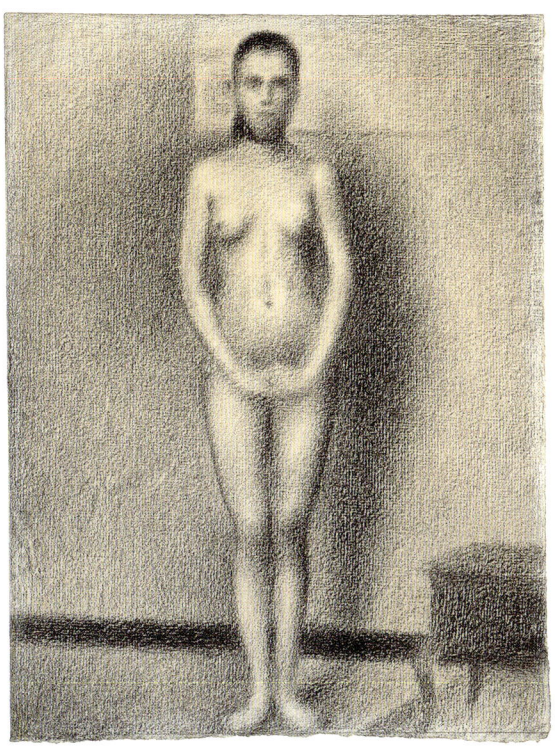

77. Georges-Pierre Seurat, *Study for "Les Poseuses,"* 1886. Conté crayon on laid paper, 11 11/16 × 8⅞ in. (29.7 × 22.5 cm). Robert Lehman Collection, 1975 (1975.1.704)

magazine *Carrefour.* Lehman reinstalled his collections on West Fifty-fourth Street in 1961 and subsequently hired George Szabo as curator, this time opening his doors to visitors by invitation. Among the many guests welcomed were graduate students at the Institute of Fine Arts.

Robert Lehman had been a trustee of the Metropolitan Museum since 1941 and vice president of the Board since 1948 and, having demonstrated distinction and loyalty, undoubtedly wished to become president. It is said that his relations with the Board cooled when Arthur Houghton was named president in 1964. Hanging in the balance was the disposition of one of the country's finest private art collections, perhaps the very finest of its time. Lehman briefly considered institutionalizing his town house in perpetuity (J. Pierpont Morgan and Henry Clay Frick had set fine examples), but the house was impractically small.

Although his ties to the Metropolitan were strained, Lehman's long-standing association with Ted Rousseau, with whom he had shared the pleasures of building the Museum's European paintings collection over many years, remained unmarred. It fell to Tom Hoving to bring him back into the fold and in so doing address with greater optimism the future of his art collection. In 1967, Lehman, already in fragile health, was made chairman of the Board of Trustees—the first trustee to bear that title (he served alongside Houghton, who remained the Board's president). The elusive honor was finally in hand. When Lehman died two years later, he had indeed bequeathed his collection to the Museum. Speaking publicly soon afterward, Houghton stated that the Lehman Collection raised the Metropolitan "from greatness to preeminence."

The gift was not unconditional. Lehman was single-mindedly determined to have his collection retain its collector's identity. It was his wish to have the works shown in galleries re-creating the ambience of his legendary town house. Ceramics and glass were to join paintings and tapestries in settings evoking their courtly past. And while no restrictions were imposed on the loan of works of art to other areas of the Museum or to other exhibitions around the world, the collection was to remain intact—a commitment that Philippe de Montebello scrupulously observed throughout his tenure as director. To house the Lehman gift a pyramidal structure of glass, limestone, and concrete was constructed by

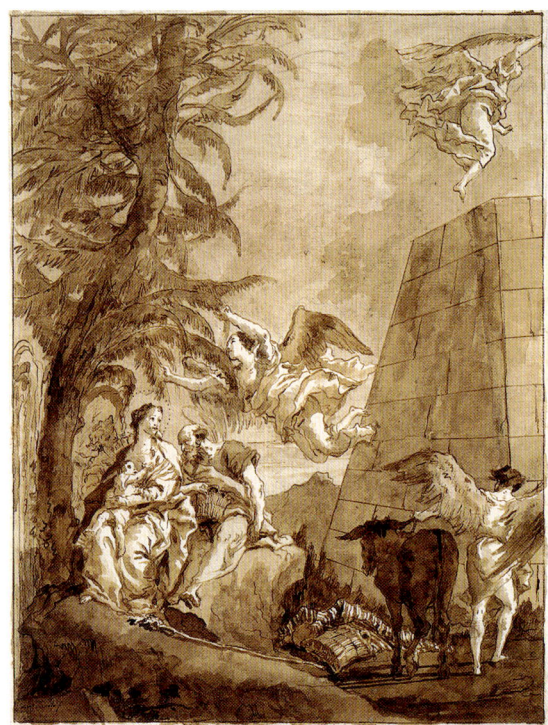

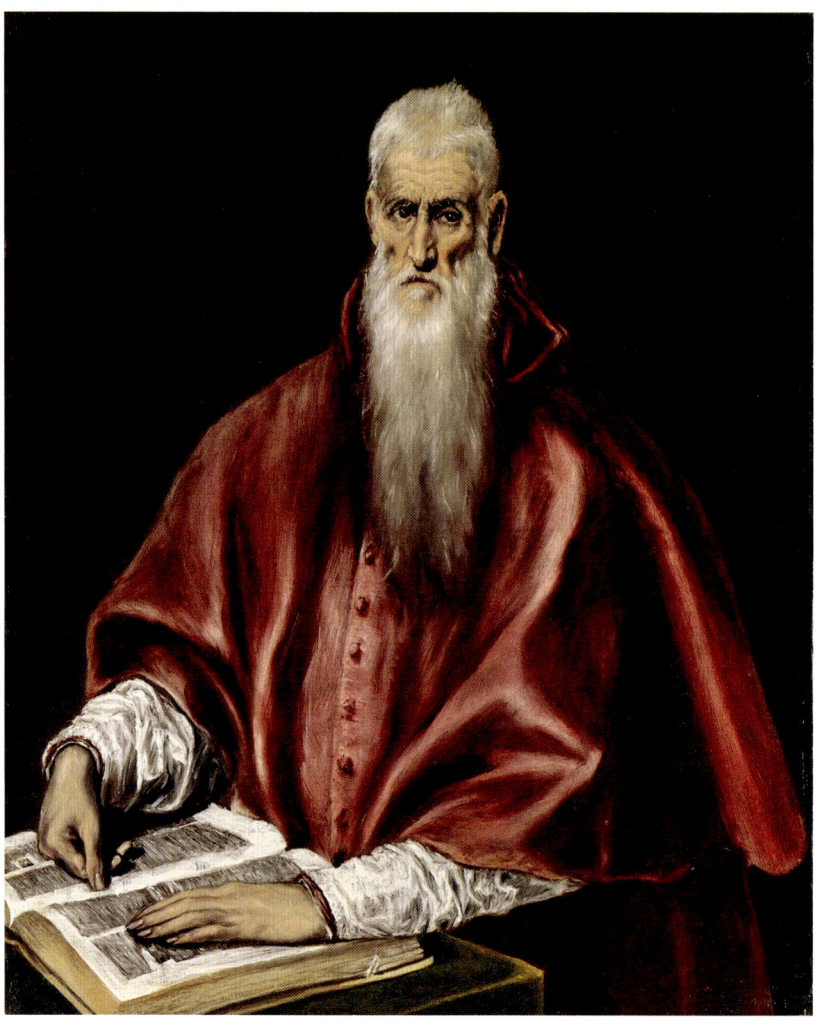

78. Domenico Tiepolo, *The Rest on the Flight into Egypt*, ca. 1770. Pen and brown ink, brown wash, and black chalk on paper, 18½ × 14¹⁵⁄₁₆ in. (47 × 37.9 cm). Robert Lehman Collection, 1975 (1975.1.474)

79. El Greco (Doménikos Theotokópoulos), *Saint Jerome as Scholar*, ca. 1610. Oil on canvas, 42½ × 35¹⁄₁₆ in. (108 × 89 cm). Robert Lehman Collection, 1975 (1975.1.146)

Kevin Roche John Dinkeloo and Associates abutting the brick western facade of the 1880 structure (fig. 75). Some of the main-floor galleries were made room size to evoke the Lehman residence and decorated with flocked-velvet wall coverings, Renaissance-style cornices, and chandeliers from the town house (fig. 73). Special exhibitions and rotations of light-sensitive objects drawn from the Lehman holdings would be shown on the floor below.

The Lehman benefaction may have carried certain demands, but the rewards were immeasurable. Only a few highlights can be cited here. In the area of early Italian painting, the gift of eleven panels by the fifteenth-century Sienese master Giovanni di Paolo doubled the Museum's holdings of works by the artist (fig. 76). With the addition of Lehman's other Sienese paintings of the fourteenth and fifteenth centuries—by Simone Martini (fig. 81), Ugolino da Siena, and the Osservanza Master, among others—the Metropolitan's collection became the finest of its kind outside Siena. Lehman's drawings by the eighteenth-century Giambattista Tiepolo and his son Domenico (fig. 78) greatly enriched the Museum's holdings of these splendid Venetian artists. Few collections can boast an assemblage of Domenico Tiepolo's graphic work as impressive as ours. In another idiosyncratic dialogue, Robert Lehman's marvelous Seurat study in Conté crayon (fig. 77) of a model for *Les Poseuses* (Barnes Foundation) joined a Museum already housing Georges Seurat's crayon drawing of still-life motifs for the same picture. Fine portraits by Rembrandt, El Greco (fig. 79), and Goya augmented the Met's significant holdings of these European masters. Now, forty years after its founding, the Lehman Wing flourishes as a reflection of taste and collecting in twentieth-century America and as the embodiment of a generous wish to return a privately assembled art collection to the public domain.

Dita Amory

PUBLISHING THE LEHMAN COLLECTION

When the Robert Lehman Collection galleries first opened at the Metropolitan Museum in 1975, the only published information on them available to the public was a general guidebook written by the collection's first curator, George Szabo, highlighting selected objects in each of the simulations of rooms from the Lehman house that then made up the display. The directors of the Robert Lehman Foundation quickly determined that a more comprehensive and scholarly catalogue of the collection was desirable, and in 1977 they approached Philippe de Montebello with a proposal for a collaborative project involving staff from the Metropolitan and New York University's Institute of Fine Arts. The project was spearheaded by Jonathan Brown, director of the Institute; Sir John Pope-Hennessy, chairman of the Department of European Paintings at the Metropolitan; and Sydney Freedberg, then in the Department of Fine Arts at Harvard University and subsequently chief curator at the National Gallery of Art in Washington. Jonathan Brown was later succeeded by Donald Posner and ultimately by Egbert Haverkamp-Begemann, who has overseen the publication of all the volumes issued to date.

The project initially divided the collection into large categories on the basis of material (paintings, drawings, decorative arts), period (modern, Renaissance, etc.), or culture (Italian, French, Asian, etc.) and assigned the supervision of each group's cataloguing to the curator in charge of the appropriate department at the Museum. Working with consultants, the curators then identified potential authors—internationally recognized experts in their fields—who were engaged to work on the catalogues through the Institute of Fine Arts and with the assistance of fellowship students at the Institute. The goal was to publish at the Metropolitan Museum a series of independent volumes, each a model of scholarship and richly illustrated, that in the aggregate would be a complete record of the holdings of the Robert Lehman Collection.

The first two volumes completed, both published in 1987, were *Italian Eighteenth-Century Drawings* by James Byam Shaw and George Knox and *Italian Paintings* by John Pope-Hennessy with Laurence B. Kanter. The former catalogued 186 works on paper, including highly significant groups by Giambattista and Gian Domenico Tiepolo, 117 of them purchased en bloc as part of the famous collection assembled by Paul Wallraf, which Robert Lehman acquired in 1962. *Italian Paintings* contains many of the most famous objects in the Lehman Collection (fig. 81). Its 112 works were bought by Mr. Lehman and his father, Philip, beginning in 1912 and continuing until the late 1960s, when Robert Lehman purchased an important pair of portraits by Jacometto Veneziano from the Liechtenstein collection for the Metropolitan Museum.

Further volumes appeared at regular intervals beginning in 1989 with Jörg Rasmussen's posthumous catalogue *Italian Majolica*. Devoted to one of the largest (157 objects) and most significant, although least well known, areas of the collection (figs. 74, 80), the publication was accompanied by a major exhibition bringing majolica pieces from two of the Museum's departments, Medieval Art and European Sculpture and Decorative Arts, and a few from other departments together with those of the Robert Lehman Collection. The nearly six hundred pieces in these combined collections constituted a panoramic survey of the art form unrivaled by the holdings of any other museum in the world. An

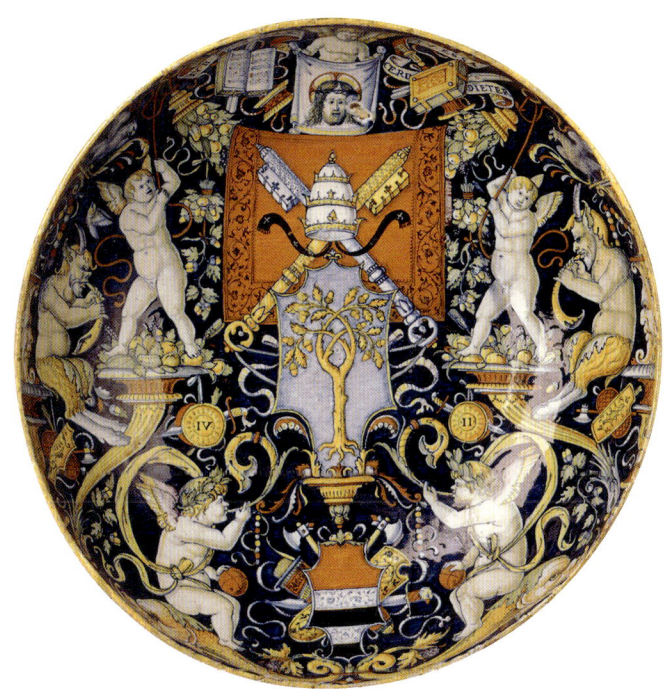

80. Majolica bowl with the arms of Pope Julius II and the Manzoli of Bologna. Italy, workshop of (or painted by?) Giovanni Maria Vasaro, Castel Durante, 1508. Tin-glazed earthenware, Diam. 12 3/16 in. (32.5 cm). Robert Lehman Collection, 1975 (1975.1.1015)

[65]

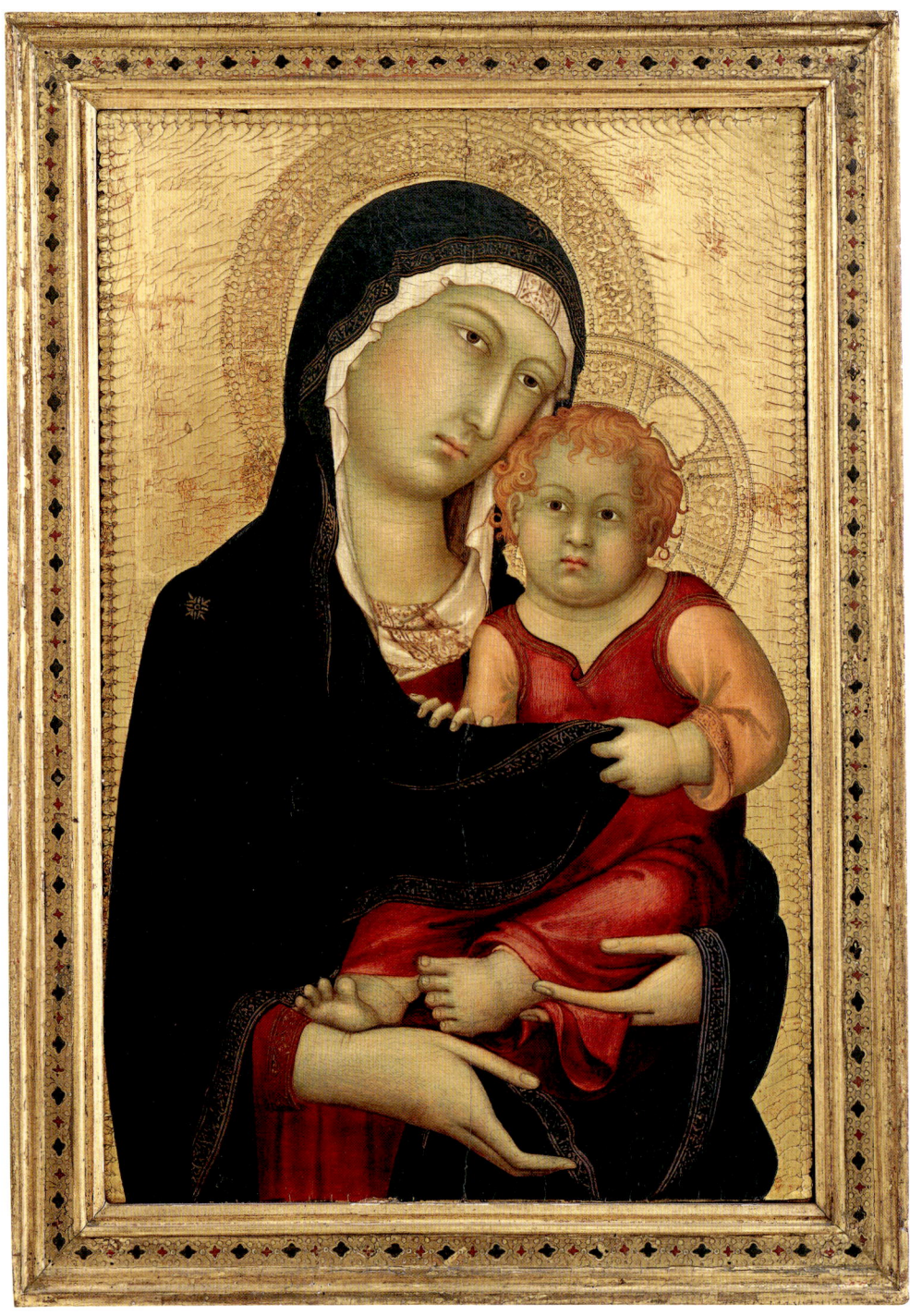

81. Simone Martini, *Madonna and Child*, ca. 1326. Tempera on wood, gold ground; overall 23⅛ × 15½ in. (58.7 × 39.4 cm). Robert Lehman Collection, 1975 (1975.1.12)

exhibition mounted the following year, "Italian Renaissance Frames," similarly combined the holdings of the Robert Lehman Collection with those of other departments in the Museum; it led to the inception of work on a Lehman volume not included in the original plans, *Frames*, authored by Timothy Newbery and eventually published in 2007. Catalogued in the volume are 371 frames, one of the largest, widest-ranging, and most historically significant assemblies of this material anywhere.

To date, twelve volumes cataloguing the Robert Lehman Collection have been published. In addition to the four already mentioned they are: *Italian Fifteenth- to Seventeenth-Century Drawings* (1991) by Anna Forlani Tempesti; *American Drawings and Watercolors* (1992) by Carol Clark; *Glass* (1993) by Dwight P. Lanmon with David B. Whitehouse; *Fifteenth- to Eighteenth-Century European Paintings: France, Central Europe, The Netherlands, Spain, and Great Britain* (1998) by Charles Sterling, Maryan W. Ainsworth, Charles Talbot, Martha Wolff, Egbert Haverkamp-Begemann, Jonathan Brown, and John Hayes (fig. 82); *Illuminations* (1998) by Sandra Hindman, Mirella Levi D'Ancona, Pia Palladino, and Maria Francesca Saffiotti; *Fifteenth- to Eighteenth-Century European Drawings: Central Europe, The Netherlands, France, England* (1999) by Egbert Haverkamp-Begemann, Mary Tavener Holmes, Fritz Koreny, Donald Posner, and Duncan Robinson; *European Textiles* (2001) by Christa C. Mayer Thurman; and *Nineteenth- and Twentieth-Century European Drawings* (2002) by Richard Brettell, Françoise Forster-Hahn, Duncan Robinson, and Janis A. Tomlinson. Two additional volumes are slated for publication within the next two years, *Nineteenth- and Twentieth-Century European Paintings* by Paul Tucker, Natalie Lee, and Richard Brettell and *Sculpture and Decorative Arts*. When these are completed more than 2,500 objects in the collection will have been studied in depth and the results made available to both a scholarly audience and the general public—one of the most ambitious publishing projects of its type ever undertaken. The success of this catalogue series is a tribute to the determination of the directors of the Robert Lehman Foundation, the unflagging support of Philippe de Montebello and the staff of The Metropolitan Museum of Art, and the tireless efforts of the faculty and students of the Institute of Fine Arts.

Laurence B. Kanter

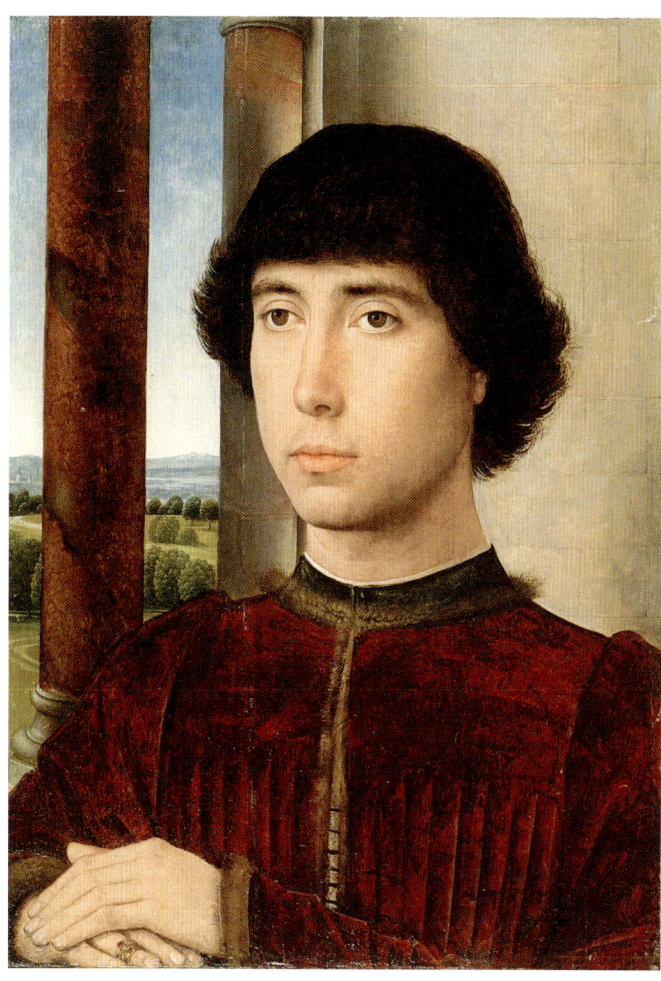

82. Hans Memling, *Portrait of a Young Man*, ca. 1482. Oil on oak panel, painted surface 15⅛ × 10¾ in. (38.3 × 27.3 cm). Robert Lehman Collection, 1975 (1975.1.112)

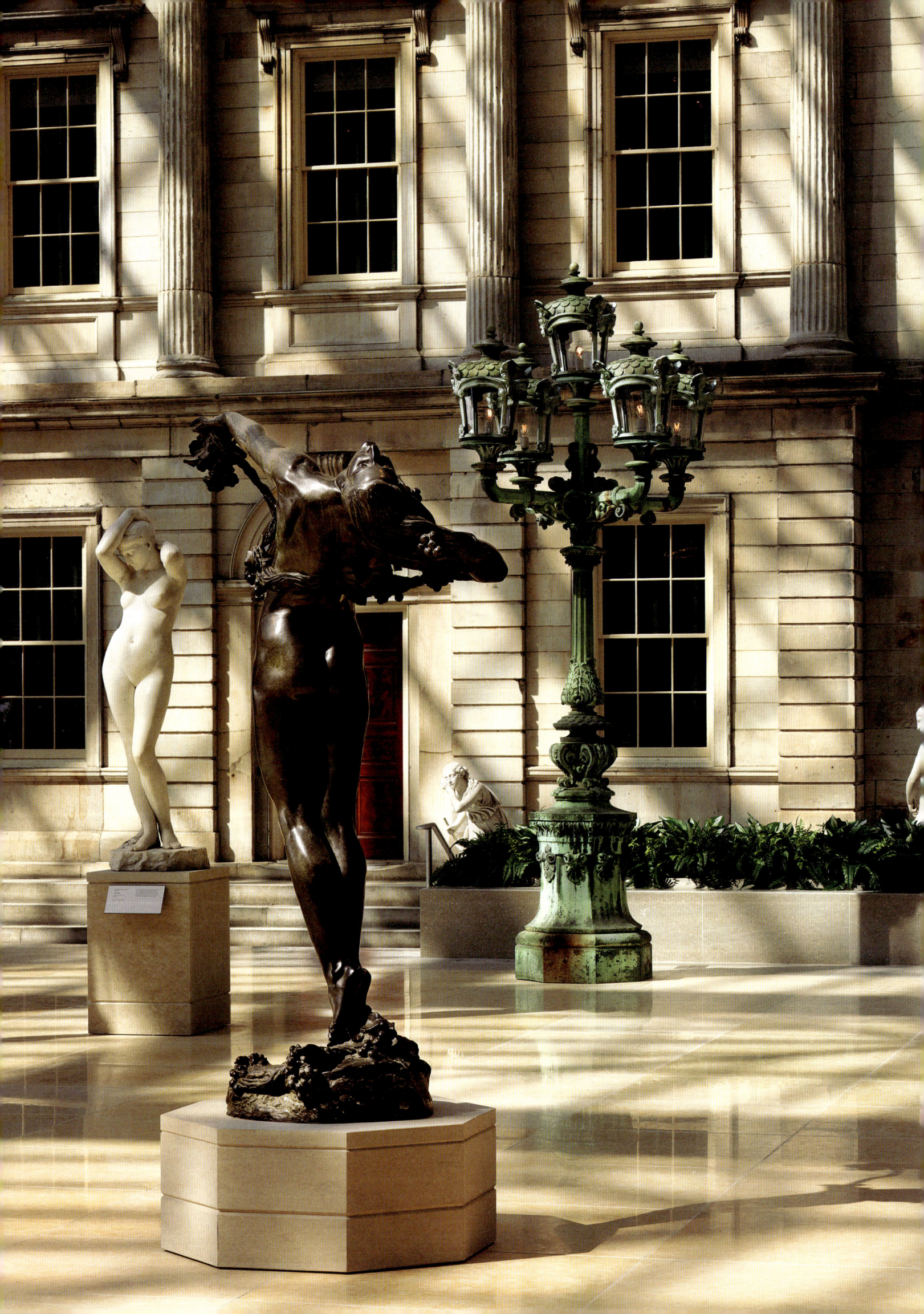

AMERICAN ART

TRANSFORMING THE AMERICAN WING, 1977–2008

Philippe could never be accused of claiming a particular affinity for the art of his adopted country, much less paying rapt attention to it. But the genius of his administration was that by virtue of his direct personal involvement with curators and their collections he enabled all the arts—American as well as European, Asian, African, or Oceanic—to flourish at the Metropolitan. During his tenure The American Wing was reinvented architecturally, its collections were much enriched, and its curators generated an unprecedented array of exhibitions and publications.

In May 1980, three years into Philippe's reign, the Museum opened its grand American Wing in accordance with the 1970 master plan. Twin focal points of the new structure were The Charles Engelhard Court, intended for the display of sculpture and stained glass, and The Joan Whitney Payson Galleries, housing American paintings and sculpture; another important component was The Erving and Joyce Wolf Gallery, for special exhibitions. Installations of all these galleries were coordinated by Berry B. Tracy, curator in charge of American Decorative Arts, until he left in 1981, and by John K. Howat, curator of American Paintings and Sculpture. "Jock" Howat, appointed Lawrence A. Fleischman Chairman of both branches by Philippe in 1982, remained in charge until 2001, at which time I became chairman.

The 1980 building was, however, far from completed. It was only over the eleven-year period 1981–92 that, with Philippe's repeated blessings, the Museum's great holdings of American architecture and decorative arts of the nineteenth and early twentieth centuries were installed on the first floor, with reserve collections going to the mezzanine level. The first floor became home to a number of permanent installations—John Vanderlyn's *Panoramic View of the Palace and Gardens of Versailles* (1818–19), endowed by Lawrence A. and Barbara Fleischman, and seven historic interiors or "period rooms": the Shaker retiring room (Mount Lebanon, New York, ca. 1835); the Greek Revival parlor (New York City, ca. 1835) and the Rococo Revival room (Astoria,

Opposite: 83. A view in the newly renovated Charles Engelhard Court, 2009

Queens, ca. 1852), both endowed by Richard and Gloria Manney; the Gothic Revival library (Balmville, New York, 1859); the Renaissance Revival parlor (Meriden, Connecticut, 1870); the McKim, Mead and White stair hall (Buffalo, 1884); and the Frank Lloyd Wright living room (Wayzata, Minnesota, 1912–14). Six of these had been lovingly installed, one at a time, by Orange County master craftsman Ezra Mills. An eighth interior, an extraordinary Aesthetic-style dressing room of 1881 from the house of John D. Rockefeller Sr. on West Fifty-fourth Street, was a generous gift from the Museum of the City of New York in 2008 and will be installed in due course. Interspersed among these rooms are two areas for the display of individual masterworks, a mid-nineteenth-century gallery endowed in honor of Martha Fleischman and a late nineteenth-century gallery for works in the Aesthetic and Arts and Crafts styles funded in honor of Deedee Wigmore.

Another, contemporaneous project was The Henry R. Luce Center for the Study of American Art. In December 1988, after four years of planning and construction, this remarkable resource opened. It occupies the entire mezzanine floor, where some thirty-five freestanding floor-to-ceiling glass cases, together with surrounding wall cases, house in orderly fashion the Wing's enormous reserve collections—works of art not displayed in the primary galleries or period rooms. And here, for the first time anywhere in the Museum, computers offered access to further information on objects in the collections.

The Erving and Joyce Wolf Gallery and later a smaller changing-display gallery in the Luce Center provided spaces in The American Wing for an ambitious exhibitions program. No director could have been more liberal in his support of this initiative than Philippe. Indeed, between 1978 and the landmark 2007 exhibition "Louis Comfort Tiffany and Laurelton Hall," The American Wing mounted exactly one hundred exhibitions, the great majority of them organized within its two curatorial departments. A third of these were small dossier displays without catalogues, such as "American Tonalism: Paintings, Drawings, Prints,

[69]

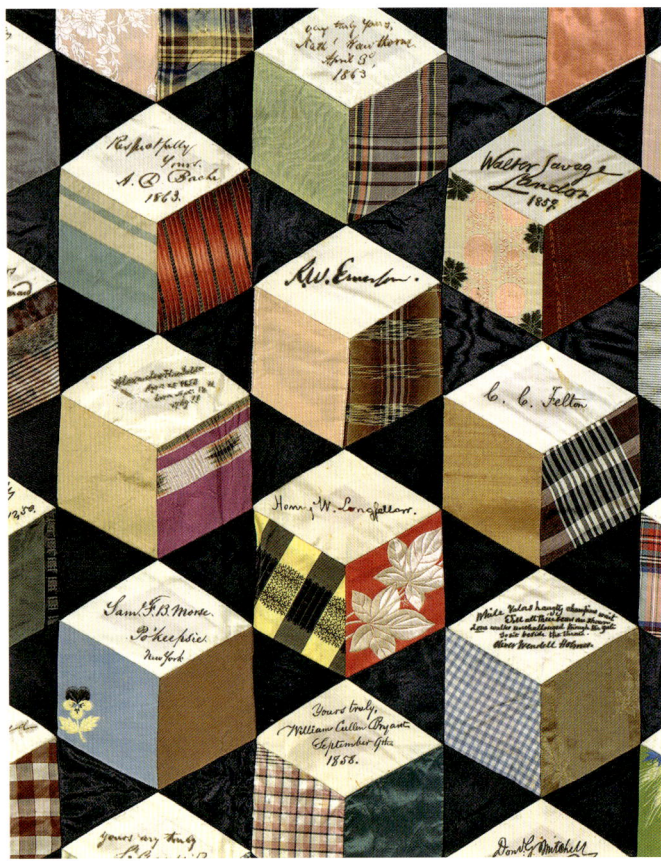

84. Detail of an autograph quilt made by Adeline Harris Sears, begun 1856. Silk, overall 77 × 80 in. (195.6 × 203.2 cm). Purchase, William Cullen Bryant Fellows Gifts, 1996 (1996.4). Among the signatures visible here are Nath. Hawthorne, R. W. Emerson, Henry W. Longfellow, Samuel F. B. Morse, and William Cullen Bryant.

and Photographs" and "American Furniture and the Art of Connoisseurship," which offered brief encounters with works presented in a new light. Since the mid-1990s, Warren and Jan Adelson have made possible many of these displays through a grant that supports The Eugénie Prendergast Exhibitions of American Art. But the bulk of our exhibitions were larger installations accompanied by special publications. Taken together, the exhibitions and their catalogues constitute a major, permanent contribution to American art scholarship.

The principal catalyst for this exhibition and publishing bonanza was the establishment of the group known as the William Cullen Bryant Fellows. Sometime around 1980 Jock Howat and Larry Fleischman had the idea of beginning a new upper-level patron group to augment the Friends of the American Wing, which since 1962 had so effectively supported our collecting of decorative arts. Principal among the new organization's founding members were Ray and Margaret Horowitz, Erv and Joy Wolf, and of course Larry and Barbara Fleischman. Named for the New York newspaper publisher and poet, who was also an early advocate for the Metropolitan Museum, the Bryant Fellows group proved particularly attractive to collectors of American paintings and sculpture. Its avowed purpose (aside from fostering fellowship among lovers of the subject) has been to support research and publications on American art. In this it has been hugely successful, generating ample funds that have facilitated the participation of American Wing curators in Philippe's ambitious publishing program.

Since 1982 Bryant Fellows funding has underwritten, in whole or in part, forty out of some fifty volumes associated with The American Wing. They include twelve permanent collection catalogues, those most venerable of scholarly museum publications: three cataloguing paintings; two each for sculpture, furniture, and drawings and watercolors; one for pastels; and one (in two separate editions) for quilts and coverlets. There have also been seven exhibition catalogues that are in-depth surveys of a particular time period or style and that, taken together, treat a considerable swath of the history of American art: *American Rococo* (Colonial art, 1750–75), *Art and the Empire City* (arts of New York City, 1825–61), *American Paradise* (Hudson River painters, 1825–75), *Americans in Paris* (painting, 1860–1900), *In Pursuit of Beauty: Americans and the Aesthetic Movement* (all the arts, 1870–90), *American Impressionism and Realism* (painting, 1885–1915), and *Design in America: The Cranbrook Vision* (1925–50). And more than a dozen exhibition-related monographs are devoted to leading artistic figures. These include painters John Singleton Copley, Gilbert Stuart, Sanford R. Gifford, William M. Harnett, J. Alden Weir, and Childe Hassam; sculptors John Quincy Adams Ward and Augustus Saint-Gaudens; architects Alexander Jackson Davis and Richard Morris Hunt; cabinetmakers John Townsend and Honoré Lannuier; and designers Herter Brothers, Candace Wheeler, and Louis Comfort Tiffany. (The catalogues for exhibitions of the works of William Merritt Chase, Thomas Eakins, Winslow Homer, George Inness, John F. Kensett, and Paul Manship were prepared elsewhere.)

Four issues of the *Bulletin* have been devoted to the Museum's holdings of works by Thomas Eakins, John Singer Sargent, Tiffany, and Frank Lloyd Wright; two to Colonial American silver and Chinese export art; and one each to the architectural history of the Museum and of Central Park. Half a dozen more issues are studies of single works, among them Vanderlyn's *Panorama*, Thomas Sully's portrait of Queen Victoria, Frederic E. Church's *Heart of the Andes*, and Sargent's Alpine sketchbooks.

Philippe's interest in acquisitions is legendary and created a positive atmosphere in which the collections of the departments of American Painting and Sculpture and American Decorative Arts grew handsomely, both in scope and in richness. Among the most compellingly American acquisitions from this period are an arresting 1789 full-length portrait of New England merchant Elijah Boardman by Ralph Earl (1979.395)—what could be more American than Boardman's obvious pride in all that stuff, the dry goods that were his stock-in-trade?—and the unique "autograph" quilt begun in 1856 by Adeline Harris Sears, which incorporates within its graphically elegant tumbling-blocks pattern the actual signatures of 360 contemporary worthies, including eight American presidents (fig. 84).

We have been the happy recipients of generous gifts (fig. 87). Some exceptional works that perfectly complement our core holdings are paintings by Hassam (*Celia Thaxter's Garden, Isles of Shoals*, 1890), Theodore Robinson (*Low Tide, Riverside Yacht Club*, 1894), and Sargent (*Mrs. Hugh Hammersley*, 1892); *Diana*, an 1894 sculpture by Saint-Gaudens; a dining table by Townsend, signed and dated 1756; and a pair of card tables by Lannuier, signed and dated 1817 (1995.377.1). With the support of the Acquisitions Committee of the Board of Trustees we have purchased major works by Copley (a self-portrait miniature, fig. 86, and pastel portraits of Ebenezer Storer and his wife, Elizabeth Green Storer), Stuart (*Captain John Gell*), Thomas Anshutz (*A Rose*), and Paul Revere Jr. (Hannah Rowe's silver tea urn, 1990.226a–d). And on occasion we have been successful in buying at public auction pieces of particular importance to the story we tell: a rare silver plateau of about 1825 by John W. Forbes, which had long been on loan as the centerpiece of our Neoclassical gallery (1993.167); a seventeenth-century oak wainscot chair from Essex County, Massachusetts, the last such in private hands and an object we had failed to win at auction some years before (1995.98); and an altogether perfect mahogany chest-on-chest from Newport, Rhode Island, labeled by Thomas Townsend, dated 1772, and passed down in a direct line through the Gardiner family of eastern Long Island (fig. 85).

Private collections that The American Wing has been able to acquire, in whole or in part, during the de Montebello years have dramatically enhanced its permanent holdings in certain areas.

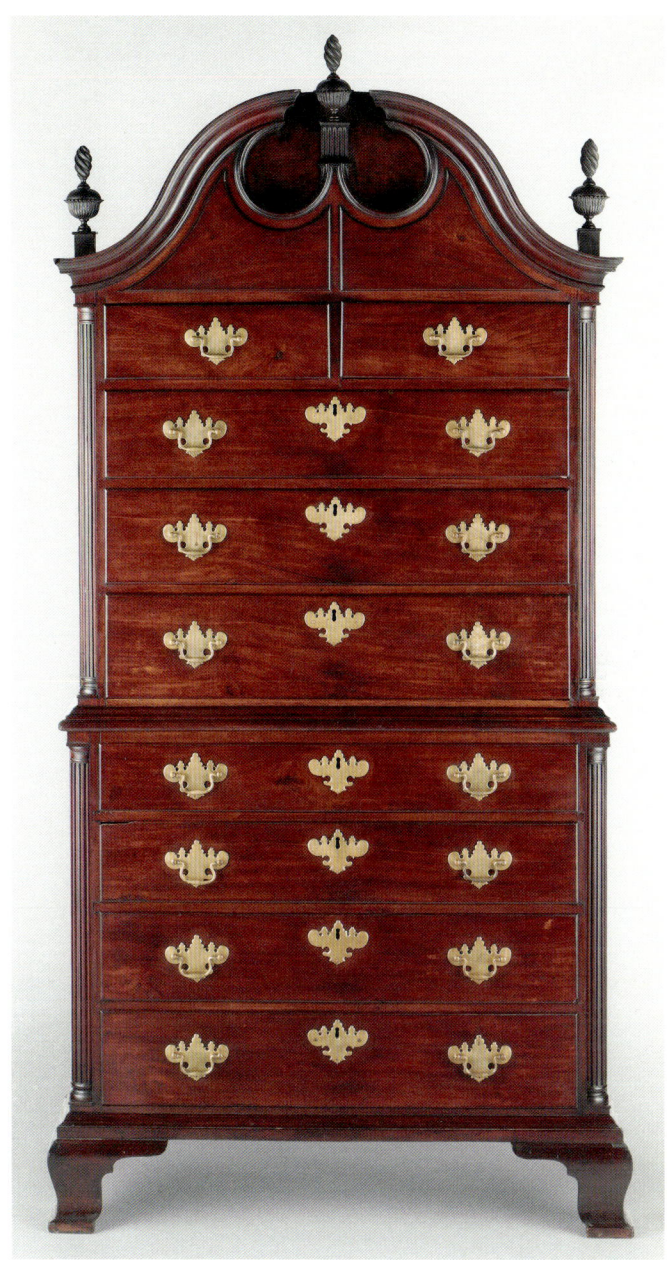

85. Thomas Townsend, Newport chest-on-chest, 1772. Mahogany, 86¾ × 44 × 21⅜ in. (220.3 × 111.8 × 54.3 cm). Purchase, Friends of the American Wing Fund, Mr. and Mrs. Robert G. Goelet Gift, Sansbury-Mills Fund, and Leigh Keno and The Hohmann Foundation Gifts, 2005 (2005.52)

For example, the Martha Gandy Fales collection of documented American jewelry inaugurated our serious collecting in this branch of art, while the purchase of 327 portrait miniatures from Richard and Gloria Manney for all intents and purposes completed our collecting of that specialty. The Barbara Sinauer gift of needlework samplers significantly strengthened our holdings of this schoolgirl art. The thoughtful and generous gift from

Philip and Ann Holzer of masterpieces of eighteenth-century Newport furniture greatly enriched our already fine collection.

But the most concentrated curatorial collecting has been of American decorative arts of the later nineteenth century, an area not much pursued by the Museum until relatively recently. Full advantage has been taken of opportunities to buy, often at very modest prices, many important and beautiful examples of glass and ceramics, and our holdings in these media are now unequaled. The same is true (except in price) of furniture and furnishings, especially those made by the Herter Brothers firm for the great houses of the Vanderbilt family. Special attention has been paid to that extraordinary artistic polymath Louis Comfort Tiffany. Building upon a core body of works that were acquired through a succession of gifts going back to the H. O. Havemeyer collection of Favrile glass in 1896, as well as through purchases, the collection has been expanded to include some six hundred works of art in glass, ceramics, paper, and other media. More than eighty of these came to the Museum in the past three decades; they range from the monumental loggia of Laurelton Hall, acquired in 1978, to an imaginative and exquisite dragonfly hair ornament given to us in 2002 (fig. 88).

Its glorious display of our national artistic heritage notwithstanding, the 1980 American Wing building has always presented a certain challenge to curator and visitor alike. The size and contours of the exterior envelope, dictated more by urban politics than by the Museum's programmatic needs, compromised the usable space, most egregiously by requiring the paintings galleries to be spread over two floors. An effort to meld the levels of the new wing with those of the previously existing three-story structure was not a total success. Indeed, Philippe always complained about getting lost while en route to—or in—The American Wing: an implicit challenge for the department to do something about it! Thus it is altogether fitting that a major initiative to modernize and improve the building was undertaken on his watch. In the spring of 2001

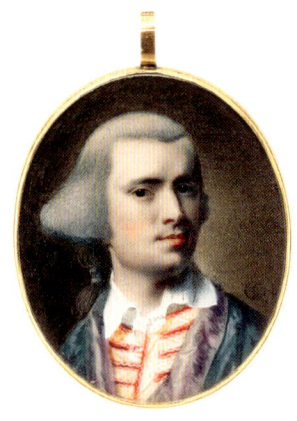

86. John Singleton Copley, Self-portrait miniature, 1769. Watercolor on ivory in gold locket, 1 5/16 × 1 1/16 in. (3.3 × 2.7 cm). Purchase, Harris Brisbane Dick Fund, by exchange, Anonymous Gift, and Virginia Marvin Stoughton Bequest, 2006 (2006.235.32)

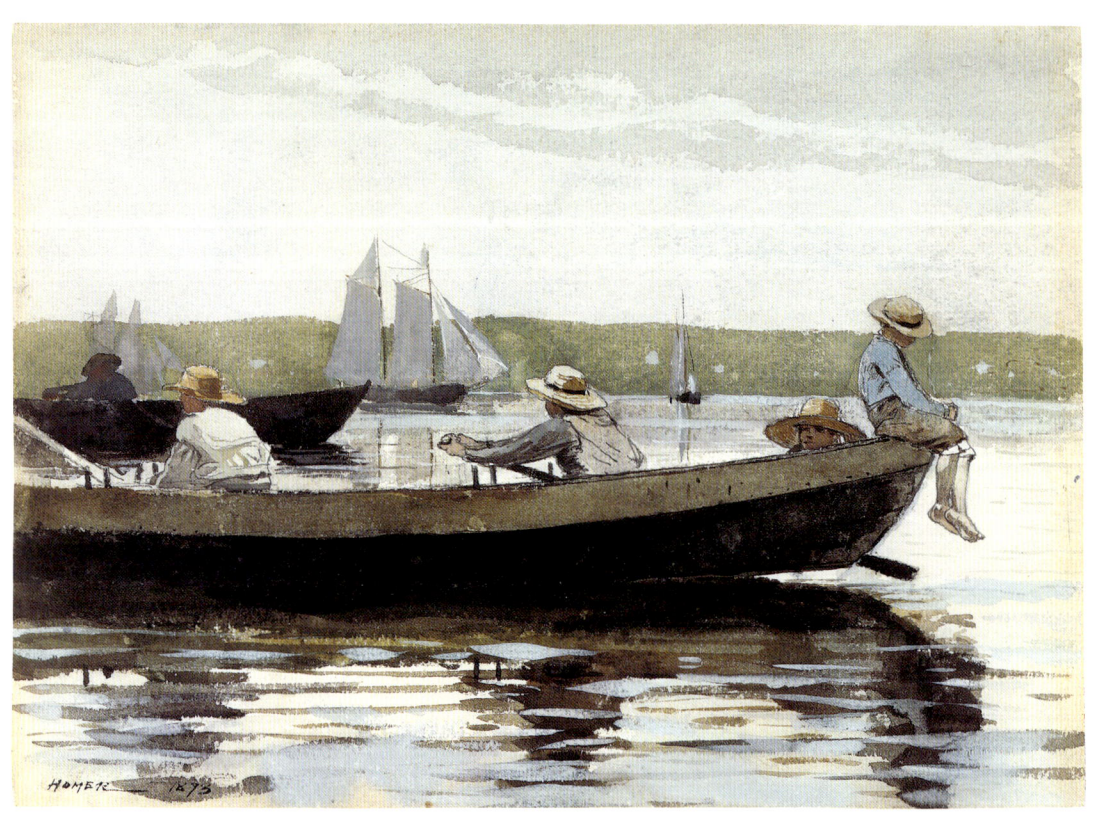

87. Winslow Homer, *Boys in a Dory*, 1873. Watercolor washes and gouache over graphite underdrawing on medium-rough textured white wove paper, 9 3/4 × 13 7/8 in. (24.8 × 35.2 cm). Bequest of Molly Flagg Knudtsen, 2001 (2001.608.1)

Philippe authorized a planning study of The American Wing. In July a contract with Jean Parker Phifer of Thomas Phifer and Partners, architects, was signed, and the first meeting of an American Wing curatorial steering committee was scheduled for September 12. It is a testament to Philippe's grit and essential optimism that after the events of September 11 he permitted, indeed encouraged, the project to go forward. The Phifer study, which among other things confirmed that the paintings could be brought together on one level, was completed in mid-2002, and shortly thereafter the design and implementation of the project were turned over to Kevin Roche of Kevin Roche John Dinkeloo and Associates, the Museum's long-standing architect and The American Wing's original designer. He took up with imagination and gusto the challenge of reconfiguring and improving his own building. By 2004, renovation of The American Wing had been incorporated into the Museum's master plan documents.

Meanwhile, Philippe had recognized a need to broaden the support for American art. First came the creation of endowed curatorial positions. Those for the Alice Pratt Brown Curator of American Paintings and Sculpture and the Anthony W. and Lulu C. Wang Curator of American Decorative Arts were established in 1998, and two more followed in 2007, for the Ruth Bigelow Wriston Curator of American Decorative Arts and the Marica Vilcek Curator of American Decorative Arts. Next on the agenda was the election to the Board of Trustees, for the first time in decades, of committed collectors of American art: Lulu C. Wang and Erving Wolf in 2001, Barrie Wigmore in 2002, Richard Chilton in 2006, and Max Berry in 2007. By making a strategically timed major pledge in 2003, Lulu and Tony Wang jump-started the renovation project, moving it out of the realm of discussion and into action. Since then more than seventy million dollars have been raised for this project, including million-dollar-and-up leadership gifts from Margaret and Raymond J. Horowitz, Anthony W. and Lulu C. Wang, The Peter J. Sharp Foundation, Juliana and Peter Terian, Mr. and Mrs. Richard L. Chilton Jr., Jan and Warren Adelson, Max and Heidi Berry, Ambassador and Mrs. W. L. Lyons Brown, Joyce Berger Cowin, Jane and Maurice Cunniffe, Barbara G. Fleischman and Martha J. Fleischman, the Peggy N. and Roger G. Gerry Charitable Trust, The Henry Luce Foundation, Elizabeth and Richard Miller, the City of New York, the Oceanic Heritage Foundation, Doris

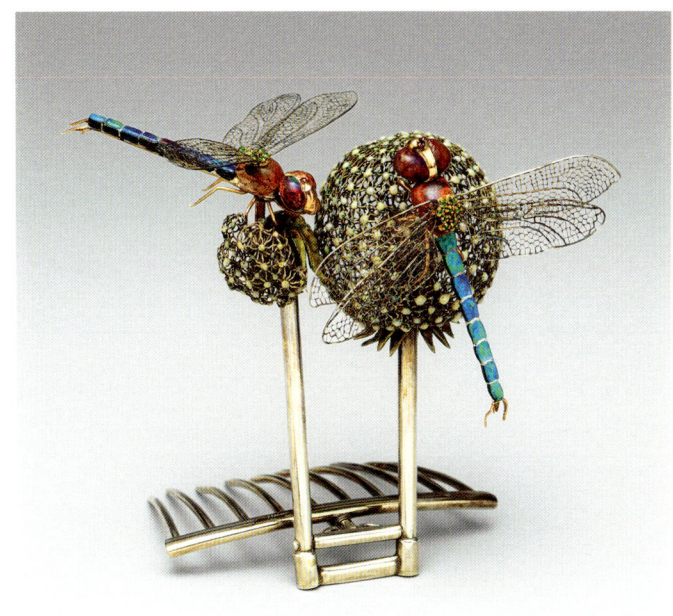

88. Louis Comfort Tiffany, Hair ornament, ca. 1904. Silver, enamel, black opal, and demantoid garnets, H. 3¼ in. (8.3 cm). Gift of Linden Havemeyer Wise, in memory of Louisine W. Havemeyer, 2002 (2002.620)

and Stanley Tananbaum, Barrie and Deedee Wigmore, and Roy J. Zuckerberg.

The first phase of the rebuilding opened in late 2006. It provided better access to The American Wing from the Temple of Dendur in The Sackler Wing and a new suite of classical galleries linking the Colonial rooms and galleries with those of the later nineteenth century. In the second phase, completed in May 2009, The Charles Engelhard Court was renovated (fig. 83) and the Colonial and early Federal period rooms were reordered and refined. Museum visitors can now experience American domestic interiors in a continuous chronological progression, beginning with a room from the Samuel Hart house (Ipswich, Massachusetts, 1680) and concluding with the living room from Frank Lloyd Wright's Francis Little house (Wayzata, Minnesota, 1912–14). The third phase of American Wing reconstruction is the complete rearrangement of the second-floor painting and sculpture galleries and adjacent eighteenth-century decorative arts galleries, scheduled for 2011, followed by upgrades to The Henry R. Luce Center. This will be the final piece of Philippe's architectural legacy.

Morrison H. Heckscher

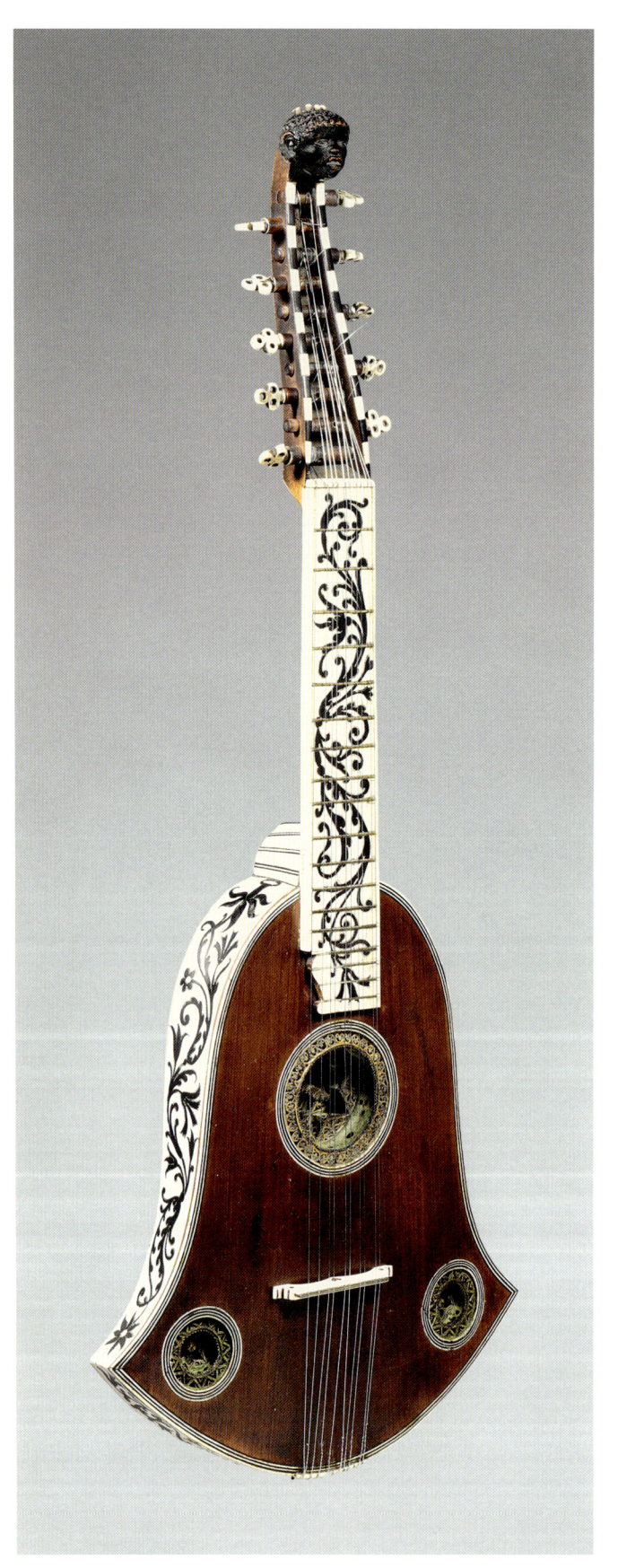 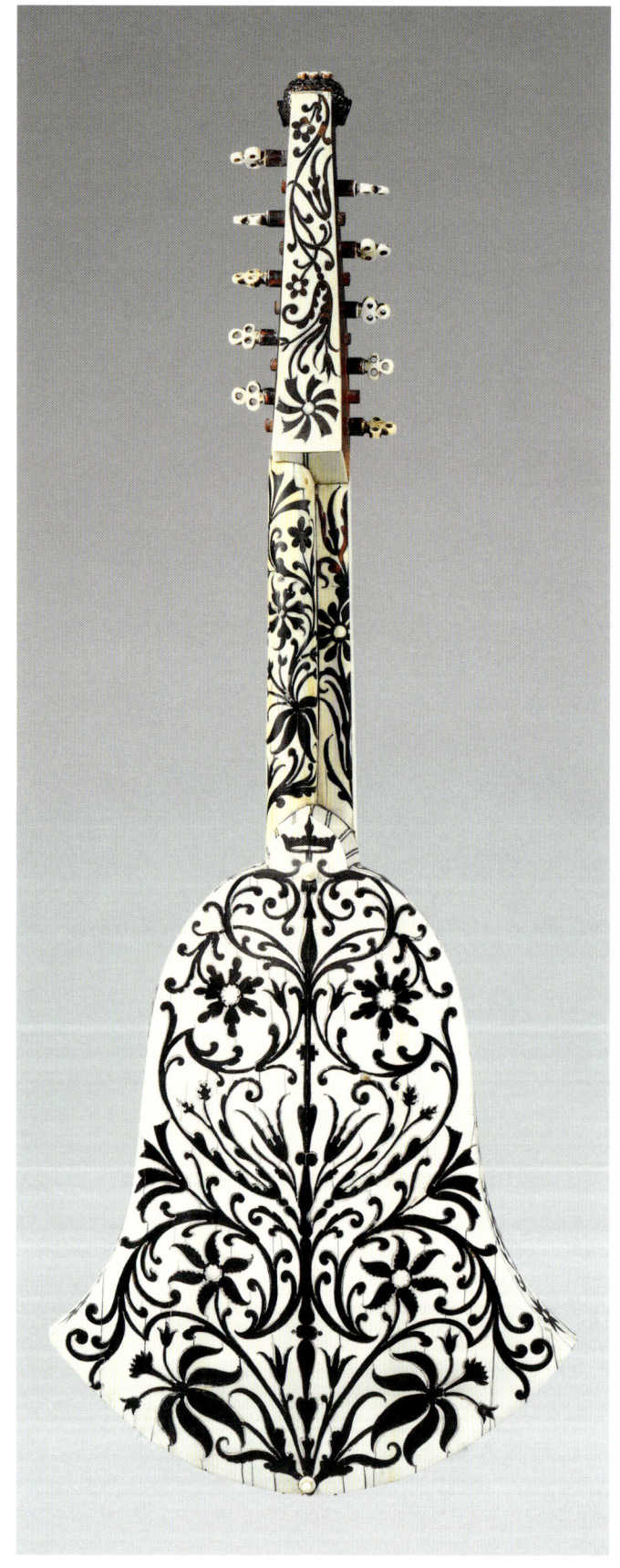

MUSICAL INSTRUMENTS

TANGIBLE EVIDENCE

The Department of Musical Instruments is unique in the Metropolitan Museum, for here one finds tangible objects that serve an intangible art, music. Some beautifully decorated and some starkly functional-looking, they represent a convergence of art, science, and craftsmanship. Instruments derive their significance from rich layers of visual and aural attributes and from the skills of performers and composers. Through subtle and seemingly mysterious processes, they produce sounds that communicate not only with mere mortals but with gods and spirits; they heal the sick and stir the emotions.

While Philippe is a great lover of music and deeply knowledgeable about its development, the word "organology"—a fairly new addition to the dictionary—had been missing from his vocabulary until we introduced him it. In organology, or the study of musical instruments, an attempt is made to explain these culture-specific symbols and processes of music making by focusing on an instrument's musical use, physical characteristics, acoustics, technologies, social role, and history. Those areas of inquiry intersect with ones familiar to sister realms in the arts and sciences: history, social science, music, art, literature, and (surprisingly) neurology are among the fields relevant to these sounding objects. Such interactions make for enriching comparative studies within the Museum, while the depictions of instruments found throughout the collections vividly connect the visual with the performing arts.

The de Montebello years have seen our field improve in a range of areas that include research, conservation, display, and interpretive methods. Musical instruments need to be discussed in terms also applicable to other works of art: maker/artist, technique (additionally, playing technique), materials, balance and tone, context, and symbol—sound being one kind of symbol. And since much of the genius of a musical instrument lies in the details, which are often concealed from the eye by casework or decoration, the curator must find ways of communicating the significance of hidden treasures.

To address these challenges we have programmed educational offerings and more than four hundred concerts (distinct from those of Concerts & Lectures) featuring music from every corner of the world, as well as recordings, radio broadcasts, publications, more than fifty audio offerings in the musical instrument galleries, and musical input to audios for other departments. Here is an introduction to a few departmental highlights—both acquisitions and activities.

The Violin Masterpieces of Guarneri del Gesù
An exhibition of twenty-five rare violins may sound a bit redundant, but when they are all by the legendary Cremonese maker Giuseppe Guarneri del Gesù (1698–1744), it is possibly the violin event of the century. Guarneri del Gesù has been dubbed the Van Gogh of violin makers—a comparison that makes reference to both his personal life and his genius, through which, despite some hasty and eccentric work in his later life, he produced instruments of astonishing tonal qualities. This 1994 exhibition was curated by Laurence Libin, then Frederick P. Rose Curator in Charge, and Stewart Pollens, then associate conservator of Musical Instruments, and underwritten by Peter Biddulph. Bringing together works from all periods of Guarneri del Gesù's life, we introduced to the general public a great maker whose instruments are considered by many to be finer than Stradivari's. Violins displayed in the exhibition had been played by the greatest virtuosi: Niccolò Paganini, Ole Bull, Joseph Joachim, Eugène Ysaÿe, Fritz Kreisler, Jascha Heifetz, Isaac Stern, Itzhak Perlman, and Elmar Oliveira, among others. The exhibition was complemented by a symposium and a remarkable concert featuring solo performances played on fifteen of the prized instruments.

"The Violin Masterpieces of Guarneri del Gesù" presented a rare opportunity to compare one artist's extraordinary instruments with those of other makers. Although rich in works by

Opposite: 89. Cittern made by Joachim Tielke, front and back views. Hamburg, Germany, ca. 1685. Wood, ivory, ebony, and other materials, L. 24⅞ in. (63.2 cm). Purchase, The Vincent Astor Foundation Gift and Rogers Fund, 1985 (1985.124)

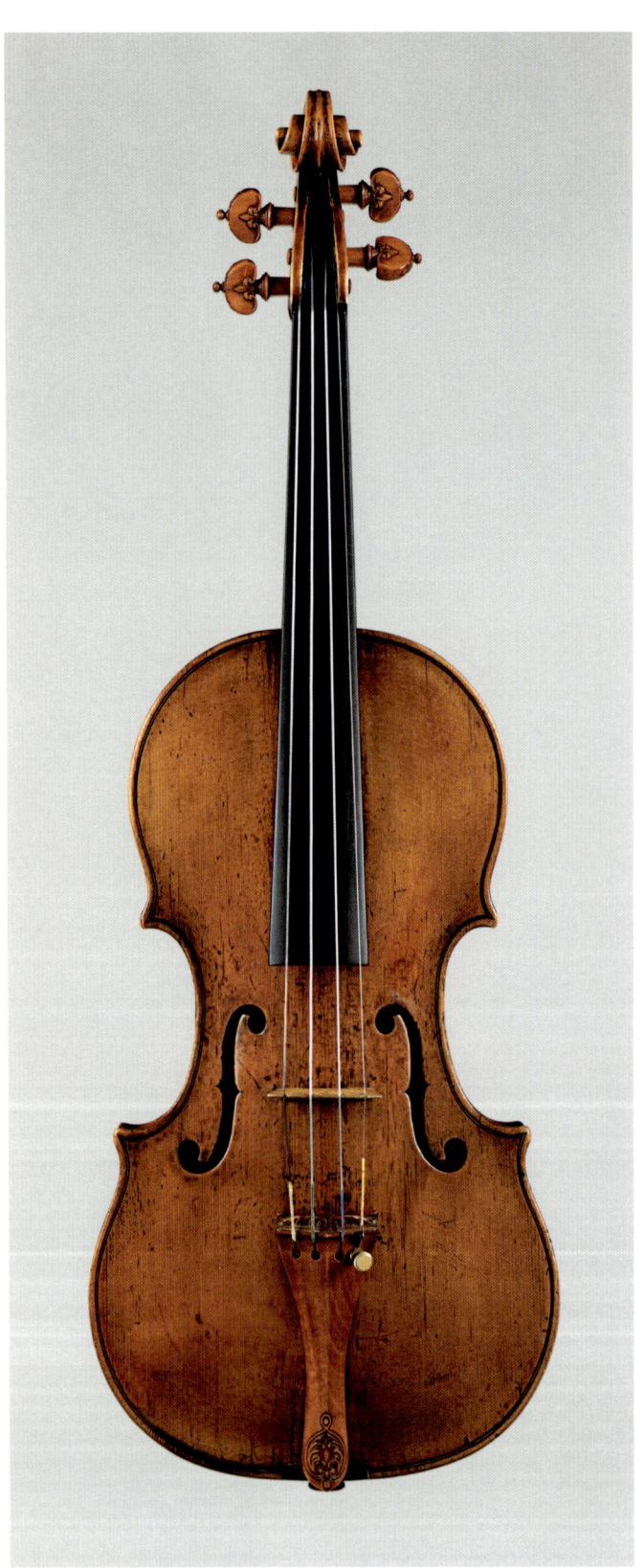

90. Violin made by Andrea Amati. Cremona, Italy, ca. 1560. Maple, spruce, and other woods, L. ca. 22⅝ in. (57.4 cm). Purchase, Robert Alonzo Lehman Bequest, 1999 (1999.26)

Stradivari the Museum does not own a Guarneri del Gesù, so we borrowed instruments from individuals and institutions, who generously permitted scholars to scrutinize them by ultraviolet light to gain insights into glues, varnishes, and alterations. The wood was dated using dendrochronology, and extremely detailed measurements were made. In addition to enhancing our presentation to the public, this research, which shed considerable light on Guarneri del Gesù's methodology, materials, and eccentricities, was later published and is a lasting resource for collectors, luthiers (stringed-instrument makers), performers, and scholars.

A Violin by Andrea Amati

If Giuseppe Guarneri del Gesù was the Van Gogh of violin makers, perhaps the much earlier Andrea Amati (ca. 1515–ca. 1580), an artist of innovation and imagination, was the Leonardo. Before Amati, bowed instruments appeared in a wide range of shapes and sizes and were often poorly crafted. Amati experimented, observing rules of proportion and using select woods and varnishes, until he had refined the design and produced the violin that we know today, with its arched top, graceful sound holes, and rich finish. The pure sound is restrained and sweet in comparison with the darker and more powerful voice of later instruments.

About twenty instruments from Amati's workshop have survived, and one of these the Museum acquired in 1999 (fig. 90). It is from a group of seven that were originally decorated similarly, with the lily of the house of Valois and a coat of arms on the back of the corners (projecting points) and a Latin motto on the sides. The coat of arms has worn off all of them except a violin in Paris, on which the device of Philip II of Spain can be discerned. Around the sides of each violin is written "QUO UNICO PROPUGNACULO STAT STABIQUE RELIGIO" (Religion is, and always shall be, the only fortress) (fig. 91). This motto was used by Catherine de Médicis, queen consort to Henry II of France and mother of the future Charles IX, and a different set of instruments bearing the motto has traditionally been associated with Charles. But current scholarship suggests that our violin and its six mates may have been intended as courtly gifts to celebrate the royal marriage in 1559 of Elisabeth of Valois—daughter of Henry II and Catherine, and sister of Charles IX—to the much older Philip II of Spain. The political union helped to end a sixty-year conflict between France and Spain and to advance Catholicism during the French Wars of Religion (1562–98). This recently proposed role for the violins would explain the appearance on them of both Philip II's coat of arms and Catherine's motto. If the theory is correct, our instrument was created as early as 1558—which would mean that it predates the set believed to have been made for Charles IX and is one of the earliest surviving violins. Despite one or two questions raised by my fellow curators, Philippe approved the recommendation to purchase this exceptional instrument.

Before coming to the Museum this violin was seldom played, but its wonderful sound quality, rather large for a violin of that period, has now been heard on several occasions. The instrument has also become the logo and namesake of the Department of Musical Instruments' friends group, the Amati—a double entendre that alludes to both the maker and the Italian word for friends.

Just as decorations, mottoes, and symbols are sometimes added to instruments, other types of meanings, such as zoomorphic and anthropomorphic ones, are often ascribed to them. The violin is not the only instrument that has a body, waist, belly, shoulders, head, neck, and tail. In some cultures the pegs that secure the strings at the upper end are known as ears; the bridge that supports the strings may be the horse or the elephant. An instrument can suggest a nationality or even a philosophy. Extramusical concepts add layers of nuance to an instrument and its music.

Qin

This is the case with the understated, iconic Chinese *qin*, a board zither that epitomizes scholarship and refinement. Endowed with cosmological and metaphysical significance and thus empowered to communicate the deepest feelings, this instrument, beloved by Confucius and other sages, is the most prestigious in China. Writers of the Han dynasty (206 B.C.– A.D. 220) asserted that the *qin* helped to cultivate character, promote an understanding of morality, supplicate gods and demons, enhance life, and enrich learning.

One of the oldest of Chinese instruments, the *qin* dates, in a slightly different form, from the Shang dynasty (ca. 1600–1100 B.C.), and in its present form from about the late eighth century B.C. By the time of the Ming dynasty (1368–1644) it had acquired a prestigious and symbolic position in Chinese society. Ming literati claimed the right to play the *qin,* which they preferred to do outdoors: in a mountain setting, garden, or small pavilion or near an old pine tree (symbol of longevity), often in the serene glow of a moonlit evening perfumed with incense. From the Tang dynasty (618–906) on, such settings appear in Chinese paintings and drawings showing a scholar playing the instrument—or with his servant, who carries it wrapped in a cloth covering—while viewing the moon or some other natural wonder. The form of the *qin* was imitated in objects such as brush boxes, fan cases, and wrist rests. The Ming-dynasty *qin* mystique encompassed metaphysics, civics, aesthetics, religion, and literature. Cosmology is ever present: for example, the upper board of *wutong* wood symbolizes heaven, while the bottom board of *zi* wood symbolizes earth. The player completes the picture, uniting heaven and earth in harmony and balance.

Playing the *qin* served as a means of contemplation and was done alone or for an intimate friend who could appreciate the depth of the player's heartfelt musical expression. Only refined and sophisticated individuals played the instrument, and if one lacked the skill, it was hung on the wall as an emblem of status. The *qin* was and remains closely tied to Confucian ritual and principles and to the Chinese literati tradition. Because of that association it was at first banned under Communist rule, but

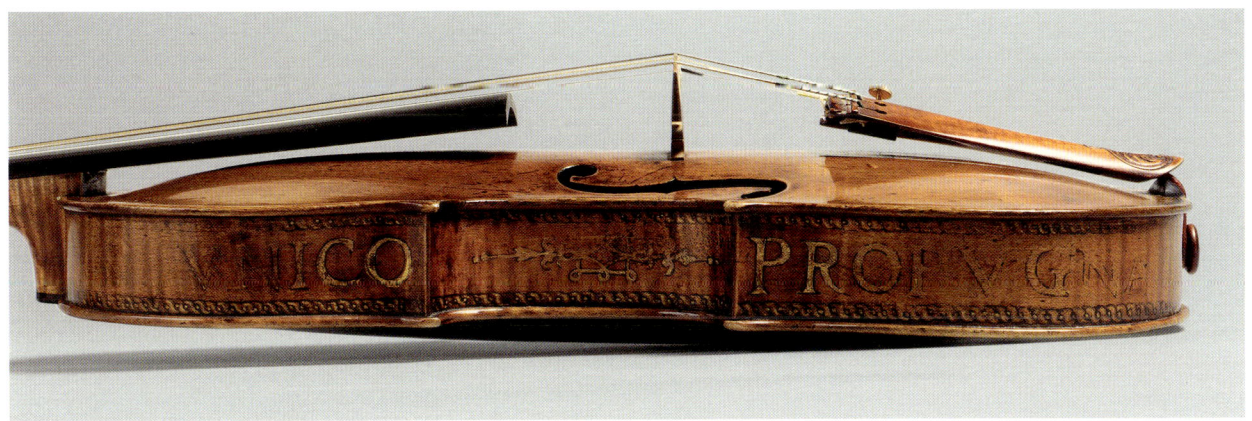

91. Amati violin, side view showing partial inscription "UNICO PROPUGNACULO"

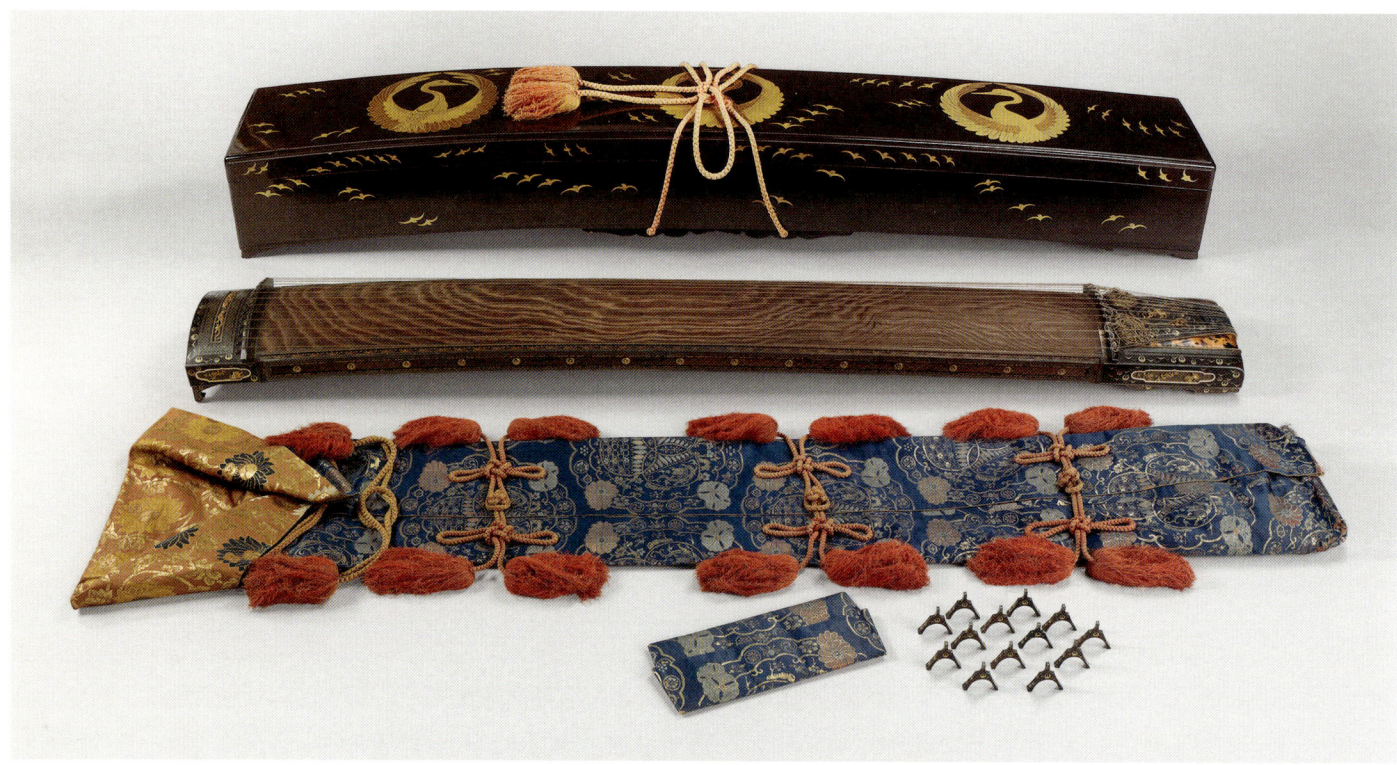

92. Koto and accessories, Japan, 17th century. Metalwork attributed to Gotō Teijo. Top to bottom: case, koto, fabric wrap, and bridges with their case. Paulownia wood and other woods, ivory, tortoiseshell, gold, silver, and other materials, cloth; koto L. 74 ⅝ in. (189.5 cm). Purchase, Amati Gifts, 2007 (2007.194a–f)

later it was revived. Today the *qin* is most often played before an audience.

The Prince Lu Qin

The *qin* acquired by the Museum in 1999 and shared by the departments of Musical Instruments and Asian Art was made by Prince Lu (act. 1624–44), one of the four best-known makers of the Ming dynasty. This rare, graceful, and still playable seven-string zither (1999.93) was produced as part of a movement to revive ancient Chinese traditions and compositions. In chapter 12 of the *History of Ming* it is written that Changfang, son of Emperor Wanli, inherited the title Prince of Lu (Lu-wang) in 1616 and later supervised the making of more than four hundred *qin*s at Hangzhou. Each one was numbered—the Museum's is number 18—and most bear dates of the Chongzhen period (1627–44). Only five Prince Lu instruments are now documented.

A *qin* is considered best if it is more than one hundred years old. Age is evidenced by cracking patterns (*duanwen*) and worn patches in the lacquered surface; these bestow a venerable appearance, document the hand movements of past players, and permit scattered russet patches and gold flecks embedded in the lacquer to peek through.

Occasionally, the edges of cracks in the lacquer rise a bit and collide with one of the silk strings. This had occurred with the Museum's instrument, producing a buzzing sound when the *qin* was played. To be playable instruments need maintenance, and in a museum setting this raises questions of conservation ethics. Does one tamper with a historic object in order to make it functional? The argument for doing so is that instruments are often restored and changed over their years of use. The violins of Stradivari are not as they were when they left the maker's hands: the angle of the neck has been changed and they have endured many adjustments. Knowing that our *qin* had been repaired over the centuries, we made the decision to render it fully playable. Our search for the right specialist to realize this repair led us to Hong Kong *qin* master Teo Kheng Chong, who arrived bearing special tools and lacquer. Working with the Museum's Department of Objects Conservation, Mr. Teo was able to smooth out the playing surface and repair areas around the thirteen mother-of-pearl studs (*hui*) running the length of one side, which locate finger positions. The strings—of diminishing gauges and secured on the lower board by two pale green jade knobs ("goose feet") and at the blunt end by seven whitish-green jade tuning pegs—now sound as they should.

The qin's lower board has two sound holes, the circular "dragon's pond" and a smaller, square "phoenix pool." The board also bears the maker's seal and date, the name Zhonghe ("Capital Peace"), and a twenty-character poem by the nobleman and scholar Jingyi Zhuren (d. 1670), which reads:

> The moonlight is reflecting in the river Yangtze.
> A light breeze is blowing over clear dewdrops.
> Only in a tranquil place
> Can one comprehend the feeling of eternity.

Koto

The aesthetics of the *qin*—subtle lines, veneration of signs of age, esoteric playing philosophy, and poetic inscriptions—are starkly contrasted by those of its Japanese cousin, the koto. Thanks to the Amati group, the Museum was able to purchase in 2007 an extraordinary early seventeenth-century koto befitting a nobleman (fig. 92) that may have belonged to Karasumaru Mitsuhiro (1579–1638); its lacquered storage box bears the Karasumaru family crest. Its exquisite metalwork is attributable to Gotō Teijo (1603–1673), a ninth-generation Gotō-family master. A number of works ascribed to this family are in the Met's Department of Arms and Armor.

Japan's national instrument, the koto is a thirteen-string zither. In its basic form it is a rectangular box of paulownia (*kiri*) wood, slightly convex on the top. Its strings, formerly of twisted silk although now often of nylon, run from one end to the other, and each is held above the board and tuned by a movable, inverted-Y-shaped bridge (*ji*) (fig. 93). Traditionally, every component of the instrument has a symbolic equivalent. Its basic construction is thought of as an arching dragon (*ryū*) with head, tongue, and tail. The bridges, when spread diagonally across the upper surface, constitute the dragon's spine.

The Museum's koto epitomizes the opulent taste of the Edo period (1615–1868). A wealth of techniques are employed in its embellishment. The instrument is not just intricately carved but also cut and singed on the wooden soundboard to create a wavelike surface of swirling grain patterns (*itame*). Materials used for the decorative inlays include dyed antler, woven bamboo, gold, silver, ivory, tortoiseshell, and exotic woods such as ebony, Bombay blackwood, sandalwood, boxwood, and rosewood. They are crafted into fanciful designs of cranes, wild geese, lions, flowers, vines, dragons, geometric patterns, a three-lobed oak leaf, and an *apsara* (celestial maiden) in a flowing robe playing a double-headed drum. When not in use the koto was kept in a cloth wrap inside a decorated case; these original accessories have been replaced by ones made later.

There is anecdotal evidence that the instrument was presented to Karasumaru Mitsuhiro, a noted poet/warrior, by the daimyo Hosokawa Sansai (1565–1645) in gratitude for his having saved the life of Hosokawa Yūsai, Sansai's father (and Mitsuhiro's father-in-law and poetry teacher). According to tradition, its completion took one thousand days. Early in the twentieth century the prized instrument was received into the Imperial Household to be viewed by the Meiji emperor Mutsuhito and his empress.

Japan's koto tradition developed from the Chinese *qin*, which was probably brought to Japan sometime around the early Nara period (710–84). Trade, war, and migration have disseminated an array of cultural manifestations, including religion, inventions, and music. Europe was the recipient of many instruments from the Middle East, for example, as was China, which also absorbed musical ideas from India.

Instruments International and Local

One aspect of such cultural interchange was explored in 1996 in "Enduring Rhythms: African Musical Instruments and the

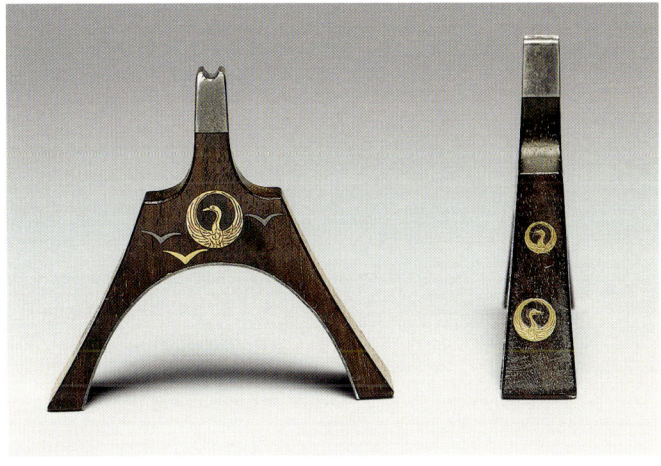

93. Bridge (*ji*) of the koto seen in figure 92, front and side views. Wood with inlays of various metals, H. 1⅞ in. (5.2 cm)

[79]

Americas," the Museum's first exhibition about the African diaspora. "Enduring Rhythms" highlighted eighty instruments from North and South America and the Caribbean that express the durability and resilience of the African-American heritage. African instruments were juxtaposed with their American counterparts, illustrating transformations in construction, use, and musical style and inviting contemplation of issues of cultural identity and continuity. Many unfamiliar instruments of the sixteenth to the twentieth century, and their sounds, were introduced to the public.

Another intriguing exhibition of the same year, presented in collaboration with the Department of American Art and, like "Enduring Rhythms," drawn largely from the Met's collections, was "Making Music: Two Centuries of Musical Instrument Making in New York." It brought together instruments ranging from folk to refined, and dating from the eighteenth century to the present day, that reflect New York's vibrant diversity: some lavishly decorated to signal social position, others the workaday tools of professional musicians or the creations of an immigrant population.

Cittern by Joachim Tielke
Some objects in our galleries are artifacts of music's passing fancies, and one such is a beautiful late seventeenth-century bell-shaped cittern (fig. 89). The instrument, a wire-strung, plucked lute, was popular during the sixteenth and seventeenth centuries. A pear-shaped cittern is wonderfully depicted in wood inlay on the wall of the Met's Studiolo from the ducal palace in Gubbio. While that Italian example has a characteristically tapering body, the specialty of luthiers in late seventeenth-century Hamburg was the bell-shaped cittern, now rare. Ours was made by Joachim Tielke (1641–1719), the foremost of these craftsmen and legendary for the sumptuous decoration of his instruments. Often string instruments were made in pairs and embellished with complementary veneered designs, one with white ivory figures on a black ebony ground and the other the reverse, as in this gracefully scrolled example. In 1973 the mate to this cittern, offered for sale to the Museum, was recognized as stolen property and returned to the Hamburg Museum für Kunst und Gewerbe; twelve years later came a second opportunity, this time to acquire the present instrument. Its typically shaped body becomes thinner in depth going from top to tail. The cypress-wood front is pierced by three sound holes bearing deeply recessed parchment rosettes; ten wire strings ascend the fingerboard to a pegbox surmounted by the carved head of a Moorish king. The neck has a coronet inlaid at its heel and on its side the engraved inscription "In Hamburg Tielke fecit."

Fashionable for one brief period in northern Europe and Scandinavia, Hamburg citterns boast only a small repertoire, of which just five musical manuscripts survive. This instrument, fortuitously preserved, testifies to a refined and idiosyncratic moment in music history.

Guitar by Hermann Hauser
A master builder is a musical mediator who uses his skills as craftsman, engineer, and acoustician to fulfill the requirements of his client and partner: the performer. One of our prized acquisitions is a guitar made in 1937 by the German maker Hermann Hauser and presented to the Museum, along with a 1912 Manuel Ramírez guitar, by Andrés Segovia as a gift from his wife, Emilita Segovia, Marquesa of Salobreña (1986.353.1). The legendary Segovia had been responsible for reviving and reinventing the classical guitar repertoire. New York City played an important role in his career, and, having given two master classes at the Met, he was familiar with our fine guitar collection. In 1986, after a brief demonstration, the maestro ceremoniously and joyously handed his guitars to Director Philippe de Montebello (fig. 94).

This Hauser guitar was Segovia's principal concert instrument from 1938 until 1962; he admired it enormously and once called it "the greatest guitar of our epoch." A long history preceded his acquisition of the instrument. Miguel Llobet, a Spanish classical guitarist/composer, introduced Segovia to Hermann Hauser in 1924. Hauser had been making guitars in the Viennese style; Llobet, however, encouraged him to adopt Spanish models. It is said that Hauser offered instruments to Segovia for twelve successive years, but none pleased him until he tried this one, after which he retired his Ramírez guitar.

The modern classical guitar is a type that emerged in mid-nineteenth-century Spain. It had a larger body than previous styles as well as a reinforced internal construction, fan bracing on the underside of the soundboard, and a bridge in which saddle and tie block are integral. Classical guitars were traditionally strung with gut, although metal-wrapped strings, invented about 1660, were often used in the bass. After World War II synthetic strings began to be used; Segovia was one of the first to experiment with and then adopt nylon strings, which are now found on nearly all modern classical guitars. The Hauser guitar has

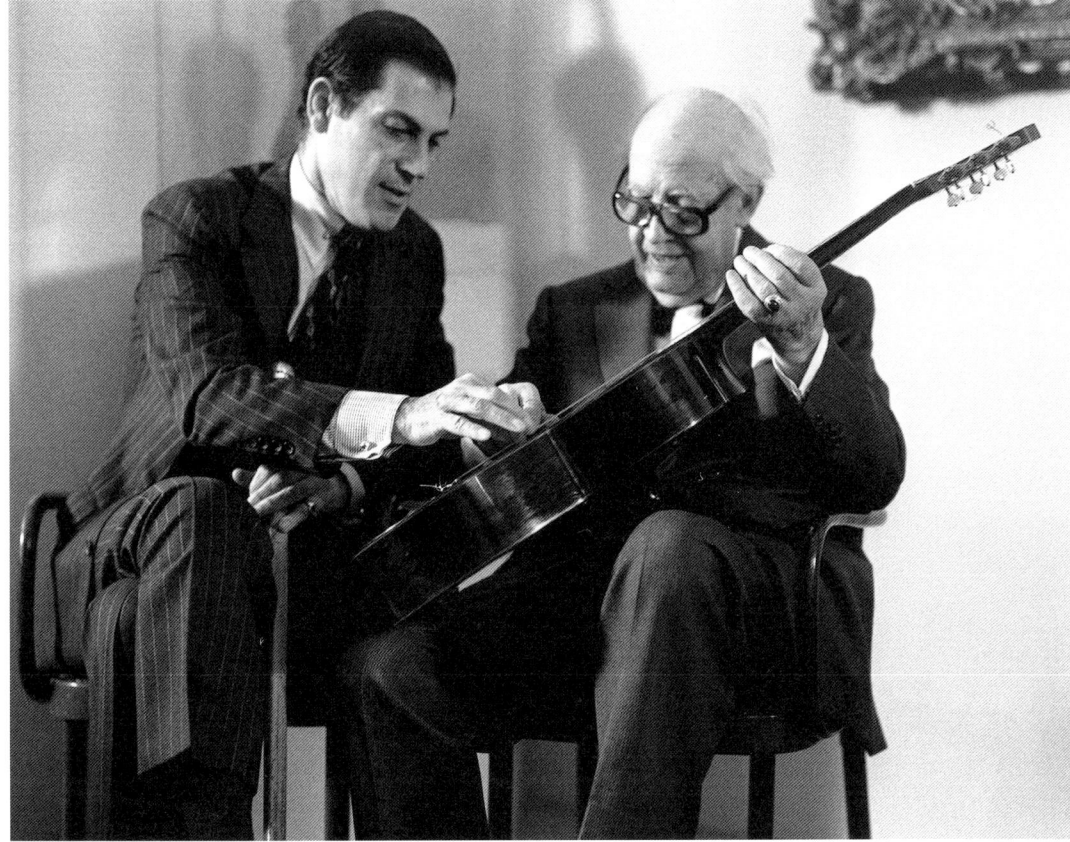

94. Philippe de Montebello with Maestro Andrés Segovia and the Hauser guitar, 1986

repeatedly been copied, and technical drawings of it with detailed measurements were recently published.

Five years after their donation, Segovia's guitars were featured here in "The Spanish Guitar/La Guitarra Española," an exhibition of thirty-five instruments ranging from a sixteenth-century vihuela (one of only two known) to a modern flamenco guitar.

Musical instruments have been a part of the Metropolitan since 1889, when the collections of Joseph Drexel and especially of Mary Elizabeth Brown (Mrs. John Crosby Brown) entered the Museum. Much more recently, the Italian composer Luciano Berio (1925–2003) wrote, "Musical instruments aren't just neutral tools: they are the concrete depositories of historical continuity, and like working tools and buildings they have a memory. They carry with them traces of the conceptual and social changes through which they were developed and transformed." Musical instruments represent music's heritage, both tangible and intangible. Like the visual arts, they hold up a mirror that reflects, by its organization of materials and symbols, our experiences, emotions, and deepest musings.

J. Kenneth Moore

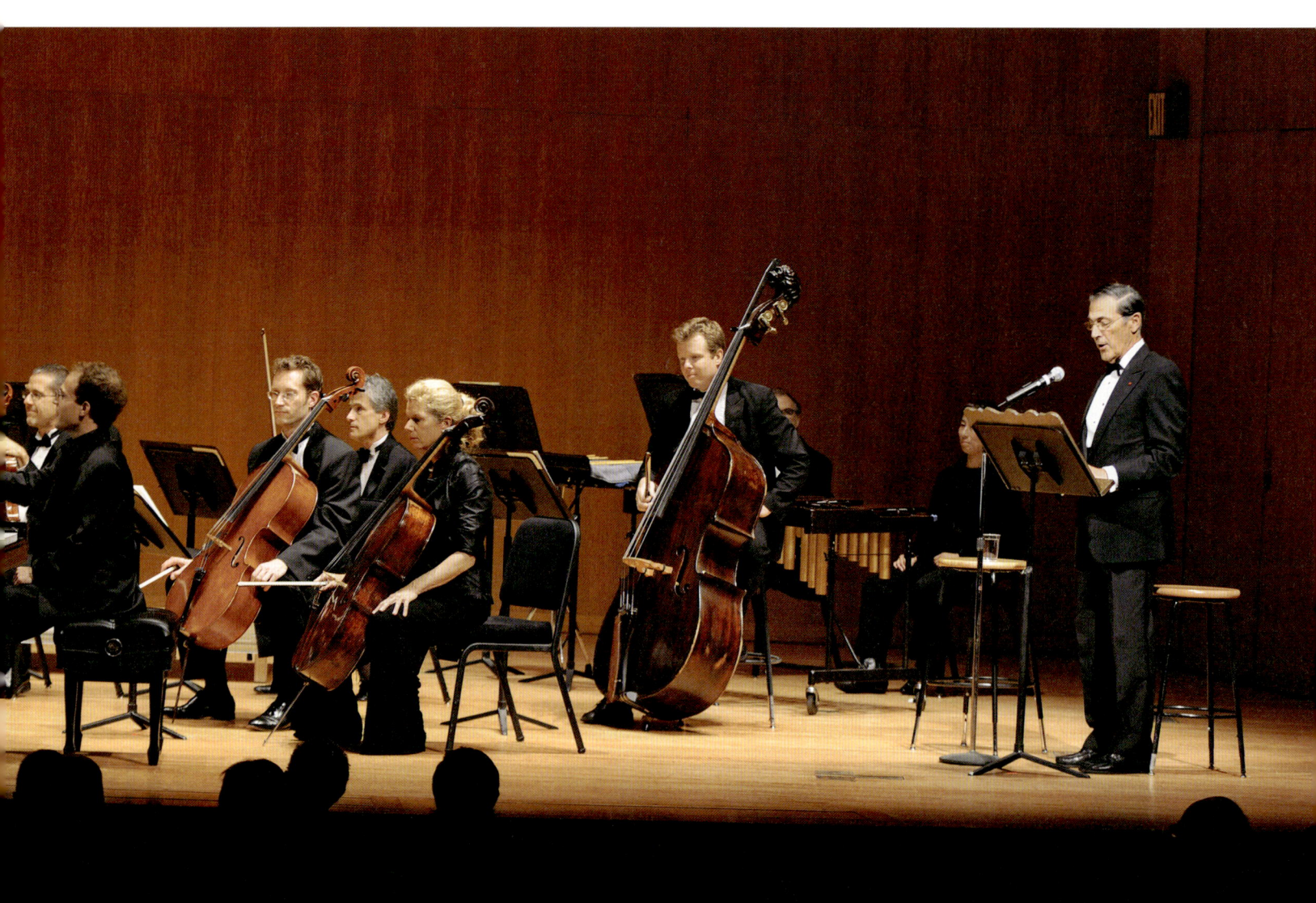

MUSIC AT THE MET

GUIDING THE CONCERTS & LECTURES PROGRAM

Shortly after Philippe de Montebello became director of the Metropolitan Museum, he and I met on a sunny May afternoon in his second-floor office overlooking Fifth Avenue. Our conversation remains sharply etched in my mind. He asked whether I had come across any outstanding recordings of the Mozart piano sonatas, an intriguing question. At the time there were few recordings of these works, with the notable cycles by András Schiff and Mitsuko Uchida still to come. We spoke about good examples that did exist: Wanda Landowska's performance on a Pleyel piano, Walter Gieseking's, and a new one by Peter Serkin. We agreed that this sector of the piano literature had not been well served by the recording industry.

I was amazed to discover that the connoisseurship Philippe possessed in art and literature also extended into the realm of music. Subsequently I would learn that music had been very much a part of his home life: his mother had been a concert pianist before her marriage, and his brother, Georges de Montebello, was a pianist of high accomplishment, whose playing I would have the pleasure of hearing. But on that spring day, our talk about Mozart was a revelation. I had gained for Concerts & Lectures not only an advocate, but a much esteemed adviser.

Along with our audiences, I have applauded the director's appearances in our series as lecturer and program host. Over the years he has brought his erudition to no fewer than twenty-six programs, speaking on a range of subjects: "The Art of Collecting," "The Fine Art of Acquisition," "The Anatomy of a Building: Multiple Architecture of The Metropolitan Museum of Art," "Art Museums, the Internet, and the New Technology," "The Making of an Exhibition," and "Museums: Why Should We Care?" to name a few. To the special delight of Metropolitan devotees, he participated in poetry readings with the actors Claire Bloom, Isabella Rossellini, Fritz Weaver, and Irene Worth.

Particularly notable was a sold-out program featuring the director in conversation with Alfred Brendel and Michael Kimmelman in April 1998. Mr. Kimmelman, an accomplished pianist, was then chief art critic of the *New York Times*. Mr. Brendel, one of the great pianists of our time, started his life in the arts as a painter and had his first public show at the age of seventeen; he is also the author of three published volumes of musical philosophy and one of prose poetry. After I mentioned to his agent that the director had read and admired Brendel's poetry, a luncheon was arranged for the three of us, during which this unique program was conceived. Onstage, Messrs. Brendel, de Montebello, and Kimmelman conversed about topics ranging from creativity and interpretation to the relationship of music to poetry and art, with Mr. Brendel illustrating a number of points at the piano.

Philippe has also personally hosted historic musical events at the Museum. Among them were a master class with the venerated classical guitarist Andrés Segovia (fig. 96); a gala benefit concert at which the pianist Murray Perahia was both conductor and soloist with the Orchestra of Saint Luke's (fig. 98); and the opening concert of the fiftieth-anniversary season of Concerts & Lectures, a performance by the Orpheus Chamber Orchestra in the Great Hall, which was capped by a champagne toast.

Ever since the Metropolitan took the first, pioneering step of presenting great music in the Museum setting, it has been imperative to obtain programs of high artistry. And for the past thirty-one years I have been driven by an internalized mantra, the starting point for every choice: Are we aspiring to the standard of quality that Philippe de Montebello has set for this institution?

Among the artists presented by Metropolitan Museum Concerts in its first fifty-four years are the singers Kathleen Battle, Marilyn Horne, Dmitri Hvorostovsky, Christa Ludwig, Birgit Nilsson, Joan Sutherland, Rolando Villazón, and Frederica von Stade; the string virtuosi Jacqueline du Pré, Gidon Kremer, Mischa Maisky, Yehudi Menuhin, David Oistrakh, Itzhak Perlman, Janos Starker, and Isaac Stern; the guitarists Julian Bream and Andrés Segovia; ensembles including the Beaux Arts Trio and the Budapest,

Opposite: 95. Philippe de Montebello as reader with the Orpheus Chamber Orchestra for its performance of Camille Saint-Saëns's *Carnival of the Animals*, September 2008

Emerson, Guarneri, Juilliard, and Tokyo string quartets; and the keyboard artists Martha Argerich, Claudio Arrau, Vladimir Ashkenazy, Jorge Bolet, Clifford Curzon, Alicia de Larrocha, Annie Fisher, Murray Perahia, Mikhail Pletnev, Sviatoslav Richter, Peter Serkin, Rudolf Serkin, Mitsuko Uchida, and André Watts. Conductors James Levine and Daniel Barenboim have also appeared on the Museum's stage in piano recitals.

Along with excellence and continuity, Philippe values innovation. Because he quite literally set the tone for our programming, I have striven to put the series in the vanguard of concert presentation, bringing new ideas to a field often weighted by tradition. With his encouragement we have developed such offerings as concerts with commentary, one-hour concerts, conversations with performing artists, exhibition-related concerts, and other events that simply would not have been possible without the support and backing of this great institution.

Thematic programming, now a norm for concert halls in New York and across the country, was a rarity in the 1970s and 1980s, when Concerts & Lectures, the only organizer to offer series exclusively of Mozart or Beethoven sonatas or Haydn trios, forged this new path. We continued to refine our approach in the de Montebello years with such events as a series during the Brahms centennial in 1983 devoted solely to the music of Brahms's predecessors, contemporaries, and followers; two contrasting series of the Bach partitas, one on piano and one on harpsichord, during the Bach tricentennial in 1985; and a weeklong festival of performances of the music of Haydn in 1991, the two hundredth anniversary of the death of Mozart, which were hailed by the *New Yorker* as "the best concerts so far in the Mozart year."

In 1985, inspired by the director's admiration for Glenn Gould, we offered the four-day film retrospective and panel discussion "Glenn Gould: An Homage." The Canadian pianist, who died in 1982 at the age of fifty, had, after a brilliant concert career, devoted the last eighteen years of his life exclusively to recordings and to performances on film and television. For months we carried out research, some of it in Toronto, where we discovered in the archives of the Canadian Broadcasting Corporation a cache of videos of television broadcasts made by the pianist over the years 1959–81. Our tribute ultimately presented a selection of these for the first time since their original airing; it also included the premiere screening in the United States of the two-hour CBC documentary *Glenn Gould: A Portrait*, as well as an evening of appreciation and reminiscence by those who had known and worked with him.

People came from across the country and as far away as Japan to attend these programs, which received considerable acclaim. The tribute was so successful that it was followed by two more, in 1987 and 1992. Edward Rothstein wrote in the *New York Times* after the last of these: "Gould, who died a decade ago at the age of 50, seemed almost palpably present. . . . The audience of this sold-out event (with listeners coming and going throughout the day) responded to the films, in fact, as if they were live performances."

In 1969, when musicians played or sang but rarely spoke to their audiences, we had asked the great Bach specialist Rosalyn Tureck to perform and also talk about the composer, a type of event that, like thematic programming, became familiar in concert halls beyond the Met. This was followed in the 1970s and 1980s by the mixed presentations of other musicians, including Jeffrey Siegel and Ruth Laredo on piano repertoire, Billy Taylor on jazz, Richard Kapp on orchestral music, and Jean-Pierre Rampal, Menahem Pressler, and Maxim Vengerov in programs devoted to one seminal work. Among the artists who have been interviewed onstage are Plácido Domingo, Luciano Pavarotti, Leontyne Price, and Beverly Sills, all of whom spoke with Speight Jenkins, and Daniel Barenboim, Valery Gergiev, and Kurt Masur, in conversation with Matthew Gurewitsch.

The great violinist Itzhak Perlman's long history at the Metropolitan Museum began when he was twenty-four. In more than three decades of performances he has appeared here with pianists Vladimir Ashkenazy, Joseph Kalichstein, and Samuel Sanders, and participated in a panel discussion about the cellist Jacqueline du Pré. At a benefit for the Concerts & Lectures series in 1994 he played a Guarneri del Gesù violin that had belonged to Jascha Heifetz. In 2007 he returned to the Museum with a concert series in which he performed with the young alumni of the Perlman Music Program, a program founded and guided by his wife, Toby Perlman. The *New York Sun*'s critic commented, "Hearing Mr. Perlman play is always a treat, but listening to him with these attentive aspirants was pure joy." As I recall, at a lunch celebrating the series, Messrs. Perlman and de Montebello, both wine connoisseurs, exchanged wine lore and bons mots.

A particularly adventurous thematic program was a series in 1969 devoted to the music of Henry Purcell. It included the final New York appearance of the legendary countertenor Alfred Deller. Early music, a thriving field today, was then viewed by the general public as impossibly long-haired, and the success of the series came as something of a surprise. The *New York Times* asked,

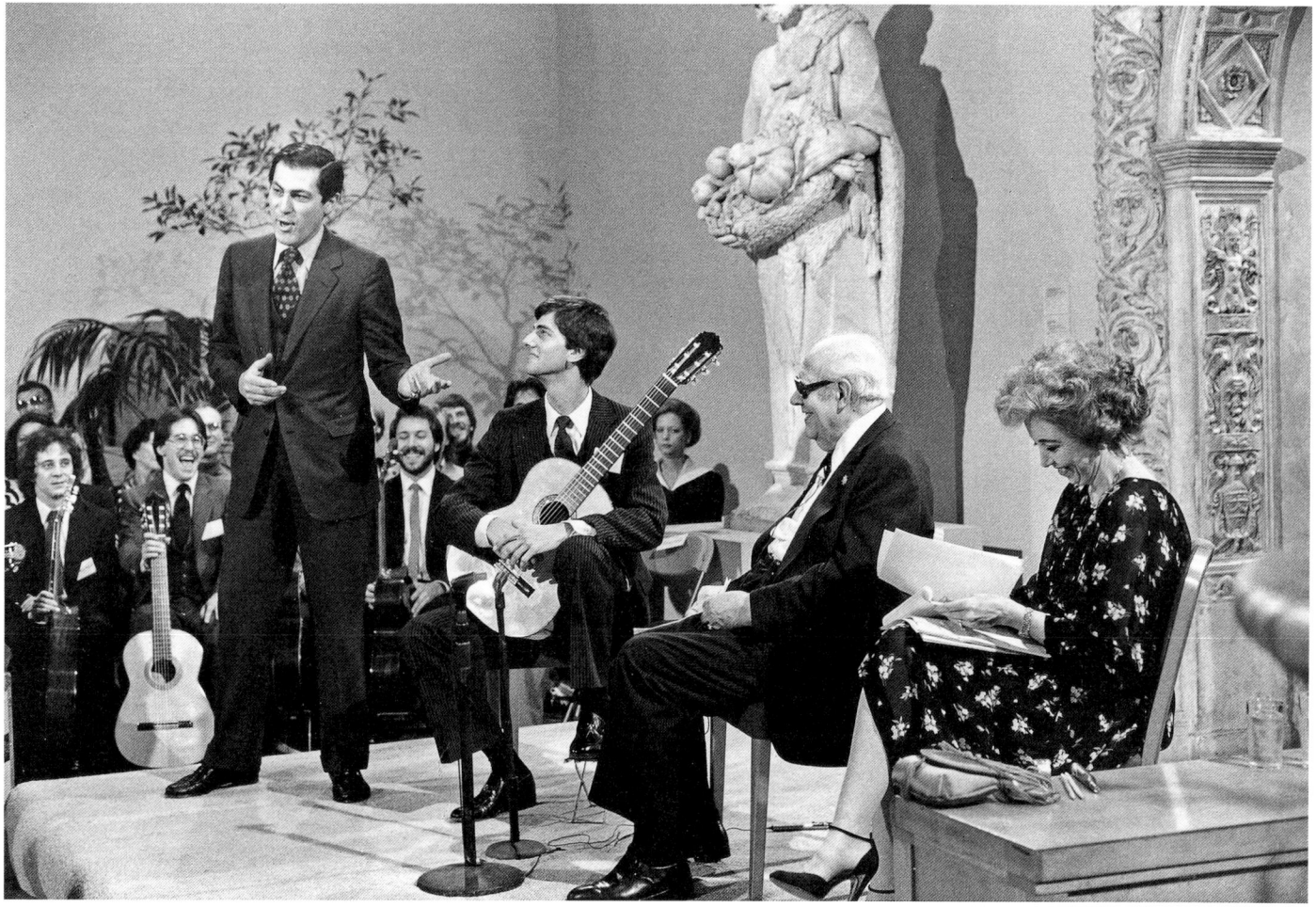

96. Philippe de Montebello introduces a master class given by Andrés Segovia in April 1982. On the podium are Director de Montebello, a student of guitar, Maestro Segovia, and his wife, Emilita Segovia.

"Who would have thought so many people still cared about such things?" Since that time the Museum has brought to the stage such early-music luminaries as Franz Brueggen, Tafelmusik, the Waverly Consort, Musica Antiqua Köln, the English Concert, Ton Koopman, and, in their New York debut appearance, Les Arts Florissants. In 2005 the Museum presented the viola da gamba master Jordi Savall, already revered in early-music circles, in a minifestival that drew sold-out crowds and galvanized the city with a new awareness of Savall. The culminating event was described by Alex Ross in the *New Yorker* as "an overwhelming experience, the concert of the year," while the *New York Times* asserted, "the Metropolitan Museum deserves gratitude."

The director was highly supportive when, to celebrate the Metropolitan Museum Concerts' fiftieth-anniversary season in 2003, I proposed that we create a resident chamber ensemble: Metropolitan Museum Artists in Concert, or "MMArtists." Characterized at its inception by Anthony Tommasini of the *New York Times* as "all that chamber music enthusiasts could hope for" and more recently by Steve Smith in the *Times* as "the most consistently satisfying chamber-music series in New York," the group appears annually and has continued to win praise for its elegant performances, its range of programming, and the intimate concert format that intersperses performance with brief commentary on the music.

But if there is one feature of the Museum's concerts that has benefited most from the director's love of music—and through which I have been most enriched by our collaboration—it is the presentation of pianists and piano recitals. Our conversation about Mozart in 1977 was just the beginning of an ongoing stream of valuable input from Philippe, culled from his vast

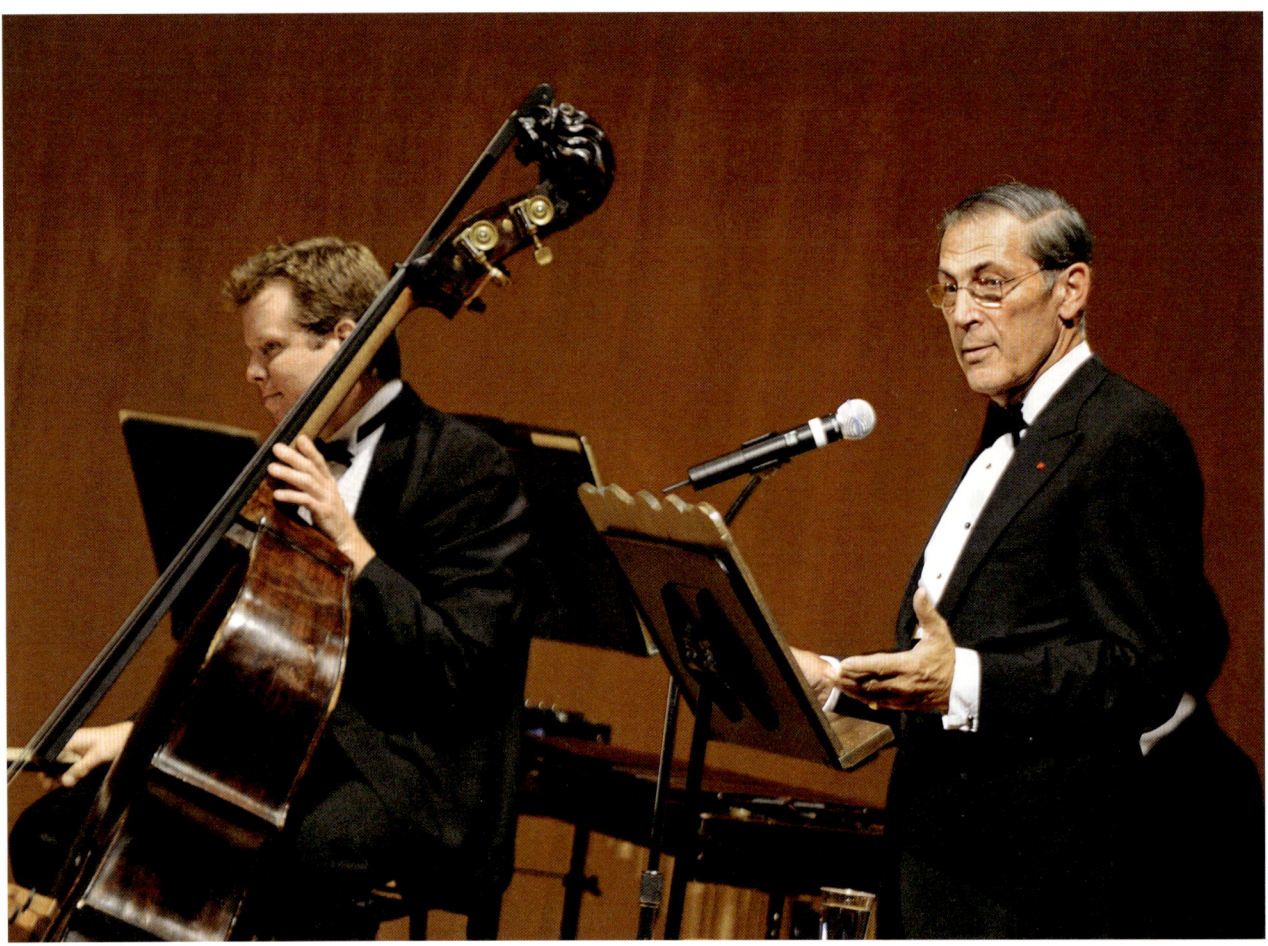

97. The director delivering lines by Ogden Nash that accompany *Carnival of the Animals*

knowledge of the musical repertoire. Surely every work in the piano repertoire can be found on his iPod—in multiple interpretations. He has from time to time brought a pianist to my attention, often with a phone call that might begin, "Hilde, have you heard . . . ?" Fazil Say was one such young artist. Say made his debut during our 2000–1 season, has performed here on three subsequent occasions, and, as the *Washington Post* wrote, "is well on his way to becoming one of the major pianists of the early 21st century." The director was impressed as well by the pianist Mikhail Pletnev, who is also a composer and the founder of the Russian National Orchestra. His appearance with us was his only New York recital in the 2002–3 season—a coup for the series, and a very special event for our audience.

In 2004 Philippe told me about a conversation he had had with his old friend Alexis Gregory about a series showcasing winners of the world's major piano competitions. The resulting event, "A Festival of International Piano Competition Winners," took place in May 2005 and featured six first-prize awardees performing over a four-day period, many of them in their United States debuts and all of them in their only New York recital appearances. That festival heralded what is today one of the crown jewels of Metropolitan Museum Concerts: the PianoForte series, which made its debut in the 2005–6 season and has created a niche for itself in the New York concert world by presenting a broad selection of keyboard artists each season, both major stars of long standing and newer musicians who are drawing interest in musical circles. This combination of variety and discernment has drawn the notice of critics. "Superbly curated," observed Alex Ross in the *New Yorker*. "When it comes to picking great pianists . . . no presenter has a better record than the Metropolitan Museum's series of Concerts & Lectures" was Charles Michener's assessment in the *New York Observer*.

In 2006 PianoForte hosted back-to-back concerts: on October 25 by the acclaimed pianist András Schiff, who had made his

New York recital debut at the Museum in 1982 and has since returned for more than twenty recitals and chamber appearances; and the next day by the piano phenomenon Ivo Pogorelich, in his Metropolitan debut and first New York appearance in a decade. Peter G. Davis articulated the value of this programming in MusicalAmerica.com: "It's difficult to think of two musicians with less in common than András Schiff and Ivo Pogorelich. Both recently gave recitals on consecutive evenings . . . at New York's Metropolitan Museum of Art, an arrangement that let piano buffs fully savor the differences between the two pianists' musical priorities and keyboard personalities."

These extraordinary piano performances have made us realize something else about music at the Museum: the acoustics of our concert hall have matured, rather like a great violin, providing a deep resonance ideal for the timbre of the piano and resulting in a velvety texture in the lower register, a singing middle register, and sparkling high notes. This is one more incitement drawing to the Metropolitan the great pianists of the world.

During Philippe's thirty-one years as director of the Metropolitan Museum, more than seven thousand concert and lecture events have been presented here—a direct reflection of his commitment to artistic excellence. Toward the end of this period he agreed to participate in a triptych of programs that paid tribute to his love for the visual arts, the spoken word, and music. He discussed art with Robert Hughes and read poetry of the Renaissance with Isabella Rossellini. And, as narrator with the Orpheus Chamber Orchestra, he read Ogden Nash's verses accompanying Saint-Saëns's *Carnival of the Animals* (figs. 95, 97) on the opening night of the fifty-fifth season of music at the Metropolitan Museum—a tradition for whose singularity and quality he has been the inspiration.

Hilde Limondjian

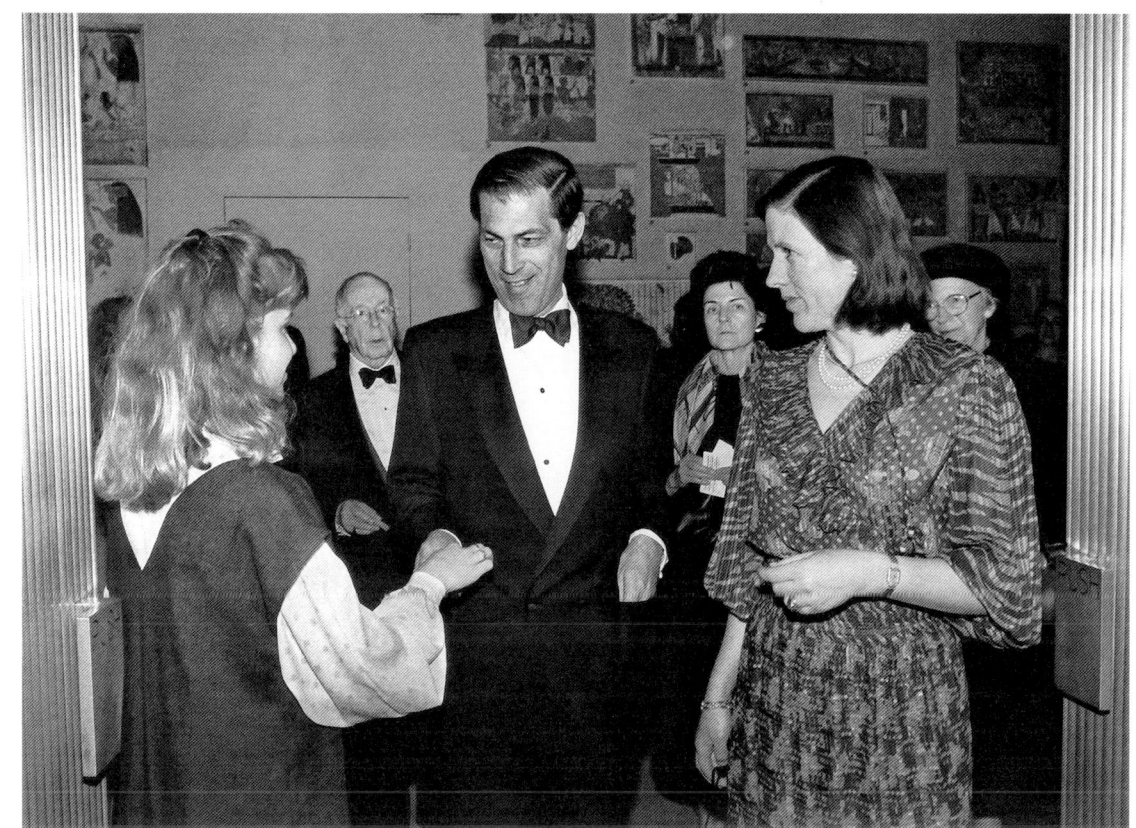

98. Philippe and Edith de Montebello arrive for a benefit concert featuring pianist Murray Perahia and the Orchestra of St. Luke's, April 1987

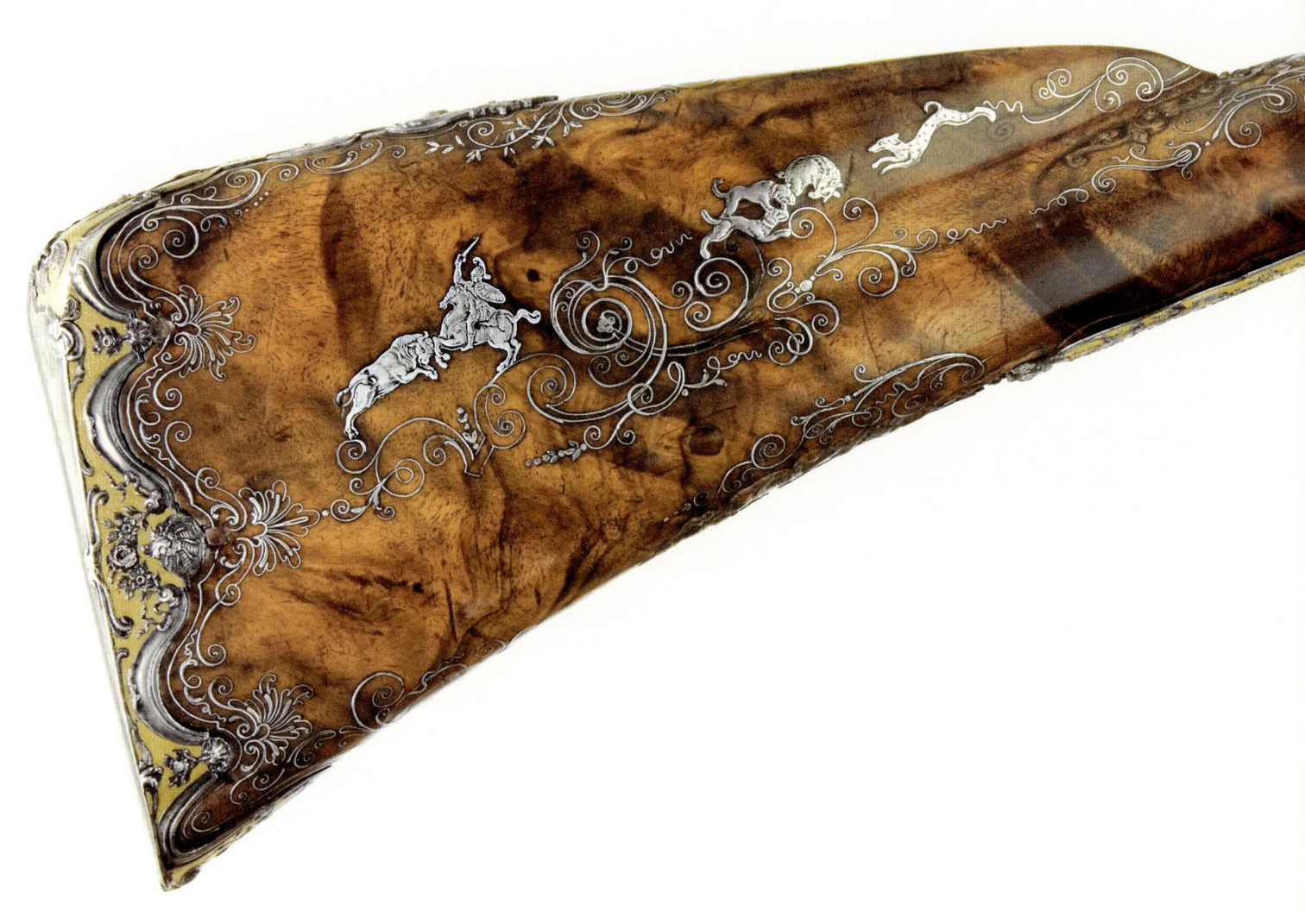

ARMS AND ARMOR

SNUFFBOXES THAT SHOOT: TWO ROCOCO FIREARMS

Philippe de Montebello's thirty-one-year tenure as director coincided with a remarkable renaissance in the Metropolitan Museum's Department of Arms and Armor. These were years of important acquisitions; scholarly publications; original, eye-opening exhibitions; the refurbishment and reinstallation of the Arms and Armor Galleries in the Pierpont Morgan Wing; and the creation of a special area for rotating departmental exhibitions, the Arthur Ochs Sulzberger Gallery. Progress was also made "belowstairs" with a much-needed augmenting of the curatorial and conservation staff and the creation of two new storerooms. All of this was accomplished with the director's support and encouragement at every step.

Philippe emphasized the primacy of collecting and encouraged curators to seek out the very best works. Taking this mandate to heart, the department acquired a wide range of objects from every part of the globe, reflecting the already encyclopedic scope of the collection. Among the most important additions are a diminutive armor made in Paris in 1712 for the five-year-old Luis, Prince of Asturias and heir to the Spanish throne (1989.3); Samuel Colt's gold-inlaid Dragoon revolver presented to the sultan of Turkey in 1854 (1995.336); and an exquisite Ottoman short sword (*yatagan*) made about 1530 in the court workshops of Süleyman the Magnificent (1993.14). These masterpieces are now highlights of the Arms and Armor Galleries. Entirely new areas of collecting, particularly Tibetan arms and armor, were developed, and the resulting acquisitions not only expanded our Asian holdings but also yielded a wealth of new research on this hitherto overlooked subject. Not since the 1920s and 1930s, a heyday for American collecting of arms and armor and the period when the department's core holdings were established, had so many important additions been made to our collection.

A curator invariably takes special satisfaction in acquiring objects in areas overlooked by his predecessors. Because earlier generations of collectors and curators favored armor and weapons of the late Middle Ages and Renaissance, the firearms of later periods had largely been ignored. While eighteenth-century decorative arts occupy a prominent place in the Museum, we had not even one exhibition-worthy long gun from that era. Thus I am particularly proud to have been able to add to our already substantial holdings of European firearms a handful of outstanding examples dating from the eighteenth century, most notably two exquisite flintlock fowling pieces, one French and the other Spanish, built for the aristocratic huntsman. Both were made in the Rococo style that became fashionable in Paris in the 1730s.

First-rate eighteenth-century firearms in good condition are extremely rare at any time. Still, when two Rococo guns became available within a few months of one another in 1987, the director and the Acquisitions Committee had to be persuaded of the necessity of acquiring both. Fortunately, the original designs, superb craftsmanship, and excellent condition of the pieces made a convincing visual argument. Each is a collaborative creation of several masters, like the finest French furniture of the period, and both display a comparable elegance of line and harmony between function and ornamentation. The locks and gunstock mounts are of bright steel chiseled in relief against a gilt ground; the complex, classically themed figural compositions are set amid swirling asymmetrical curves, rocks, shells, and flowing water. Close examination yields pleasant surprises and occasional humor. The obvious relationship between the French gun (fig. 99) and other decorative arts of the period inspired one member of the Acquisitions Committee to call it "a snuffbox that shoots."

Made in 1735 in Saint-Étienne, a town in southeastern France known primarily for the manufacture of military arms, this gun surpasses even the finest Parisian works. Likely a special order for a high-ranking aristocrat, it bears an unprecedented number of makers' names, attesting no doubt to pride of workmanship as well as the importance and prestige of the commission. There are the usual barrel- and lockmaker's marks, but, quite exceptionally,

Opposite: 99. Butt of a flintlock gun. Saint-Étienne, France, 1735. Chiseled and gilt steel, wood (walnut), silver, L. overall 57½ in. (146.1 cm). Harris Brisbane Dick and Rogers Funds, 1987 (1987.274)

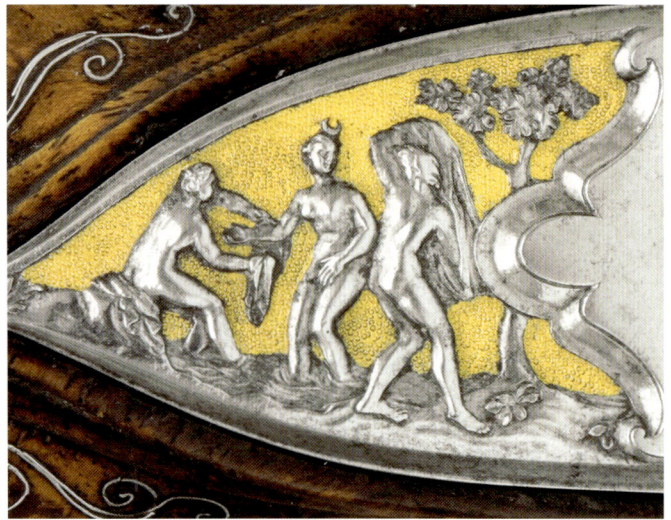

100. Diana discovered at her bath by Actaeon. Chiseled steel and gilt decoration on the lock plate of the French gun (1987.274)

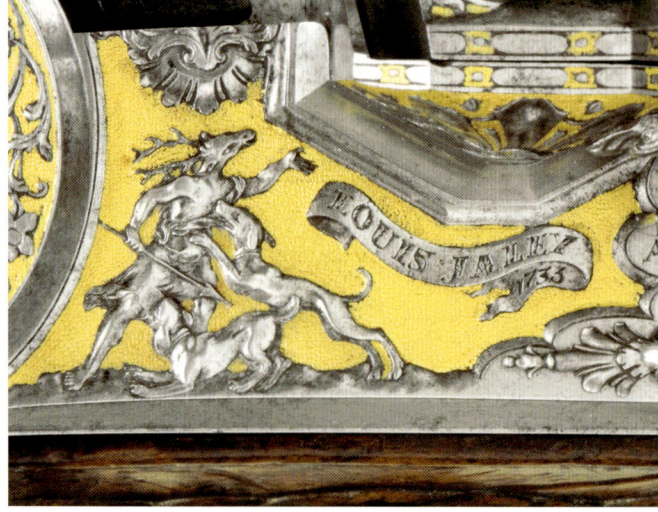

101. Actaeon transformed into a stag and set upon by his dogs. Chiseled steel and gilt decoration on the lock plate of the French gun

the iron chiseler Louis Jaley also signed two of the gun's parts (see fig. 101), and another decorator, Joseph Blachon, added his name in silver wire inlaid into the stock beneath the side plate. The construction is unexpectedly complex and sophisticated, for the gun appears to have been assembled without screws. To dismantle it one must release the barrel from the stock by sliding each ramrod pipe forward, a highly idiosyncratic method of attachment that takes the place of the usual transverse pins. Removal of the barrel reveals a hinged bolt that releases the side plate, and from that point each mount can be taken off sequentially as hidden pins become visible. The lock also has an unusual safety device: a pivoting L-shaped steel, or frizzen, that prevents accidental discharge. Often used in northern Europe, particularly Russia and Sweden, the feature is uncommon on French guns.

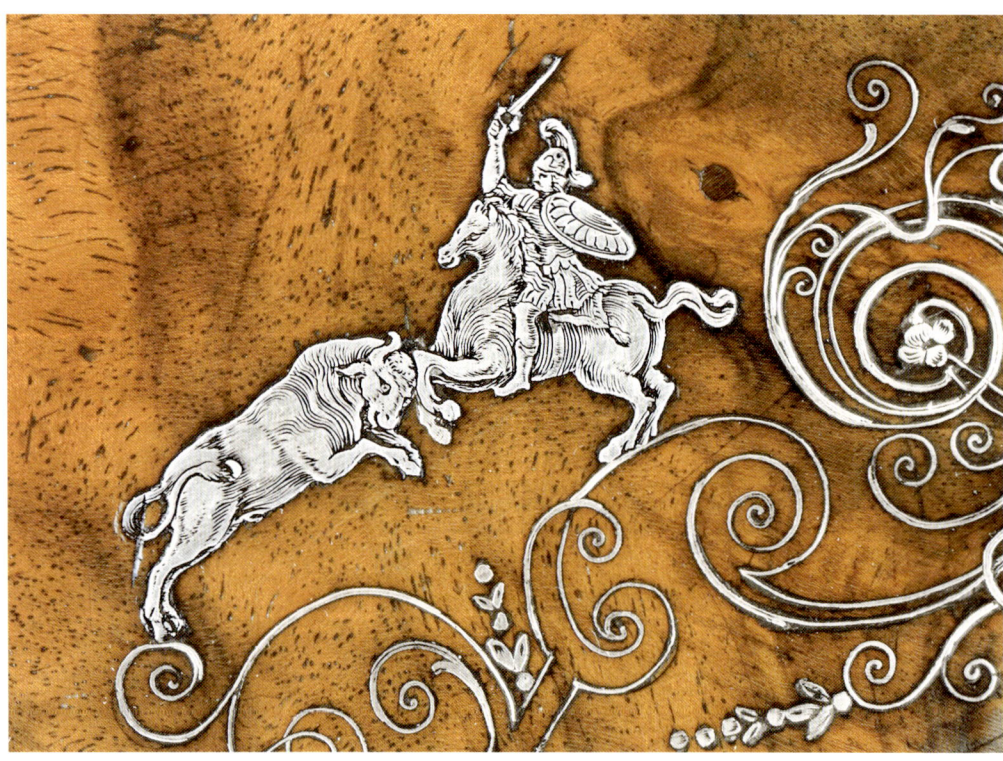

102. Horseman battling a bull. Detail of silver inlay decoration on the butt of the French gun

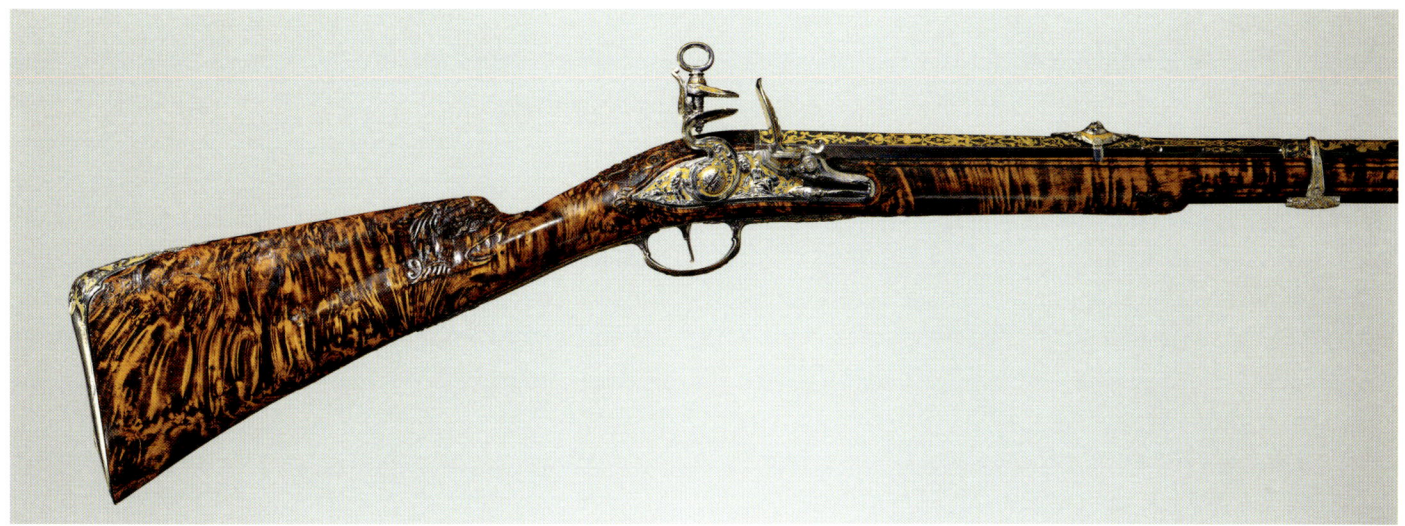

103. Flintlock gun (partial view). Madrid, Spain, made by Gabriel de Algora, 1744. Chiseled, blued, and gilt steel, wood (figured maple), L. overall 53¾ in. (136.5 cm). Purchase, Gifts of George D. Pratt, Charles M. Schott Jr., and Bashford Dean, and Bashford Dean Memorial Collection, Funds from various donors, by exchange, 1987 (1987.397)

The exquisitely chiseled steel mounts are inhabited by mythological figures drawn from Ovid's *Metamorphoses*. On the lock plate, Diana is discovered naked at her bath (fig. 100) by the hunter Actaeon, who as punishment is thereupon transformed into a stag and set upon by his own dogs (fig. 101), a cautionary tale for any hunter. The flintlock mechanism presents chiseled figures of Jupiter and Semele, a maiden seduced by the god, whose lovemaking proved so intense that the poor girl was incinerated. When the flintlock's hammer (on which Jupiter is depicted), with a spark-producing flint in its jaws, snaps forward against the upright steel (where Semele is shown tumbling from the clouds), the gun fires and simultaneously reenacts the incendiary coupling. Minerva adorns the breech of the barrel, Venus and Cupid are on the trigger guard, and a seated Mars, with legs nonchalantly

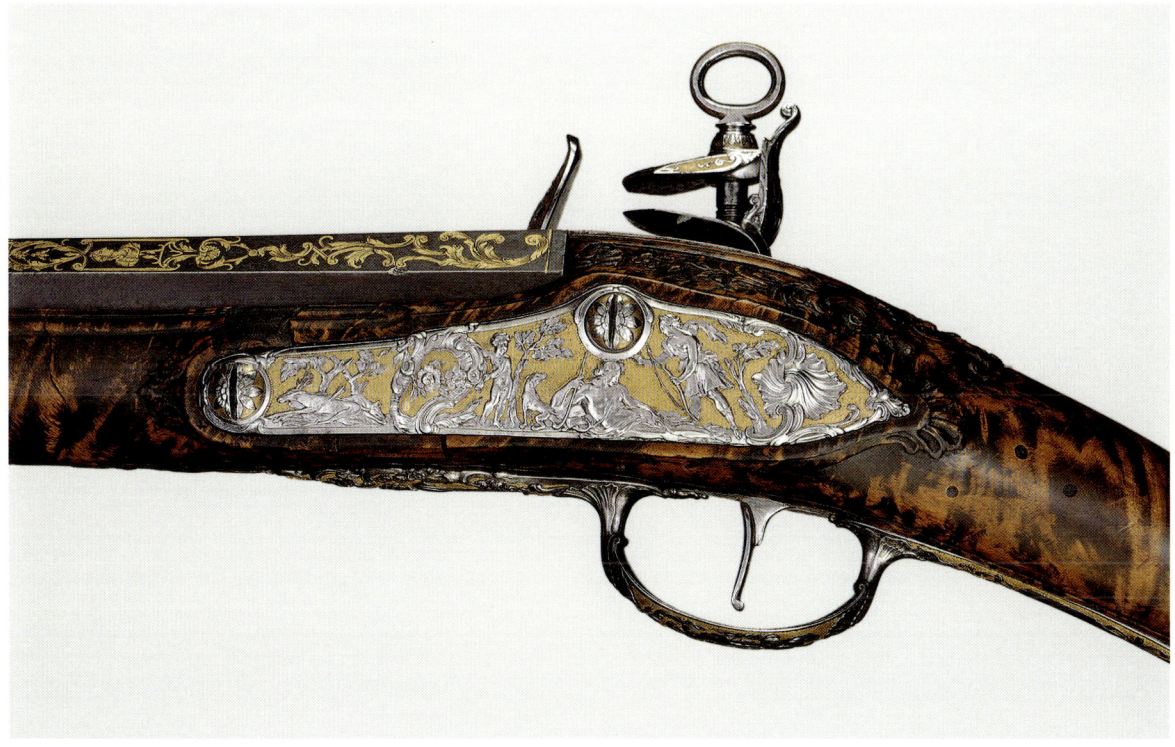

104. Diana and the sleeping Endymion. Chiseled steel and gilt decoration on the side plate of the Spanish gun

crossed and head haloed by a shell, appears on the side plate. On the butt of the gun, Hercules stands on a dripping shell that is itself precariously perched on an asymmetrical rocky outcropping; these fanciful elements drawn from nature were leitmotifs of the Rococo style then just emerging. Its 1735 date makes this flintlock one of the earliest and most distinguished examples of Rococo gunmaking in Europe.

The silver decoration inlaid into the walnut stock seems to include allusions to contemporary political events. On one side of the butt a bull charges a horseman in classical armor (perhaps emblematic of the duchy of Lithuania) (fig. 102), and on the other side a lion and a dog attack a two-headed eagle (signifying either Russia or the Holy Roman Empire)—possibly references to political concerns in France over the Polish throne. The gold escutcheon, cast with figures that include Fame blowing her trumpet and a grimacing devil-like figure in free fall, may also have political overtones. The center of the escutcheon was intended to be engraved with the owner's arms or monogram but was unfortunately left blank, leaving us to guess at the circumstances of the gun's commission.

The Spanish gun (fig. 103), dated 1744, is as fine as any French example. Indeed, since the accession of Philip V in 1700, establishing a Bourbon monarch on the Spanish throne, French taste had dominated the royal court in Madrid. The Museum's gun was made by Gabriel de Algora, the leading Madrid gunsmith, whose mastery was recognized with his appointment in 1749 as royal gunmaker. Spanish gun barrels were highly prized throughout Europe, and Algora's superb example retains its original blued and gilt surface and its crisply engraved ornament, which includes figures of Mars and Juno. The stock, of figured maple with an emphatic marbled pattern, was left undecorated. The lock and mounts are the work of a specialist iron chiseler, and their brightly polished low-relief ornament against a stippled gold ground reflects Parisian inspiration. Mythological figures including Minerva, Adonis, Diana and Endymion (fig. 104), and Eros and Anteros are framed by Rococo foliage and shell motifs. The exquisite chiseling of the mounts and their original designs—apparently composed without recourse to the exported French gunmakers' pattern books on which Madrid masters usually relied—establish this fowling piece as one of the finest of the period. Fleurs-de-lis stamped on the underside of the stock, presumably an ownership or arsenal marking, suggest that it was a royal weapon.

Even a few important acquisitions, such as guns of the caliber of these two, can have a transformative effect. The outstanding additions made to the Museum's holdings in arms and armor during the last thirty years reflect a supportive Acquisitions Committee, generous individual donors, and, perhaps most of all, Philippe's commitment to excellence.

Stuart W. Pyhrr

THE ART OF WAR ON THE ROOF OF THE WORLD

The exhibition "Warriors of the Himalayas: Rediscovering the Arms and Armor of Tibet," held at The Metropolitan Museum of Art in 2006, included approximately 135 items drawn mostly from the permanent collection of the Museum and augmented by major loans from several institutions in Great Britain and the United States (fig. 105). It is doubtful whether a topic so specialized, not to say obscure, could have become the subject of an international loan show and a substantial exhibition catalogue—with all the expense, time, and labor such projects demand—at any place other than the Metropolitan.

"Warriors of the Himalayas" was the culmination of more than ten years of what began as very speculative and exploratory research and a few tentative acquisitions (fig. 106). This grew in an ongoing process unique to a great museum like the Metropolitan, in which research into the permanent collection leads to new acquisitions, and the acquisitions in turn inspire further original research benefiting both the permanent collection and scholarship in the field. In the best of circumstances, as in this instance, the combination of research and acquisitions develops to the point at which an in-depth exhibition becomes possible.

This was only the second major international loan exhibition in the hundred-year history of the Department of Arms and Armor, the first having been the widely acclaimed "Heroic Armor of the Italian Renaissance: Filippo Negroli and His Contemporaries"

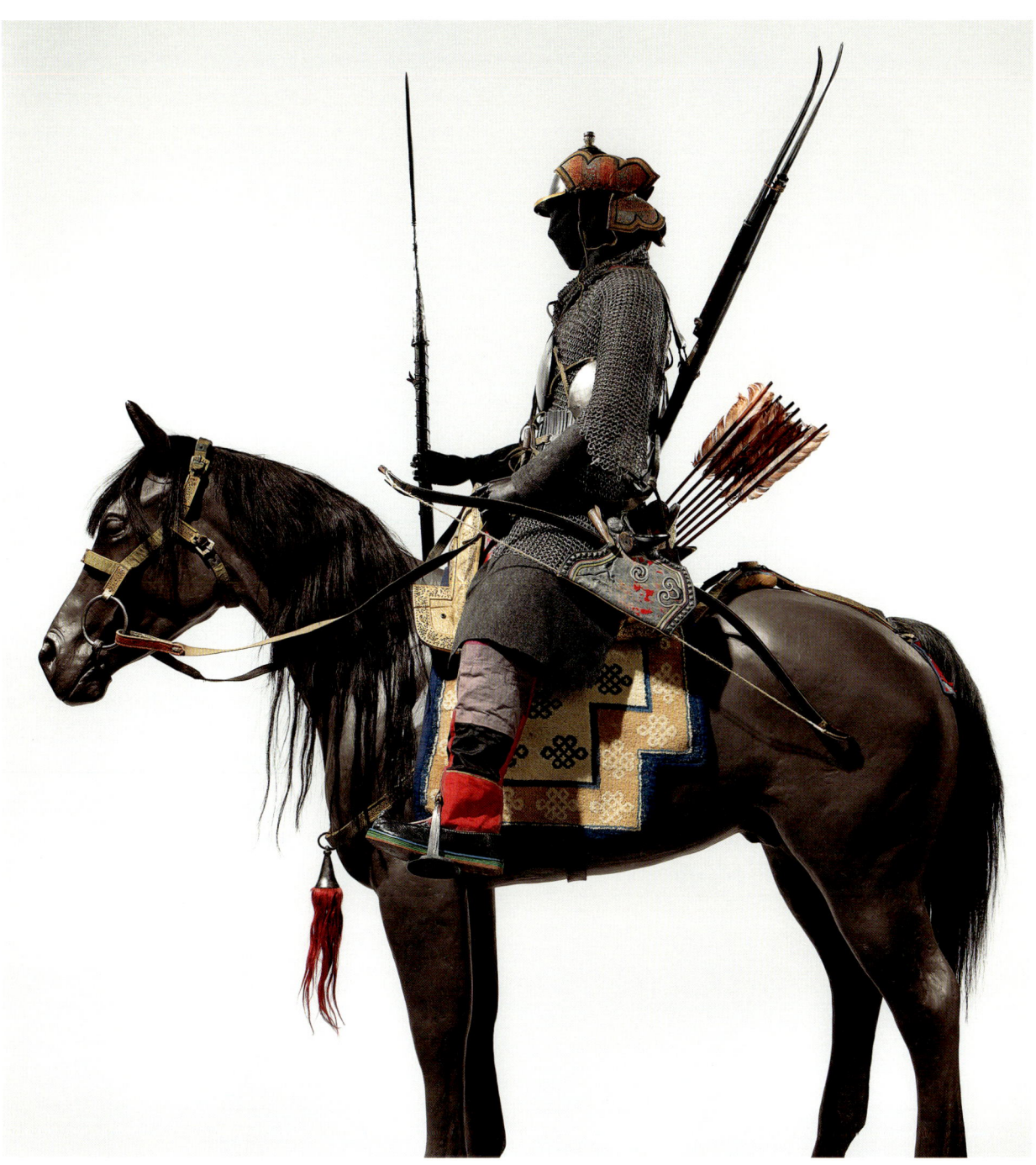

105. Arms and equipment of an armored cavalryman. Tibetan and possibly Bhutanese and Nepalese, 17th–19th century. Iron, gold, silver, copper alloy, wood, leather, and textile. Bequest of George C. Stone, 1935 (36.25.25, .28, .351, .476, .583a–c, h–k, .842a–c, .2174, .2461, .2505, .2557); Bequest of Joseph V. McMullan, 1973 (1974.160.10 [saddle rug]); Gift of Mrs. Faïe J. Joyce, 1970 (1970.164.74a, b [boots])

(1998) organized by Stuart W. Pyhrr, Arthur Ochs Sulzberger Curator in Charge. The idea from which the Tibetan project grew, however, came about more or less by chance during preparations for a small in-house exhibition in the mid-1990s, "The Gods of War: Sacred Imagery and the Decoration of Arms and Armor" (1996). That show was an exploration of religious iconography as manifested on armor and weapons from areas dominated by the world's most widespread religions: Hinduism, Buddhism, Catholicism, and Islam. Because of the encyclopedic nature of the department's collections, such a survey could be drawn

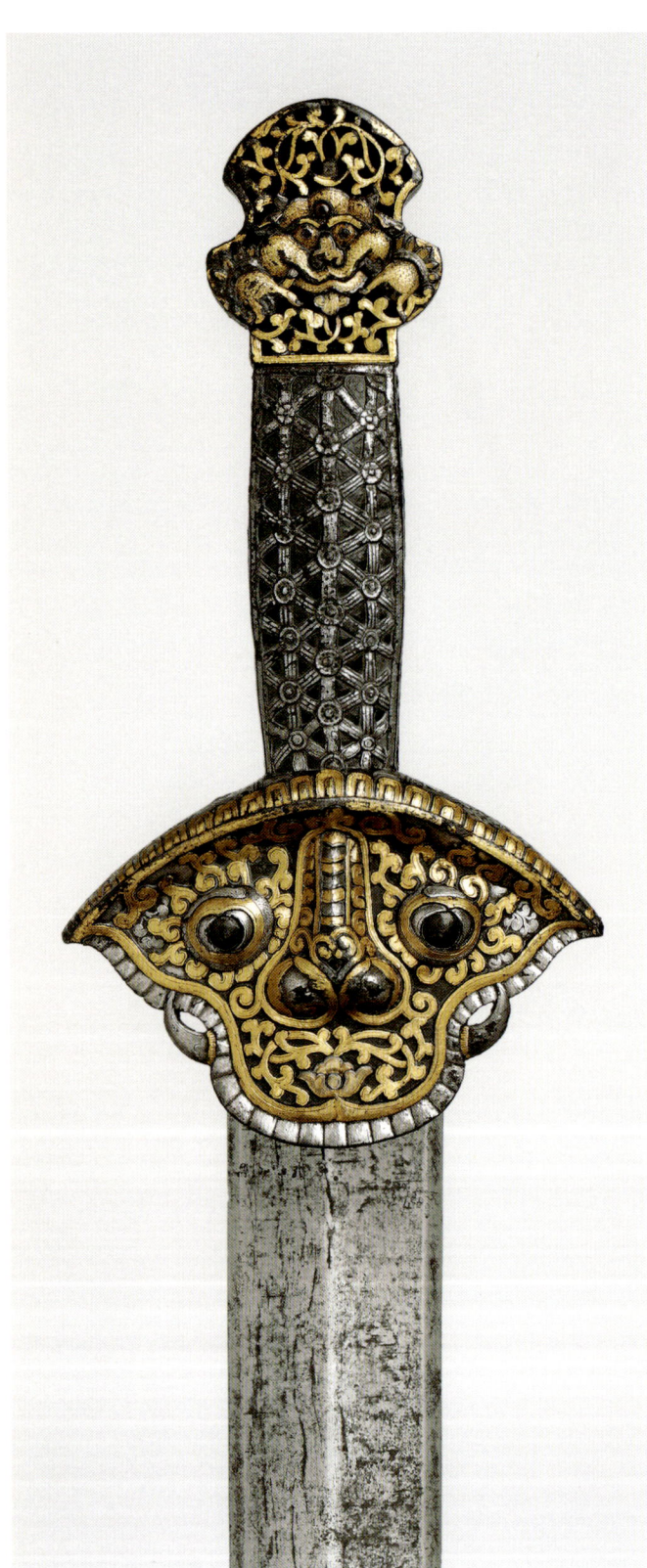

106. Hilt of a sword. Tibet or China, 14th–16th century. Iron, steel, gold, and silver, sword L. overall 34⅞ in. (88.6 cm). Purchase, Rogers Fund and Fletcher Fund, by exchange, 1995 (1995.136)

entirely from objects in storage; the result was an evocative and tightly packed display of sixty-five items and a short catalogue. This was the first installation in the department's newly created small gallery for rotating installations, which was designated the Arthur Ochs Sulzberger Gallery in 2002.

In "The Gods of War" were three objects—a dagger, a saddle, and a sword—catalogued as Tibetan or Sino-Tibetan. When doing research for the catalogue entries I was surprised by the apparent lack of literature relating to these pieces. Arms and armor as a field of study in the modern sense began in the late eighteenth century. In the time since then almost every culture, period, or style pertinent to arms and armor has been the subject of at least one article if not a monograph or book, so I naturally assumed that I had not yet found the relevant publications. Further digging, however, revealed that beyond scattered references and a few short surveys, nothing of depth had been written on the subject of Tibetan arms and armor. Intrigued by the objects I had seen in our own collection and by the allure of a fairly unexplored area of study, I began to look into the subject more consistently, as time and other duties allowed, starting with the core group of about fifty Tibetan and Himalayan pieces that had come to our department in 1935 as part of the bequest of George Cameron Stone (1859–1935). Between 1995 and 2009, with full support from the department and the encouragement of the director, we were able to more than triple our holdings of Tibetan and related arms and armor (fig. 107) and to vastly increase the collection's variety, rarity, and quality—to such an extent that it now constitutes one of the most comprehensive and important groups of such objects anywhere in the world.

In hopes of finding specialized Tibetan terms concerning arms and armor and in order to better understand the cultural context of the objects, I attempted to acquire a rough working knowledge of literary Tibetan. This was done first through private study after hours, starting in 1998. The generous support of the Museum then made it possible for me to take a summer Tibetan language immersion course at the University of Virginia in 2001 and to enroll in, and also intermittently audit, Tibetan classes at Columbia University between 2001 and 2006. The access this provided, even in a limited capacity, to historical Tibetan literary sources added a depth and dimension to my research, and subsequently to the exhibition and catalogue, that otherwise would have been impossible. In addition, through a series of Museum-funded travel grants I was able to carry out the very necessary task of visiting museums, collectors, and dealers in the United States, Great Britain, and Europe in search of comparable objects, both for study and, when appropriate, for possible acquisition. The high point of this phase of the research was a 2003 trip to the Buddhist monasteries, museums, and historic sites in Ladakh, a culturally Tibetan enclave in northwestern India.

The basic goal of "Warriors of the Himalayas" was to bring to the general public, to those interested in Tibetan history and culture, and to students of arms and armor an awareness of the amazingly wide range of armor, weapons, and associated materials, most of them overlooked or virtually unknown, that were used in Tibet as early as the seventh century and until the mid-twentieth century. The objects surveyed were considered not simply as types but also with attention to their quality, materials, decorative techniques, iconography, and historical significance. The hope was to establish such works as an important aspect of Tibetan material culture and a significant area of arms and armor studies—as well as to exhibit and publish an important, largely unrecognized body of objects, many of them works of inherent beauty and fine craftsmanship (fig. 108).

I believed that the goals of the exhibition could be accomplished most clearly by presenting these rare and important objects on their own intrinsic merits, an approach rooted in the study and connoisseurship of the works themselves. Such object-based scholarship has been the heart and soul of the Metropolitan Museum since its founding and also of the study of arms and armor since its inception as a field of scholarly investigation. In this way we can promote an accurate and compelling understanding of the works of art in our care and prevent them from being used in publications and exhibitions as mere didactic illustrations of a particular theme, educational fad, or political agenda.

The Department of Arms and Armor represents a long and unbroken tradition of scholarly research, publication, acquisition, exhibition, and permanent display, now carried out with more continuity and on a more solid footing than by any comparable collection in the world. Our success at what we do and how we do it rests on the support of superb staff, an enlightened administration, generous trustees, and a devoted public, for which we are very grateful. The steadfast nurturing of this type of activity, which today exists in very few institutions, has nowhere been stronger than at The Metropolitan Museum of Art during the tenure of Philippe de Montebello.   *Donald J. La Rocca*

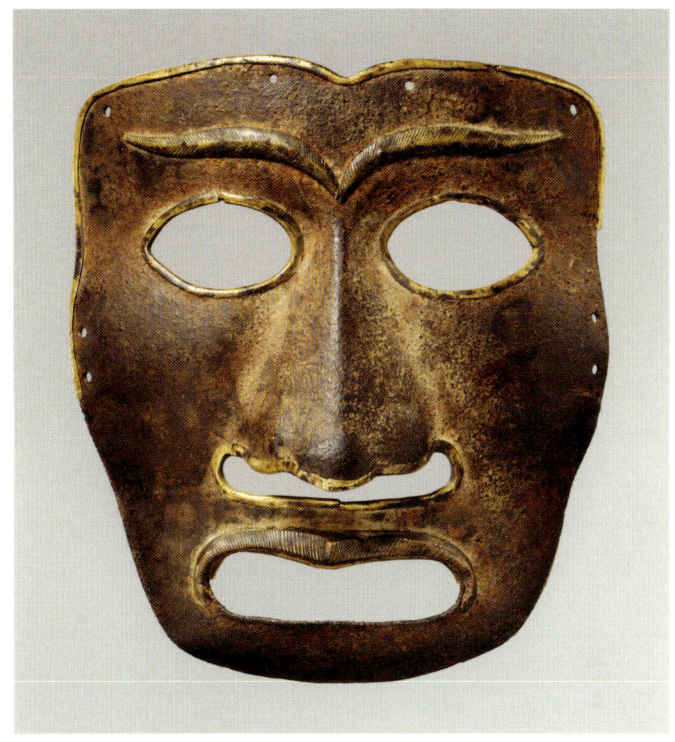

107. War mask. Mongolia or Tibet, 12th–14th century. Iron and copper alloy, 6½ × 5¾ in. (16.5 × 14.6 cm). Purchase, Arthur Ochs Sulzberger Gift, 2007 (2007.10)

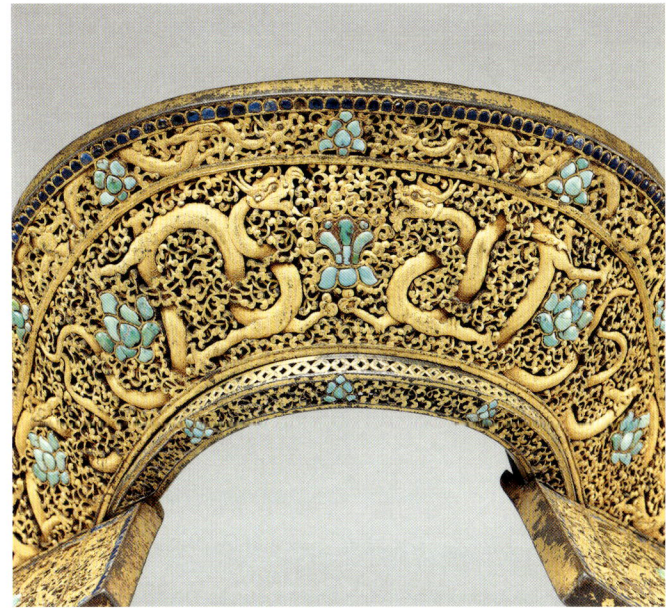

108. Detail of a ceremonial saddle. Tibet or China, ca. 1400. Iron, gold, lapis lazuli, and turquoise, H. overall 9⅞ in. (25 cm). Purchase, Gift of William H. Riggs, by exchange, and Kenneth and Vivian Lam Gift, 1999 (1999.118)

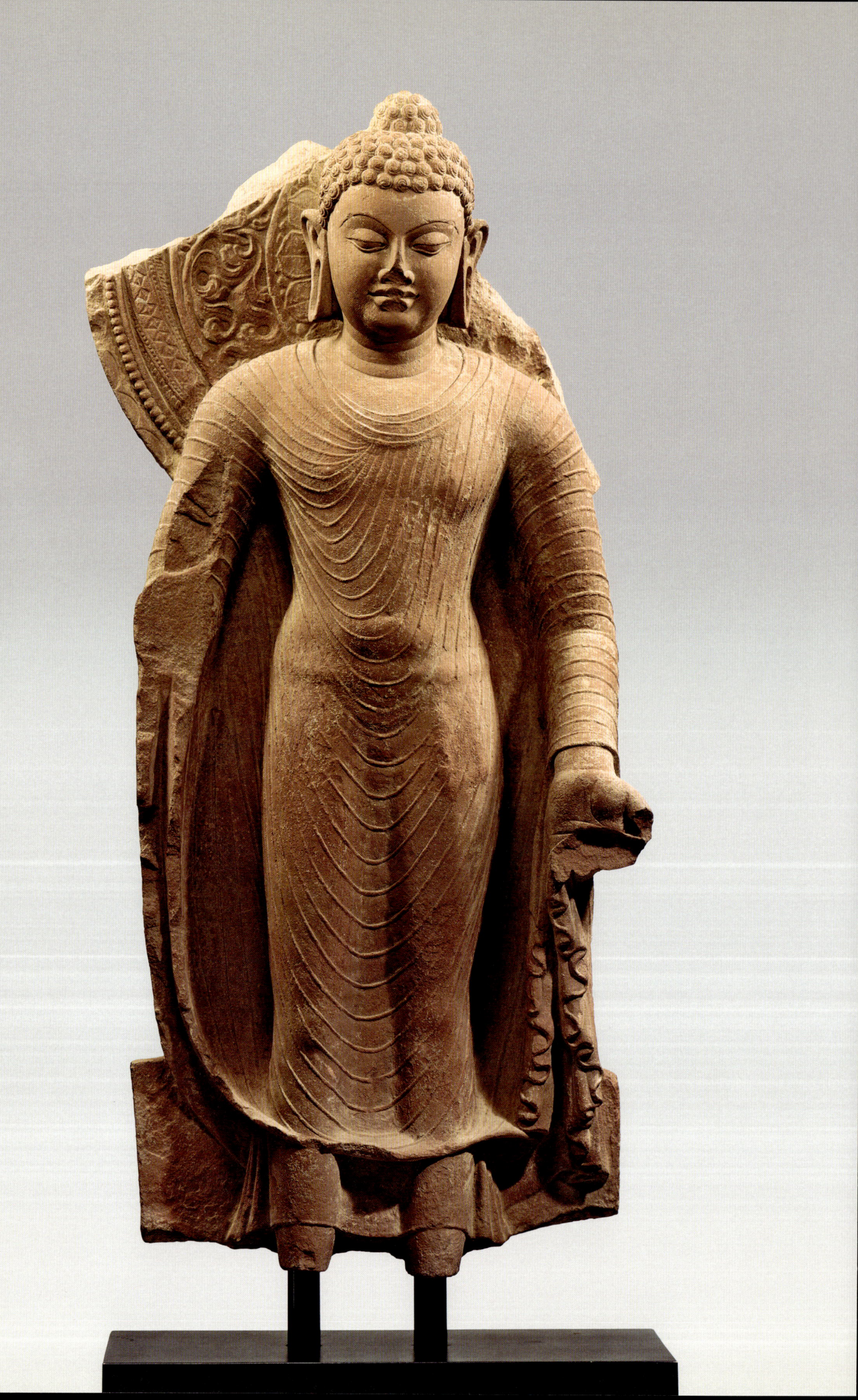

ASIAN ART

THE FIRST DECADE, 1977–87

Shortly after Philippe de Montebello assumed the acting directorship of the Metropolitan Museum in July 1977 he presided over the acquisition of perhaps the greatest horse painting in Chinese art, *Night-Shining White*, by the eighth-century master Han Gan (fig. 111). For decades the painting had been in the collection of Sir Percival David, a British connoisseur who had acquired it from descendants of the Qing royal family.

Its acquisition was approved by Philippe and supported by Douglas Dillon, chairman of the Board of Trustees, and The Dillon Fund. During the next three decades Philippe worked closely with department chairs Wen Fong, who retired in 2000, and James Watt, overseeing a complete transformation in the area of Asian art at the Metropolitan. What emerged was, in the director's words, "a museum within a museum" that has fifty galleries (some 64,500 square feet of display space) and one of the world's most comprehensive collections of the arts of Asia.

In the late 1970s, however, this remarkable growth of the Department of Far Eastern Art (as it was called from 1915 to 1986) was mostly in the future. The Museum had made some important acquisitions—notably The Harry G. C. Packard Collection of Asian Art, in 1975, and twenty-five masterworks of Song and Yuan dynasty painting (tenth to fourteenth century) from the C. C. Wang Family Collection, in 1973—and new curators had been appointed. But there were still many lacunae in both the departmental staff and the collections, while permanent exhibition space was limited to cases around the Great Hall balcony, for the display of Chinese ceramics, and a single gallery of early Chinese Buddhist sculpture. The acquisition of the Han Gan painting signaled the new director's willingness to move decisively and elevate our Asian holdings to a level commensurate with that of other departments in the Museum.

By early 1979 Philippe was actively assisting with acquisitions of Asian art as well as overseeing exhibition organization and plans for permanent galleries. In January he approved two major additions to the collection: a monumental 45-foot Chinese handscroll, one of twelve that make up the masterwork *The Kangxi Emperor's Southern Inspection Tour* by Wang Hui (1632–1717), purchased with the help of The Dillon Fund (1979.5); and a sublime Mathuran standing Buddha carved from red sandstone in the fifth century, the gift of Enid Haupt (fig. 109). In February, Philippe, Wen Fong, and I traveled to China to finalize selections to be lent by the Chinese government for a major exhibition, "The Great Bronze Age of China." In touring Chinese museums the director demonstrated his connoisseur's eye and astonished his hosts by consistently identifying the bronzes that were modern replicas. This aesthetic acumen also played a crucial role in his successful negotiation for the inclusion in the exhibition of certain extremely important objects. The 105 masterworks that thus came to the United States, among them many of the most significant archaeological finds of the preceding thirty years, constituted a chronicle of the brilliant artistic achievements of China's Bronze Age, from its beginnings sometime after 2000 B.C. to its final flowering in the second century B.C., early in the Han dynasty. Included were ritual bronze vessels, jades, and, displayed for the first time in the West, eight lifesize terracotta figures from the funerary complex of the First Emperor of Qin (221–210 B.C.). The exhibition subsequently traveled to Chicago, Fort Worth, San Francisco, and Boston and attracted over 1.3 million visitors.

On the same trip we visited Suzhou, where craftsmen charged with maintaining the city's many traditional gardens had been engaged by the Museum to create the planned Astor Court. After viewing a full-scale prototype that had been built in Suzhou and recommending several changes in material (such as granite instead of marble for the moon-viewing terrace), Philippe approved the project. And early in 1980, twenty-six Chinese craftsmen and engineers—and a chef—arrived in New York, where, for the next five months, handcrafted components were assembled to become a courtyard and reception hall modeled on seventeenth-century Ming-dynasty prototypes. The first step in

Opposite: 109. Standing Buddha. India, Gupta period, 5th century. Mottled red sandstone, H. 33 11/16 in. (85.5 cm). Purchase, Enid A. Haupt Gift, 1979 (1979.6)

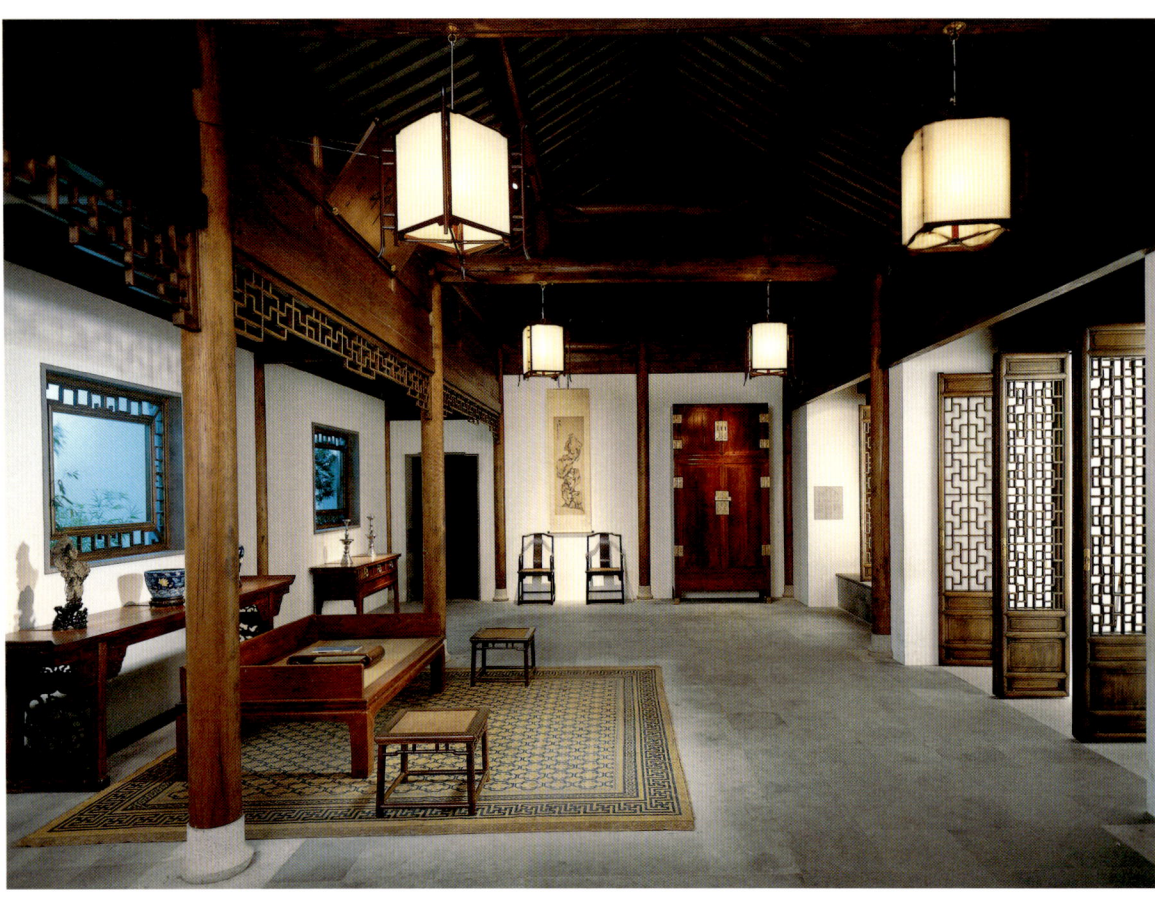

110. The Ming Room, adjoining The Astor Court

the creation of an entire wing for Asian art, The Astor Court was the inspiration of trustee Brooke Russell Astor, who had lived in Beijing between the ages of seven and twelve. Both the garden court and the adjoining Ming Room (fig. 110) were built with the generous support of The Vincent Astor Foundation as the setting for a suite of Ming-dynasty furniture that the Museum had acquired in 1976, also with the foundation's help. Mrs. Astor, ever the perfect hostess, helped transform a portion of the newly finished departmental offices into a temporary dining room for the workers, complete with TV and Ping-Pong table. Mrs. Astor, Philippe, and Zhang Biaorong, head of the Chinese delegation, hosted a number of dinner parties for visiting dignitaries, including Mayor Ed Koch and Henry Kissinger. On one such occasion Philippe demonstrated the breadth of his skills by vanquishing all his Chinese challengers in Ping-Pong.

The garden was the first permanent cultural exchange between the United States and the People's Republic of China. It has long been one of the most beloved spaces in the Museum—an idyllic place of repose and contemplation for visitors that sets the mood for the appreciation of the artworks in the surrounding galleries. It opened in June 1981 together with the flanking Douglas Dillon Galleries, which are devoted primarily to the exhibition of the Museum's Chinese paintings; the inaugural display featured many of the gifts and purchases made by Mr. Dillon and The Dillon Fund in the preceding decade. The scale of the galleries is daunting—they are the largest display space for such paintings outside of Asia—and at the time there were not enough paintings in the collection suitable for exhibition to fill a second rotation (light-sensitive works on paper and silk must be rotated after a short while). Fortunately, the Museum's evident commitment to Asian painting was rewarded that same year with the promised gift of the renowned collection of John M. Crawford Jr., which was unrivaled among private collections in this country for its wealth of extraordinary early paintings and calligraphies. The 215 works from the Crawford collection, added to the paintings acquired by Mr. Dillon (eventually numbering 133), immediately elevated the Museum's holdings in this area to the top tier of collections worldwide.

In tandem with the planning and opening of The Astor Court and Dillon Galleries, exhibitions of other aspects of Asian art were finding a place on the Museum's busy calendar. In December 1980 The Costume Institute presented "The Manchu Dragon: Costumes of China—The Ch'ing Dynasty," an in-house exhibition overseen by special consultant Diana Vreeland and Textile Study Room curator Jean Mailey. It featured 150 robes drawn entirely from the Museum's extensive holdings of Qing-dynasty robes, augmented by jades, ceramics, and paintings from the collection. In January 1981 the Museum opened "5,000 Years of Korean Art," a major government loan exhibition coordinated by assistant curator Julia Meech-Pekarik that included 256 works dating from 3000 B.C. to modern times. And April 1982 saw the opening of an exhibition organized by curator Martin Lerner, "Along the Ancient Silk Routes: Central Asian Art from the West Berlin State Museums," which featured 150 wall paintings, sculptures, and temple hangings dating from the fifth to the tenth century.

Another major initiative of the early 1980s was the creation of a permanent display of Japanese art. The acquisition in 1975 of the Harry Packard collection—more than four hundred Japanese works ranging from the Neolithic period to the nineteenth century—became an important catalyst in this process. In 1979 the Japanese government presented the Museum with a gift of one million dollars toward the new installation. In the following years fund-raising in both Japan and New York was taken up by a committee of prominent Japanese government and business leaders. Meanwhile, Wen Fong, assisted by associate curator Barbara Ford, was working with Kevin Roche of Kevin Roche John Dinkaloo and Associates to plan and execute the new Arts of Japan galleries; they opened in The Sackler Galleries for Asian Art in April 1987 (fig. 113). The Museum is now able to present the full range of Japanese art, from Neolithic pottery (ca. 2500–300 B.C.) to woodblock prints and textiles of the Edo period (1615–1868) to contemporary ceramics, in a chronologically ordered sequence of eleven display spaces.

Along the way there were also a number of special exhibitions, and one, "Selections from the Permanent Collection of Indian and Southeast Asian Art," which opened in October 1983, was an early indication of our remarkable growth in this area under the leadership of Martin Lerner. On display were fifty works dating from the first century B.C. to the thirteenth century A.D.—including fourteen important early bronze and stone sculptures acquired in 1982 from the renowned Pan-Asian Collection, exemplified by a superb early twelfth-century Chola bronze image of Yashoda and the infant Krishna (fig. 112). A monumental granite figure from the eighth-century Pandian culture, *Garuda Seated in Royal Ease* (1983.518), a gift from Alice and Nasli M. Heeramaneck, was another highlight of the exhibition.

By 1984 Philippe was able to observe that although Indian and Southeast Asian art had previously been poorly represented, with the appointment of Martin Lerner as curator in 1979 the Museum had acquired a strong advocate for this area of collecting. Succinctly the director characterized this development: "As museums are in effect a palimpsest of successive curatorial biases, it was inevitable that the imbalance would eventually be

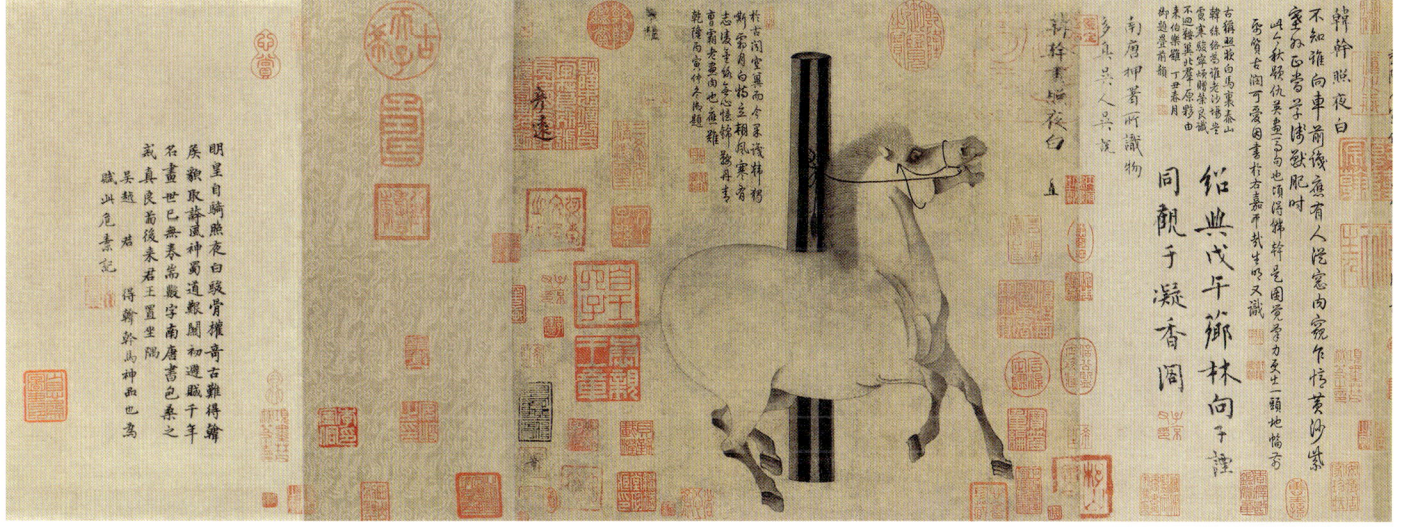

111. Han Gan, *Night-Shining White*. China, Tang dynasty, ca. 750. Handscroll, ink on paper, 12⅛ × 13⅜ in. (30.8 × 34 cm). Purchase, The Dillon Fund Gift, 1977 (1977.78)

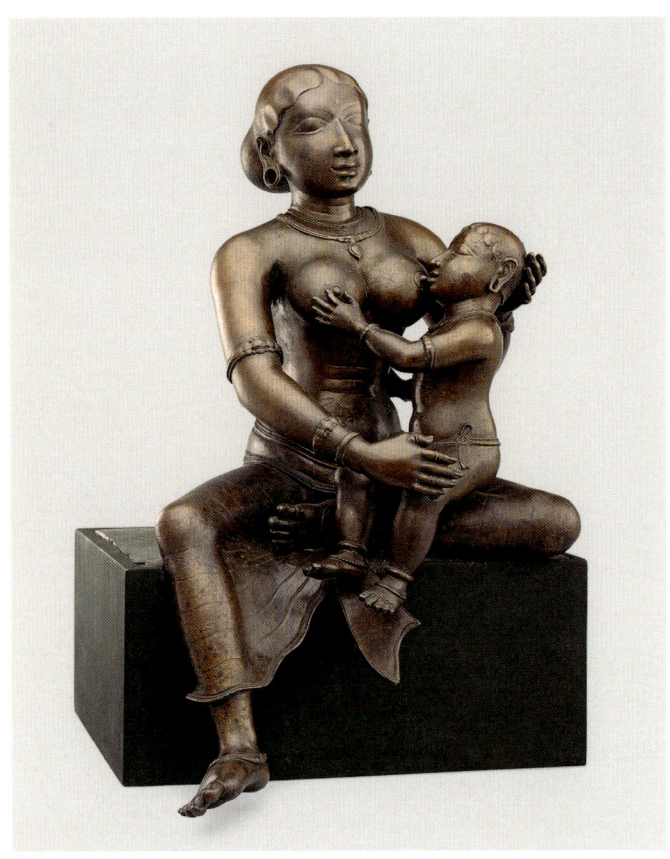

112. *Krishna's Foster Mother, Yashoda, with the Infant Krishna*. India, Chola period, early 12th century. Copper alloy, H. 17½ in. (44.5 cm). Purchase, Lita Annenberg Hazen Charitable Trust Gift, in honor of Cynthia Hazen and Leon B. Polsky, 1982 (1982.220.8)

more than 440 works in the Ellsworth collection added to the gifts and purchases of the preceding decade—most notably those of John Crawford Jr. and Douglas Dillon—the size of the Museum's holdings in Chinese painting and calligraphy had more than doubled within a few short years.

These transformations were accompanied by one of name: in 1986 Philippe announced that the Department of Far Eastern Art was henceforth the Department of Asian Art, a name that "more accurately reflects the broad geographic origins of the collections assembled there." At the same time he appointed James Watt, formerly chairman of the Asiatic Department of the Museum of Fine Arts, Boston, to be senior consultant for Chinese antiquities and decorative arts at the Metropolitan, with "responsibility for the collection and installation plans for the arts of ancient China." Philippe pointed out that planning for these future galleries coincided with the gift from the Ernest Erickson Foundation of Erickson's Chinese bronzes, ceramics, and jades, "which at one stroke has given the Department of Asian Art one of the premier collections of archaic and early Chinese art." I catalogued the collection, which comprises some 150 choice works in jade, bronze, bone, silver, and amber, principally from China's Bronze Age, as well as early porcelains and three paintings of the Yuan and Ming periods; it was exhibited in the Notable Acquisitions Gallery in 1987.

Maxwell K. Hearn

redressed." The Museum's renewed commitment resulted in two major donations of South and Southeast Asian art in the mid-1980s: in the fall of 1984 "The Flame and the Lotus: Indian and Southeast Asian Art from The Kronos Collections" celebrated seventy exquisite gifts and loans from Steven M. Kossak and his family, and in 1987 the Museum acquired through gift and purchase over 425 objects from Samuel Eilenberg, former chairman of the Department of Mathematics at Columbia University. Assembled over thirty years, the Eilenberg collection has brought to the Museum, in Philippe's words, "the best representation of Javanese bronzes outside Jakarta and of smaller Gandharan arts outside of Pakistan, in addition to important Indian, Nepali, and Thai works."

In 1986 Philippe also announced Robert H. Ellsworth's gift of his collection of nineteenth- and twentieth-century Chinese paintings, which "not only complement our strong holdings in classic Chinese painting prior to 1800 but extend the field much closer in time than was imaginable just a few years ago." With the

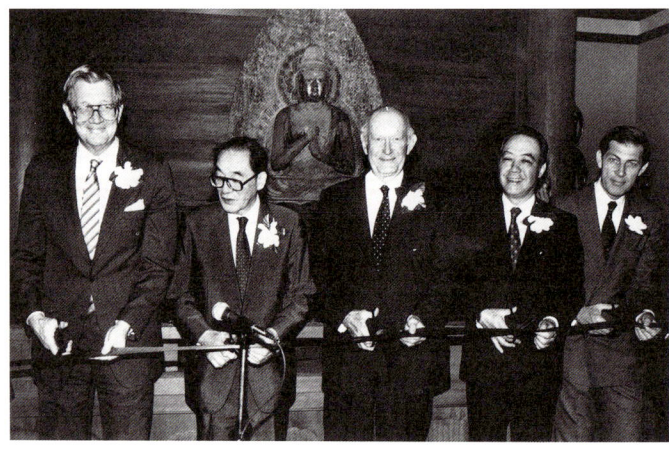

113. Ribbon-cutting ceremony at the opening of The Arts of Japan in The Sackler Galleries for Asian Art, 1987. Participants were President William H. Luers; The Honorable Takeshi Yasukawa, former ambassador of Japan to the United States, counselor, Mitsui and Co., and chairman, The Cooperative Committee in Japan for the Construction of the Japanese Galleries at The Metropolitan Museum of Art; Trustee Emeritus Douglas Dillon; His Excellency Ambassador Hidetoshi Ukawa, consul general of Japan in New York; and Director Philippe de Montebello.

THE IRVING WING

One afternoon in late 1988, the director paid a visit to Herbert and Florence Irving at their home in Old Westbury on Long Island. Everywhere he looked his gaze was met by Chinese and Japanese paintings, Indian sculptures, and objects of all sorts, large and small. In the sitting room they were arranged on tables, perched on stands, set on shelves. In the study there were chests with drawers full of jade carvings, while cabinets normally kept closed for reasons of conservation housed the lacquer collection. The finest small carvings of jade and hard stone were in the bedroom. The Irvings had been collecting for close to thirty years. At the end of the visit Philippe left with a large box of cookies. But much more was to come—for the Metropolitan Museum.

Among the many topics of conversation on that pleasant afternoon were the Irvings' interest in Indian art and the Museum's intention to create new galleries for its collections of South and Southeast Asian art. The easy rapport established between collectors and director led naturally to a meeting shortly afterward in Philippe's office on the mezzanine floor of the Museum (now part of the Greek and Roman Galleries), at which the Irvings agreed to fund the construction of the galleries for Indian art and offered to lend a number of masterpieces of Indian sculpture from their collection for display in these galleries. All of these would soon be promised or outright gifts. It was also proposed that the Museum stage an exhibition of the Irvings' East Asian lacquer. This subject was chosen because with a show drawn from a private collection, works of art of a single type seemed preferable to a heterogeneous assemblage of objects; at the same time, the lacquers, which included representative pieces from all areas of East Asia, would demonstrate the richness and diversity of the Irvings' holdings. As it happened, lacquer objects then constituted the fastest-growing part of the couple's collection. They agreed to this proposal. A little later, their gift for the construction of the Indian galleries was extended to cover all the South and Southeast Asian galleries.

In the fall of 1991, while the new galleries were still under construction, the exhibition of East Asian lacquer opened. It included 180 objects from China, Japan, Korea, and the Ryukyu Islands, which are usually regarded as a distinct group (Okinawa had developed its own tradition of lacquer making before it was annexed by Japan in 1609). This was the first comprehensive presentation devoted to a particular East Asian art form in New York City, if not in the entire country. In addition to masterpieces of Chinese and Japanese lacquer, the exhibition featured superb examples of Korean lacquer of a quality seldom seen outside Korea and Japan (fig. 117). The group of Ryukyuan pieces in the collection is so representative and complete that when Okinawa commemorated the twentieth anniversary of its return to Japanese sovereignty in 1992, many of the objects in its celebratory exhibition were loans from the Irvings.

The Florence and Herbert Irving Galleries for South and Southeast Asian art opened in 1994 (fig. 114). In them the Museum is able to display fine examples of every major school of Indian sculpture from the first to the sixteenth century. Equally comprehensive is the coverage of Southeast Asian sculpture, complemented by smaller artifacts in various media. On an upper floor that houses galleries for the arts of later India and the Himalayas, paintings, sculptures, and decorative arts are displayed. The opening of these galleries was a major step toward the realization of Philippe's vision of a universal museum. The donors of the greatest number of works of art displayed in these galleries were the Irvings themselves; however, it should also be mentioned that

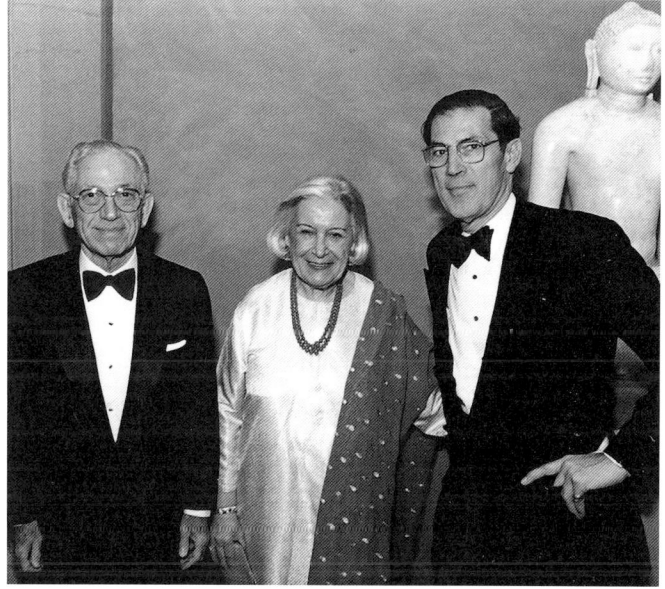

114. Herbert and Florence Irving with Philippe de Montebello at the opening of The Florence and Herbert Irving Galleries for South and Southeast Asian art, 1994

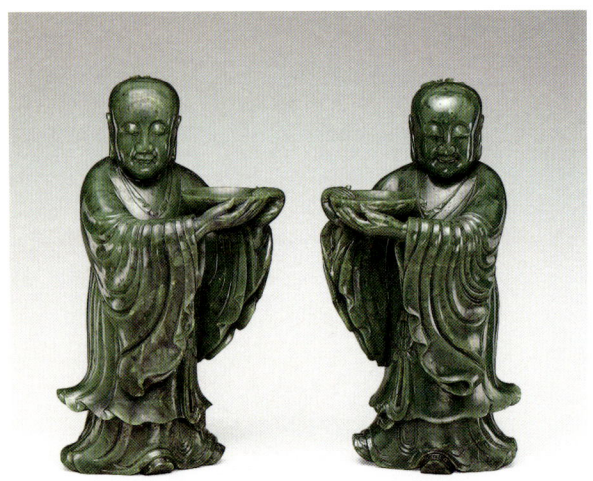

115. Temple attendants. China, Qing dynasty, 18th century. Jade (nephrite), H. 11 15/16 in. (30.3 cm). *Left*, Gift of Heber R. Bishop, 1902 (02.18.411); *right*, Florence and Herbert Irving Collection

Right: 116. Cosmological mandala with Mount Meru. China, Yuan dynasty, 1271–1368. Silk tapestry (*kesi*), 33 × 33 in. (83.8 × 83.8 cm). Purchase, Fletcher Fund and Joseph E. Hotung and Michael and Danielle Rosenberg Gifts, 1989 (1989.140)

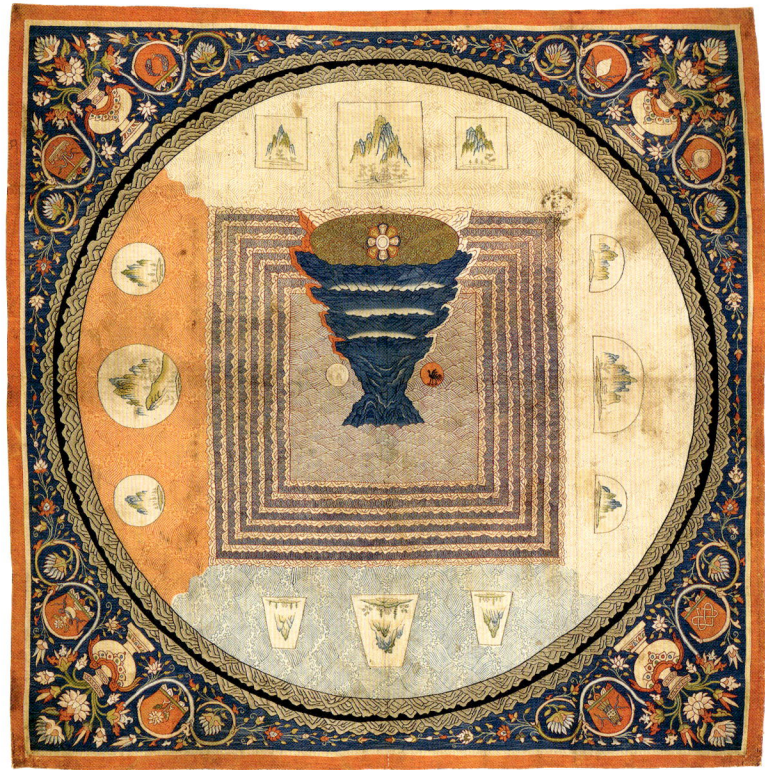

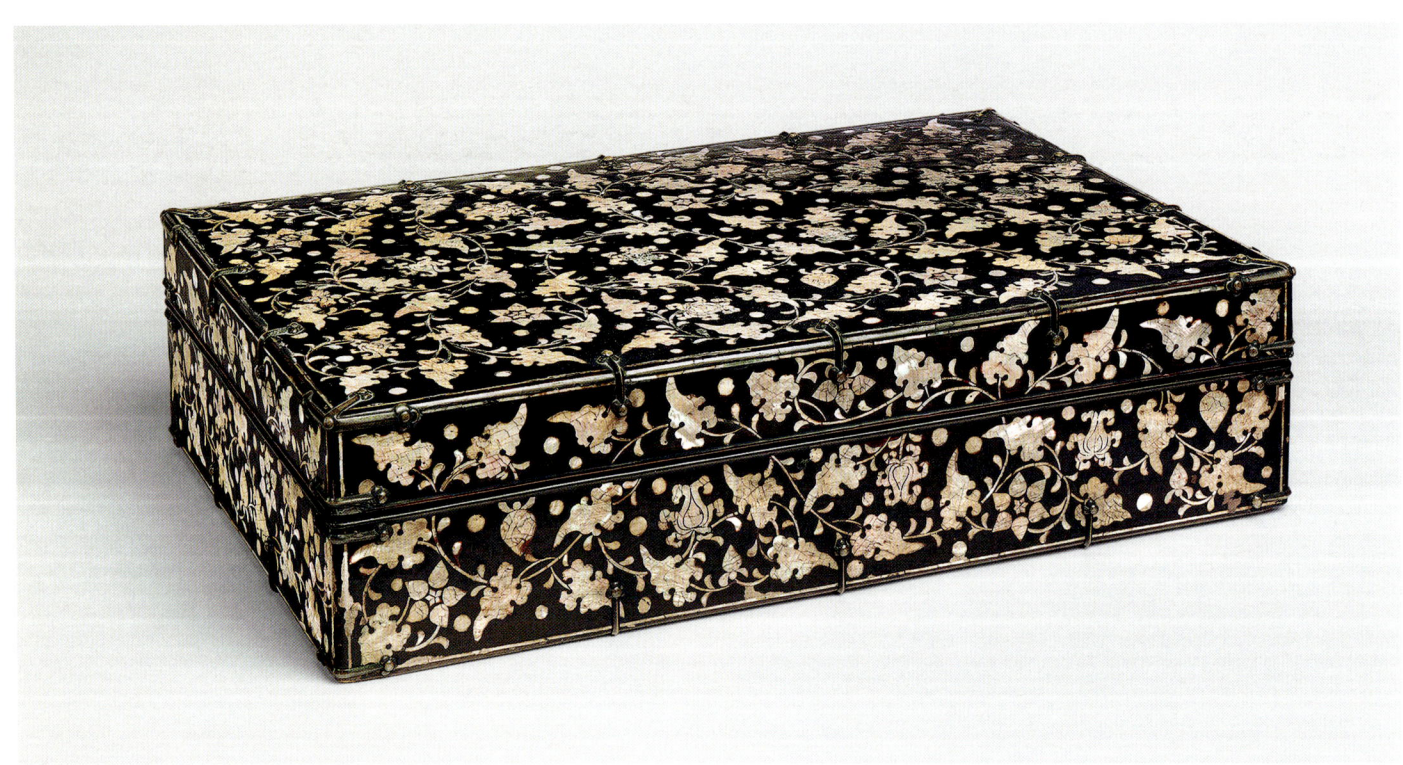

117. Stationery box with decoration of peony scrolls. Korea, Joseon dynasty, 15th century. Lacquer with mother of pearl inlay, 3½ × 14⅜ × 9½ in. (9 × 36.5 × 24.1 cm). Promised Gift of Florence and Herbert Irving

several of the most important Indian and Southeast Asian sculptures in our collection were gifts of Mr. and Mrs. Walter Annenberg and members of their family (fig. 112). All came to the Museum through Philippe's efforts.

In 1997 the Douglas Dillon Galleries for Chinese Paintings were renovated and the two arms were connected by the new Frances Young Tang Gallery, which had an additional upper floor to house the collections of Chinese decorative arts. Florence and Herbert Irving once again not only funded this construction but also supplied the majority of objects shown. One of the four rooms is devoted to the now-famous lacquer collection and another to *Kleinkunst*, small objects carved in bamboo, ivory, jade, or rhinoceros horn, together with articles for the Chinese scholar's desk. A third room contains a display of the Museum's collection of textiles (fig. 116), which until then were not on view. And the last gallery houses the Heber R. Bishop collection of jade—with one additional item that is the first piece of Chinese jade the Irvings ever acquired. Decades ago, before beginning to amass their vast holdings, the Irvings used to visit the Met to view, among other things, the Bishop jades. One day while browsing in a commercial gallery they chanced upon a green jade figure that they immediately recognized as a mate to one in the Bishop collection. They bought it on the spot. In 1997, after at least a century apart, the paired figures were reunited in the Florence and Herbert Irving Galleries for Chinese Decorative Arts (fig. 115). The Irving jades are otherwise notable for including a number of superb carvings of the Tang to the Yuan dynasty (seventh to fourteenth century), an era from which jades are rarely seen.

In the meantime, gifts kept coming from the Irvings to other sections of the Asian Art department as well (fig. 118). In the Japanese galleries these range from early pottery to Buddhist sculpture to Edo-period paintings and are constantly on display. Gifts also abound in the gallery for the arts of Nepal and Tibet. The majority of galleries of the Department of Asian Art belong to what has now been named the Florence and Herbert Irving Asian Wing.

To the good fortune of the Metropolitan Museum, the immense enrichment of its Asian Art collection in recent years is a direct consequence of the friendship that began twenty years ago with an afternoon visit to Old Westbury.

James C. Y. Watt

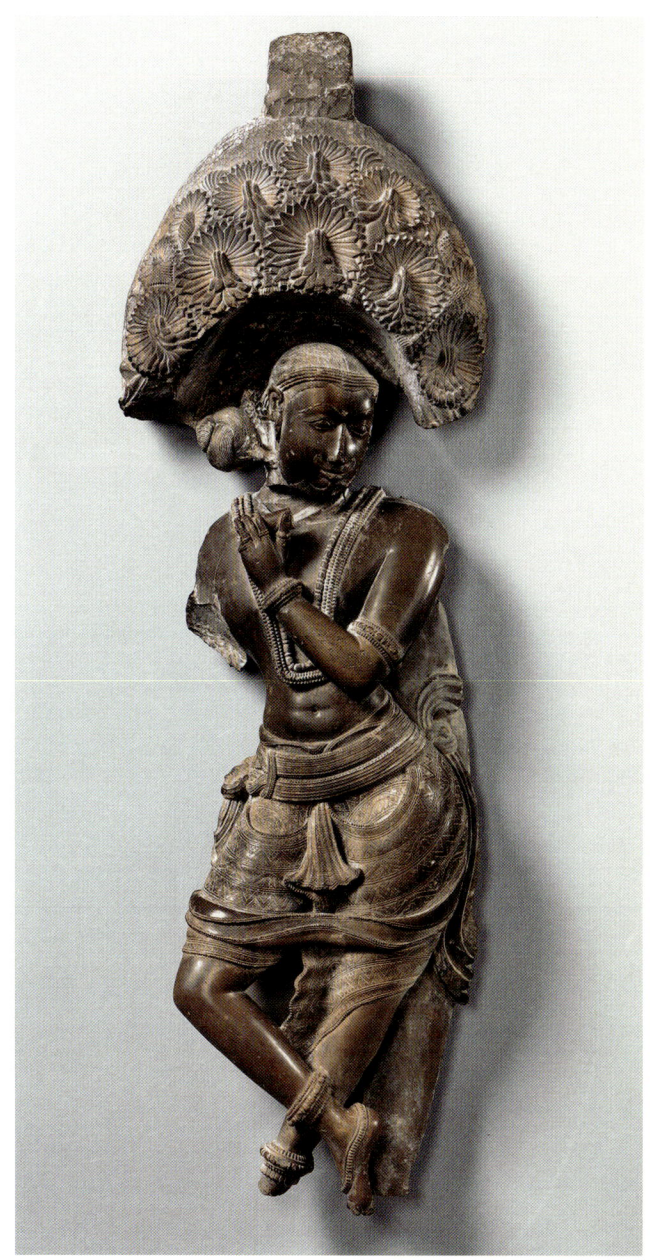

118. Celestial flutist (Gandharva). India, Hoysala period, 11th century. Slate, H. 40¾ in. (103.5 cm). Gift of Florence and Herbert Irving, in honor of Philippe de Montebello, 2008 (2008.537)

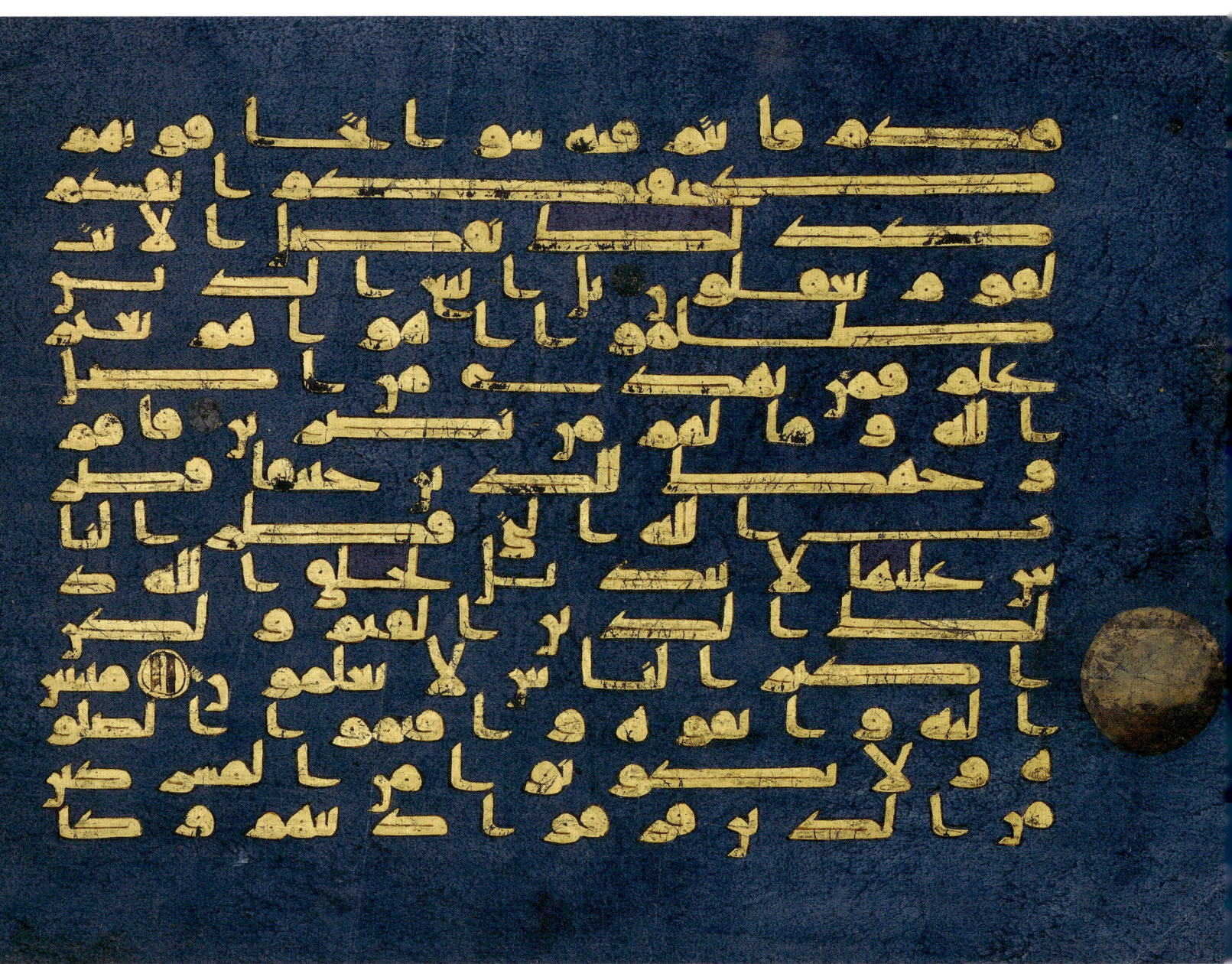

ISLAMIC ART

A "PRINCE" TO THE DEPARTMENT OF ISLAMIC ART

Debbe ancora uno principe monstrarsi amatore delle virtù, et onorare li eccellenti in una arte. Appresso, debbe animare li sua cittadini di potere quietamente esercitare li esercizii loro, e nella mercanzia e nella agricultura, et in ogni altro esercizio delli uomini, e che quello non tema di ornare le sua possessione per timore che le li sieno tolte, e quell'altro di aprire uno traffico per paura delle taglie; ma debbe preparare premi a chi vuol fare queste cose, et a qualunque pensa, in qualunque modo ampliare la sua città o il suo stato.

Debbe, oltre a questo, ne' tempi convenienti dell'anno, tenere occupati è populi con le feste e spettaculi. E, perché ogni città è divisa in arte o in tribù, debbe tenere conto di quelle università, raunarsi con loro qualche volta, dare di sé esempli di umanità e di munificenzia, tenendo sempre ferma non di manco la maestà della dignità sua, perché questo non vuole mai mancare in cosa alcuna.

Niccolò Machiavelli, *Il Principe*, chapter 21: "Che si conviene a un principe perché sia stimato"

I am not sure whether Philippe holds Machiavelli in high esteem; unlike the more traditional philosophers and political analysts of medieval and Renaissance Italy—who believed there was a necessary relationship between legitimate authority and moral goodness—the author of *The Prince* saw no particular link between the two and criticized this ethical view in his perhaps unjustly celebrated treatise. But recently I was amused, and thought of Philippe, when I reread the passage cited above, which is taken from the twenty-first chapter, entitled "What a Ruler Ought to Do in Order to Be Well-Regarded." During his long tenure, Philippe has often been described as a prince or king—sometimes with endearing intent, sometimes unsympathetically. It is a characterization that I have always found off the mark, given his accessibility to senior staff members and his generosity with his time. Nonetheless, a kingly "aura" is present. And

Opposite: 119. A page from the "Blue Qur'an." Tunisia, Fatimid period, late 9th–early 10th century. Gold and silver on indigo-dyed parchment, 11¹⁵⁄₁₆ × 15¹³⁄₁₆ in. (30.4 × 40.2 cm). Purchase, Lila Acheson Wallace Gift, 2004 (2004.88)

I like the applicability of Machiavelli's words because it brings up the French–Italian connection between us. Although Philippe speaks Italian fluently, with only a slight French accent, whenever he introduced me he would invariably call me "Stephanoh Carbonee"—as if I had been born of Italian ancestry in Marseille. My response, of course, was always to pronounce his family name with the most crystalline Italian accent!

To return to the "prince": throughout this brief essay, which is just one piece of a big puzzle celebrating Philippe's legacy at the Met, I intend to use citations from the paragraph above as a rhythmic guideline. They are meant to highlight his contributions to the life of the department I served in a curatorial capacity for over sixteen years, from 1992 to 2008.

A prince ought to show himself a patron of merits and honor the proficient in every art.

When Philippe became acting director, the Department of Islamic Art was blooming under the leadership of Richard Ettinghausen, one of the most revered, sometimes feared, and utterly respected scholars of Islamic art, whose legacy in our field of studies is still very much alive, especially in the United States. The expanded Islamic galleries had been opened in 1975 on the second floor of the southeastern wing of the Museum, establishing new benchmarks for the display of Islamic art in scale, chronological range, geographical breadth, museology, and academic depth. This exemplary offering continued for an entire generation and was the envy of many other institutions with holdings of Islamic art.

Dr. Ettinghausen must have been one of the most senior department heads "inherited" by the new director. Philippe has often remarked that their meetings during the period they overlapped (brief because of Ettinghausen's failing health) were always poignant, that the scholar had an authoritative and at the same time charming personality, that he commanded respect but was also able to show intimate and lighter aspects of his character, and that from him Philippe learned much about the beauty and

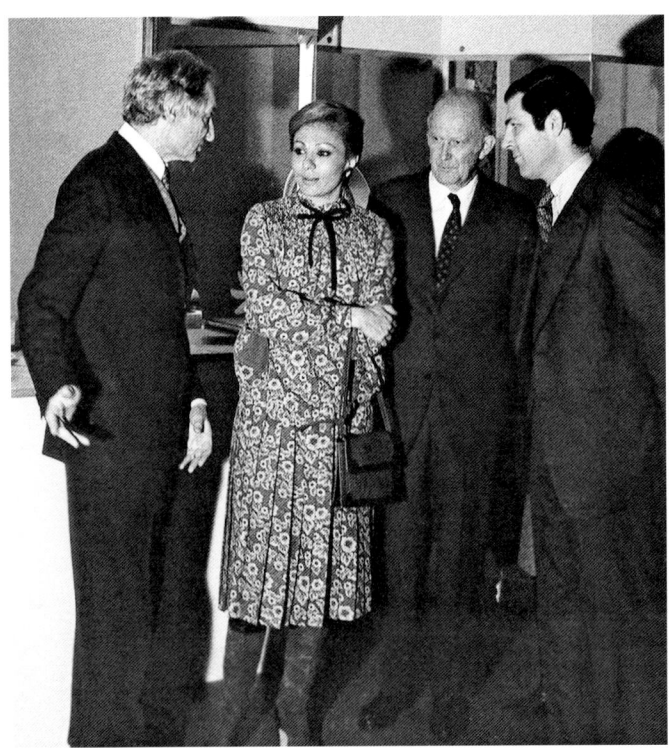

120. Richard Ettinghausen; Farah Pahlavi, Empress of Iran; Douglas Dillon; and Philippe de Montebello during the empress's visit to the Metropolitan Museum, January 13, 1978

artistic value of Islamic art (fig. 120). An immigrant from Germany with the traditional classical education of his generation, Ettinghausen was indeed "proficient in every art"; Philippe recognized his merits and honored him, and continues to do so.

His widow, Elizabeth Ettinghausen—herself a scholar of Islamic art—is still today a generous donor to the department, an adviser, and a member of its Visiting Committee, providing as well a constant reminder of her husband's legacy, fostered during the last few years of his tenure by Philippe. Among the major acquisitions of the Department of Islamic Art in the brief period 1977–79 were a small wooden ceiling from medieval Spain (1977.93)—a Hearst Foundation gift—that was promptly installed in the introductory room of the recently opened galleries, as well as several gifts from important donors who included Edwin Binney 3rd; Ettinghausen's predecessor and former head of the Ancient Near Eastern and Islamic departments, Charles K. Wilkinson, and his wife, Irma; the young and fervent collector Shaykh Nasser al-Sabah, from Kuwait, now a Museum honorary trustee; Nelly, Violet, and Elie Abemeyor in memory of Michael Abemeyor; and Richard Ettinghausen himself, who regularly made gifts of objects from his collection to the department.

The list of acquisitions in the period before Dr. Ettinghausen died on April 2, 1979, at the age of seventy-one, is, by and large, a tribute to his leadership and scholarship. Gifts in his honor came from Norbert Schimmel; Adrienne Minassian; Charles and Irma Wilkinson; Elizabeth Ettinghausen—the first of many from her throughout the years (see fig. 123), the most recent being a Deccani illustrated manuscript acquired in 2008 (2008.251); and many others. Perhaps the most important acquisition of these years is the so-called Seley Carpet, one of the finest late sixteenth-century Persian rugs known today, which was presented in memory of Richard Ettinghausen partially as a gift of Louis E., Theresa S., Hervey, and Eliot Jay Seley (1978.550).

At the same time he should encourage his citizens to practice their callings peaceably, both in commerce and agriculture, and in every other following, so that the one should not be deterred from improving his possessions for fear lest they be taken away from him, or another from opening up trade for fear of taxes; but the prince ought to offer rewards to whoever wishes to do these things and designs in any way to honor his city or state.

The successor to Richard Ettinghausen was Stuart Cary Welch, the first department head appointed by Philippe. Like Ettinghausen, Welch influenced more than an entire generation of younger Islamists (and did so until his very recent death, in the summer of 2008). In background and life paths Welch was very different from his predecessor, however, as well as in his personality, which was spontaneous, with a bursting and infectious enthusiasm. An American-born, self-taught lover of Islamic art—especially that of Mughal India and Safavid Iran—Welch had a fantastic eye and the passionate spirit of a true collector. Whichever of Welch's qualities particularly appealed to Philippe or prompted the offer to join the Museum, it is certain that his appointment to the Department of Islamic Art brought a change of pace: a step on the accelerator.

The eight years of Welch's tenure were a period of high visibility for the department, no doubt accomplished with Philippe's help, encouragement, and benign eye. Contacts with donors, collectors, and trustees were intensified, and Welch's drive toward continuous, almost obsessive, collecting resulted in enormous improvements of the department's holdings. At this moment Islamic art was ever more fashionable and in demand; meanwhile the great donors of earlier days—the likes of Edward C. Moore,

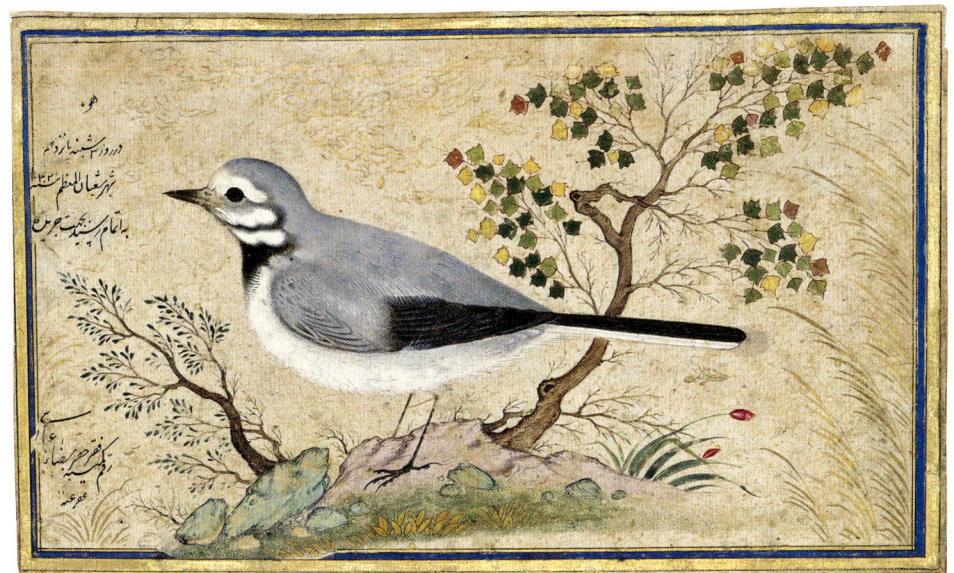

121. Riza-i ʿAbbasi, Study of a bird. Iran, Safavid period, 1634. Ink, colors, gold, and silver on paper, 4¼ × 7¼ in. (10.8 × 18.4 cm). Louis E. and Theresa S. Seley Purchase Fund for Islamic Art, and Rogers Fund, 1985 (1985.2)

122. Dagger and sheath. India, Mughal period, 17th century. Jade (nephrite) and steel, L. of dagger 15 in. (38.1 cm). Gift of Alice Heeramaneck, in memory of Nasli Heeramaneck, 1985 (1985.58a, b)

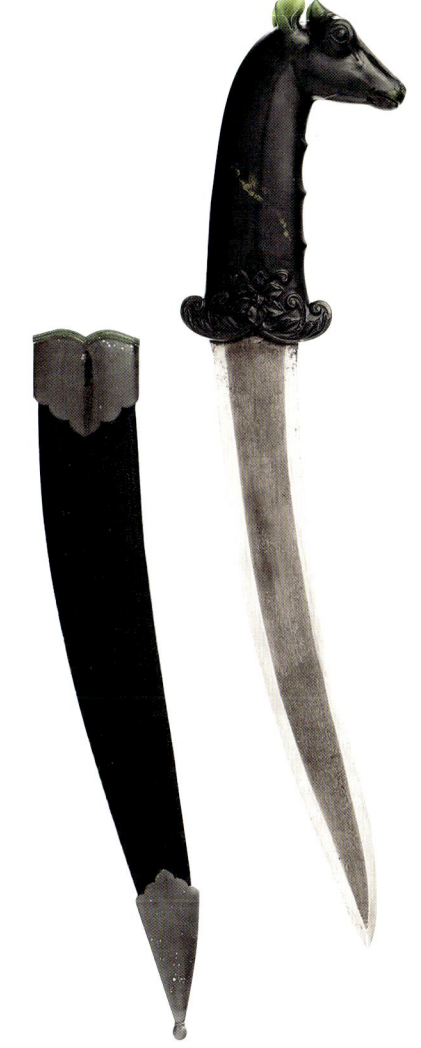

J. Pierpont Morgan, Alexander Smith Cochran, James Ballard—had become a thing of the past. Consequently, prices rose sensibly, and the market grew much more competitive. It is a tribute to Philippe and Cary Welch that in this new and challenging environment both the program and the quality of acquisitions—mostly devoted to improving the holdings of later, especially Indian, Islamic art—continued unabated. Acquisitions during the period 1980–87 reflect Welch's efforts not only to cultivate donors but also to persuade Philippe and the trustees to acquire significant Indian works with Museum funds. Among the most spectacular one might mention the Deccani painting *The House of Bijapur* (1982.213), a Mughal marble *jali* screen and carved basin (1984.193,.213), and a *bidri* water-pipe base (1984.221), all Indian; also a study of a bird made in early seventeenth-century Iran by the celebrated artist Riza-i ʿAbbasi (fig. 121). An especially generous donor in the Welch years was Alice Heeramaneck, who gave to the department a quantity of jewelry, manuscripts, individual folios, and textiles, and also, remarkably, masterpieces such as a Mughal dagger with a carved jade hilt in the shape of a blue nilgai (fig. 122) and the late sixteenth-century Akbar period painting *Lion at Rest* (1985.221). Welch's close relationships with dealers and collectors as well as members of the corporate world are reflected in the large number of gifts proceeding from Ruth Blumka, Habib Anavian, Margaret Mushekian, Mrs. Nelson Doubleday, Marguerite McBey, Edith Macy Schoenborn-Buchheim, Beatrice Kelekian, Nanette R. Kelekian, George Blumenthal, Nathaniel Spear, Mrs. Hayford Pierce, Nasser David Khalili, The Kronos

Collections, and the Mobil Foundation, Inc. Cary Welch and his wife, Edith, donated several objects from their own collection, including a set of seventeenth-century Mughal bridle or belt ornaments in the shape of two interlocking fish (1987.254); it inspired a design for earrings that became one of the most popular items in the Met gift shop for years thereafter. Throughout this period, Philippe assuredly "encouraged his [Islamic department] citizens to practice their callings peaceably" and "improve their possessions," often also "offering rewards" by helping identify new donors and funds so that the department's desires to improve its collection could be fulfilled.

Further, he ought to entertain the people with festivals and spectacles at convenient seasons of the year.

Welch's tenure coincided with the enactment of Philippe's fine idea that, in addition to mounting unavoidable blockbuster exhibitions, the Met should "entertain the people" and especially educate them through "spectacles" that combined a scholarly approach, strong aesthetic appeal, and a novel subject. For our department, the first of a steady stream of such exhibitions was "India! Art and Culture: 1300–1900" (1985–86), a spectacular display of Indian art—both Islamic and non-Islamic—through the centuries and up to the British period. It revealed Welch's grasp and depth of knowledge on the subject and, especially, his passionate enthusiasm for India and Indian art. Welch's obituary in the *New York Times* contained this quotation from the late John Russell's 1985 review: "The best exhibitions are acts of love, and *India!* is one of them."

"India!" increased the visibility of the department and prompted further organizing of major international exhibitions. Such endeavors, conducted under Philippe's watchful eye, represent perhaps the highest achievements of the department during the leadership of Welch's successor, Daniel Walker, who was curator in charge from 1988 to 2005. In addition to a regular program of exhibitions highlighting the department's collections and held within the Islamic art galleries—in The Hagop Kevorkian Fund Special Exhibitions Gallery endowed in 1989, thanks to Ralph Minasian's continuing generosity and interest in the activities of the department—Islamic art exhibitions have frequently appeared in Museum-wide gallery spaces, to public and critical acclaim. Among those generated or co-organized by departmental curators were the landmark projects "Al-Andalus: The Art of Islamic Spain," a collaboration with the Patronato de la Alhambra y Generalife in Granada (1991–92); "Flowers under Foot: Indian Carpets of the Mughal Era," Daniel Walker's brainchild (1997–98); "Glass of the Sultans," which I organized with David Whitehouse of the Corning Museum of Glass (2001); and "The Legacy of Genghis Khan: Art and Culture in Western Asia, 1256–1353," organized by me and Linda Komaroff of the Los Angeles County Museum of Art (2002). The most recent, also initiated during Walker's tenure, was my "Venice and the Islamic World, 828–1797," co-organized with the Institut du Monde Arabe in Paris and subsequently brought to the Doge's Palace in Venice (2006–7). To these major endeavors can be added several other exhibitions of works borrowed from important collections around the world that emphasized the active role of the department in promoting knowledge of Islamic art among American and international publics. Among them were "Pages of Perfection: Islamic Paintings and Calligraphy from the Russian Academy of Sciences, St. Petersburg" (1995); "King of the World: A Mughal Manuscript from the Royal Library, Windsor Castle" (1997); "Letters in Gold: Ottoman Calligraphy from the Sakıp Sabancı Collection, Istanbul" (1998); and "Treasure of the World: Jeweled Art of India in the Age of the Mughals," from the holdings of the Al-Sabah Collection in Kuwait (2001).

In this discussion of exhibitions it might be mentioned that the tragedy of September 11, 2001, occurred at a particularly intense moment for the department. On the morning of that day several trucks were ready to leave the Corning Museum of Glass in upstate New York to deliver all the works associated with

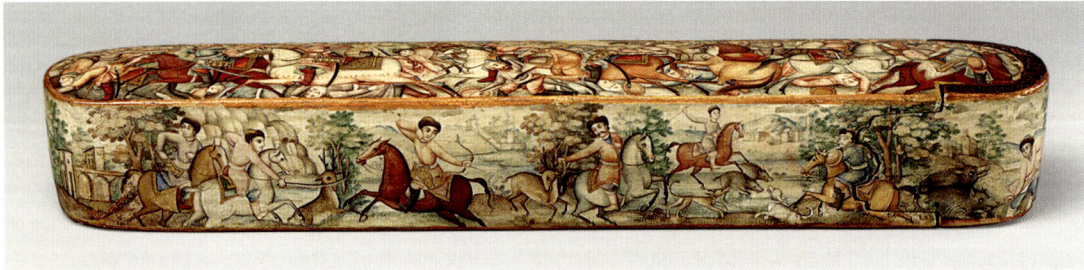

123. Box depicting Shah Ismaʿil at war with the Uzbeks. Attributed to Iran, early 19th century. Papier-mâché, painted and lacquered, L. 10⅛ in. (25.7 cm). Purchase, Elizabeth S. Ettinghausen Gift, in memory of Richard Ettinghausen; and Stephenson Family Foundation Gift, 2006 (2006.523a, b)

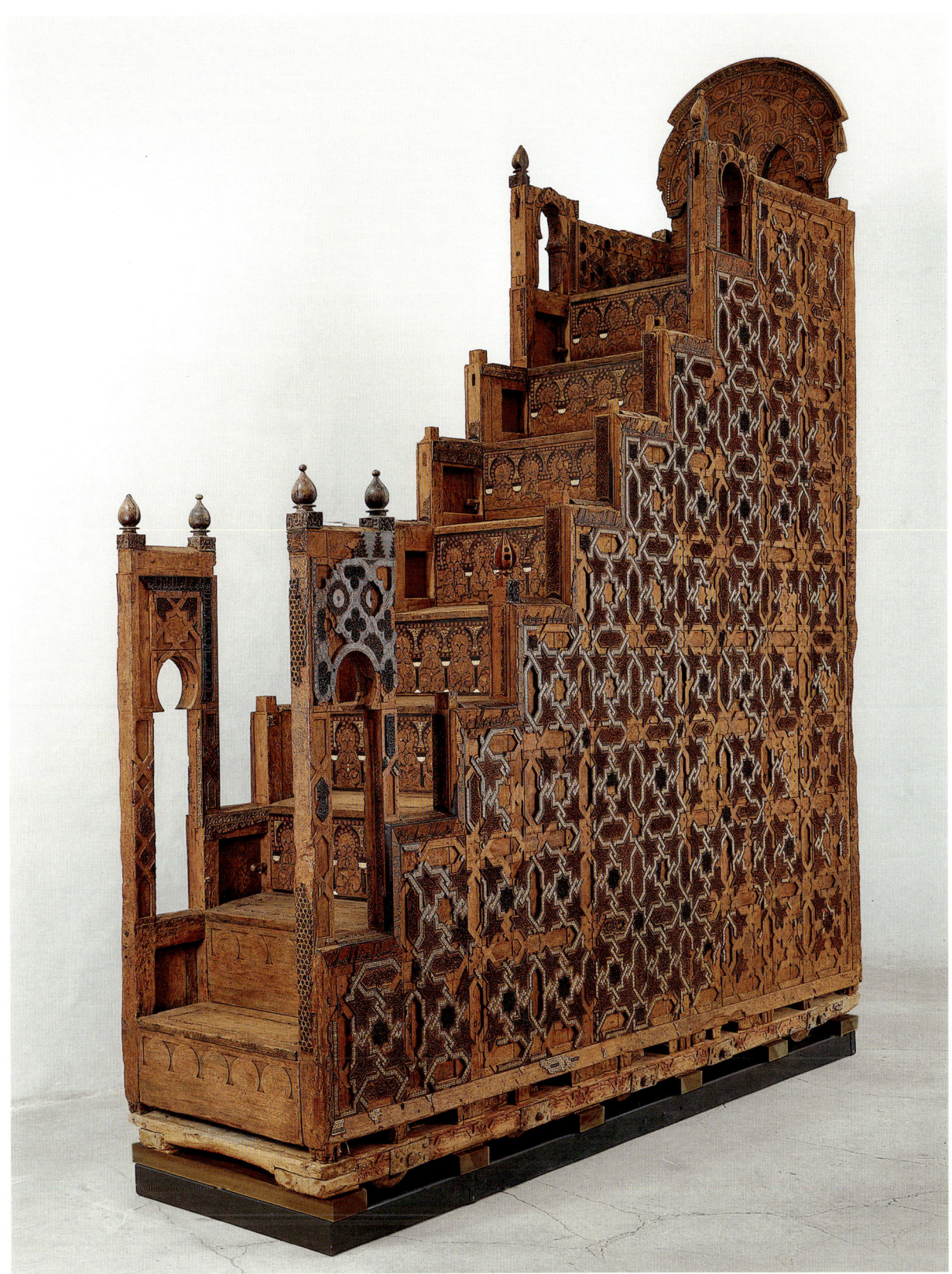

124. *Minbar* (pulpit) from the Kutubiyya Mosque. Córdoba, Spain, 1137–ca. 1145; now in the Badiʿ Palace, Marrakesh. Cedar, pine, and other woods, H. 12 ft. 8 in. (386.1 cm). The *minbar* was restored and installed in 1997–98 by conservators and curators of the Metropolitan Museum.

"Glass of the Sultans," which was due to open on October 2. When the terrible news reached Corning the delivery was suspended, and in the following days it became imperative for Philippe and the Met's administration to decide whether the exhibition should be canceled altogether, postponed indefinitely, or carried out as planned. This was an "Islamic" show, and there was a legitimate fear of possible violent incident or at least negative publicity; in addition, many international lenders were involved in the project. To my great relief and gratitude, Philippe's enlightened thinking, and his reasoning that art is able to bring solace in a moment of distress, led to a decision to go forward as scheduled. An exhibition of Islamic art could serve as a powerful medium of communication and at the same time offer reassurance. Our success in convincing all the lenders to confirm their loans for the exhibition was further evidence of the strength of this reasoning and the rightness of the decision.

And as every city is divided into guilds or into societies, he ought to hold such bodies in esteem, and associate with them sometimes, and show himself an example of courtesy and liberality; nevertheless, always maintaining the majesty of his rank, for this he must never consent to abate in anything.

During this long period, the individual curatorial departments—or "guilds" or "societies"—were increasingly competing for Philippe's attention and approval of acquisitions, at the same time renewing their efforts to ensure other sources for departmental funds. This was particularly true of the smaller departments. In appointing Daniel Walker to head the Department of Islamic Art, Philippe had chosen a relatively young curator but proven administrator from the Cincinnati Art Museum whose field of expertise, Islamic carpets and textiles, seemed to many—and perhaps to Philippe himself—somewhat peripheral to the field. On the other hand, about one-third of the department's collection was indeed composed of textiles, and this choice was probably also an attempt to break from the extravagant personalities of the past years and encourage a long-term, steady development of the department's curatorial experience, acquisition policies, and fund-raising.

Walker can be associated in his early days with the late Patti Cadby Birch (d. 2007), one of the staunchest and most enthusiastic supporters of the Department of Islamic Art over the past three decades. She and her husband, Everett B. Birch, had donated a series of belt plaques (1981.232.5a–kk) in 1981 during Welch's tenure, and in 1988 she had given a Safavid glazed ceramic water-pipe base in Mr. Birch's memory (1988.247). A well-known former dealer, discoverer of talents, and collector, with a broad interest in the arts and a recently acquired passion for Morocco, Patti Birch grew to be a sort of godmother for the department, eventually becoming an honorary Museum trustee. Among much else, she was behind the reestablishment of the Friends of Islamic Art, a support group that has been instrumental in the acquisition program of the department since 1994 and is still going strong; she endowed a curatorship whose first incumbent was Daniel Walker, in 1997; and she sponsored the 1997–98 restoration, publication, and installation in Marrakesh by Met conservators and curators of the twelfth-century wooden *minbar* of the Kutubiyya Mosque, one of the indisputable masterpieces of Islamic art (fig. 124).

Walker had been a student of Cary Welch at Harvard, and it was shortly after his arrival that one of the masterpieces of early Safavid painting, Sultan Muhammad's *Allegory of Worldly and Otherworldly Drunkenness* (1988.430), became a promised gift from Welch and his wife, to be jointly owned with the Arthur M. Sackler Museum of Harvard University. Walker continued Welch's policy of improving the holdings in Mughal and Deccani Indian art and did so in dramatic fashion: first by steering Friends funds in that direction (the very first such acquisition was a pair of palanquin finials, 1995.258a, b); and subsequently, under Philippe's guidance, by drawing on the generosity of another inspired supporter of the Museum and in particular of its Asian collections, the elective trustee Cynthia Polsky. Together with her husband, Leon, she established an acquisitions fund to assist the Asian and the Islamic departments, and from 2000 to 2006 the Cynthia Hazen Polsky and Leon B. Polsky Fund greatly helped us fill important gaps in the Indian Islamic collection. Recently she also generously contributed to the department's prominent purchase of the impressive Company painting *Giant Indian Fruit Bat* (2008.312).

Deepening our relationships with supporters in the Friends group was key to the success of the department under Walker, and after his departure in 2005 to become director of the Textile Museum in Washington, D.C., I tried to follow his lead. One of the most important and active supporters of the department, soon to become chairman of the Visiting Committee, is Harvey B. Plotnick, a Chicago-based collector who fell in love with Islamic ceramics and was guided by Walker in the first stages of his interest. Additionally, the names of several others in the

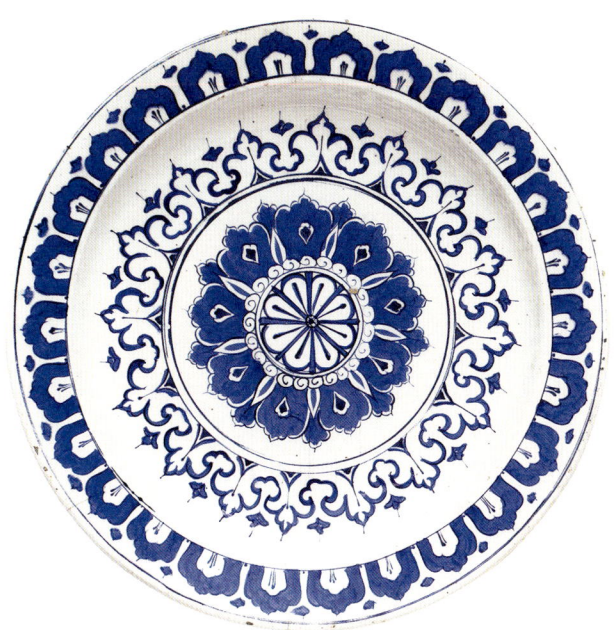

125. Plate. Iznik, Turkey, ca. 1580. Fritware, painted and glazed, Diam. 13¾ in. (34.9 cm). Gift of Philippe and Edith de Montebello, 1991 (1991.172)

Friends group—among whom I would like to mention Rebecca and Richard Lindsay, Gemma and Lewis Hall, and Shamina Talyarkhan—can often be spotted in the credit lines of recent purchases or as contributors to conservation projects.

Of the department's 450-odd acquisitions since 1988, it is appropriate to mention the large gift of textile fragments donated by Nanette Kelekian in honor of Olga Raggio, which includes well over one hundred Islamic works; the many objects acquired through the Bequest of Adrienne Minassian; and especially the gift, ongoing since 2005, of Turkoman jewelry—thus far a vastly underrepresented category in the collections—by other great supporters of the Friends group, Marilyn and Marshall Wolf, who had begun by donating some textiles in 1997. In addition, James and Diane Burke, the latter another generous honorary trustee of the Museum, have contributed a substantial sum for acquisitions in honor of former curator Marilyn Jenkins-Madina, making it possible to add to the collection, for example, two pages from the splendid "Nurse's" Qur'an (2007.191). Walker's best-known acquisition, however, supported by Philippe and the trustees of the Acquisitions Committee using Museum funds, is a celebrated early Ottoman "animal" carpet, one of the most important discoveries in the field in the recent past (1990.61). Through Philippe's generous attitude toward the department, the acquisition of works of Islamic art has been greatly facilitated by the utilization of general Museum funds: the Rogers Fund, Harris Brisbane Dick Fund, Joseph Pulitzer Bequest, Pfeiffer Fund, Louis V. Bell Fund, and in several instances the very important Louis E. and Theresa S. Seley Purchase Fund for Islamic Art as well as the Lila Acheson Wallace Gift (fig. 119).

In 2005 the focus of departmental effort switched dramatically to planning for the reopening of the Islamic Galleries in 2011. Therefore, rather than naming a curator in charge, Philippe brought in a consultative chairman, Michael Barry, who applied his extensive knowledge of the Arab, Persian, and Central Asian worlds to developing a historical and cultural approach for planning the new galleries. During Barry's three-year tenure, his multifaceted perspective helped curators, designers, architects, project managers, and of course the director move conclusively forward with one of the most important long-term projects the field of Islamic art has seen in the past decades.

Ultimately it is thanks to Philippe's encyclopedic approach to improving the collections and educating the public through temporary exhibitions that the Department of Islamic Art has grown steadily in depth, numbers, quality, and especially visibility in the past thirty years. Although much smaller than many other curatorial departments, it has its permanent place in the constellation of worldwide art history that is The Metropolitan Museum of Art, exactly as the academic discipline of Islamic art history has come of age and has gained its status as a proper scholarly field of studies in the past two or three decades. As a good art historian and a museum man, Philippe was fully aware of these developments. Not surprisingly, he quietly collected Islamic art himself during his tenure. Over the years he and Edith donated several works to the department, including the Iznik plate that was featured in the recent exhibition in his honor (fig. 125) and, in one of his final acts of generosity as director, an early sixteenth-century Qur'an page from India that—appropriately making it all come full circle—he had acquired following the advice of Richard Ettinghausen in the late 1970s (2008.336).

Thus—speaking for the Department of Islamic Art—Philippe was indeed a patron of merits, honored the proficient, did not deter the citizens from improving their possessions, entertained people with spectacles, and often associated with the (Islamic art) guild. And while he did so "always maintaining the majesty of his rank," perhaps my quotation from *Il Principe* and the lighthearted game I played around it will make him smile after all.

Stefano Carboni

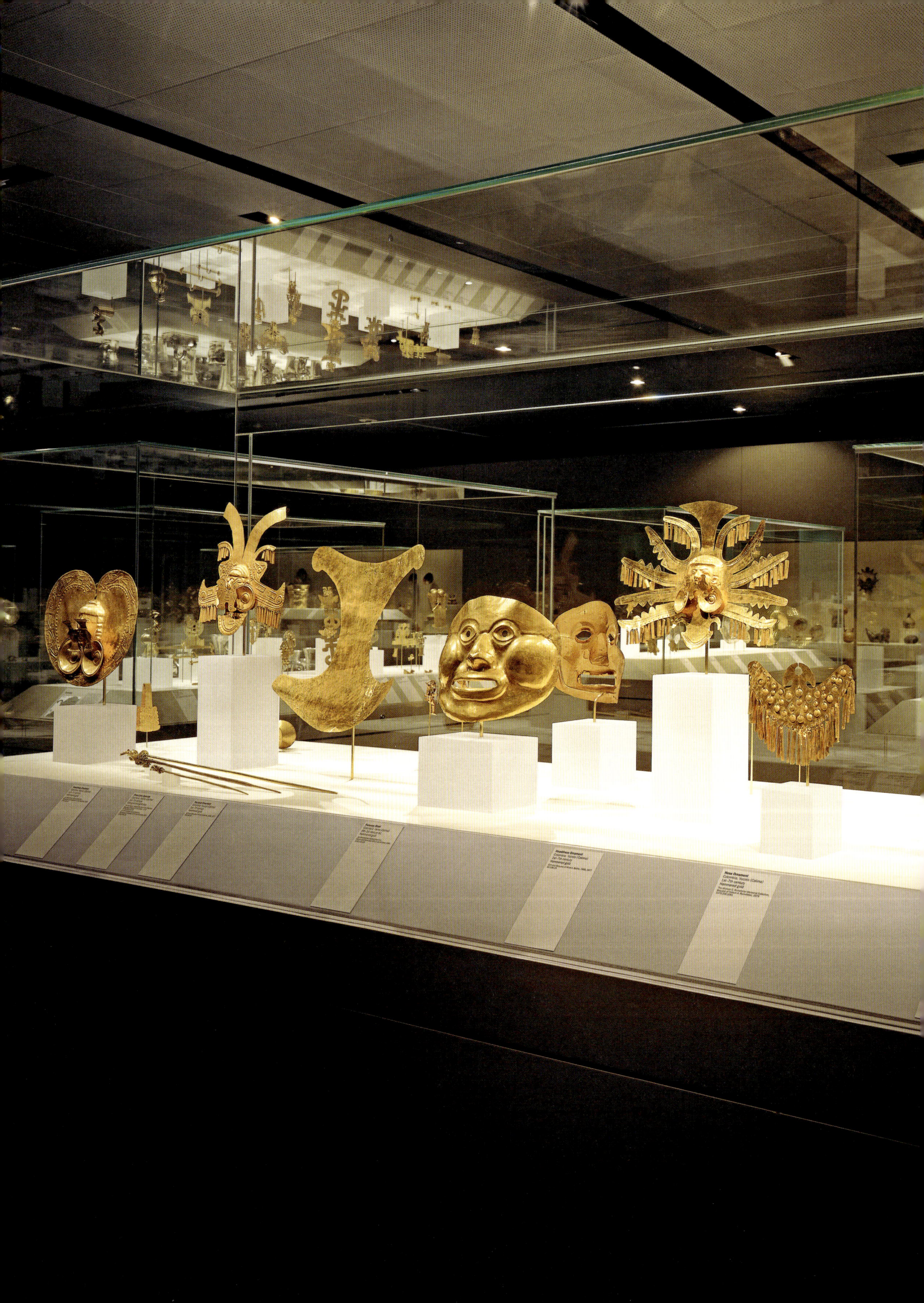

AFRICA, OCEANIA, AND THE AMERICAS

THE JAN MITCHELL TREASURY OF PRECOLUMBIAN GOLD

When The Jan Mitchell Treasury for Precolumbian works of art in gold opened to the public in 1993, it held some 250 objects from the ancient Americas (fig. 126). They had been coming to the Museum since the 1880s, but the pace of acquisition picked up considerably in the twentieth century, particularly in the 1950s and 1960s. At that time major New York collectors, supporters of the Metropolitan, were active in the field, among them Jan Mitchell, Alice Bache, and Nelson Rockefeller. Jan Mitchell's collection was first exhibited at the Metropolitan in 1985 in the special exhibition "The Art of Precolumbian Gold: The Jan Mitchell Collection," and six years later many of the works that had been in the show were given to the Museum.

To exhibit the large number of new acquisitions as their quality deserved and integrate them with those already on display, additional viewing space was needed. We decided that the existing installation of Precolumbian gold objects in the permanent South American Galleries of The Michael C. Rockefeller Wing had to be completely rethought. The shadow boxes were replaced with newly designed standing cases that allowed their contents to be seen from all four sides, not only providing greater visibility for exhibited works but also making it possible for more objects to be placed in each case. The now-expanded collection was installed in the new Treasury, which had been underwritten by Jan Mitchell and named in his honor. At the May 1993 inauguration Mr. Mitchell, after expressing delight that his collection was now in the Metropolitan, which he considered the best museum in the world, voiced the hope that "many, many thousands of people" would view these rare and rich objects and be as thrilled by their unique beauty as he had been for thirty years. As Philippe then observed, the Jan Mitchell gift solidified the Metropolitan's preeminence in this area.

The Mitchell Treasury holds the most representative exhibit of Precolumbian gold to be found in the Americas. Its contents come from all the goldworking regions in ancient America, from Peru in the south to Mexico in the north; they date from the last centuries of the first millennium B.C. to the fifteenth century A.D. and the coming of the Spaniards. Over those many centuries and across that great geographic expanse, gold was worked in a variety of techniques and in distinct styles. Its primary but not exclusive use was for personal ornament. There were embellishments for the head—diadems and crowns, headdress frontals and crest extensions; and for the chest—necklaces and pendants; and decorations for the ears and nose as well. The privilege of wearing precious metals was reserved for persons of high status, power, and wealth, or for the gods they revered. Objects of gold were worn at religious rituals and private ceremonies, in warfare and in death. They were declarative and protective.

The works in the Treasury are organized by region and period, following a timeline based on current archaeological information. Peru, where handsome gold ornaments were first placed in burials in the first millennium B.C., was home to the earliest goldsmiths. Also on the west coast but farther north, the metalsmiths of Colombia soon began a similar production. Ecuador, between Peru and Colombia, had meaningful relationships with both. The knowledge of goldworking spread as both metalworking techniques and the objects themselves crossed the isthmus from northern Colombia to Panama and Costa Rica, then continued northward. Eventually gold objects were fabricated in Mexico for the first time, some fifteen hundred years after their origination in Peru.

Within the overall picture they present of ancient American goldwork, the Treasury holdings have particular strengths. One is the gathering of works from Colombia's Calima area, where some pieces were designed with compelling simplicity while others display complex imagery. A sheet-gold funerary mask with apple-round cheeks (at the center in fig. 126), which was made shortly before the time of Christ, exemplifies the straightforward depiction of humans characteristic of hammered-gold Colombian objects of the period. Also of sheet gold are headdress ornaments with a multiplicity of elements, including elegant side extenders and danglers; they too feature a human face, but one entirely hidden

Opposite: 126. The Jan Mitchell Treasury, inaugurated in 1993. Calima works in gold from Colombia, 2nd century B.C.–A.D. 7th century, in foreground

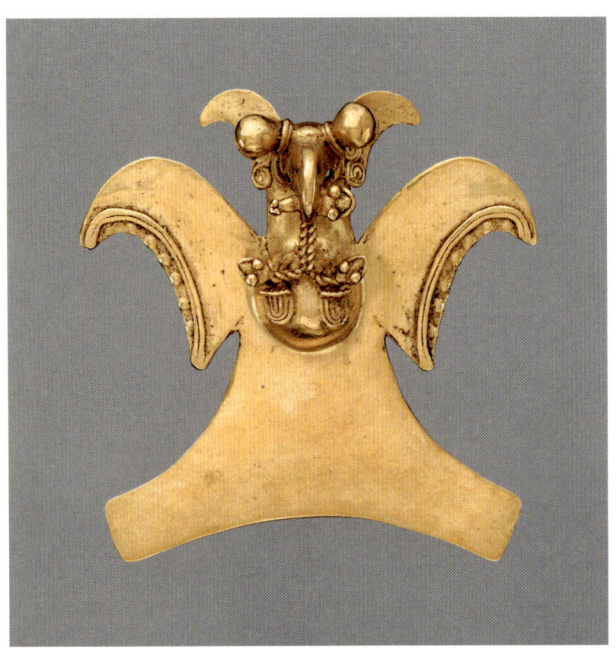

127. Eagle pendant. Costa Rica, Chiriqui, 11th–16th century. Gold, 4⅜ × 4⁷⁄₁₆ in. (11.1 × 11.2 cm). Bequest of Alice K. Bache, 1977 (1977.187.22)

Right: 128. Standing figure. Colombia/Ecuador, Tumaco/Tolita, 1st century B.C.–A.D. 1st century. Gold, H. 9 in. (22.9 cm). Jan Mitchell and Sons Collection, Gift of Jan Mitchell, 1995 (1995.427)

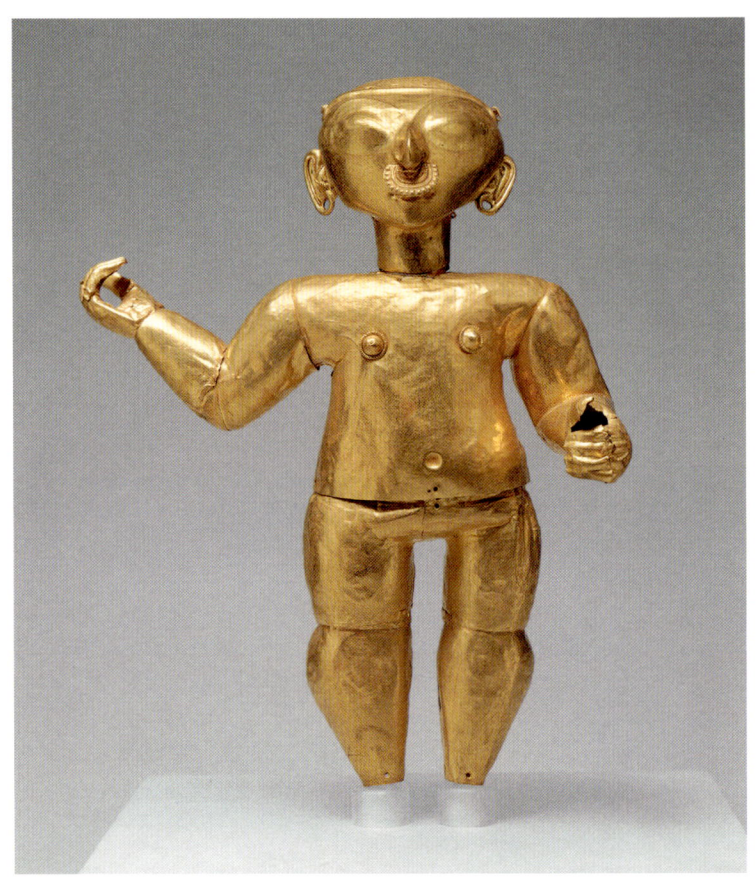

by elaboration. They were made several hundred years later than the mask, at a time period when gold was also being cast.

A noteworthy group of Peruvian gold works in the Treasury, among them the largest pieces on view, are known as Lambayeque after the northern coastal valley in which they were discovered. They date from the tenth and eleventh centuries, when royalty in the region lived well and died grandly, taking their gold objects with them. Large golden burial masks, crowns, impressive beakers, and inlaid ritual knives were all among the astonishingly rich mortuary offerings.

Isthmian gold eagles are yet another strength of the Treasury (fig. 127). These bird-form pendants were first called eagles by Christopher Columbus himself, who observed them being worn by inhabitants of Costa Rica when he sailed down its coast in the early sixteenth century. Like all Precolumbian cast-gold objects, they were manufactured by the lost-wax process. Made in a variety of sizes, the eagles were suspended from a cord around the wearer's neck. While in Precolumbian times ornaments were cast in countless shapes, the eagle was very frequently the design chosen for pendants.

One especially significant object, which Jan Mitchell added to the Treasury after it opened to the public, is a hollow, three-dimensional figure made of sheet gold (fig. 128) that dates to about the time of Christ. With elegant features and worked in extremely thin gold, it is a striking technical achievement. The figure's personal appeal is great: its elongated head has a small chin, large eyes, and wide cheekbones that impart the remote expression appropriate to an individual of high status, which it was surely meant to represent. The intricate nose ornament is still in place, although the ear ornaments are missing, as are the figure's cap, clothes, and staffs, all of which would have proclaimed their wearer's position in society. The sense of importance and self-possession remains.

Jan Mitchell's association with the Metropolitan Museum was strengthened by his admiration for Philippe de Montebello. The Mitchell collection was first exhibited in the Museum in the mid-1980s, when the de Montebello years were moving into full swing; the gift of this important collection came when Philippe's directorship was very well established. The Jan Mitchell Treasury for Precolumbian works of art in gold is the visible evidence of a mutual respect.

Julie Jones

TOWARD A FULLER APPRECIATION OF AFRICAN ART

African art at the Metropolitan has undergone a significant metamorphosis since the incorporation of Nelson A. Rockefeller's collection from the Museum of Primitive Art in 1978 and its installation here as The Michael C. Rockefeller Memorial Collection. The finest private assemblage of African art of its time, the collection has expanded here in ways that reflect the Museum's mandate as an encyclopedic institution. Important additions have enhanced already-existing areas of strength, and many gaps have been filled, enabling the scope of Africa's artistic heritage to be far more fully represented.

Nelson Rockefeller's collection had been composed of works available on the art market in the 1950s and 1960s. Its signature pieces, acquired with the advice of his curator, Robert Goldwater, were principally from Mali, Ivory Coast, the Kingdom of Benin in Nigeria, and Gabon—then regarded as the principal sources of classical African art. Emphasis had been placed on refining the collection by focusing on single outstanding examples of key genres. This differed substantially from the Metropolitan's general practice of collecting an array of works from a given cultural milieu, making it possible to compare distinctive artistic approaches of contemporary individuals within their shared tradition.

In the Rockefeller holdings, Mali's exceptional sculptural legacy was especially impressively represented, a key example being a Dogon lifesize standing male figure with arms raised in a gesture of prayer (1978.412.322). Additional Dogon works given to the Metropolitan by Lester Wunderman between 1977 and 1987 provide a superb context, situating the heroic, volumetric figure among a cast of other characters rendered on a more intimate scale for family altars. Notable among these is the angular *Primordial Couple* (1977.394.15), a linear, bilaterally symmetrical twosome articulated by a number of details that underscore both the distinctions and the parallels between its male and female halves.

In Mali's arid climate wood is very well preserved, and analysis indicates that many of our Dogon sculptures may date as early as the sixteenth century. In 1981 the historical scope of the Museum's collection was extended back to the early thirteenth century by the acquisition of a Dogon terracotta figure (1981.218) identified with the precolonial urban center of Djenne-Djeno in Mali's Inland Niger Delta, southwest of the Bandiagara Escarpment. Like the later, neighboring tradition of Dogon devotional wood sculpture, such Djenne creations appear to have been conceived for placement on domestic altars to embody prayers for ancestral protection and sustenance. Shaped from malleable clay, this work is both fluid and compressed in form. The figure bends forward, its back curving extravagantly over crossed legs—a folded posture that conveys intense introspection and vulnerability.

Among the masterpieces collected by Nelson Rockefeller were works made in the sixteenth century for the Court of Benin in present-day Nigeria by artists belonging to the royal guilds of brass casters and ivory carvers. They include an ivory pendant

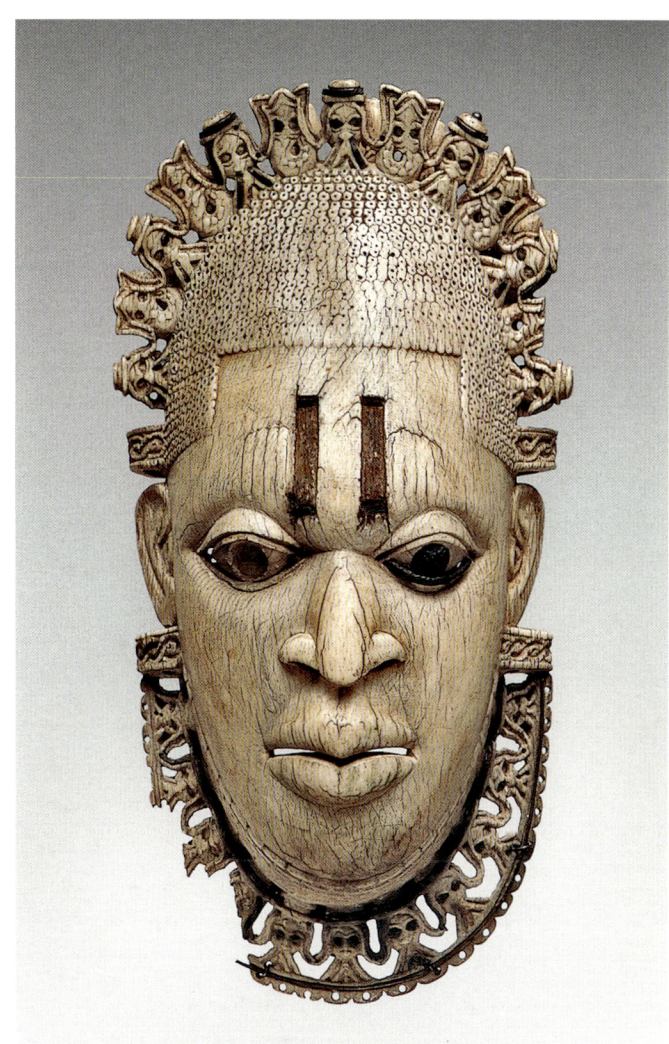

129. Pendant mask (Iyoba). Nigeria; Edo peoples, Court of Benin, 16th century. Ivory, iron, copper(?), 9⅜ × 5 × 3¼ in. (23.8 × 12.7 × 8.3 cm). The Michael C. Rockefeller Memorial Collection, Gift of Nelson A. Rockefeller, 1972 (1978.412.323)

[115]

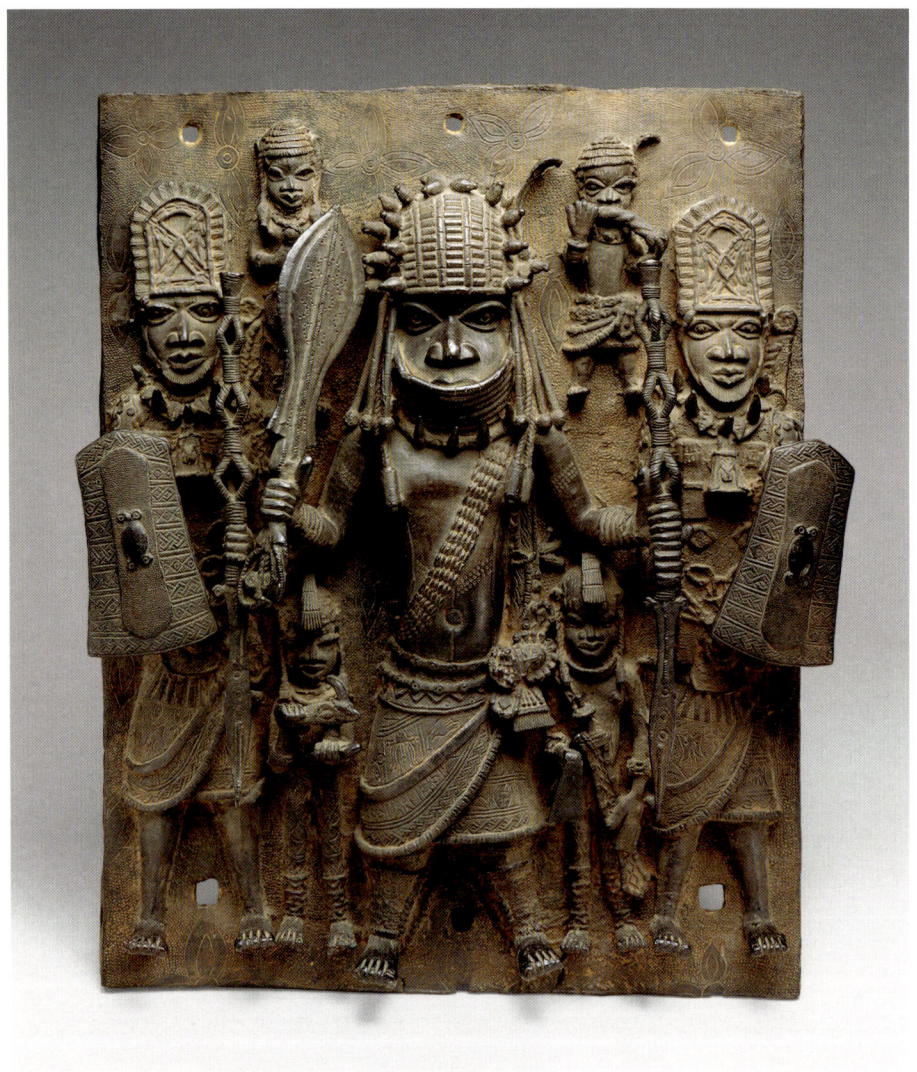
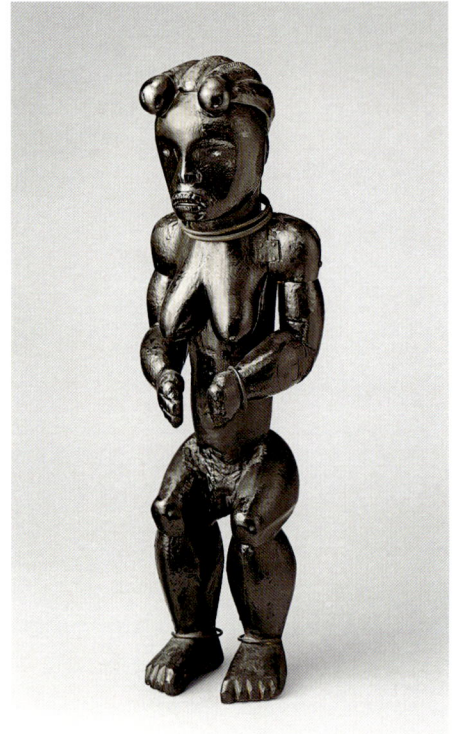

130. Female figure from a reliquary ensemble. Gabon or Equatorial Guinea; Fang peoples, Okak group, 19th–20th century. Wood and metal, 25 3/16 × 7 7/8 × 6 1/2 in. (64 × 20 × 16.5 cm). The Michael C. Rockefeller Memorial Collection, Gift of Nelson A. Rockefeller, 1965 (1978.412.441)

Left: 131. Plaque with warrior and attendants. Nigeria; Edo peoples, Court of Benin, 16th–17th century. Brass, H. 18 3/4 in. (47.6 cm). Gift of Mr. and Mrs. Klaus G. Perls, 1990 (1990.332)

mask, thought to portray queen mother Idia (fig. 129), a commemorative head for the altar of an oba, or king (1979.206.86), and a brass plaque depicting an oba seated on a horse and flanked by attendants and warriors (1978.412.309). In 1991 Mr. and Mrs. Klaus G. Perls's gift of over one hundred works created in the Kingdom of Benin between the fifteenth and twentieth centuries enriched the Museum's holdings with an array of precious regalia worn by the oba and his courtiers and also works by later generations of artists that reflect significant stylistic changes introduced over time. Especially notable was the addition of eighteen plaques depicting emblems of divine kingship and many personages at the court (fig. 131), including the Portuguese merchants who served as the court's earliest European trading partners (1991.17.18).

At Benin it was customary for each oba to commission a commemorative head that was placed on a royal altar at the time of his ascension to the throne, in honor of his predecessor. These idealized depictions present their subjects at the prime of youthful adulthood and with the trappings of leadership. Analysis of the six altar heads now in the collection suggests that as metals gradually became more available through trade, greater quantities were used in the casting process. The sixteenth-century Rockefeller head is highly naturalistic and makes sparing use of its precious material, while four works from the Perls collection created in this tradition in the eighteenth and nineteenth centuries show progressively heavier casting and a gradual deemphasis of the physiognomy in favor of increasingly elaborate trappings of leadership, such as complex crowns and tall beaded collars.

Chief among Rockefeller's works from central Africa are two masterpieces of Fang sculpture, a freestanding head (1979.206.229)

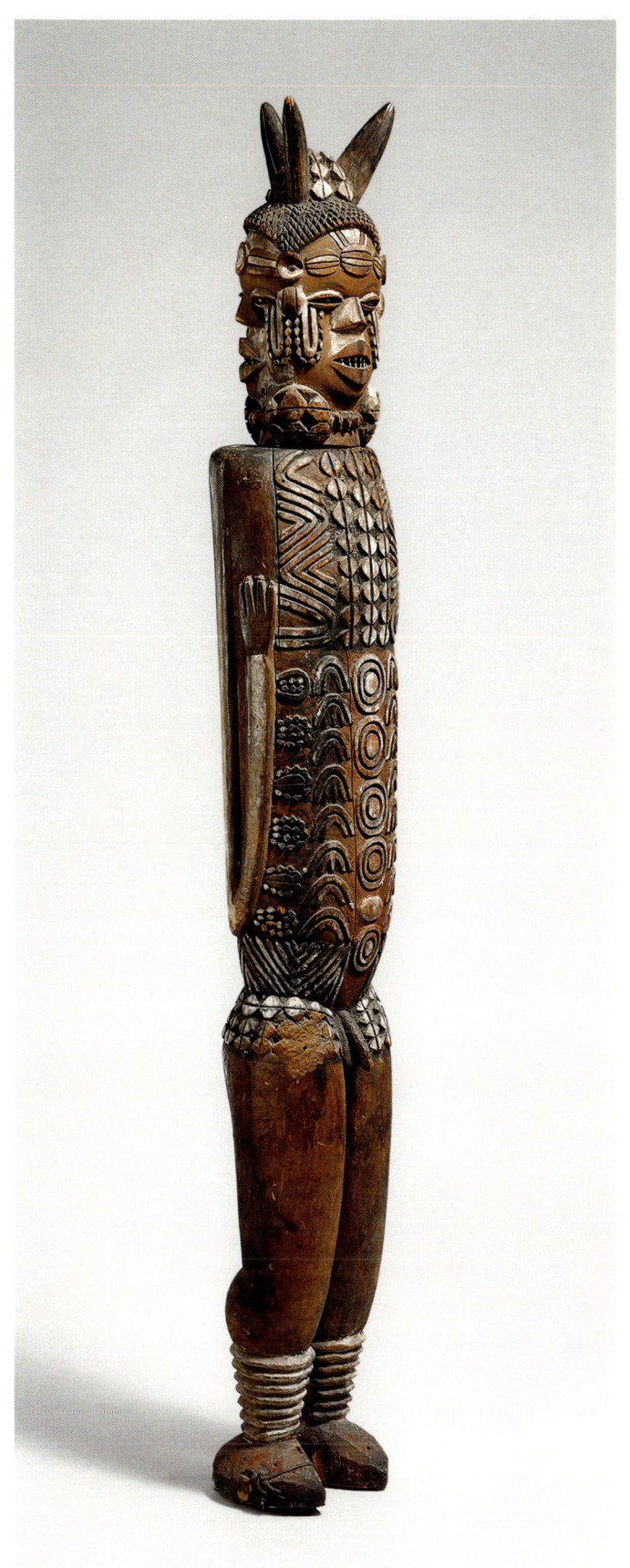

and a female figure (fig. 130), acquired, with Goldwater's skillful negotiation, from the estate of the sculptor Sir Jacob Epstein. Created, probably in Gabon during the nineteenth century, to amplify the power of receptacles for sacred relics, these schematic, dynamic evocations of founding ancestors inspired Western Modernist artists. Indeed, Rockefeller had developed his collection partly to celebrate art that played this role. The Museum's collection lacked works of comparable importance from elsewhere in central Africa, however, until the most recent acquisition of two exceptional sculptures. The first is a large three-headed Kuyu figure (fig. 132) from the Republic of Congo acquired from the Pierre Verité collection in Paris, its surface characteristically carved with abstract graphic designs and enlivened by brilliant polychromy. The second—the single most important addition to this collection in the last three decades—is the N'kondi power figure from the Democratic Republic of the Congo (2008.30). Electrifying and majestic, it personifies an all-powerful force of jurisprudence that presides over the resolution of disputes and the ratification of agreements, and embodies the highest level of a Kongo community's legal system. Its menacing and confrontational demeanor was intended to deter those who might overstep established codes of social conduct. Every element of a bristling forest of fearsome hardware was individually added by a ritual specialist as he invoked the power residing within to bear witness to the dissipation of multiple conflicts—through the ratification of treaties or the dissolution of familial contracts—under the figure's penetrating and omniscient gaze.

While collectors such as Nelson Rockefeller were guided by the once-pervasive notion that African art consists of wood sculptures produced in isolation from outside influences, the Museum's approach today includes attention to the ways Africa's arts have reflected its engagement with the world at large. A striking example is the embrace of Christianity by ancient Ethiopia's leadership in the fourth century, which bore artistic fruit in devotional works painted on parchment and wood panels, and carved or cast processional crosses, from northern Ethiopia. The centerpiece of the Museum's collection in this area is a fifteenth-century illuminated Gospel (1998.66) with twenty-four full-page

132. Three-headed figure. Republic of Congo; Kuyu peoples, 19th–early 20th century. Wood and pigment, H. 53¾ in. (136.5 cm). Purchase, Funds from various donors, Daniel and Marian Malcolm Gift, and Laura and James J. Ross Gift, 2006 (2006.447)

paintings, in two distinct hands, presenting scenes from the life of Christ and portraits of the evangelists. Lavish manuscripts such as this were commissioned from monastic scriptoria and given to churches by abbots, nobles, or emperors as acts of devotion. While drawing primarily on Byzantine models, the artists also departed from them decisively to develop their own distinctive idiom characterized by bold colors and flat, abstract design.

Finally, yet another important dimension was added to our collection with the acquisition of the Madagascar Couple (fig. 133) of the late eighteenth century or earlier. From the island of Madagascar off the coast of East Africa, it reflects a blend of African and Pacific Island influences and constitutes an eloquent bridge between the African and Oceanic galleries. In this work of quiet power and lyrically balanced symmetry a man and woman are represented standing side by side, gazing intently at the viewer. This couple and a closely related one by the same artist, now in the Louvre, were the crowning elements of a pair of ritual wood posts that stood facing each other at the center of a Malagasy community. The Metropolitan's example became widely known in Parisian avant-garde circles by the early twentieth century and was one of the rare works from its tradition to influence Western artistic development. Acquired, like the Fang sculptures, by Jacob Epstein, it was recognized as an artistic landmark by Robert Goldwater, but Rockefeller let it pass and ultimately it entered the Carlo Monzino collection in Milan in 1961. Its acquisition exactly forty years later by the Metropolitan was a major contribution to the growth of the collection, which now, in extent and in caliber, exceeds even Rockefeller's ambitions.

Alisa LaGamma

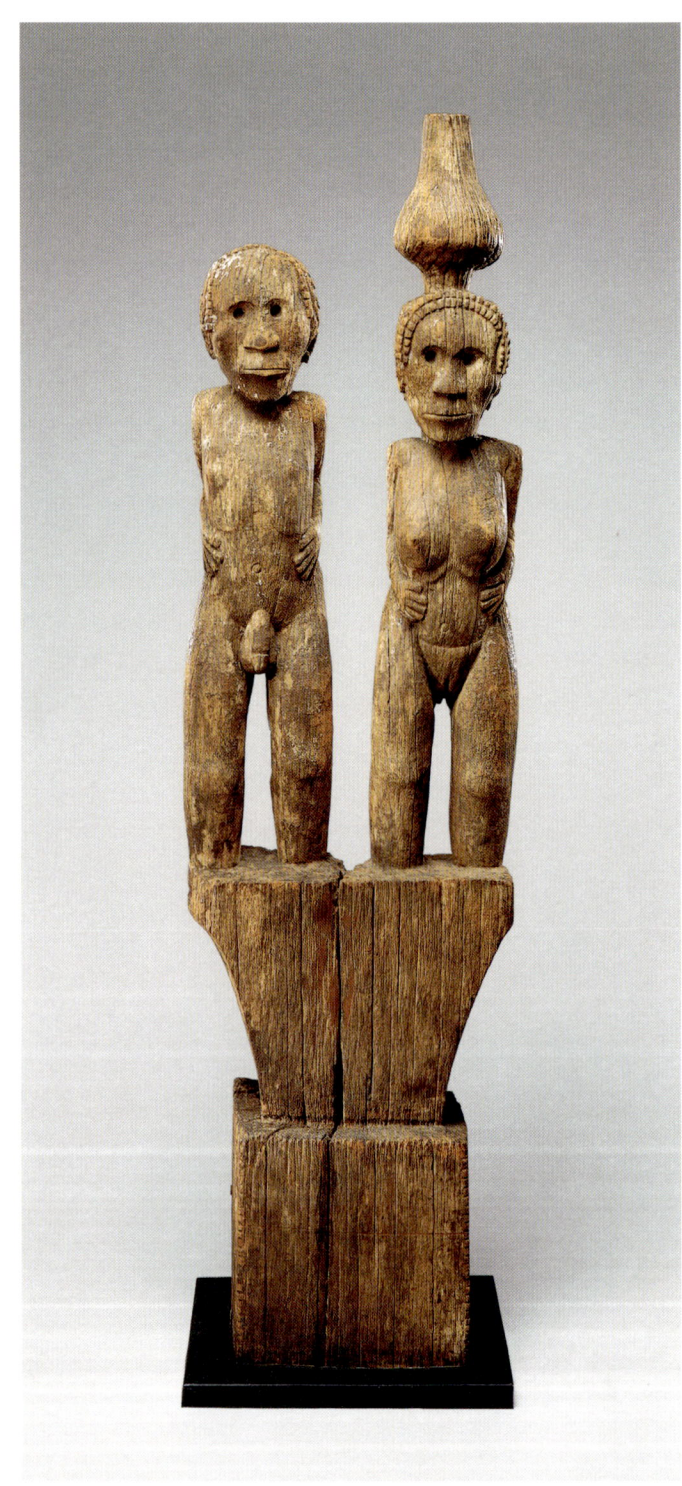

133. Couple. Madagascar, Menabe region; Sakalava peoples, 17th–late 18th century. Wood and pigment, H. 39 in. (99.1 cm). Purchase, Lila Acheson Wallace, Daniel and Marian Malcolm, and James J. Ross Gifts, 2001 (2001.408)

OCEANIC ART

In both scope and presentation, the Metropolitan's Oceanic collection was enormously enhanced under the directorship of Philippe de Montebello. Two central events marked those years: the establishment of a collection of works representing the extremely important indigenous artistic traditions of Island Southeast Asia, and the redesign and reinstallation of the permanent galleries for Oceanic Art.

The indigenous arts of Island Southeast Asia had not been represented among the Museum's Oceanic holdings until, in 1987 and 1988, Fred and Rita Richman donated the greater part of their extensive collection of sculpture and decorative arts from the region. Since then the Richmans have continued their generosity to the department both through additional donations of art and by supporting the purchase of works from Oceania (fig. 134). In 1990 the burgeoning Island Southeast Asian collection was further enhanced by a spectacular group of textiles and other works given by Anita E. Spertus and Robert J. Holmgren in honor of Douglas Newton, then Evelyn A. J. Hall and John A. Friede Chairman of Primitive Art. There followed, in 1999 and 2000, John B. Elliott's bequest of a large collection of textiles and decorative arts from Island Southeast Asia and other regions.

The de Montebello years saw as well the continuing enrichment of the department's holdings from many parts of Oceania. Gifts include highly important groups of Melanesian and Polynesian works presented by Evelyn A. J. Hall in 1981 and 1986 and works of art from the Papuan Gulf region of New Guinea given jointly in 1983 by Evelyn A. J. Hall and John A. Friede. In 1984 one of the Metropolitan's signature works of Polynesian sculpture, an exquisite male figure from Rapa Nui (Easter Island), was donated by Faith-dorian and Martin Wright, longtime supporters of the department (fig. 136). In 2002 came the gift of an important work of Micronesian sculpture from the Wright family in memory of Douglas Newton (2003.243).

Philippe's dedication to the best possible display of the permanent collections was elegantly embodied in the completely redesigned galleries for Oceanic Art, which opened in 2007. The goal of the new installation was twofold: to ensure, with reconceived gallery layout, casework, and lighting, that the works in the Oceanic collection are seen to their best advantage; and to allow the display of a substantially larger proportion of the collection than had previously been on view. The installation is divided into three galleries encompassing more than four hundred works that represent all five major artistic regions of Oceania: Melanesia, Polynesia, Micronesia, Australia, and Island Southeast Asia.

The signature area is the spacious gallery for Melanesian art, dedicated to works from New Guinea, Island Melanesia (the

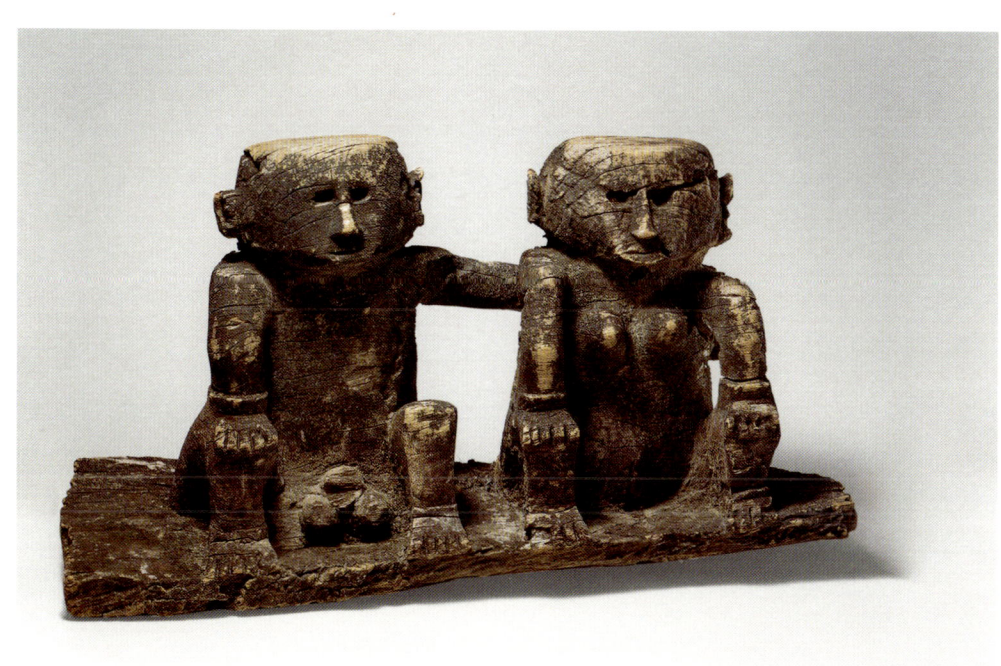

134. Ancestral couple (Ana deo). Nage people; Indonesia, Nusa Tenggara, central Flores Island, 19th–early 20th century. Wood, H. 11¾ in. (29.8 cm). Gift of Fred and Rita Richman, 2006 (2006.510)

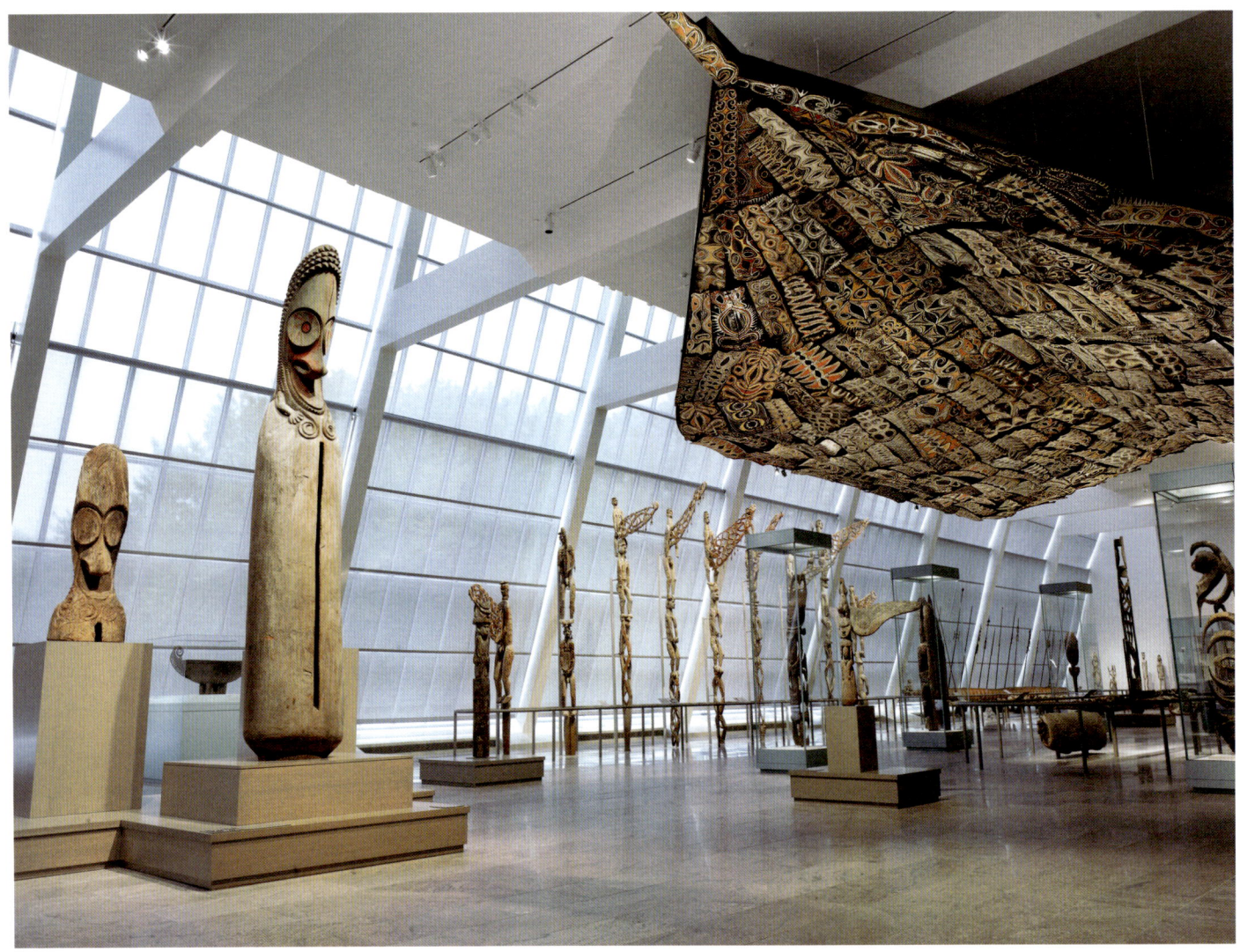

135. The newly reinstalled gallery for Melanesian art in The Michael C. Rockefeller Wing, opened in November 2007

islands of the southwest Pacific), and Australia (fig. 135). Employing an open floor plan that enables many of the major works to be seen in the round for the first time, this grand space houses objects ranging from monumental sculptures to intimately scaled personal ornaments and accessories. At the center hangs the soaring, brilliantly polychromed ceiling of a ceremonial house from the Kwoma people of New Guinea; some 80 feet long and 30 feet wide, it is composed of more than 270 individual paintings. In the previous installation, space constraints had meant that only a portion of the ceiling could be presented. Now, mounted on a specially designed armature and raised to an appropriate height, the ceiling is displayed in its entirety for the first time. It brings a cathedral-like grandeur to the new space.

The center of the Melanesian gallery is given over to a dramatic display of sculpture from the Sepik region of New Guinea, one of the great strengths of our Oceanic collection. Nearby are nine monumental ancestor poles (*bis*) from the Asmat people of New Guinea and the Museum's well-known Asmat canoe, over 48 feet long and capable of carrying up to twenty people. These and the other Asmat works in the gallery were primarily collected by Michael C. Rockefeller in 1961.

Featured in the Island Melanesia section is a rare and newly restored work: a monumental bark-cloth effigy, towering more than 15 feet, from New Britain (1978.412.1495). This otherworldly figure, which portrays a powerful female spirit, is the only one of its kind in the United States and had not been on exhibition for nearly four decades. Also returned to view in the Island Melanesian installation is our monumental slit gong from the nation of Vanuatu (1975.93). More than 14 feet tall and among the largest freestanding musical instruments on earth, the gong is carved in the form of a powerful ancestor, whose voice was heard in its resonant beats. Another section of the Melanesian gallery is devoted to the arts of Aboriginal Australia.

The adjoining gallery for Polynesian and Micronesian art is more intimate in scale and atmosphere. It showcases, with redesigned casework and lighting, sculpture and decorative arts from the islands of the central and eastern Pacific, including Hawai'i, Tahiti, and Rapa Nui. A highlight is the renowned figure from the island of Mangareva, one of the great masterworks of the Metropolitan's Oceanic collection (1979.206.1466). In the Polynesian displays are presentations of different regional traditions and also thematically arranged cases dedicated to sacred images, decorated bark cloth, and luxurious ornaments and accessories created for elite chiefs. The Micronesian section contains rare examples of the region's wood sculpture, including our well-known female figure from the nation of Belau (1978.412.1558a–d), as well as two significant recent acquisitions, a weather charm and a seated figure from the Caroline Islands (2003.243, 2003.8).

An entirely new element of the installation is the gallery designed for our collection of indigenous arts of Island Southeast Asia. The dramatically lit space contains a rich variety of works, among them sculpture, gold and silver jewelry, and textiles. Encompassing objects from Indonesia, the Philippines, Taiwan, and adjoining regions, this array spans diverse artistic traditions. The entire reinstallation represents the culmination of the project to broaden the Museum's presentation of Oceanic art, an undertaking with a lasting legacy that had Philippe's support throughout.

Eric Kjellgren

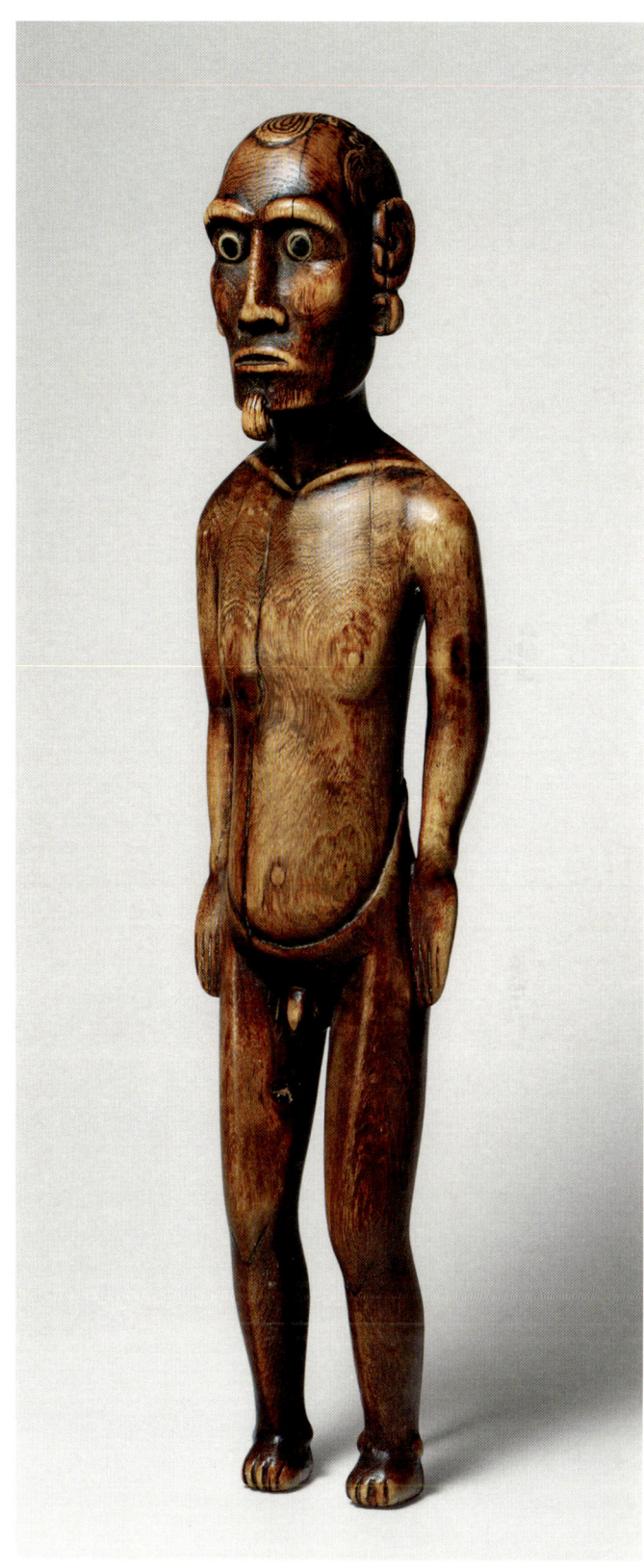

136. Male figure (Moai tangata). Rapa Nui people; Rapa Nui (Easter Island), early 19th century. Wood, obsidian, and bone, H. 16 in. (40.6 cm). Gift of Faith-dorian and Martin Wright, in honor of Livio Scamperle, 1984 (1984.526)

EXPANDING THE CANON: PHOTOGRAPHY AND THE ARTS OF AFRICA, OCEANIA, AND THE AMERICAS

Since its invention in France and England and announcement in 1839, photography has been practiced by artists, travelers, ethnologists, and scientists and researchers in many disciplines. The new medium's range of subjects thus quickly expanded. Traditional activities and works of art from diverse cultures attracted the interest of photographers, and images of this type can be found in the Photograph Study Collection of the Museum's Department of the Arts of Africa, Oceania, and the Americas.

The Photograph Study Collection was set up in 1958 at the Museum of Primitive Art in New York as a resource to aid in the understanding of traditional arts and cultures. In 1978, when the collections acquired by that landmark museum were transferred to the Metropolitan, 30,000 photographs came to us as well. During Philippe de Montebello's tenure the number grew to over 120,000. The scope of the collection has become more comprehensive and perceptions of it have been transformed through the director's guidance and his support of curatorial ideas.

Until recent years this type of collection occupied a secondary place in the connoisseurship of photography. These pictures of art, people, and cultural activities were erroneously categorized as "field" photographs made in the service of anthropology or pejoratively characterized as "documentary" or "archival," and presumed to be of little aesthetic value.

The first exhibition to make the Metropolitan's public aware of these previously hidden-away photographs was held in 1985–86 in the mezzanine gallery of the newly opened Michael C. Rockefeller Wing and titled "Frank Hurley in New Guinea." Hurley was well known for surviving a shipwreck with Ernest Shackleton in Antarctica and photographing its icy terrain. His photographic accomplishments had been investigated in a publication by scholar James Specht, which inspired the exhibition. However, Hurley's images of Papua New Guinea were not yet familiar to the public; here the beauty of this Pacific island and its traditional arts were revealed in lyrical and bold gelatin silver prints made from his glass-plate negatives at the Australian Museum, Sydney.

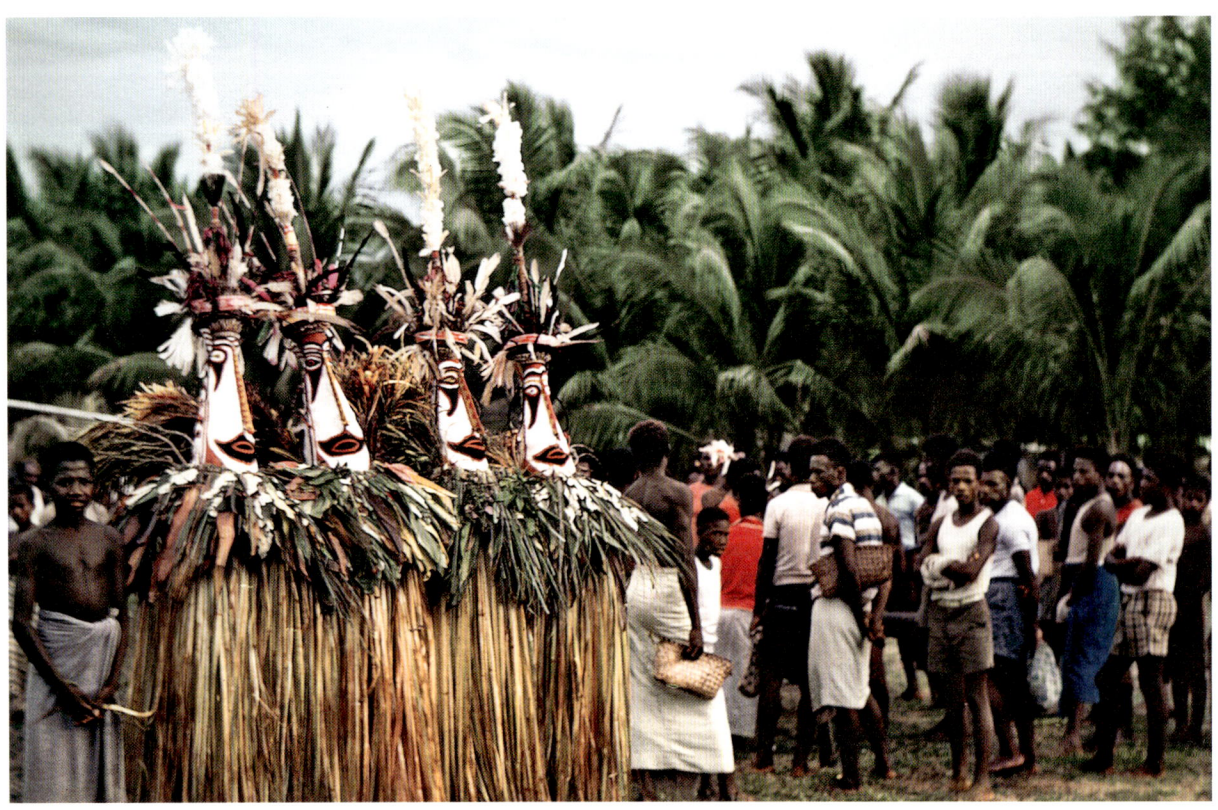

137. Philip J. C. Dark, *Nataptavo Masqueraders at Cape Gloucester, New Britain*, December 8, 1966. Chromogenic print, 6½ × 10 in. (20.3 × 25.4 cm). Promised Gift of Philip J. C. Dark and Mavis H. Dark

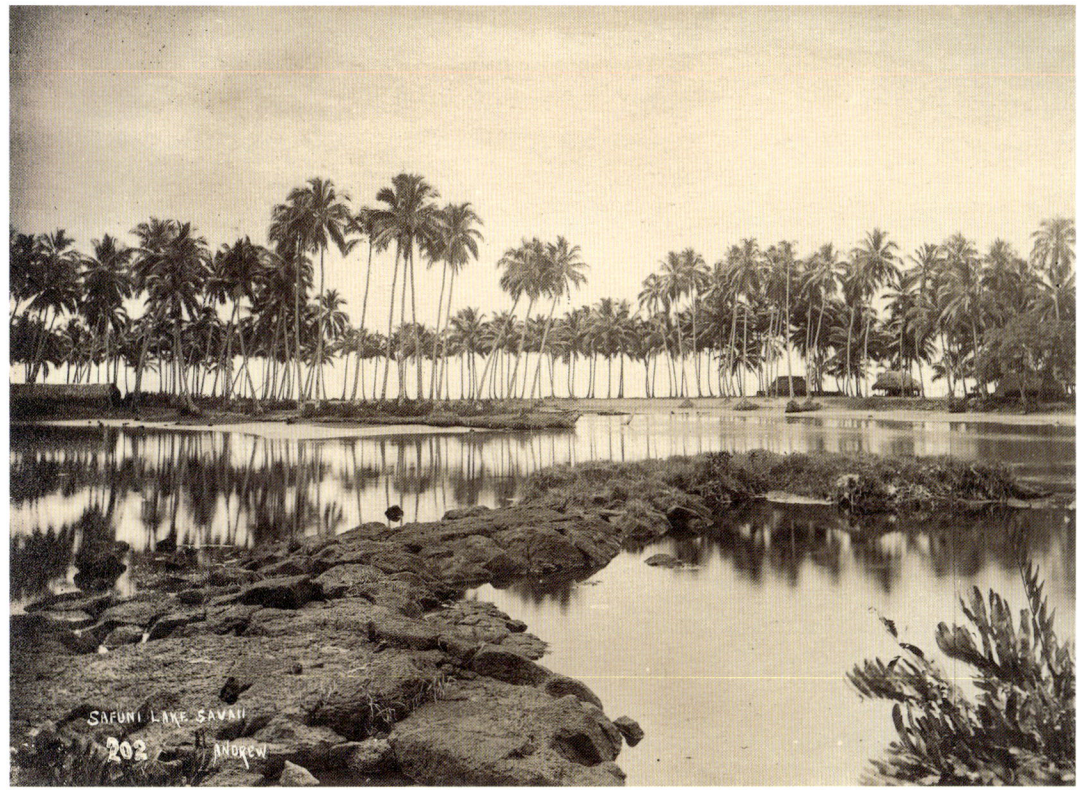

138. Thomas Andrew, *Safuni Lake, Savaii*, Samoa, 1905–6. Platinum print, 5½ × 7¾ in. (14 × 19.7 cm). The Photograph Study Collection, Department of the Arts of Africa, Oceania, and the Americas (PSC 1987.24.18)

Between 1985 and 2003, twelve exhibitions and gallery rotations from the Photograph Study Collection presented exquisite images that were often the fruits of new research on hitherto unidentified photographers. Most addressed the cultural context of the works of art pictured and the objectives of the artists who photographed them. With the director's support, these displays brought the obscure or anonymous artists to the public's attention and elucidated the contexts in which the pictures were made. Photographs by Paul Gebauer, a missionary who collected and studied art in Cameroon; Lester Wunderman's pictures of Dogon art and ceremony in Mali; and Philip Dark's images of brilliantly colored Kilenge sculptures and performances in New Britain (fig. 137) were among the exhibited works. Mythical characters depicted on ceramics by Maya painters were made clearly visible through inventive "rollout photographs" by Justin Kerr that have significantly expanded our interpretation and understanding of the art of this complex culture.

In March 1996, "Picturing Paradise: Colonial Photography of Samoa 1875–1925" opened in the changing exhibition space in the Rockefeller Wing, displaying there for the first time photographs—mostly by New Zealand, Australian, and European artists—of Samoan people, landscape, art, and architecture (fig. 138). The exhibition raised questions about taste and artistic practice, suggesting that fallacies and subjective notions were likely to accompany any colonial presentation of Pacific peoples and art. Scholarly research had made it possible for unidentified studio photographers who created copious bodies of work to be named and profiled and their careers illuminated. The subjects and contexts of the images were investigated, and it became apparent that while some portraits and depictions were sensitive and honorable, others, especially those used for tourism and commercial purposes, promoted erroneous stereotypes. A version of the exhibition was shown in Apia, the capital of Samoa, and copies of the photographs were shared with contemporary Samoan communities, giving them access to images of their ancestors and an opportunity to comment on their pictorial representation.

The question of photographs as "evidence" or "documents" was posed in an exhibition in 2000 about the renowned American photographer Walker Evans. "Perfect Documents: Walker Evans and African Art, 1935" brought to light a portfolio of

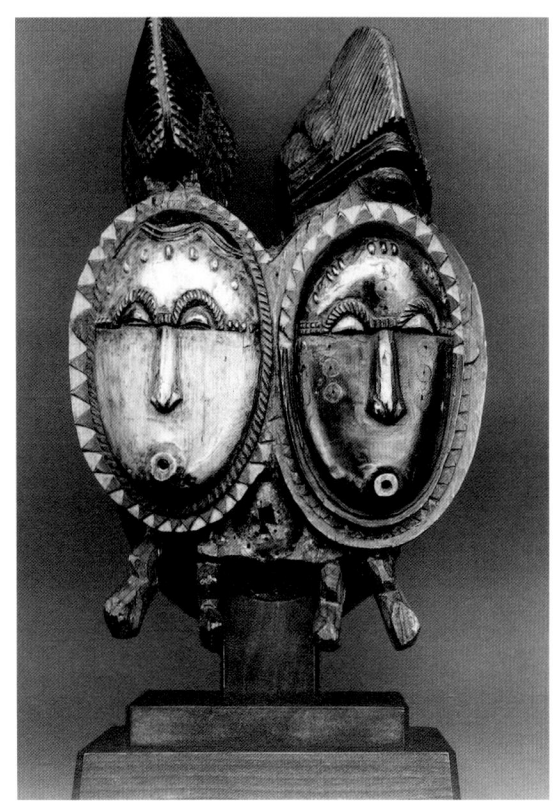

139. Walker Evans, *Double Mask*, 1935. Gelatin silver print, 8¾ × 7⅛ in. (22.2 × 18.1 cm). The Michael C. Rockefeller Memorial Collection, Gift of Robert Goldwater, 1961 and 1962 (1978.412.1961)

images in the Metropolitan's collection that had been dismissed as insignificant by art historians. It was Philippe's mandate to investigate and research the Museum's collections that had led to the discovery of an important and neglected part of Evans's career. Among the works presented were his minimalistic and eccentric photographic depictions of masterpieces of African art and a selection of the sculptures themselves that were part of a historic show at the Museum of Modern Art (several of these sculptures are now in the Metropolitan's collection). The notion of the photograph as a mere record made without creativity or point of view was challenged by Evans's singular images (fig. 139) and by exhibiting the actual sculptures next to them. These juxtapositions revealed that the photographs were highly stylized and artistically linked to the classic pictures Evans began making for the U.S. Resettlement Administration during the same period— and thus that they were equally molded by the photographer's pictorial ideas. This exhibition and its publication added much to our knowledge of the way African art has been understood, exhibited, and depicted in the United States.

"Coaxing the Spirits to Dance: The Art of the Papuan Gulf" (2006–7) presented sculpture by and photographs of the Papuan Gulf cultures to nearly 250,000 people. The exhibition asked how authentically photographs convey their subjects. Sculptures and

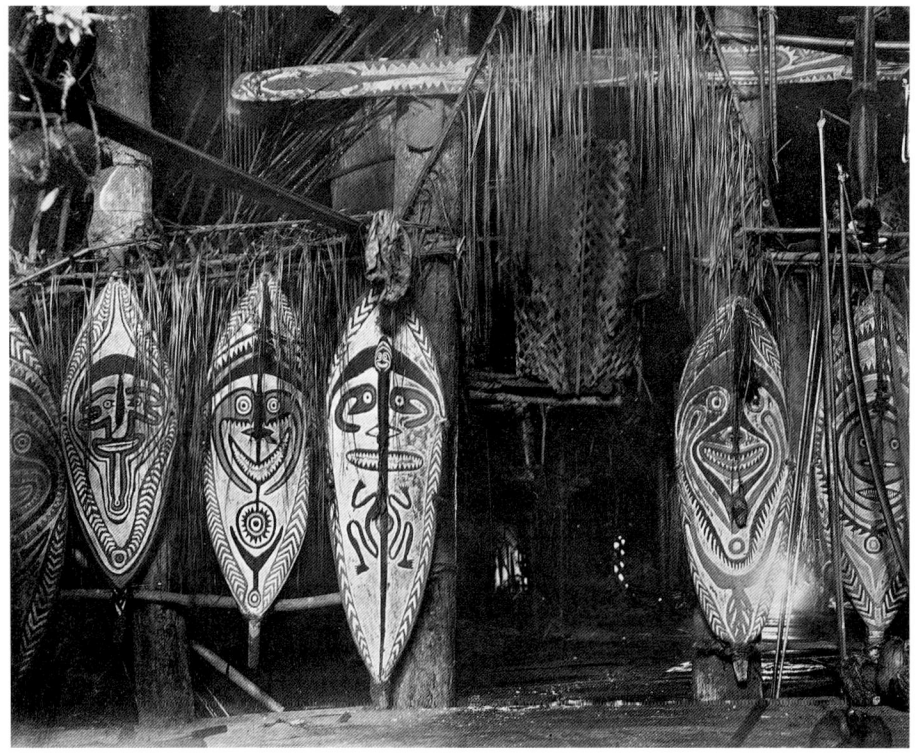

140. A. B. Lewis, *Interior of an Elema Men's House with Spirit Boards (Hohao)*, Orokolo Village, Papua New Guinea, May 1912. Gelatin silver print, 8 × 10 in. (20.3 × 25.4 cm). The Photograph Study Collection, Department of the Arts of Africa, Oceania, and the Americas (PSC 2006.41). Copyright The Field Museum, Chicago

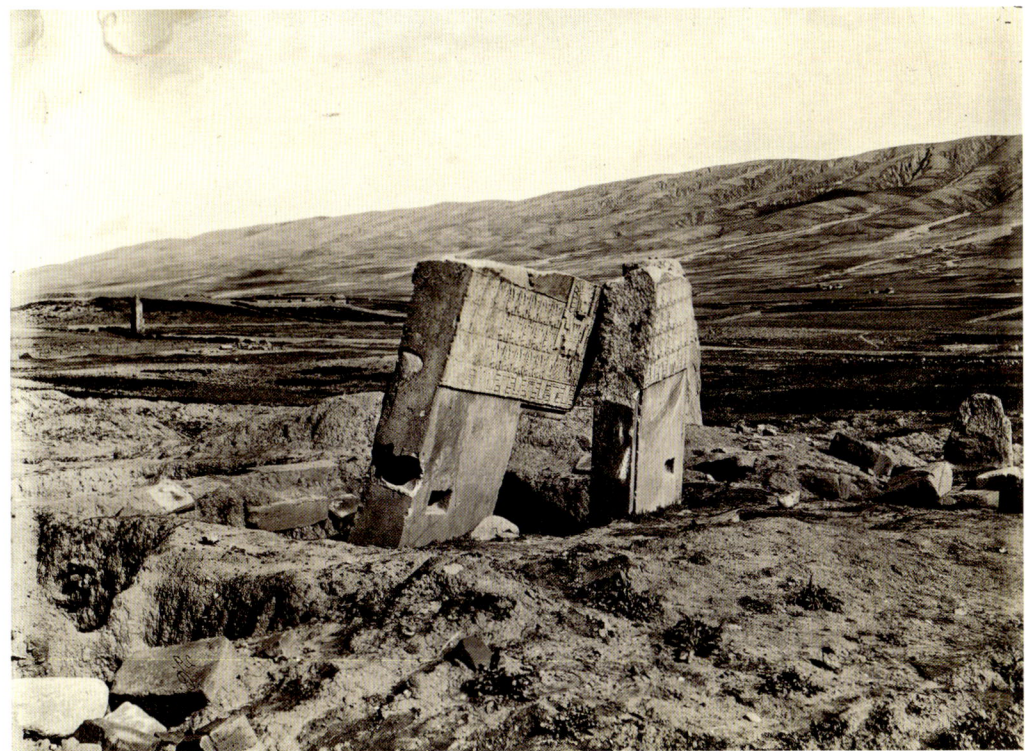

141. Arthur Posnansky, *Sun Door, Tiahuanaco*, Bolivia, 1904. Gelatin silver print, 8⅝ × 11¾ in. (21.9 × 8 cm). Purchase, Stephanie H. Bernheim Gift, 2007 (2007.395)

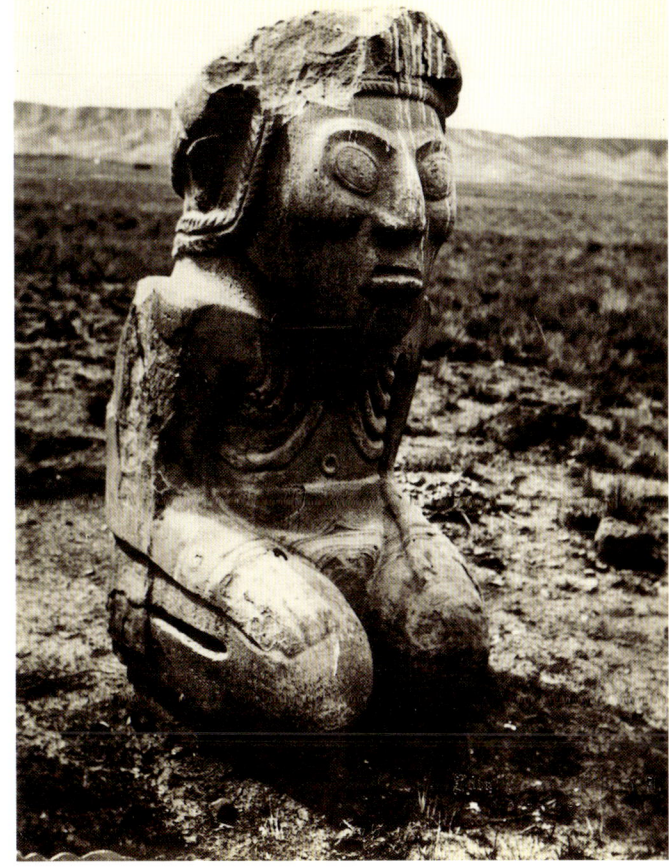

142. Martín Chambi, *Tiahuanaco*, Bolivia, ca. 1940s. Gelatin silver print, 8¾ × 6¾ in. (22.2 × 17.1 cm). Purchase, Arthur M. Bullowa Bequest, 2007 (2007.23)

photographs were displayed together, creating parallel historical narratives; the term *in situ* was rigorously examined. Ultimately, the use of photographs was seen to be a tool in the responsible investigation of provenance, allowing works of art to be tracked through images. Biographies of individuals and works of art have been assembled by examining the exquisite, now-identified photographs in which they appear (fig. 140).

Under Philippe's leadership, photographs of traditional arts and culture in Africa, Oceania, and the Americas (figs. 141, 142) have moved out of the archive and into the art-historical narrative placed before the public—broadening our knowledge, opening our eyes to talented photographic artists, and expanding the canon of art.

Virginia-Lee Webb

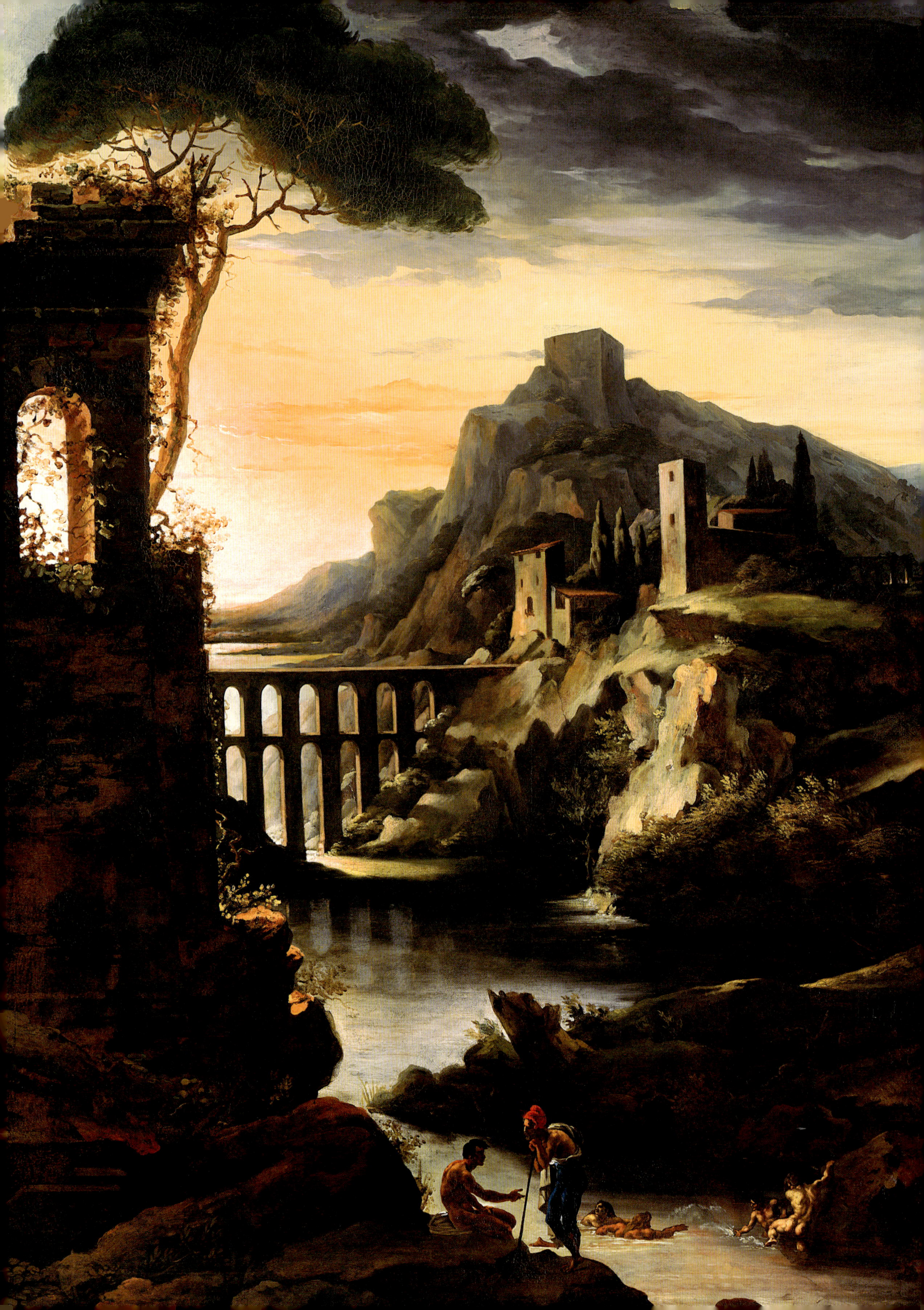

THE MODERN ERA

THE MET, MONTEBELLO, AND MODERN ART

The Department of Nineteenth-Century, Modern, and Contemporary Art did not exist when Philippe de Montebello became director of the Metropolitan Museum. Like so many of the developments that occurred during Philippe's tenure, its establishment would have been almost inconceivable then. It is a remarkable, even paradoxical fact that the director who has been most criticized for resisting the charms of contemporary art was the director most responsible for the enormous growth of our collection of nineteenth- and twentieth-century art and of the space devoted to its display. It was he who assigned the balcony of the Rockefeller Wing, which opened as the André Meyer Galleries in 1980, to the display of nineteenth-century European paintings and sculpture (arranged by John Pope-Hennessy); it was he who determined that the Lila Acheson Wallace Wing, inaugurated in 1987, would be given over to modern art; and it was he who conceived the idea of constructing, literally out of thin air, a new set of rooms for nineteenth- and early twentieth-century art, the Henry J. Heinz II Galleries, which opened in 2007 in the airspace high above the Oceanic art display. These last galleries, Philippe recognized, would help bridge the growing gap between nineteenth-century art and that of the twentieth century. The same need gave rise to the creation, in 2004, of the new department that I head.

The range of works now displayed in these commodious spaces was far less extensive in 1977. Since then, some one hundred nineteenth-century European paintings have been purchased and almost another hundred received as gifts, promised gifts, and bequests. And in modern art the growth has been truly astounding: 2,533 purchases and 5,237 gifts and bequests.

Though the New York art community has long cherished a belief that the Metropolitan Museum was always hostile to contemporary art, that myth ignores one of the primary motivations of the artists and collectors of contemporary art who founded the

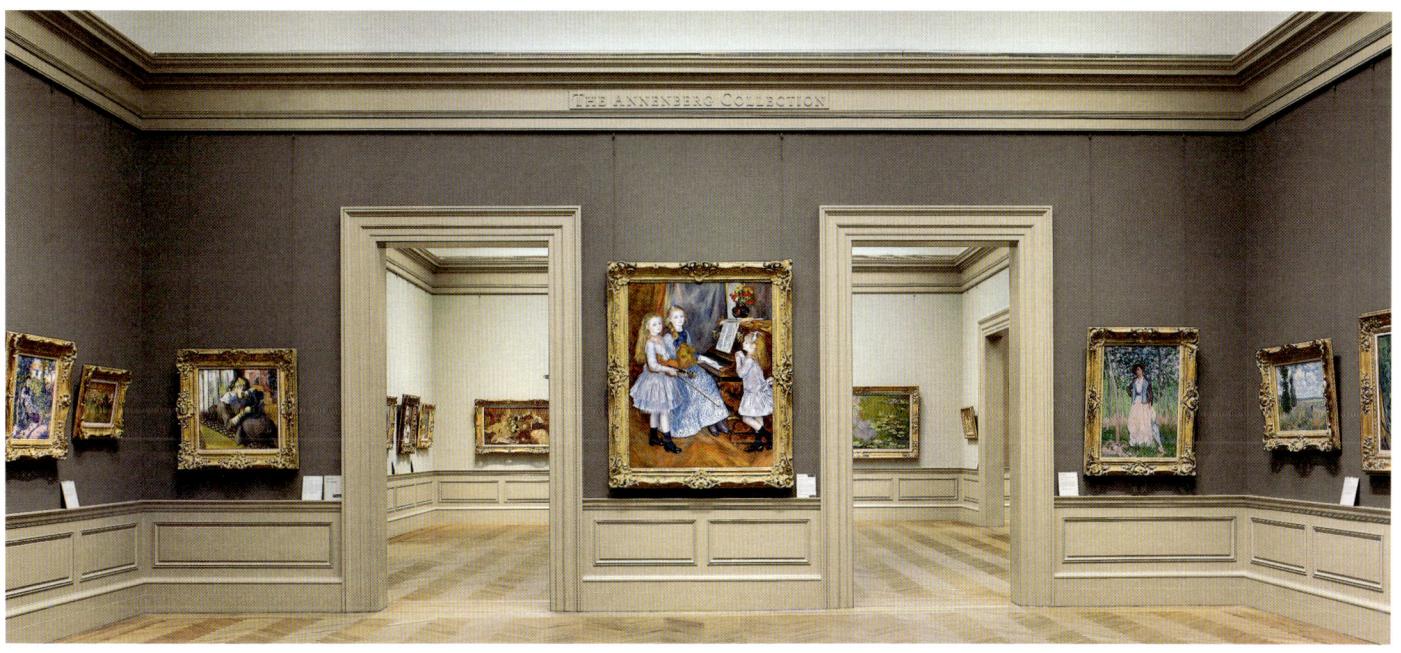

143. The Walter H. and Leonore Annenberg Collection Galleries

Opposite: 144. Théodore Gericault, *Evening: Landscape with an Aqueduct*, 1818. Oil on canvas, 98½ × 86½ in. (250.2 × 219.7 cm). Purchase, Gift of James A. Moffett 2nd, in memory of George M. Moffett, by exchange, 1989 (1989.183)

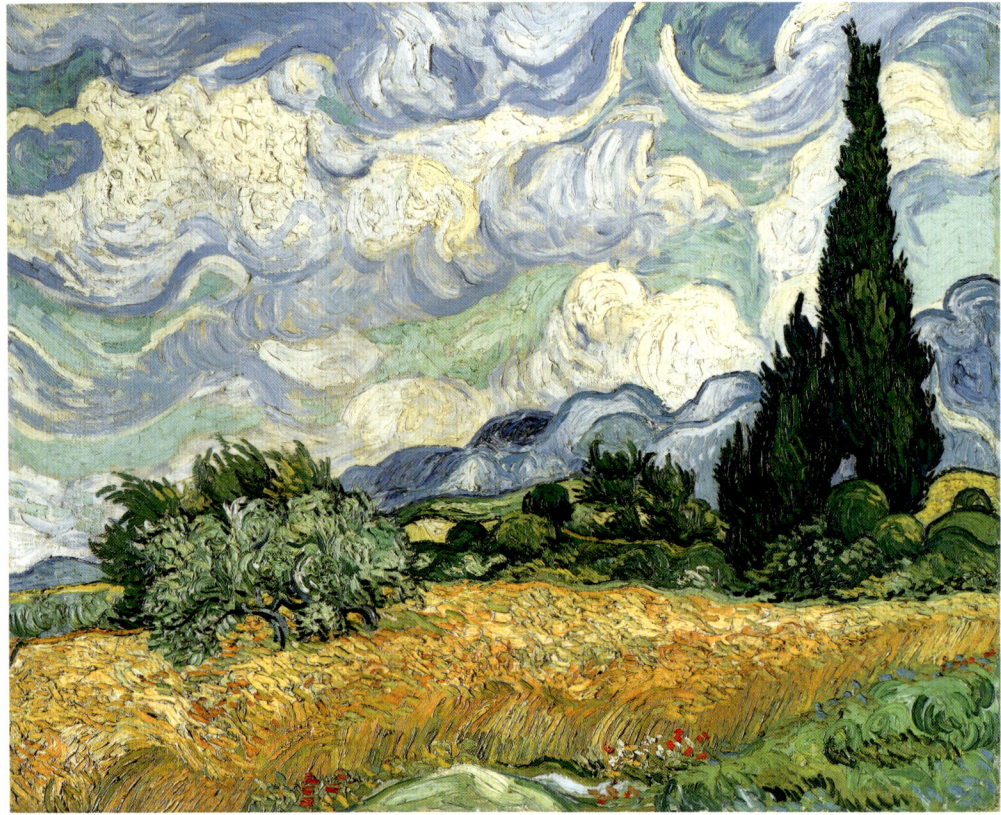

145. Vincent van Gogh, *Wheat Field with Cypresses*, 1889. Oil on canvas, 28¾ × 36¾ in. (73 × 93.4 cm). Purchase, The Annenberg Foundation Gift, 1993 (1993.132)

Museum in 1870. The inaugural exhibition in the new Central Park building in 1880 featured works by living artists both European and American; the first important gift of works of art, the Catharine Lorillard Wolfe bequest in 1887, was a group of 143 paintings by contemporary, mainly European, artists; and, excepting antiquities, the most significant purchases of the years before 1914 were paintings by Auguste Renoir and Paul Cézanne, sculptures by Auguste Rodin, and many fine works by American painters and sculptors. Although the almost instant success of the Museum of Modern Art after its founding in 1929 might have obviated the need for contemporary art at the Metropolitan, the Museum's trustees were quick to realize that their new sister institution could provide an opportunity for the eventual enrichment of the Met's collections. In 1931 the president of the Museum addressed his counterpart at the Modern: "When the so-called 'wild' creatures of today are regarded as the conservative standards of tomorrow, is it too much to hope that you will permit them to come to the Metropolitan Museum of Art, leaving space on your walls for the new creations of the new day?"

In 1947 Director Francis Henry Taylor and his trustees at the Metropolitan signed a noncompetitive, tripartite agreement with the officers of the Museum of Modern Art and the Whitney Museum of American Art. The acquisition of European and American "modern art" was assigned to MoMA and that of American contemporary art to the Whitney; the Met would purchase works from its sister institutions once they were no longer wanted. The Whitney withdrew from the pact just a year later because of disagreements over policy and disappointment that a proposed Whitney Wing at the Metropolitan was not progressing. The arrangement with MoMA lasted five years, ending in 1952 as MoMA trustees lamented their museum's sale of Picassos and Cézannes to the Met in order to purchase works by avantgarde New York painters. After the breakup with the Whitney the Met established a Department of American Paintings and Sculpture (1949), and its first curator, Robert Beverly Hale, who served until 1966, did buy works by modern American artists, including monuments such as Pollock's *Autumn Rhythm*, and organized exhibitions and even prizes for work by living artists. But since the cultural conservatism of the McCarthy era extended as far as the Museum's Board, the postwar enthusiasm for modern art palpably diminished in the ensuing years. By 1967, when Thomas Hoving created for curator Henry Geldzahler a Department of

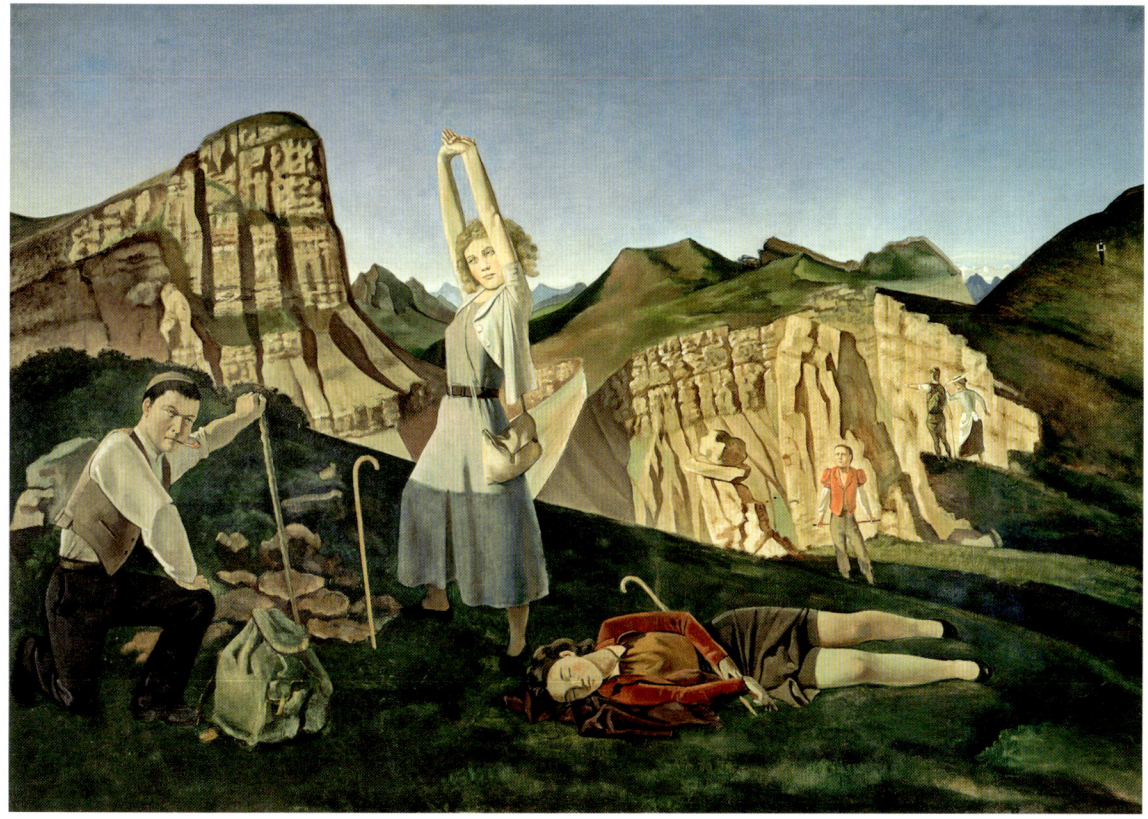

146. Balthus, *The Mountain*, 1936–37. Oil on canvas, 98 × 144 in. (248.9 × 365.8 cm). Purchase, Gifts of Mr. and Mrs. Nate B. Spingold and Nathan Cummings, Rogers Fund and The Alfred N. Punnett Endowment Fund, by exchange, and Harris Brisbane Dick Fund, 1982 (1982.530)

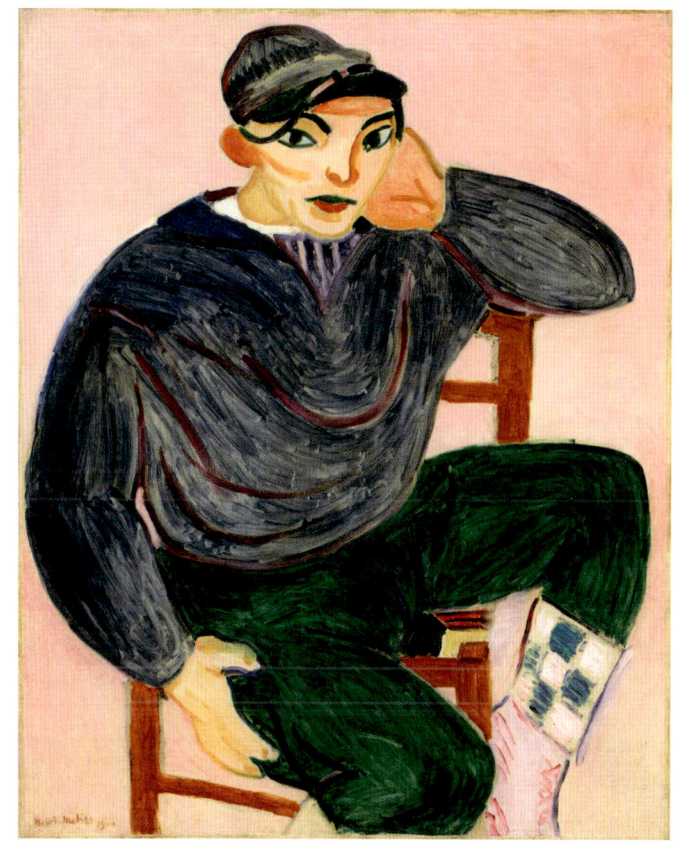

147. Henri Matisse, *The Young Sailor II*, 1906. Oil on canvas, 40 × 32¾ in. (101.6 × 83.2 cm). Jacques and Natasha Gelman Collection, 1998 (1999.363.41)

Contemporary Art (renamed Department of Twentieth-Century Art in 1970), most other large art museums—those in Boston, Chicago, Cleveland, Detroit, Los Angeles, Philadelphia, Saint Louis, and elsewhere—had already formed similar departments. By the time that New York could be accurately described as the capital of the art world, the Metropolitan had fallen out of step with its own environment.

Despite the enormous, unprecedented success of Geldzahler's landmark 1970 exhibition "New York Painting and Sculpture: 1940–1970," our trustees remained uncomfortable with modern art; major acquisitions were rarely approved. In all, Geldzahler purchased some three dozen paintings and sculptures and the same number of works on paper during his tenure (none from his famous friends Andy Warhol, Frank Stella, Robert Rauschenberg, or Jasper Johns). (Later, curator Lowery Sims was able to continue Robert Hale's tradition of encouraging and buying works from young, not-yet-recognized artists.) In those days the contemporary art collection was enlarged primarily through gifts from patrons, who included Peter Brant, Joseph Hazen, and Robert and Ethel Scull. Nevertheless, as commissioner of cultural affairs, Geldzahler did leave a lasting legacy: he persuaded the

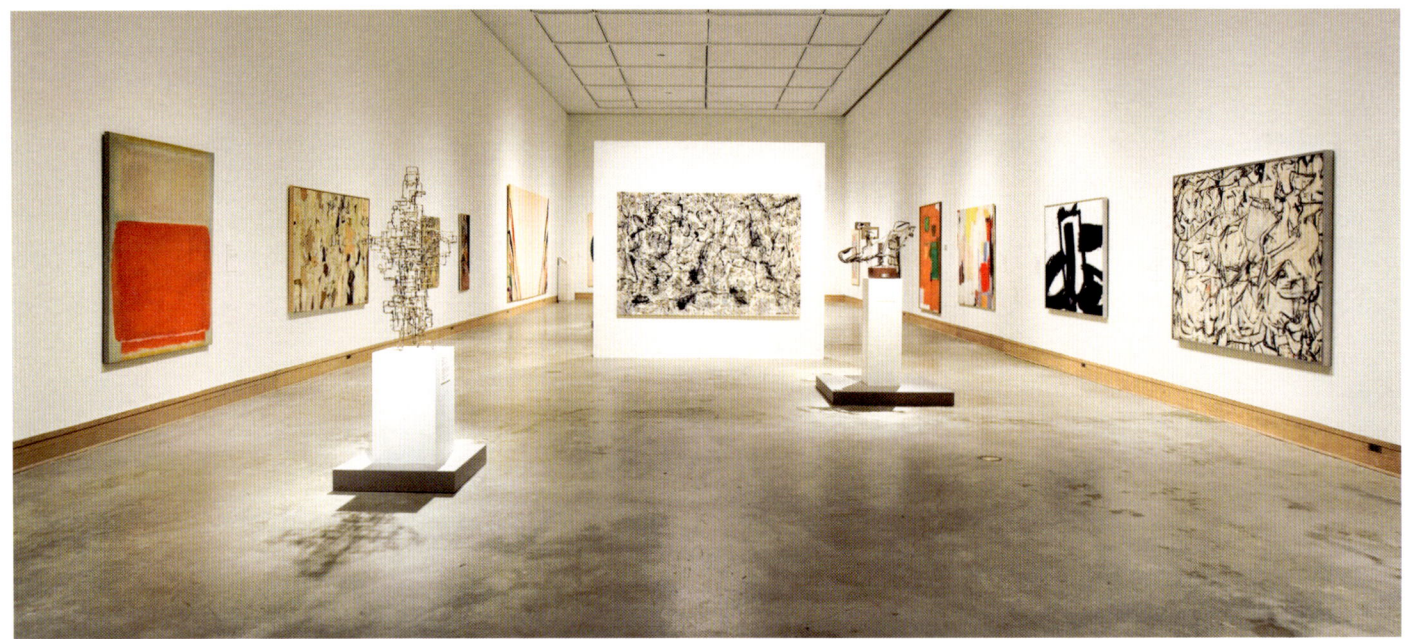

148. Gallery view of the exhibition "Abstract Expressionism and Other Modern Works: The Muriel Kallis Steinberg Newman Collection in The Metropolitan Museum of Art," 2007

city fathers and Barnabas McHenry, adviser to Lila Acheson Wallace (cofounder of Reader's Digest), that the Museum's southwest wing should be devoted to modern and contemporary art. With support from these sources and the administrative guidance of Kay Bearman, the Lila Acheson Wallace Wing came into being.

It was not until Philippe appointed William S. Lieberman chairman of the department—a position he held for twenty-five years, from 1979 to 2004 (in 1990 he became Jacques and Natasha Gelman Chairman)—that the modern collection began to be transformed. (To succeed Geldzahler, Philippe had first appointed Thomas Hess, consultative chairman from February 1978 until his death in April 1979.) The list of significant gifts and bequests welcomed by Philippe and Bill Lieberman still boggles the mind: the Muriel Kallis Steinberg Newman Collection, principally of American abstract expressionist works (promised 1980, conveyed 2006) (fig. 148); Heinz Berggruen's collection of works by Paul Klee (1984); Italian Futurist works from Lydia Winston Malbin (1989); Florene M. Schoenborn's School of Paris paintings (1996); the Mr. and Mrs. Klaus G. Perls Collection of European and American modernism (1997); the Jacques and Natasha Gelman Collection of French twentieth-century painting, drawing, and sculpture (1998) (fig. 147); the Pierre and Maria-Gaetana Matisse Collection of European modernism and surrealism (2002); and John C. Waddell's collection of modern design (promised in 1999 and given over time). In addition there were gifts from the estates of Pollock, Mark Rothko, and Clyfford Still, and significant gifts of individual works from Jane and Robert E. Carroll, Barbaralee Diamonstein Spielvogel, Lincoln Kirstein, Arnold and Milly Glimcher, Cynthia Hazen Polsky, Stanley Posthorn, Barbara Schwartz, Kenneth Tyler, Dave and Reba Williams, and others. There were also key purchases, ranging from Balthus's *The Mountain* (fig. 146) to a large group of drawings and watercolors and one great painting by Anselm Kiefer (fig. 149) to Jasper Johns's magisterial *White Flag* (fig. 153). Unlike Hale and Geldzahler, who had focused on modern American art, Lieberman placed an emphasis on European art prior to World War II—as did Philippe.

The Museum's collection of nineteenth-century European painting was of course formed long before Philippe's appointment as director: with the great bequests of the Havemeyers, the Lewisohns, Stephen C. Clark, and Robert Lehman, as well as other smaller but no less fine bequests, its shape and character had been defined by generations of New York collectors. Philippe's tenure was marked, however, by the arrival of a collection that lifted the museum's holdings of nineteenth-century French painting to a new level: the promised gift and eventual bequest from the Honorable Walter H. and Leonore Annenberg (fig. 143). Wrongly

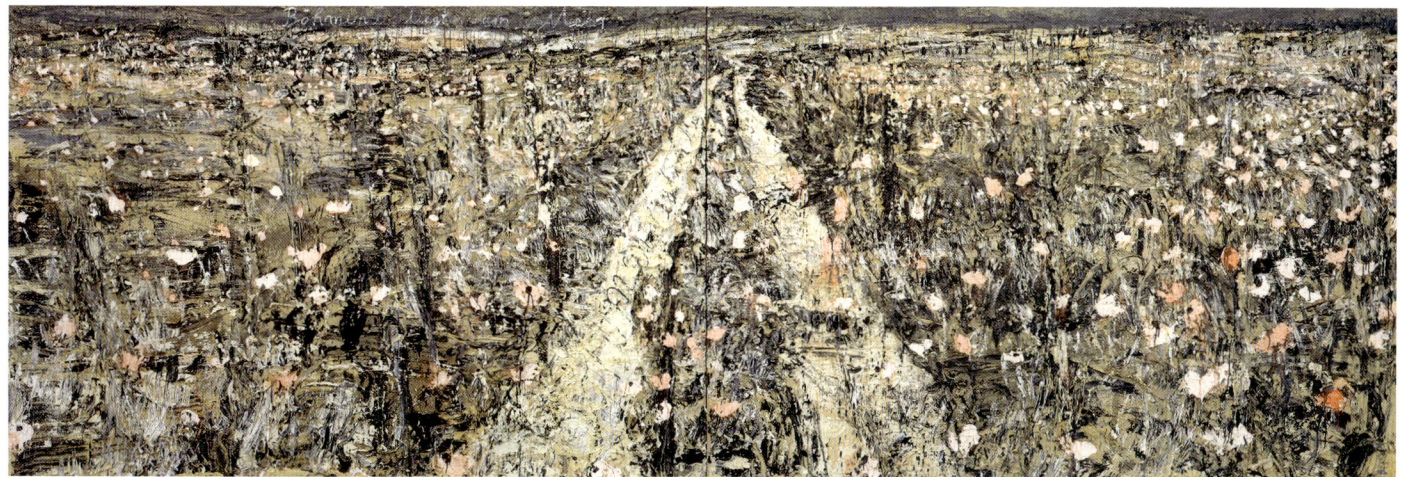

149. Anselm Kiefer, *Bohemia Lies by the Sea*, 1996. Oil, emulsion, shellac, charcoal, and powdered paint on burlap, 75¼ × 221 in. (191.1 × 561.3 cm). Purchase, Lila Acheson Wallace Gift and Joseph H. Hazen Foundation Purchase Fund, 1997 (1997.4ab)

called by some "coals to Newcastle," the addition of the Annenberg collection in fact completed the Museum's array of Impressionist and Post-Impressionist paintings with works of extraordinary quality: figure paintings by Renoir, Édouard Manet, and Claude Monet; large, late landscapes and water-lily paintings by Monet; masterpieces by Cézanne, Georges Seurat, Vincent van Gogh, Paul Gauguin, Pablo Picasso, Georges Braque, and Henri Matisse. The Annenbergs also generously purchased for the Museum two additional paintings by Van Gogh, *Shoes* and *Wheat Field with Cypresses* (fig. 145); the latter, bought in 1993, remains the most expensive single work of art ever purchased by the Museum.

Huge increases in the price of Impressionist and Post-Impressionist paintings in recent years meant that the Museum could buy a Van Gogh only with the support of a patron such as Ambassador Annenberg. But significant works were within our reach in another area, one underrepresented at the Metropolitan: French painting of the first half of the nineteenth century. It was only after the Civil War that New Yorkers began to buy modern French art of significance, and as a result, few Neoclassical or Romantic paintings had come to the Museum as gifts or bequests. We do have a few masterpieces from that period—Jacques-Louis David's *Death of Socrates*, Jean-Auguste-Dominique Ingres's portraits of Monsieur and Madame Leblanc, and Eugène Delacroix's *Abduction of Rebecca*, all purchased before World War II with the Wolfe Fund. Over the past twenty-five years, strengthening our holdings in this field has been a priority for me and Philippe, and one shared by Everett Fahy, John Pope-Hennessy Chairman of

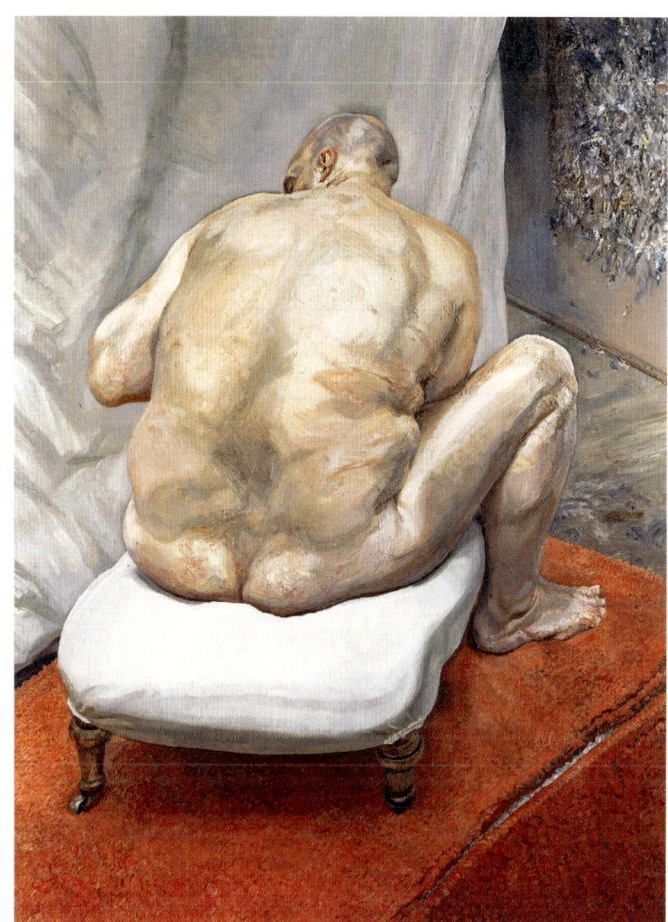

150. Lucien Freud, *Naked Man, Back View*, 1991–92. Oil on canvas, 72¼ × 54⅛ in. (183.5 × 137.5 cm). Purchase, Lila Acheson Wallace Gift, 1993 (1993.71)

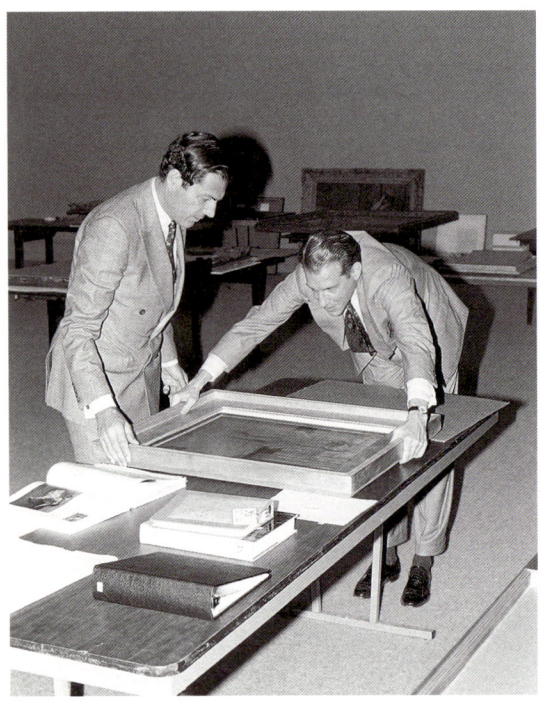

151. Philippe de Montebello and Gary Tinterow in the Degas galleries, 1988

152. Robert Rauschenberg, *Winter Pool*, 1959. Oil, paper, fabric, wood, metal, sandpaper, tape, printed paper, printed reproductions, handheld bellows, and found painting, on two canvases, with ladder, 89½ × 58½ × 4 in. (227.3 × 148.6 × 10.2 cm). Jointly owned by Steven A. Cohen and The Metropolitan Museum of Art; Promised Gift of Steven A. Cohen, and Purchase, Lila Acheson Wallace Gift, Bequest of Gioconda King, by exchange, Anonymous Gift and Gift of Sylvia de Cuevas, by exchange, Janet Lee Kadesky Ruttenberg Fund, in memory of William S. Lieberman, Mayer Fund, Norman M. Leff Bequest, and George A. Hearn and Kathryn E. Hurd Funds, 2005 (2005.390)

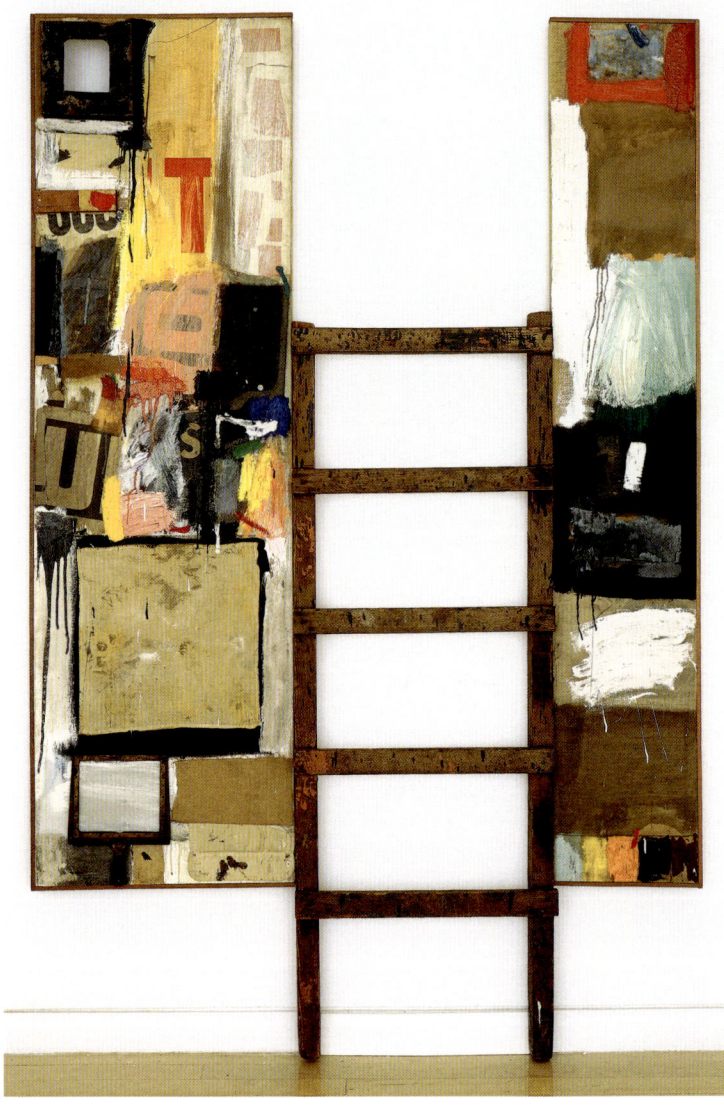

the Department of European Paintings. Thanks to the remarkable vision and generosity of Jayne Wrightsman, extremely fine paintings by Pierre-Paul Prud'hon, François Gérard, Théodore Chassériau, and Delacroix were added to the collection; Mrs. Wrightsman also made possible the acquisition of a memorable Caspar David Friedrich, and our first, *Two Men Contemplating the Moon*. In addition, an enormous painting by Théodore Gericault, *Evening: Landscape with Aqueduct* (fig. 144), and a fine one by Delacroix, *The Natchez*, were bought at auction.

After Philippe endorsed in 2003 the purchase of a half interest in Wheelock Whitney's oil sketches by French and Belgian artists (the remaining interest is a promised gift of Mr. Whitney), Eugene V. Thaw felt encouraged to consider the Metropolitan a fitting home for his much larger collection of landscape oil sketches, which we will share with the Morgan Library. These additions, together with individual works given by Mrs. Wrightsman and Karen Cohen, constitute a veritable department within a department. They offer a history of the development of European landscape painting in the Romantic era unequaled anywhere in the country and matched only at the Kunstmuseum Winterthur (Switzerland) and the Musée Granet (Aix, France). Built to house them, the Heinz Galleries opened in December 2007, just weeks before Philippe announced his retirement, adding almost ten thousand square feet to the previous thirty thousand. In the combined galleries for nineteenth- and early twentieth-century art it is now possible to display, for the first time in at least a century, almost all of the Museum's holdings in an area that is one of its legendary strengths. These galleries

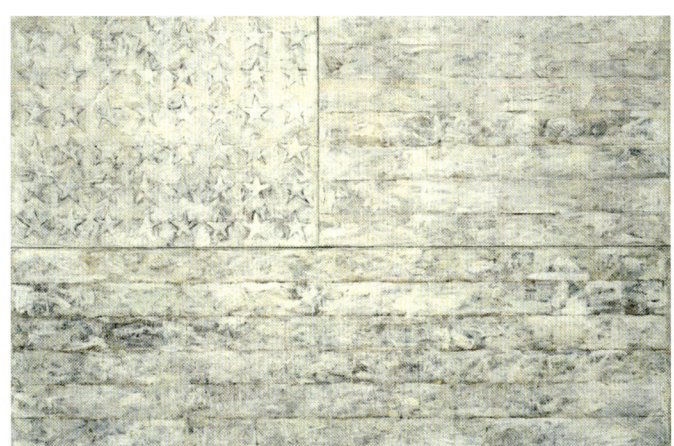

153. Jasper Johns, *White Flag*, 1955. Encaustic, oil, newsprint, and charcoal on canvas, 78 5/16 × 120 3/4 in. (198.9 × 306.7cm). Purchase, Lila Acheson Wallace, Reba and Dave Williams, Stephen and Nan Swid, Roy R. and Marie S. Neuberger, Louis and Bessie Adler Foundation Inc., Paula Cussi, Maria-Gaetana Matisse, The Barnett Newman Foundation, Jane and Robert Carroll, Eliot and Wilson Nolen, Mr. and Mrs. Derald H. Ruttenberg, Ruth and Seymour Klein Foundation Inc., Andrew N. Schiff, The Cowles Charitable Trust, The Merrill G. and Emita E. Hastings Foundation, John J. Roche, Molly and Walter Bareiss, Linda and Morton Janklow, Aaron I. Fleischman, and Linford L. Lougheed Gifts, and gifts from friends of the Museum; Kathryn E. Hurd, Denise and Andrew Saul, George A. Hearn, Arthur Hoppock Hearn, Joseph H. Hazen Foundation Purchase, and Cynthia Hazen Polsky and Leon B. Polsky Funds; Mayer Fund; Florene M. Schoenborn Bequest; Gifts of Professor and Mrs. Zevi Scharfstein and Himan Brown, and other gifts, bequests, and funds from various donors, by exchange, 1998 (1998.329)

constitute a fitting tribute to Philippe's belief in the primacy of the Museum's collection and permanent displays, and I hope that they will be seen as one of the great legacies of his tenure.

Many other signal achievements in our department can be cited, among them superb, prize winning, record-breaking exhibitions organized, and catalogues written, by the curators of nineteenth-century and modern art, who include Kathryn Galitz, Rebecca A. Rabinow, Susan A. Stein, Sabine Rewald, Nan Rosenthal, Anne L. Strauss, Lisa Messinger, Jane Adlin, and Jared Goss. And then there is our recent foray into the presentation of work by significant but still-contested young artists, of which Damien Hirst's *The Physical Impossibility of Death in the Mind of Someone Living* is the most prominent example. The appearance of that formidable work of art in the first room of the Lila Acheson Wallace Wing in 2007 (fig. 154) announced to the art community that we were shaking off some very old dust. It also represented a dramatic turnabout for Philippe, who had famously, publicly, and in hindsight perhaps regrettably denounced that same work in an Op-Ed piece for the *New York Times* when it was exhibited at the Brooklyn Museum in 1999. (I have been careful to save the email I received from Philippe in April 2005: "Can you get the Shark?") Although Philippe continues to profess a calculated distance from "the decisions of his curators," his willingness to revisit and revise earlier decisions and his uncanny instinct for what the Met's public might enjoy remain two of his most remarkable qualities.

Gary Tinterow

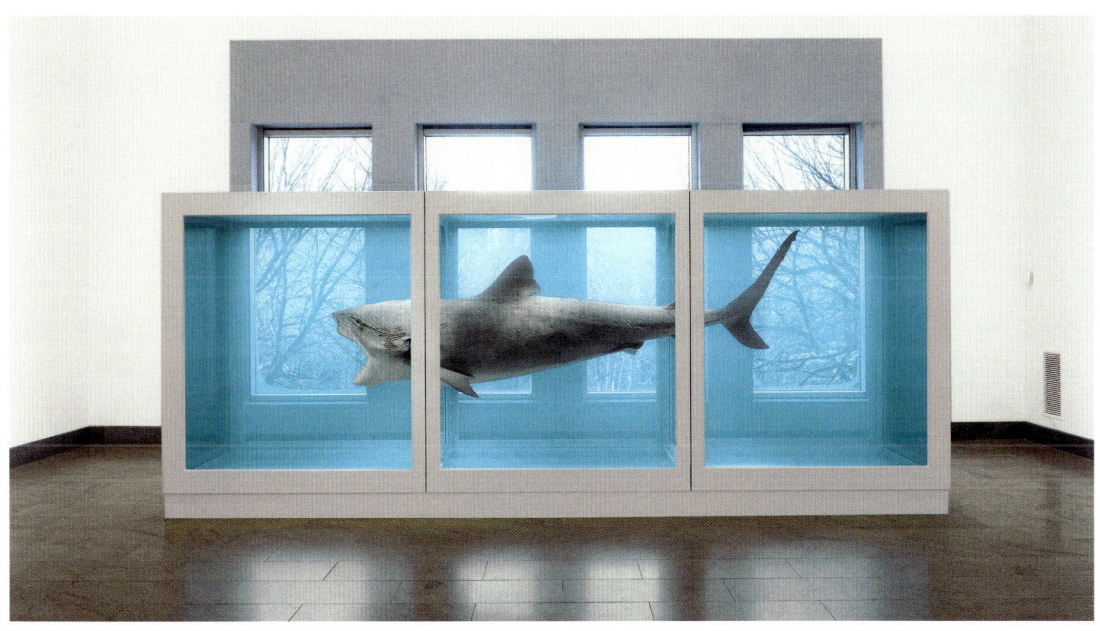

154. Damien Hirst, *The Physical Impossibility of Death in the Mind of Someone Living*, 1991. Glass, steel, formaldehyde solution, shark, 85 1/16 × 212 5/8 × 70 7/8 in. (216 × 540 × 180 cm). On loan from the Steven and Alexandra Cohen Collection

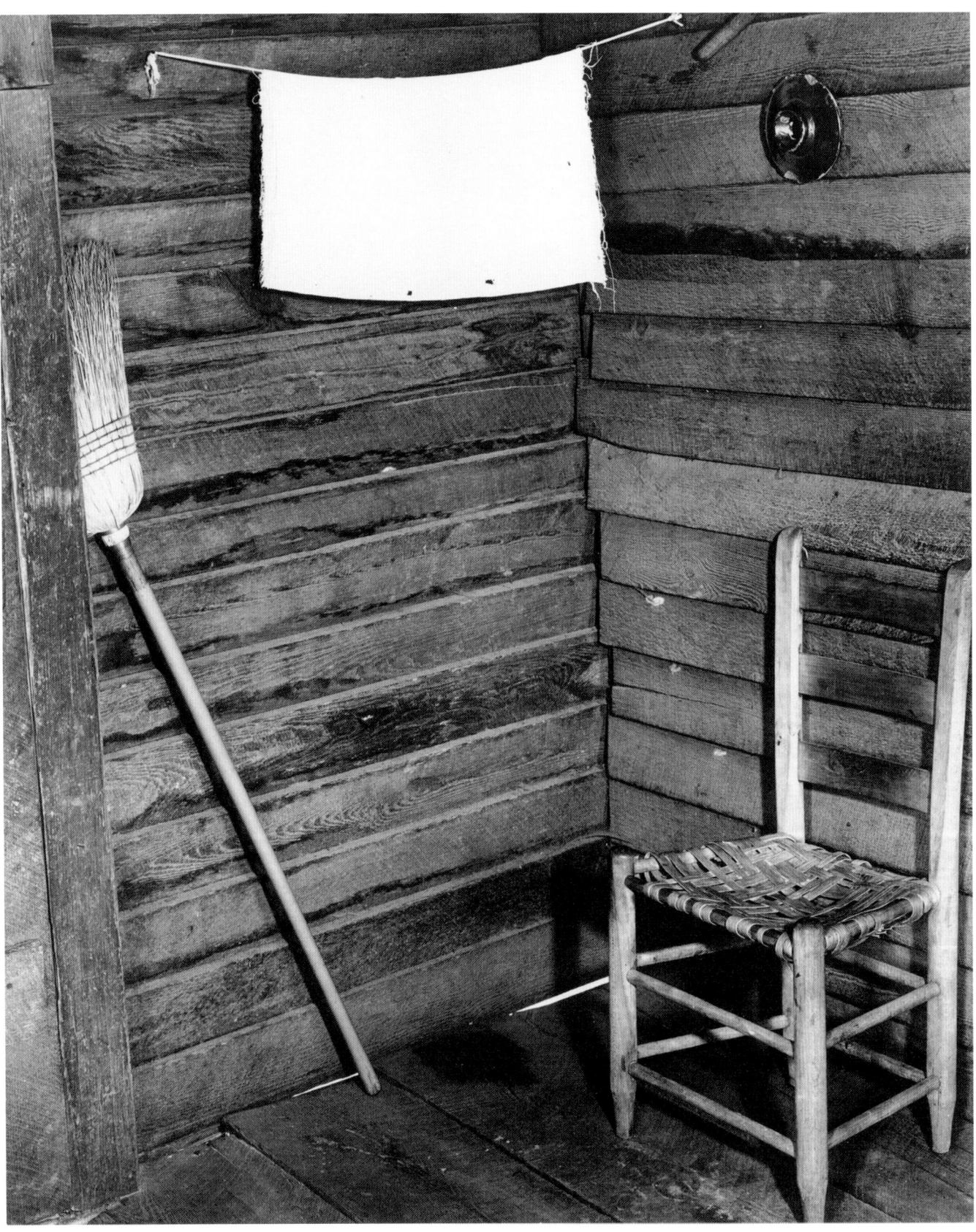

PHOTOGRAPHS

THE MUSEUM'S NEWEST DEPARTMENT

When Philippe de Montebello began his directorship of the Metropolitan Museum in 1977, a single associate curator, Weston Naef, had staked out photography as his bailiwick, and a single paper conservator had some knowledge of photograph conservation. The photography collection, then part of the Department of Prints and Photographs, consisted of Alfred Stieglitz's magnificent gift and bequest of some six hundred photographs by various artists that he had published in *Camera Work* and shown in his Little Galleries of the Photo-Secession; also a smattering of nineteenth- and twentieth-century photographs acquired by the founding curator of that department, William Ivins, and his successors A. Hyatt Mayor, John McHenry, and Colta Ives. Today, Philippe leaves in place an independent Department of Photographs with a staff of twelve; a world-class collection; permanent exhibition galleries devoted to photography; a state-of-the-art photograph conservation lab; an active exhibition and publication program; a devoted group of photography supporters; and an avid public. Without the director's active support, none of those achievements would have come about.

The Trustees created the Department of Photographs in 1992 on Philippe's recommendation. It was led by Maria Morris Hambourg, whom he had hired to be an associate curator six years earlier and who worked to build the collection in the areas preceding and following the 1895–1915 period represented by the Stieglitz Collection. Because she was a historian of early French photography, as was I when I was hired in 1990 as a curatorial assistant, our focus fortuitously coincided with the director's well-known Francophilia and, more important, with the Museum's exceptional strengths in nineteenth-century French painting, drawing, and graphic arts. Among Maria's first acquisitions in this area, in 1987, was a photograph made by Gustave Le Gray in the Forest of Fontainebleau. In it he departed from his more usual subject, the noble, aging oaks for which the forest was famous, and instead, pointing his camera into the light, captured an image of seemingly insignificant brush springing from a tree trunk. The picture is a momentary epiphany of observation—a sparkling display of life rendered in the golden hues characteristic of Le Gray's prints from the mid-1850s (fig. 158). A fine, unique print of an aesthetically innovative image that is also large, visually engaging, beautifully preserved, and by one of the medium's undisputed masters, it met the standard that the director had set: photographs entering the collection should hold their own with the Museum's treasures in other media. Acquisitions of early French photographs that followed included Charles Marville's views of Paris neighborhoods slated for demolition; portraits of the left-wing politician Eugène Pelletan, the painter Pierre-Luc-Charles Cicéri, and the composer Gioacchino Rossini by the famed Second Empire portraitist Nadar; a magnificent album of photographs by Edmond Bacot, assembled by Victor Hugo and his son Charles; studies of the female nude by Vallou de Villeneuve; a group of superbly preserved landscape, architectural, and industrial compositions by Édouard Baldus; and works by Adolphe Braun, Eugène Cuvelier, Henri Le Secq, Charles Nègre, Charles Soulier, and others.

Early in her tenure Maria proposed, and the director and trustees helped fund, acquisitions of major works by two of the greatest American landscape photographers: Timothy O'Sullivan's *Geographical and Geological Explorations and Surveys West of the 100th Meridian. Season of 1871,* a volume with thirty-five photographs; and a beautifully preserved group of mammoth-plate landscapes of the American West by Carleton Watkins, including a stunning triptych of the Yosemite Valley's sweeping expanse as seen from Sentinel Dome.

The department also built its collection with works by established twentieth-century photographic masters such as André Kertész, Bill Brandt, Helen Levitt, Robert Frank, William Klein, Aaron Siskind, and Shomei Tomatsu. And photography's central role in the art of our own time was underlined by the acquisition

Opposite: 155. Walker Evans, *Kitchen Corner, Tenant Farmhouse, Hale County, Alabama*, 1936. Gelatin silver print, 7 11/16 × 6 5/16 in. (19.5 × 16.1 cm). Purchase, The Horace W. Goldsmith Foundation Gift, through Joyce and Robert Menschel, 1988 (1988.1030)

of large contemporary photographs rivaling paintings in scale and seductiveness: Cindy Sherman's untitled self-portrait as a monk and Doug and Mike Starn's *Horses* in 1991; Jean-Marc Bustamante's *Lumière* and Sigmar Polke's highly abstract photograph from his São Paulo series in 1992; Andreas Gursky's *Schiphol* in 1995; and Thomas Struth's *San Zaccaria, Venice* (fig. 157) in 1996. The Struth photograph, which brings contemporary art and its antecedents into rich harmony, seemed particularly appropriate for the Metropolitan. A luminous altarpiece of 1505 by Giovanni Bellini, at the center of the picture, reigns over the adjacent paintings and the entire space. Bellini's illusionism had made the painted altarpiece seem to be a niche beyond the church wall; but Struth uses photography's trompe l'oeil effect to bring Bellini's saints and the other painted figures into a space shared with the tourist-pilgrims viewing them—a single sensuous, orderly world, washed in Venetian light.

In the late 1990s and early 2000s we made a concentrated effort to acquire important contemporary photographs by several groups of artists: those who worked at the intersection of photography and conceptual art, earth art, and performance art, such as Vito Acconci, Dennis Oppenheim, Robert Smithson, Felix Gonzalez-Torres, Gordon Matta-Clark, On Kawara, and Douglas Huebler; artists of the "Düsseldorf School," including Bernd and Hilla Becher and their students Thomas Ruff, Gursky, and Struth; photographers of the "Pictures Generation," among them Richard Prince, Sherman, Louise Lawler, and Laurie Simmons; and other artists who use photography, including Jeff Wall, Rodney Graham, Charles Ray, and Tom Friedman, as well as younger emerging artists.

All these important purchases depended upon Philippe's support. The dramatic leaps forward in the Museum's photographic holdings, however, came in a series of large acquisitions that required from the director not only assent but sustained commitment.

The 1987 gift of the Ford Motor Company Collection—five hundred avant-garde American and European photographs from between the two world wars, assembled by New York collector John C. Waddell—picked up where the Stieglitz Collection had left off, charting the urban, technological, and psychological revolutions of the modern age. Waddell had collected strong bodies of work by American photographers Berenice Abbott, Margaret Bourke-White, Walker Evans, and Man Ray, as well as superb individual photographs such as Paul Strand's *Abstraction, Twin Lakes, Connecticut*. And in European photography, the Ford Collection strengthened the Museum's representation of Brassaï, Henri Cartier-Bresson, August Sander, and László Moholy-Nagy, among others. Moholy's *Photogram* of 1926 (fig. 156) exemplifies the flexible approach to the medium adopted by some of the most progressive European photographers of the 1920s. Working without a camera, Moholy simply placed his hand, a paintbrush, and other objects on a sheet of photographic paper and exposed it to light. Unorthodox methods such as this freed photography from its customary role as recorder of the visible world and opened it to highly personal and expressive uses. A gift of the Ford Motor Company and Waddell, the collection was presented in an exhibition, "The New Vision," in 1989, 150 years after the invention of photography was announced.

A decade later another opportunity arose to enrich the Museum's collection in a difficult-to-collect area. The 1997 purchase and gift of seventy-eight masterpieces from the Rubel Collection contained major works by each of the four pillars of early British

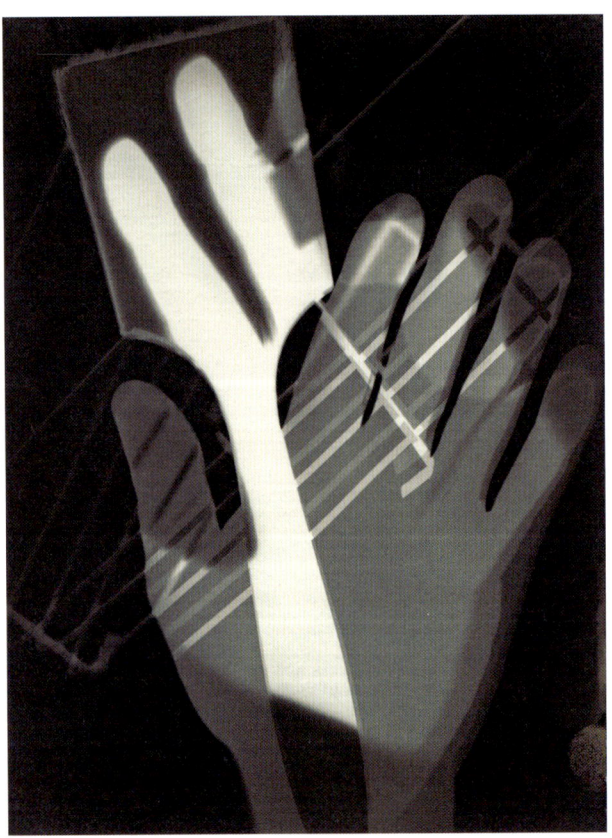

156. László Moholy-Nagy, *Photogram*, 1926. Gelatin silver print, 9⁷⁄₁₆ × 7¹⁄₁₆ in. (23.9 × 17.9 cm). Ford Motor Company Collection, Gift of Ford Motor Company and John C. Waddell, 1987 (1987.1100.158)

[136]

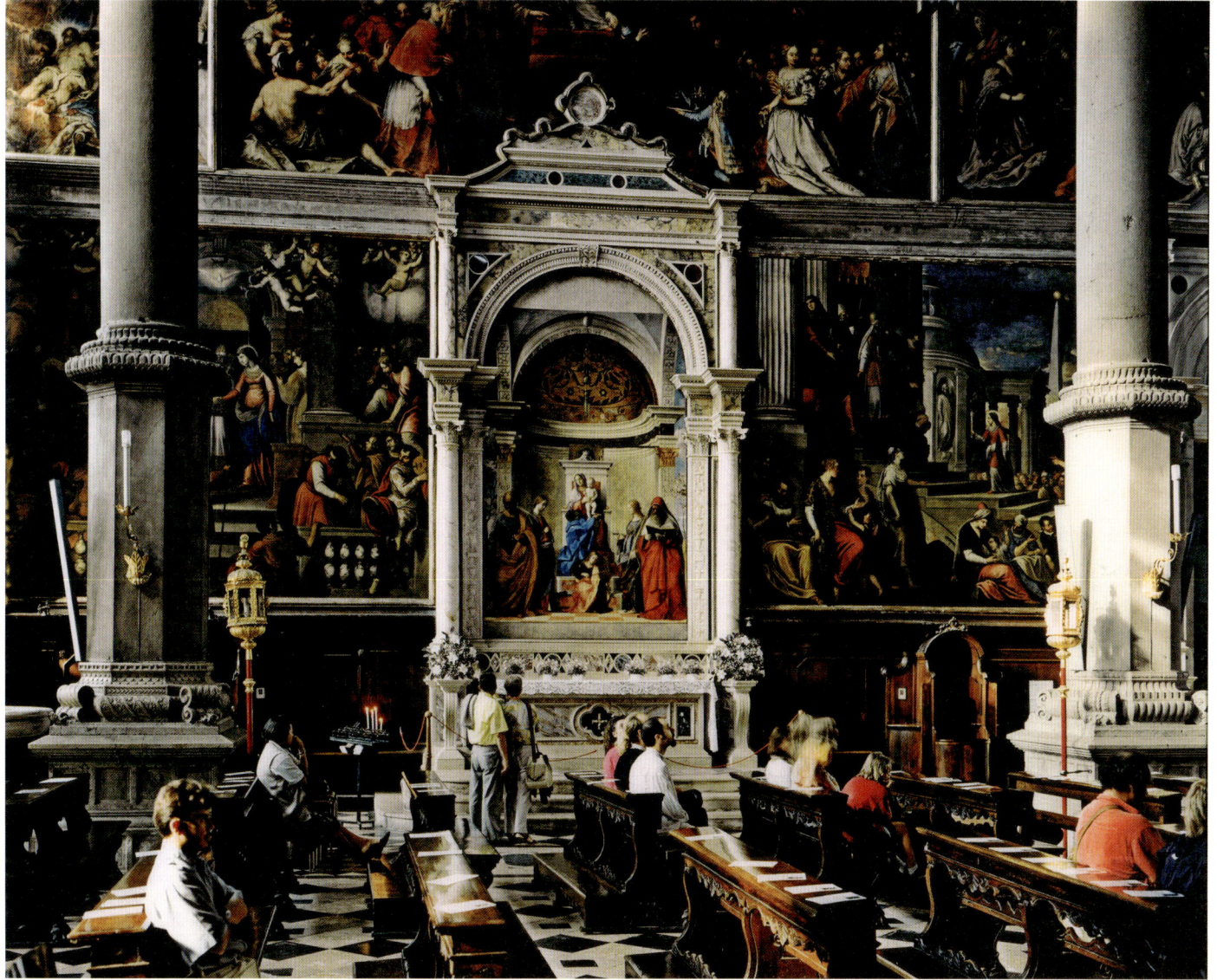

157. Thomas Struth, *San Zaccaria, Venice*, 1995. Chromogenic print, 71⅝ × 90¾ in. (181.9 × 230.5 cm). Purchase, The Howard Gilman Foundation Gift, 1996 (1996.297)

photography: early experiments by the medium's inventor, William Henry Fox Talbot, and his circle; Rembrandtesque portraits from the 1840s by the Scottish painter-photographer team David Octavius Hill and Robert Adamson; an enchanting odalisque and sublime landscapes by Roger Fenton, a key figure during the 1850s; and deeply spiritual portraits from the 1860s by Julia Margaret Cameron. Because Fenton's work is especially scarce—previously the Museum had only a single exhibitable print, acquired by Maria Hambourg in 1988—the Rubel Collection's two expansive cloudscapes by Fenton were particularly prized. Descendants of Constable's cloud studies and Turner's explorations of atmosphere and light, these are intensely felt private meditations on man's spiritual connection to nature, each printed once and kept in the artist's personal albums.

Also in the late 1990s and early 2000s, several important bodies of work by individual artists entered the collection. The acquisition of works by Stieglitz had been a long time in the making. In 1949, not long after his death, and again in 1976 for an exhibition here, the painter Georgia O'Keeffe, Stieglitz's widow, made a long-term loan to the Museum of seventy-three of his portraits of her—part of Stieglitz's extraordinary composite portrait of O'Keeffe, a series of more than three hundred images produced between 1917 and 1937 that document a famous and intimate artistic collaboration and that he considered among his greatest achievements. After O'Keeffe's death in 1986, the fate of the images she had chosen for the Met remained in jeopardy until their definitive donation through a gift from Jennifer and Joseph Duke and the Georgia O'Keeffe Foundation in 1997.

In 2002 the Museum received major gifts from the two premier fashion photographers of our time, in both cases of works more personal and expressive than the fashion images for which they are best known. Indeed, the earthy physicality of Irving Penn's nudes made in 1949 and 1950 might best be understood as an artistic antidote to the fantasy and artifice of the work for ladies' magazines that filled his days. In these photographs the models and poses are highly unorthodox: their fleshy torsos are folded, twisted, and stretched, with extra belly, mounded hips, and puddled breasts. In thanking Penn for his gift of sixty-six photographs from this series, Philippe placed the 1949–50 nudes in "a tradition that began with the earliest depictions of the human form, the archaic fertility idols found in sites scattered around the world." These "sisters of Titian's and Rubens's Venus," are, he said, "among the most ambitious and successful nudes ever made in any medium."

The gift of 128 photographs that the Museum received from Richard Avedon in the same year was the entire contents of his landmark exhibition of portraits held at Marlborough Gallery in New York in 1975. Unlike his commissioned fashion work, most of Avedon's portraits were of subjects chosen by the artist himself, including Igor Stravinsky, Ezra Pound, Isak Dinesen, Jean Genet, Marilyn Monroe, and Buckminster Fuller: a modern-day pantheon of intellectual, artistic, and political luminaries of the late 1950s through the early 1970s. Most spectacular are three enormous murals, *The Mission Council*, *The Chicago Seven*, and *Andy Warhol and Members of The Factory, New York City* (the last some 35 feet wide)—friezes of Vietnam War architects, radical left leaders, and avant-garde artists, filmmakers, actors, and performers that constitute a powerful collective portrait of 1960s America.

No photography acquisition was as transformative as the 2005 purchase and gift of the famed Gilman Paper Company

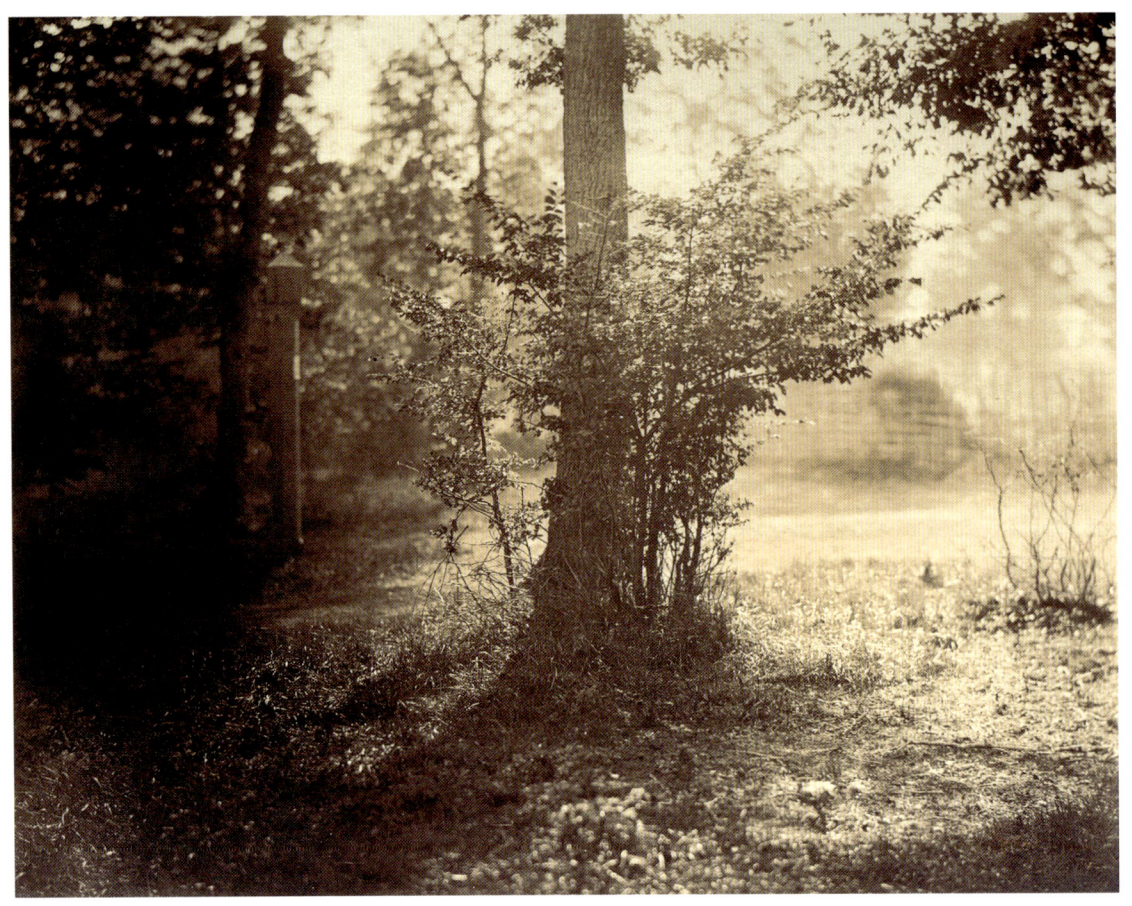

158. Gustave Le Gray, Tree Study, Forest of Fontainebleau, ca. 1856. Albumen silver print from glass negative, 12½ × 16⁵⁄₁₆ in. (31.8 × 41.4 cm). Purchase, Joyce and Robert Menschel, The Howard Gilman Foundation, Harrison D. Horblit, Harriette and Noel Levine and Paul F. Walter Gifts and David Hunter McAlpin Fund; and Gift of Mr. and Mrs. Harry H. Lunn Jr., 1987 (1987.1011)

Collection. Widely regarded as the world's finest collection of photographs in private hands, it had been amassed over two decades, beginning about 1977, by Howard Gilman, chairman of the Gilman Paper Company, and his visionary curator, Pierre Apraxine. During the 1990s Maria Hambourg worked closely with Gilman and Apraxine to help shape the collection so it fit in perfect jigsaw-puzzle fashion with the Metropolitan's. In 1993, hoping to become a permanent home for Gilman's treasures, the Museum organized a landmark exhibition of some 250 masterpieces from his collection. "The Waking Dream" was the first photography exhibition presented in second-floor galleries normally reserved for the likes of Velázquez and Van Gogh. The majestic Neoclassical rooms, the matting and framing of each photograph in keeping with its individual aesthetics, the scholarly catalogue, and most of all the supreme quality of the works themselves made the exhibition a pivotal event, and the Met a major presence, in the field of photography.

Gilman died unexpectedly in January 1998, before any arrangements for a hoped-for gift to the Museum could be finalized, and the fate of the collection remained uncertain through seven years of negotiation with his estate and foundation. When a purchase/gift arrangement was eventually agreed to in March 2005, it brought to the Museum some 8,500 photographs, primarily from the medium's first century, 1839–1939. In many areas the Gilman Collection had been far stronger than the Met's; together they constitute a deep, rich trove of work by many of the greatest artists of the medium. In one leap the Metropolitan's photography collection soared to the highest ranks worldwide.

A particular strength of the Gilman Collection is nineteenth-century French photography, with high points that include early daguerreotypes such as Choiselat and Ratel's dazzling *Pavillon de Flore and the Tuileries Gardens*; photographs by the famed Nadar and his brother Adrien Tournachon, whose *Self-Portrait* reveals a curiously sly artist in a sketching hat and smock; twenty-one images by Le Gray, including dramatic seascapes and dappled forest scenes (fig. 158); and extensive explorations of Egypt and the Holy Land by Maxime du Camp, Félix Teynard, John Beasley Greene, Auguste Salzmann, and Louis de Clercq. Among the exceptional nineteenth-century English photographs are more than twenty by Talbot, spanning his career from earliest experiments to mature work; more than two dozen masterworks of landscape, architectural, still-life, portrait, and documentary photography by Fenton; mesmerizing portraits by Cameron; and

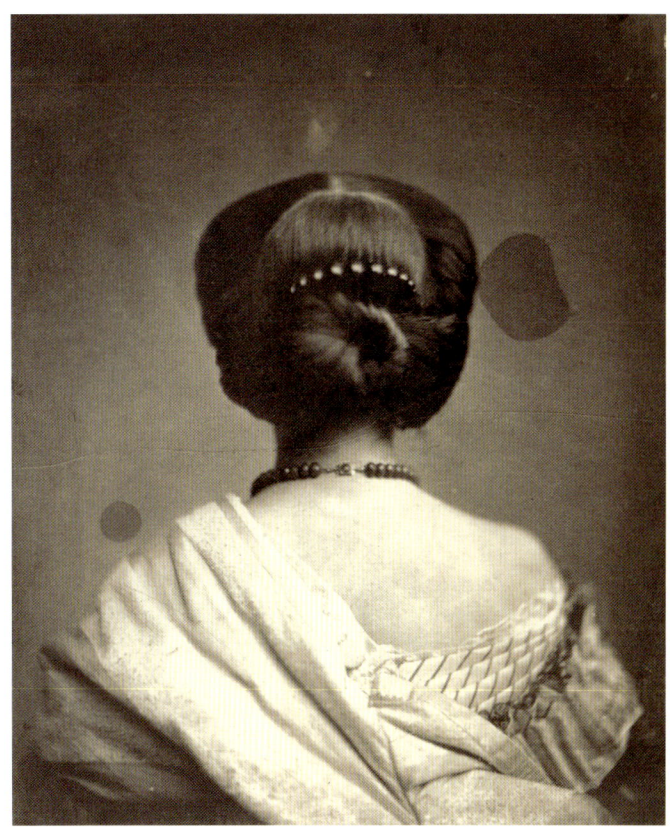

159. Onésipe Aguado, Woman Seen from the Back, ca. 1862. Salted paper print from glass negative, 12⅛ × 10³⁄₁₆ in. (30.8 × 25.8 cm). Gilman Collection, Purchase, Joyce F. Menschel Gift, 2005 (2005.100.1)

fine examples of Lewis Carroll's photographs of children, most notably his portrait of the girl made famous by his Alice stories, *Alice Liddell as "The Beggar Maid."*

The themes of slavery, the abolitionist movement, and the Civil War are hauntingly present in American photographs from the Gilman Collection. Among such works are a rare and particularly sensitive portrait of the fifty-one-year-old Abraham Lincoln in Springfield soon after he received his first nomination for the presidency; an anonymous portrait, unexpectedly noble for its time, of an unknown African-American youth; a group portrait of emancipated slaves, some of them branded on the forehead by their former owners; portraits of major political figures by Mathew Brady; photographs of the terrain and casualties of battle by Alexander Gardner; a display of artifacts from the notorious Andersonville Confederate prison, where thirteen thousand Union soldiers died of starvation and disease; a photographically illustrated broadside for the capture of John Wilkes Booth and his coconspirators; and Gardner's photograph of the execution of the Lincoln conspirators on July 7, 1865. There are also extensive holdings of American daguerreotypy and magnificent landscape views of the American West by Watkins, O'Sullivan, and William Bell.

Turn-of-the-century photographs in the Gilman Collection include Edward Steichen's large and painterly composite image *Rodin—The Thinker*, a unique exhibition print made from two negatives that the photographer referred to as "mon chef d'oeuvre, mon enfant"; George Seeley's highly abstract *Winter Landscape*; and nearly fifty prints by Eugène Atget. From the fertile period of visual experimentation that followed are three unique exhibition prints from Paul Strand's most creative moment, about 1916; ten works by Man Ray, including the large cameraless and abstract *Rayograph*; the sole known print of Charles Sheeler's *Upper Deck* (ca. 1928), the photographic model for one of his signature paintings; more than two dozen photographs by Walker Evans; and major works by Alexander Rodchenko, El Lissitzky, Moholy-Nagy, Sander, Cartier-Bresson, Brassaï, and others.

Finally, the Gilman Collection includes remarkable photographs by little-known and even unknown masters. One of these, Onésipe Aguado's *Woman Seen from the Back* of about 1862 (fig. 159)—an obscure work before it appeared on the cover of *The Waking Dream*—is among the most elegant and enigmatic portraits of its time. The elaborate chignon, discreet jewelry, and luxurious fabrics all indicate a woman of rank, while the bare neck and shoulder tantalize the imagination and add to the mystery of her hidden identity.

As Philippe made clear when announcing it in March 2005, the Gilman Collection's acquisition depended not only on allocations from the Museum's general art acquisition funds but also on a broad array of major gifts from Joyce F. Menschel, a Museum trustee and chair of the Department of Photographs Visiting Committee, and The Horace W. Goldsmith Foundation; Ann Tenenbaum and Thomas H. Lee; Harriette and Noel Levine; Mr. and Mrs. Andrew M. Saul; Mrs. Walter H. Annenberg and The Annenberg Foundation; Joseph M. Cohen; Jennifer and Joseph Duke; Mr. and Mrs. Henry R. Kravis; Cynthia Hazen Polsky; and, collectively, The Alfred Stieglitz Society, the Friends group of the Department of Photographs. Generous support also came from the Estate of Jacob S. Rogers, the William Talbott Hillman Foundation, Robert Rosenkrantz, the Marlene Nathan Meyerson Family Foundation, W. Bruce and Delaney H. Lundberg, the Sam Salz Foundation, Heidi S. Steiger, and two anonymous donors. The Museum is profoundly indebted to The Howard Gilman Foundation, which donated a substantial portion of the collection.

Two other notable and unusual recent acquisitions are the personal archives of the seminal twentieth-century master photographers Walker Evans and Diane Arbus. Both acquisitions were spearheaded by curator Jeff Rosenheim and accomplished through the generosity of the artists' estates and the Museum's trustees and supporters.

Through gift and purchase the Museum had for many years collected the work of Walker Evans, best known for his Depression-era photographs such as *Kitchen Corner, Tenant Farmhouse, Hale County, Alabama* (fig. 155). This work is from Evans's 1936 collaboration with writer James Agee, *Let Us Now Praise Famous Men* (1941), their study of cotton farmers in the American South. In respectful and unsentimental portraits of three sharecropper families and in views of their homes, furniture, clothing, and rented land, Evans recorded the everyday experiences of the common man. His study of a clean-swept corner recalls Agee's observations that "general odds and ends are set very plainly and squarely discrete from one another . . . [giving] each object a full strength it would not otherwise have."

It was the 1994 acquisition of Evans's archives, however, that offered a wide-ranging view of the artist's methods and achievement, with its forty thousand negatives and transparencies dating from the late 1920s to the early 1970s, personal and professional correspondence, papers, diaries, family photo albums, and the artist's collections of books, picture postcards, clippings, roadside signs, and works by other artists. Research in the archives underlay the 2000 retrospective exhibition "Walker Evans," its catalogue, and a series of subsequent publications.

The 2007 purchase of twenty exhibition prints of iconic images by Diane Arbus enriched the Museum's already prominent collection of her photographs, many acquired through the generosity of Jennifer and Joseph Duke and as gifts from David and Danielle Ganek. The purchased works include such masterpieces as *Russian midget friends in a living room on 100th Street, N.Y.C.* (1963) and *Woman with a veil on Fifth Avenue, N.Y.C.* (1968), as well as prints ranging in date from her earliest 35mm street photographs—such as *Masked boy with friends, Coney Island, N.Y.* (1956)—to one of her last pictures, *Blind couple in their bedroom, Queens, N.Y.* (1971). At the same time, the artist's estate designated the Metropolitan Museum as the permanent repository of her archives, making gifts and promised gifts of

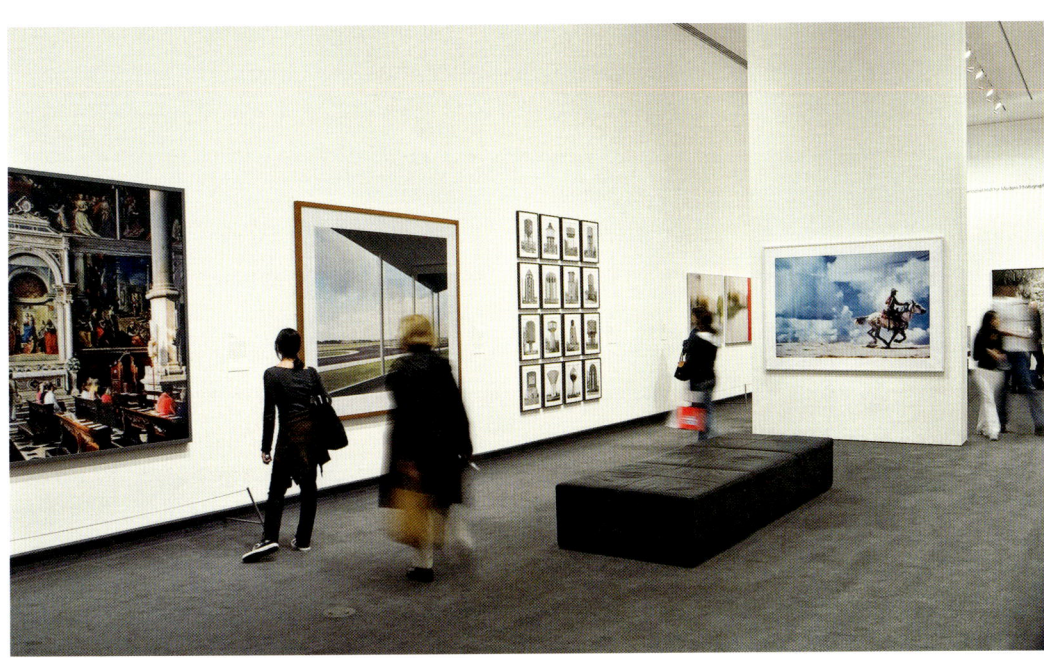

160. The Joyce and Robert Menschel Hall for Modern Photography

hundreds of early and unique photographs by Arbus, negatives and contact prints of 6,500 rolls of film, glassine print sleeves annotated by the artist, and her photography collection, library, and personal papers including appointment books, notebooks, correspondence, writings, and ephemera. The Metropolitan is now the essential locus for study of Arbus's achievement.

Philippe's directorship of the Metropolitan coincided with radical changes in the very nature of photography: new technologies that allowed the production of photographs on a scale previously the domain of painting; the rapid shift from analog to digital capture, manipulation, and output; a blurring of the boundaries between photography and other media; and an expanded artistic use of time-based photographic media such as video. In 2001 the department acquired the Museum's first work of video art, Ann Hamilton's *abc*, and since then we have continued to collect judiciously in this area. "Closed Circuit" (2007), with eight works from the permanent collection, was the Museum's first multiartist exhibition of video and new media.

The department has had a very visible role in the Museum's galleries. Among our special exhibitions were monographic presentations of the work of Talbot, Le Gray, Baldus, Nadar, Cuvelier, Fenton, Watkins, Degas, Stieglitz, Strand, Sheeler, Sander, Evans, Levitt, Avedon, Penn, Arbus, Struth, Tomatsu, and Hiroshi Sugimoto. There have also been thematic shows on subjects that include New York City, spirit photography, French daguerreotypes, and British calotypes. In 1992 the Robert Wood Johnson Jr. Gallery was designated a space for rotating installations of prints, drawings, and photographs; in 1997 The Howard Gilman Gallery became the first space in the Metropolitan devoted exclusively to photography, with a design that especially suited it for nineteenth-century and small twentieth-century works; and 2007 saw the opening of The Joyce and Robert Menschel Hall for Modern Photography (fig. 160), a cleanly designed, high-ceilinged gallery made for the display of contemporary photography, including large-scale color photographs by Wall, Struth, Gursky, and other modern masters.

The growth of our collection and changes in the nature of the medium have also necessitated increased attention to preservation, analysis, and conservation. Under Philippe's leadership a new lab for photograph conservation was built and equipped, with the assistance of the Sherman Fairchild Foundation and the Andrew W. Mellon Foundation; conservators specializing in photography were hired; a research scholarship in photograph conservation was endowed with the support of the Andrew W. Mellon Foundation; and important research projects in collaboration with the Museum's conservation scientists have begun.

Philippe's creation of a Department of Photographs and his encouragement of its rapid growth have yielded startling results. The Metropolitan's achievements in the collecting, scholarly study, exhibition, and conservation of photography are now on a par with those in other long-established curatorial areas of the Museum, and with activities of premier photography collections worldwide.

Malcolm Daniel

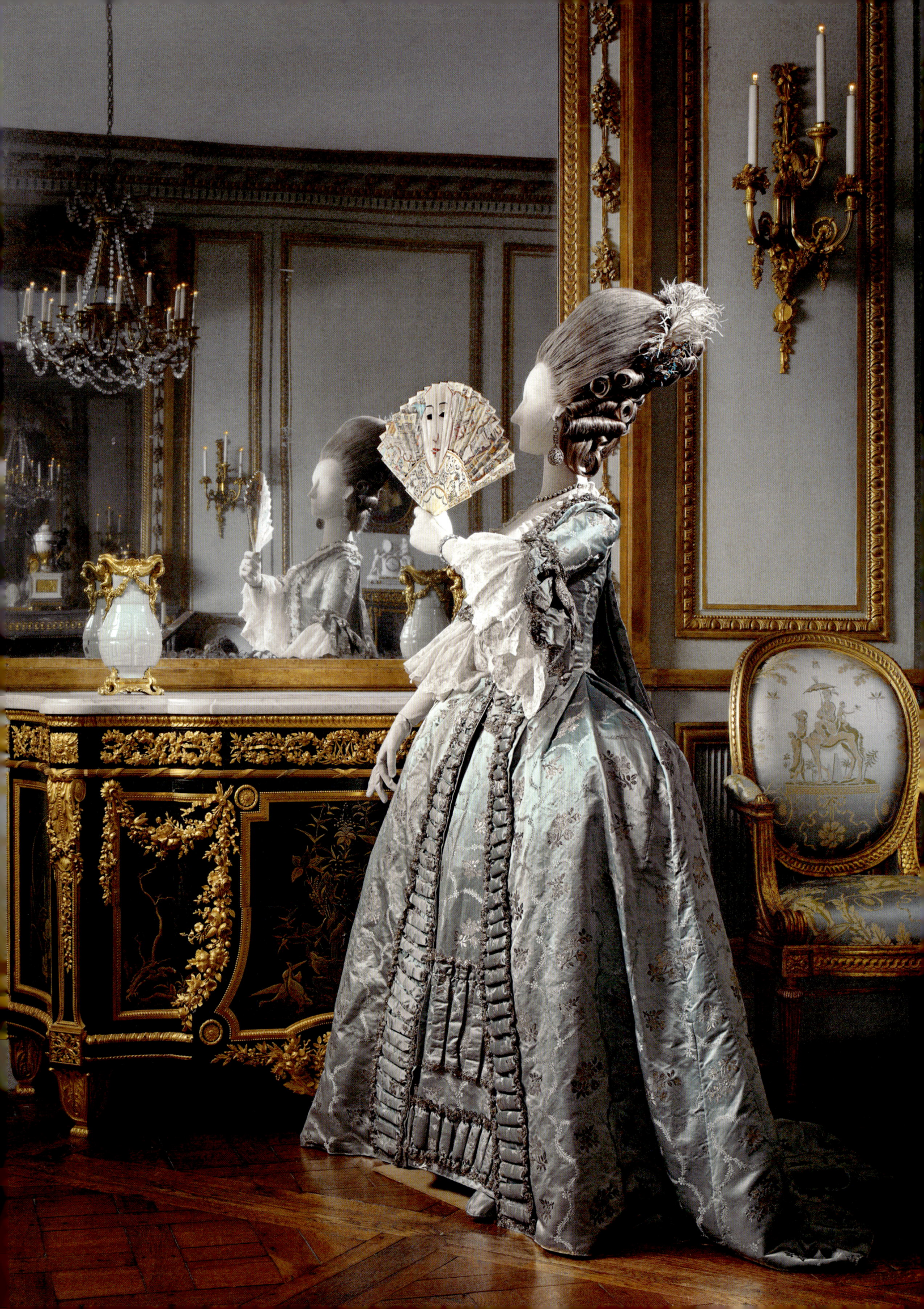

COSTUME

DE MONTEBELLO FASHION

When dealing with The Costume Institute, Director Philippe de Montebello generally began by acknowledging his unfamiliarity with the subject at hand. His expertise in fashion seemed to reside in a preference for bespoke Thomas Pink shirts and a late-night addiction to "Full Frontal Fashion," although this somewhat limited range rarely deterred him from offering an opinion about our exhibition titles, the images on our posters, or the allure of our mannequins. Typically he weighed in on any project with a decisively articulated opinion, especially when he had reservations about it; then, in a gesture familiar to his staff, he would glance down obliquely—shoulders raised, hands lowered, palms forward in a defensive position like a child pushing away a plate of peas—and say, "But do what you think best." Curators understood this to mean: Mull this further and come back with a stronger argument for your position.

From the beginning, The Costume Institute has had a distinctive place within the Museum. It originated as a collection of period and regional dress acquired by the Neighborhood Playhouse, a drama group associated with a settlement house on the Lower East Side, and by the 1930s had become an archive of considerable historical significance. Recognizing the valuable and irreplaceable nature of the garments, the cofounders of the playhouse, Irene Lewisohn and her sister Alice Lewisohn Crowley, and the theatrical designers, Aline Bernstein and Lee Simonson, withdrew the collection from use in theater productions to preserve it as a study resource for design specialists, scholars, and the public. With this collection as its core and with the participation of important members of the New York fashion community, the Museum of Costume Art was founded in 1937. Its collection was housed in the storage rooms of Saks Fifth Avenue.

A few years later the museum's trustees determined that their holdings would be better served if they were placed under the wing of a well-established institution. In 1946, with the explicit understanding that its operating expenses would be borne by the fashion industry (the primary fund-raising mechanism for this support is the annual benefit gala popularly known as The Party of the Year), the Museum of Costume Art became a study collection in The Metropolitan Museum of Art. The Costume Institute was recognized as a curatorial department in 1959.

By the time that Philippe was named director of the Metropolitan, The Costume Institute had become a vigorous department. In 1972 new storage facilities had been created to accommodate a collection that had expanded from 5,000 to more than 17,500 accessioned items. That year the fashion editor and writer Diana Vreeland was appointed special consultant to the department. Vreeland not only elevated The Costume Institute to a new level of public visibility but also transformed the somnolent world of costume display. Her exhibitions introduced the ambition and excitement of a blockbuster to the department's galleries in the Museum's ground floor. For many museumgoers the Vreeland era had the glamorous aura of a golden age, but the exhibitions of those years were not without controversy. Her predilection for audacious visual effects, sometimes at the expense of historical details, and her embrace of anachronistic interpretation were criticized by many of the scholars whose conventional approach to costume presentation she had so dramatically upended. Today, many of her innovations—gallery walls saturated with color, dramatic lighting, abstract mannequins in animated poses, and ambient period music—have been adopted by some of the very institutions that once repudiated her approach. Other, more exotic ideas, such as placing open vats of fragrance in the Museum's air-conditioning ducts, fell victim to practical considerations.

Philippe supported Vreeland's successful programming but at the same time encouraged the curatorial team to judiciously apply as much art-historical methodology as possible to her exhibitions. In the mid-1980s, when ill health forced Vreeland to retreat from day-to-day involvement in the department, a series of exhibitions balancing innovation with a high level of scholarly

Opposite: 161. "Dangerous Liaisons" exhibit: Dress (robe à la française). French or Austrian, ca. 1765. Pale blue silk satin with hammered-silver floral brocade and silver bobbin-lace trim. Purchase, Irene Lewisohn Bequest, 2001 (2001.472a, b)

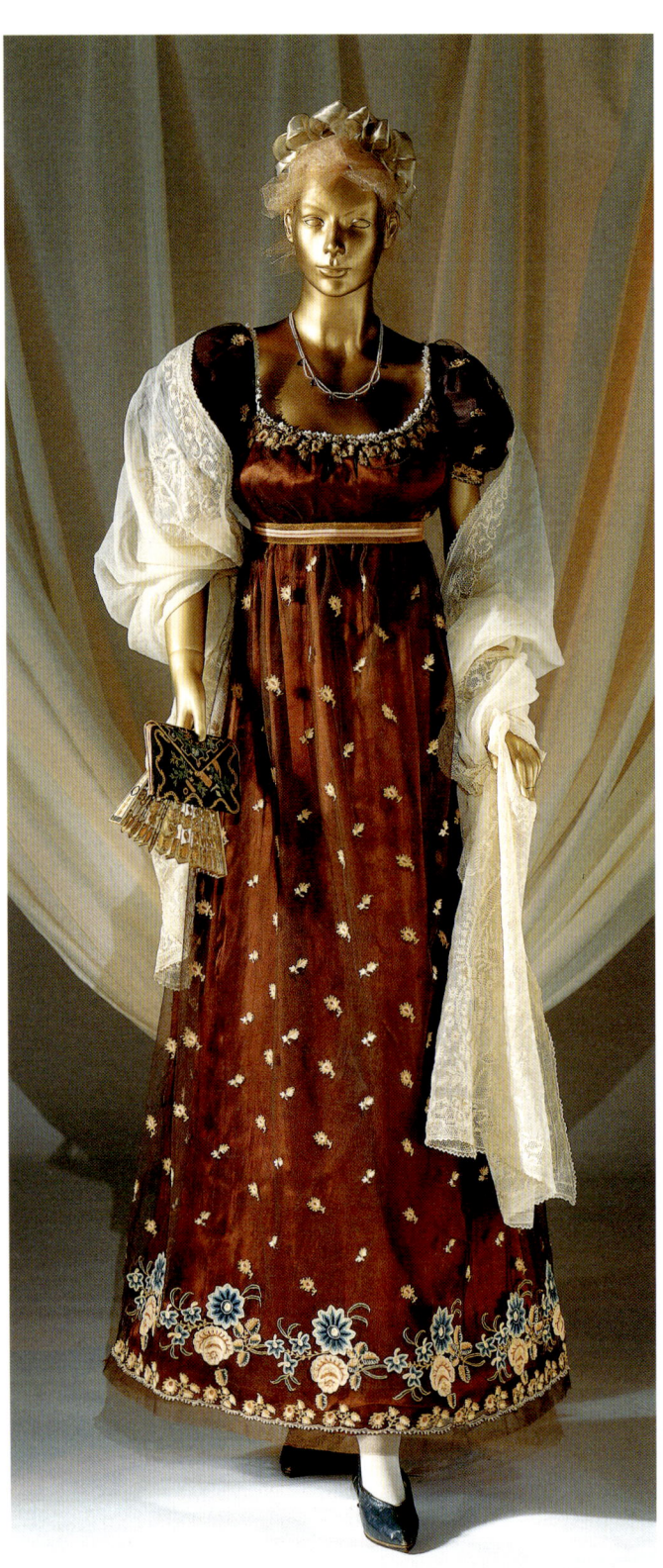

162. "The Age of Napoleon" exhibit: Dress. French, ca. 1808–10. Brown silk net with embroidered floral point de chainette and deep floral and foliate border. Purchase, Irene Lewisohn Bequest, 1959 (C.I.59.5)

rigor quietly entered the planning stage. "In Style: Celebrating 50 Years of The Costume Institute" (1987), developed by Jean Druesedow, and "From Queen to Empress: Victorian Dress, 1837–1877," curated by Caroline Goldthorpe and presented in 1988–89, focused on areas of strength in the collection. Philippe's ambitions for the department are perhaps best characterized by another show of the late 1980s, "The Age of Napoleon: Costume from Revolution to Empire, 1789–1815" (fig. 162). The exhibition was comprehensive in its reach, incorporating works from throughout the Museum, and the curator, Katell le Bourhis, positioned dress for equal consideration alongside the other decorative and fine arts. In addition to its emphasis on the aesthetic refinement, originality, and provenance of each work, the display offered a compelling interpretation of the cultural and political factors that influenced fashions of the period.

Beginning with Diana Vreeland's first installation for the Museum in 1973, The Costume Institute's exhibitions, which typically remained on view for nine months, had been heavily reliant on loans. Over the years, as lending institutions grew increasingly concerned about the exposure of their garments for extended periods of time, it became difficult to secure agreements to borrow exceptional objects or large numbers of objects from a single museum. In the mid-1980s The Costume Institute established a three-month borrowing limit on its outgoing material, and other institutions soon followed suit. To address these changing circumstances and others having to do with distribution of Museum space, the director asked the curators of the institute to develop a new model for its exhibition programming. In response the department created a small permanent gallery where selections from the collection could be presented in seasonal rotation. It was understood that on occasion, use of the special exhibition galleries elsewhere in the Museum might be possible. When the permanent gallery opened in 1992, the public response was something less than enthusiastic. A reduction of the earlier gallery space by two-thirds and the creation of vitrines in which mannequins could be placed in unprecedented proximity to the viewer, inviting an almost intimate scrutiny, were interpreted as evidence of the collection's secondary status in the Museum.

Philippe may have professed himself an innocent in the world of costume specialists, but his choice of Richard Martin to head the department in 1992 was both felicitous and shrewd. Editor-in-chief of *Arts Magazine* and director of the Shirley Goodman Resource Center at the Fashion Institute of Technology, this well-regarded art historian had animated the field of costume study and display with a series of conceptually rich and visually seductive exhibitions and catalogues. At the Met he initiated a program of thematic presentations built around little-seen works from The Costume Institute's holdings. Exhibitions that featured fashions inspired by military uniforms or focused on the trend to turn underwear into outerwear alternated with monographic shows on designers such as Madame Grès (fig. 163) and Christian Dior. Martin also aggressively solicited the participation of contemporary designers in his exhibitions. Visitors were thus exposed to a wide variety of costumes from the Museum's historical holdings and also introduced to compelling contemporary works.

Throughout his tenure at the Metropolitan, Philippe encouraged the institute to integrate its activities with those of the Museum at large. Diana Vreeland had relied on interdepartmental loans to demonstrate the inseparability of the fine and decorative arts. Philippe pressed for an even closer and more frequent collaboration. In 1999 The Costume Institute partnered with the Department of European Paintings to present "Costume and Character in the Age of Ingres" in tandem with one of the Museum's major loan exhibitions, "Portraits by Ingres: Image of an Epoch." Five years later, again at the behest of the director, the department originated an installation in the Wrightsman Galleries, "Dangerous Liaisons: Fashion and Furniture in the Eighteenth Century," in which exquisitely dressed mannequins were posed to illustrate scenes of aristocratic daily life during the ancien régime, based on the engravings of Jean-Michel Moreau (fig. 161). It was the first time since the 1960s that costume had been presented in any of the museum's period rooms. The exhibition relied primarily on the Museum's own rich holdings of costumes, paintings, sculpture, and decorative arts and was jointly developed by the curators of two departments.

"Dangerous Liaisons" is a good example of both the director's large institutional vision and his interest in the details of curatorial expression. By introducing into each vignette a narrative with an undercurrent of decadence, eroticism, and excess, we were attempting to address his concern that period mannequins rarely communicate the seductive intention of much fashionable dress. We were successful—the show sparked a flurry of titillating reviews—but in one case we perhaps overshot our mark. Viewing the tableaux as they were being finalized with moody lighting and the usual last-minute primping of the gowns, Philippe paused, pondered for a minute or two, and then observed that

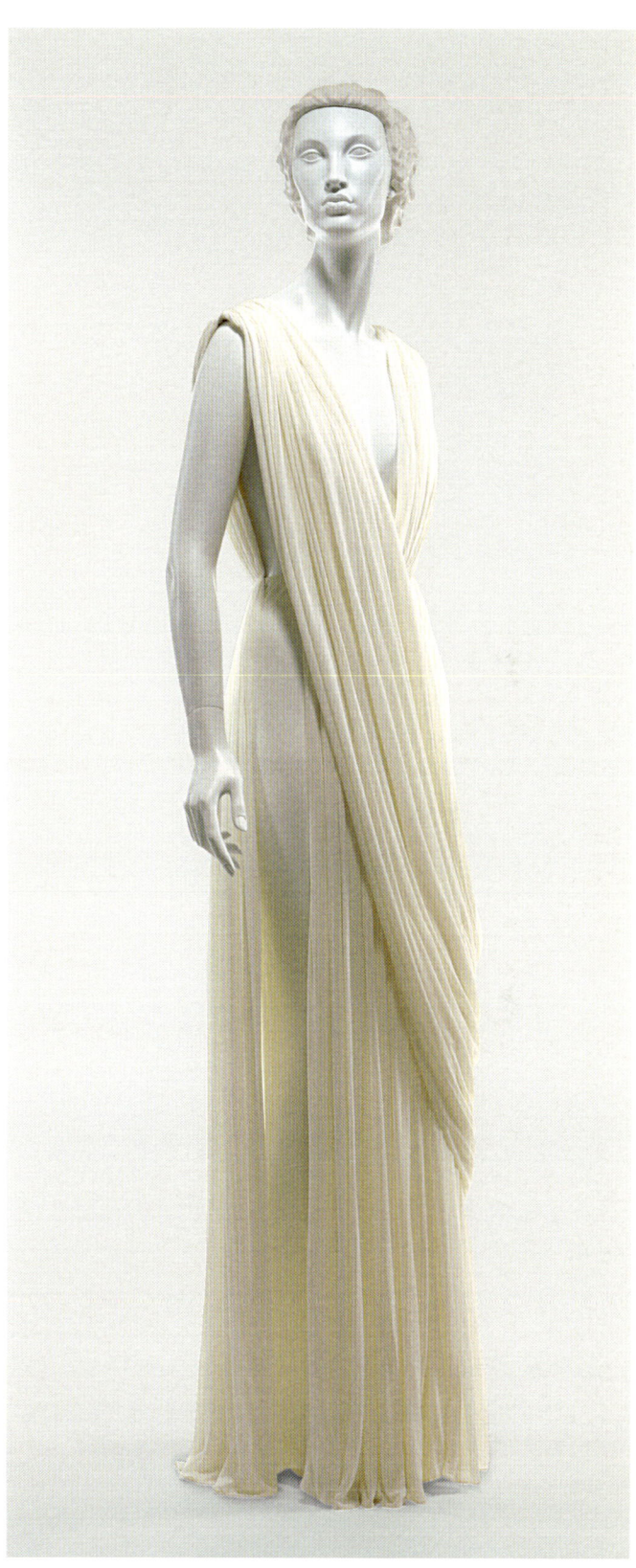

163. Evening dress. French, by Madame Grès [Alix Barton], ca. 1965. White silk jersey. Gift of Mrs. Oscar de la Renta, 1994 (1994.192.12)

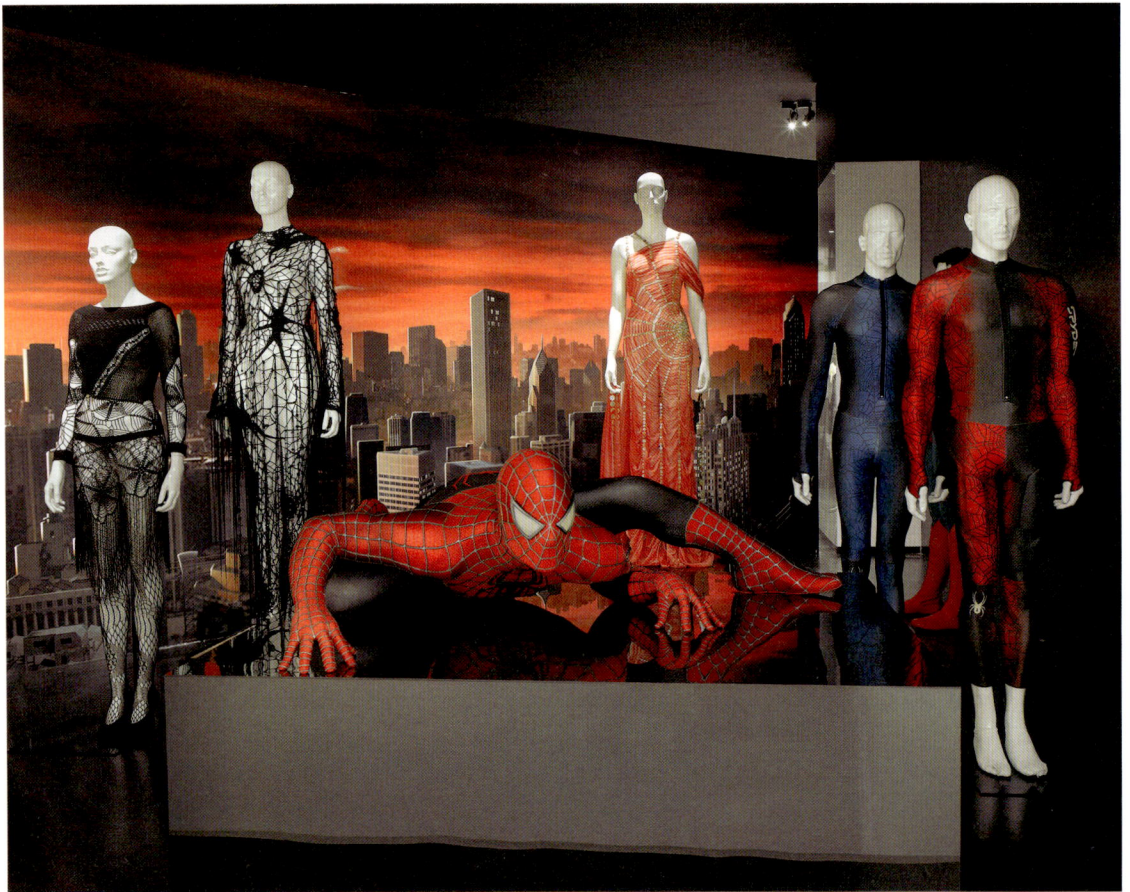

164. "Superheroes" exhibit: Garments by Julien Macdonald, Thierry Mugler, James Acheson (on Spider-Man), Jean Paul Gaultier, and two by Spyder Active Sports, Inc.

one scene—intended to suggest the denouement of amorous surrender—was, in his words, a bit too "gynecological." The careless disarray of the mannequin's petticoat was quickly adjusted to a level of discretion more typical for the Museum (fig. 165).

On other occasions Philippe surprised his staff by revealing a showman's side to his appreciation of feminine fashions. For a press luncheon he preferred a photograph of a Tom Ford deconstructed "goddess" dress on a model as sleek and lacquered as a Peking duck to one showing the department's quieter display of the same dress on a tailor's form. In another instance he criticized the presentation of a 1950s Jacques Fath evening gown because the strapless and very décolleté bodice of the dress, heavily structured with wires, boning, and pads, did not conform to the mannequin's molded-fiberglass bosom. This phenomenon—the failure of the contours of a mannequin from one period to match the shaping of dresses from another—is commonly referred to in our field as the "generation gap." It is now standard practice at The Costume Institute to avoid or at least attempt to mediate the "gap." The final detailing of a mannequin has come to be called "philippe-ing" a bustline, a term that has not yet entered the *Oxford English Dictionary*.

Another of the director's bêtes noires has been the lighting of our exhibitions: the five foot-candle restrictions imposed on our designers to protect light-sensitive objects virtually ensures a low-contrast effect, and when mannequins are crowded together, the visual blandness is exacerbated. Philippe repeatedly voiced his opinion that our objects would benefit from more dramatic illumination. Over the years, certain manipulations of design—dark walls and the placement of mannequins either considerably separated or in defined clusters with "drop-away" zones—helped add visual drama (fig. 164).

In 2000, after the critically successful and popular Costume Institute show "Jacqueline Kennedy: The White House Years" opened in the Iris and B. Gerald Cantor Exhibition Hall, Philippe began to revisit the idea that we use The Costume Institute's permanent galleries as a rotational space for dossier installations and mount exhibitions with a more general appeal in areas outside the department, including the French and English period rooms. He

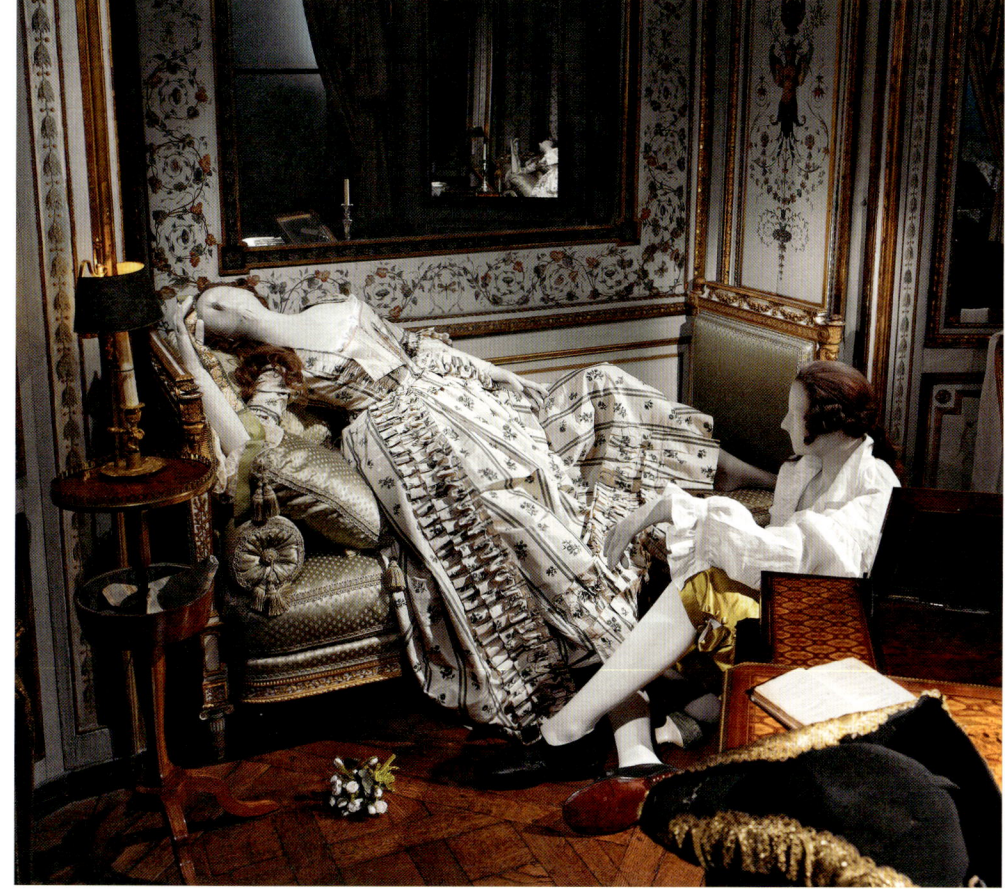

165. "Dangerous Liaisons" exhibit: Dress (robe à la française). French, late 18th century. Hand-painted green-and-white woven striped silk taffeta. Purchase, Irene Lewisohn Bequest, 1954 (c.i.54.70a, b)

believed that larger spaces would encourage the creation of ambitious exhibition schemes and also permit a more hospitable accommodation of the public; his point was supported by swelling attendance figures and approving comments in the Museum's visitor surveys. At the same time came the realization that the storage facilities of the department were nearly full to capacity. Plans for a radical transformation of our physical plant, now being studied, call for an ambitious new design for a state-of-the-art storage facility to house the collection and offer various options for the reconfiguration of the department's offices.

In connection with this capital project, the director insisted that The Costume Institute reexamine its collecting philosophy and undertake a rigorous editing of its works. He had always emphasized the primacy of artistic merit in the consideration of works for the collection but had also given the department a mandate to represent fully the history of Western dress—one reason our holdings have almost doubled since he came to the Museum. It is ironic that although Philippe disavowed any deep knowledge of costume history, he had to exercise his judgment on many of our most important acquisitions without consulting the trustees. Because until recently even the rarest costume pieces have been of relatively small value, the institute has usually been exempted from the general acquisitions review process and has only had to secure approval from the director. In the past few years, however, as competition for important examples of historical costume has increased, a number of extraordinary works of considerable value have been presented to the Acquisitions Committee. Only once did Philippe have reservations about a departmental submission: an extremely unusual set of panniers, the eighteenth-century hoops that underpinned the airy volume of a court gown. It speaks to his faith in and support of his curators that throughout the review process he maintained an uncharacteristic silence, however provocative may have been the temptation to speak—the panniers were French, they were expensive, they were underwear—and left it to the expertise of his staff and the exceptionality of the object to make the argument.

The department made perhaps its most important major acquisition in 2005, when the wardrobe of Denise Poiret, the wife of designer Paul Poiret, suddenly appeared on the market.

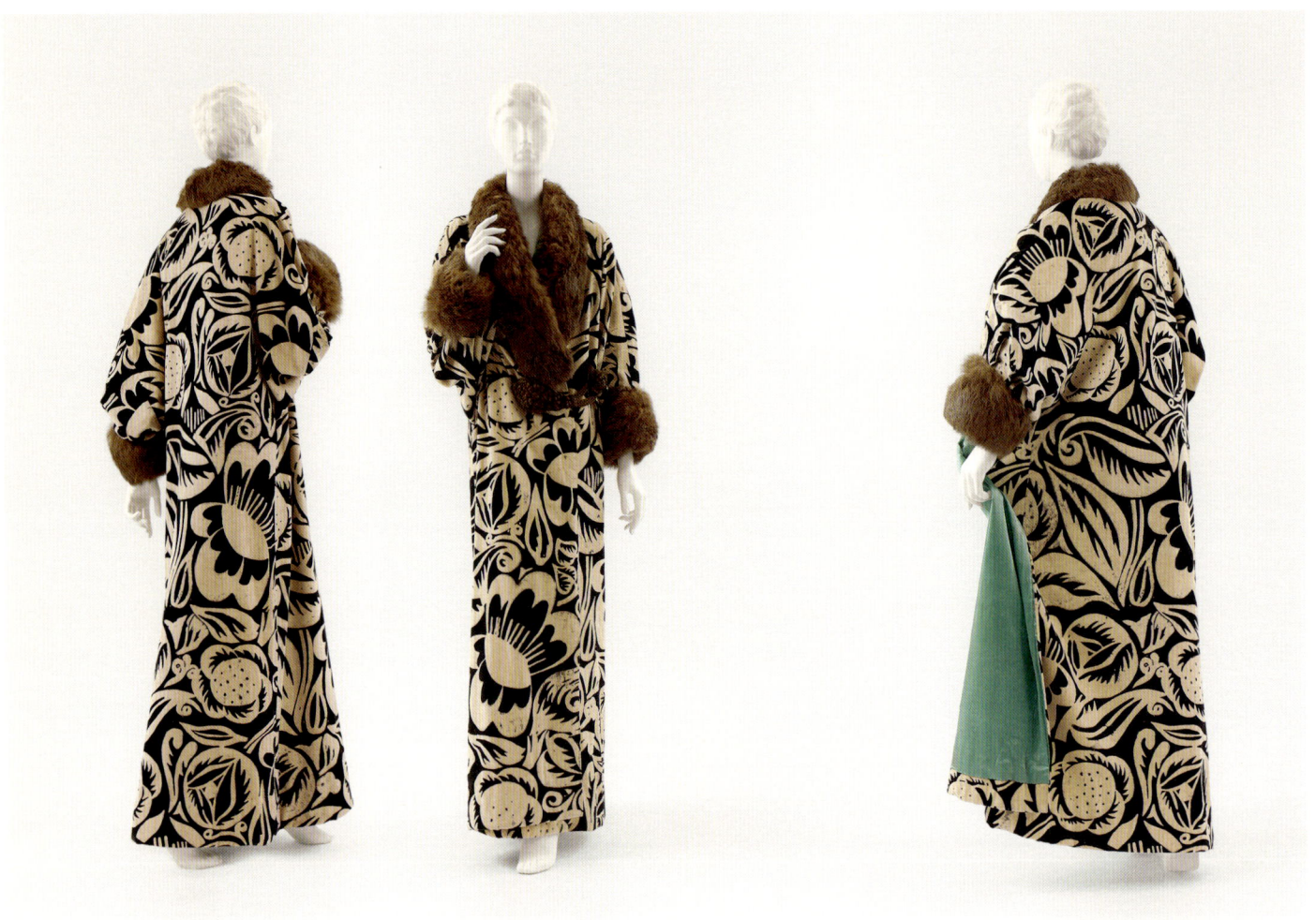

166. "La Perse" coat worn by Denise Poiret. French, by Paul Poiret, 1911. Textile design by Raoul Dufy. Ivory and blue-black block-printed cotton velvet with brown rabbit fur trim. Purchase, Friends of The Costume Institute Gifts, 2005 (2005.199)

Poiret was the first modernist couturier of the twentieth century, and his late work was already more than adequately represented in the collection. With the exception, however, of one fancy dress, the institute had no designs from his most influential period, the years just preceding World War I. For some of Poiret's most iconic works, with their impeccable provenance, to be offered at auction was an unprecedented opportunity. The director immediately mobilized the Acquisitions Committee and released enough funding to allow the Museum to purchase the most important pieces in the Denise Poiret collection. The new acquisitions, supplemented by a minimal number of loans, became the basis of the award-winning 2007 exhibition "Poiret: King of Fashion" (figs. 166, 167, 168).

During his last years as director, Philippe encouraged the department to pursue a partnership with the Brooklyn Museum, in which its magnificent costume collections would be pooled with our own. Clearly such a merger would result in an expansion of our storage needs. The director's support for this potential enhancement of the collection, over the pressing (but manageable) pragmatics of a capital project, gives an idea of his priorities and ambitions. To underscore our interest in the possible partnership, Philippe arranged a meeting with Arnold Lehman, director of the Brooklyn Museum. Arriving early, he stopped at a small coffee shop near the museum. The burly chef, his back to the counter, must have heard Philippe place his order. He turned and asked, "Aren't you Philippe de Montebello, the

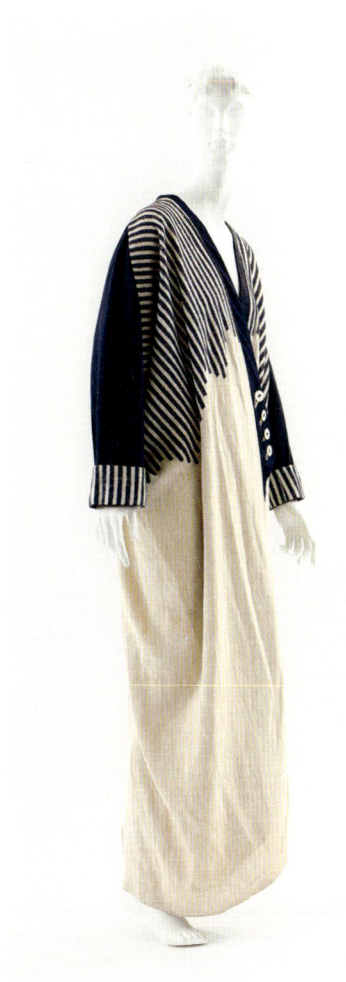
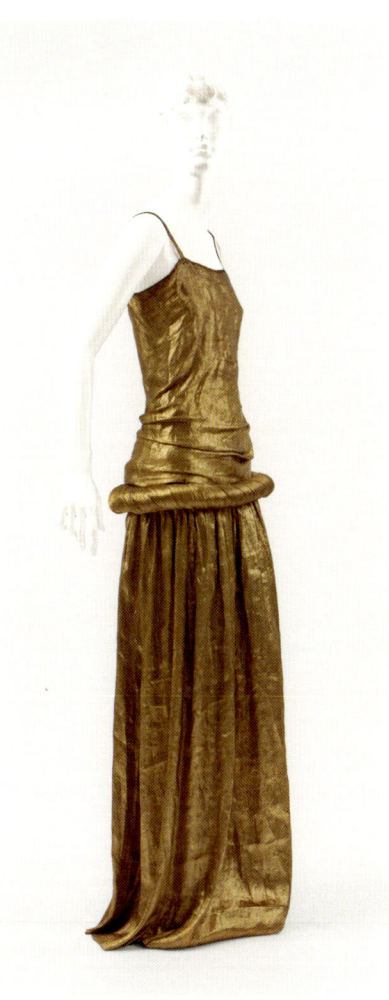
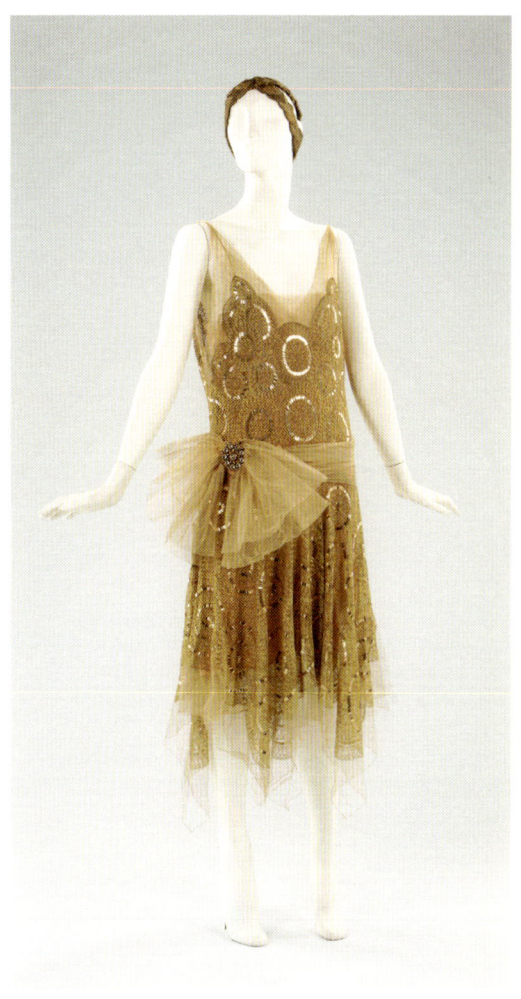

167. "Manteau d'Auto" coat worn by Denise Poiret. French, by Paul Poiret, 1912. Textile by Rodier. Blue-and-oatmeal striped woven linen and blue silk. Isabel Shults Fund, 2005 (2005.200)

168. "Irudrée" evening gown. French, by Paul Poiret, ca. 1922. Gold lamé. Purchase, Friends of The Costume Institute Gifts, 2007 (2007.146)

169. Evening ensemble. French, by Jeanne Lanvin, summer 1923. Silk, sequins, metallic, rhinestones. Brooklyn Museum Costume Collection at The Metropolitan Museum of Art, Gift of the Brooklyn Museum, 2009; Designated Purchase Fund, 1984 (84.4a–c)

director of the Metropolitan Museum?" It was a trivial moment and had no bearing on the later discussion, but it augured well for a successful outcome. On December 16, 2008, Lehman announced that the "landmark collaboration" between the Brooklyn Museum and the Metropolitan Museum would become effective in January 2009 (fig. 169).

Early in his tenure Philippe remarked, with more candor than tact, that an Aubusson chair seat might be said to have a higher position in a hierarchy of the arts than any dress. Even today, after three decades of his encouraging this department's efforts and, on more than one occasion, indulging our requests, it is unlikely that Philippe could with conviction equate a couture masterpiece with a painting or sculpture. It speaks to his philosophy as director that during the past thirty years his commitment to the department was, nonetheless, sustained and often passionate.

Under Philippe's directorship, the staff of the institute more than doubled, its archives were fully catalogued, and its exhibition programming was enhanced. At his behest, the curators initiated an ongoing review of the collection. Not only have pieces of secondary interest been identified and deaccessioned or otherwise disposed of, but a body of masterworks has been assembled that constitutes a timeline of Western high fashion. To put it differently, The Costume Institute has evolved into an archive not only encyclopedic in breadth but also rich in iconic examples of the last three centuries.

Harold Koda

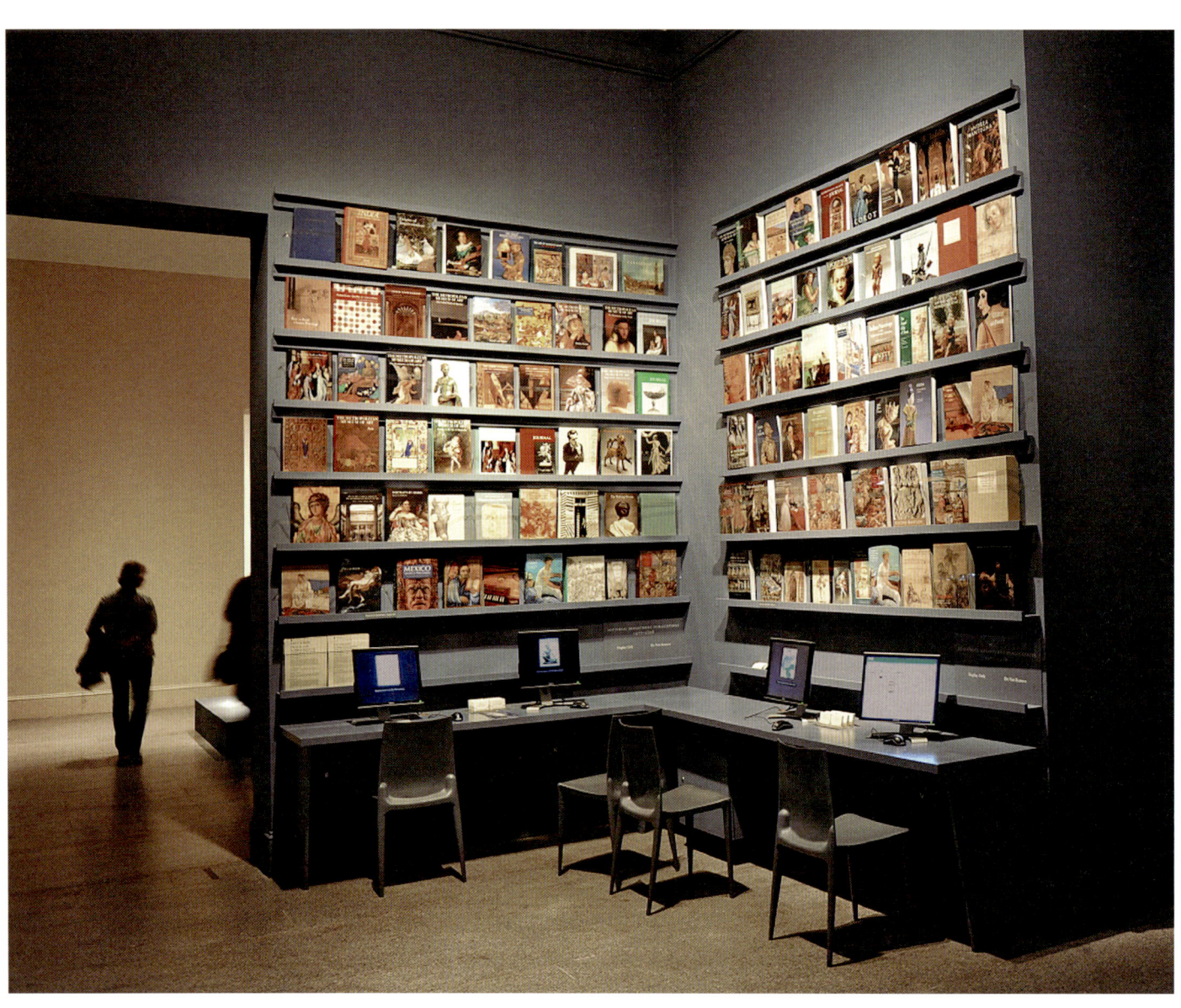

PUBLICATIONS

PUBLISHING AT THE METROPOLITAN MUSEUM

The Metropolitan Museum publications program is based upon the Museum's first publication, the *Charter, Constitution, and By-Laws of 1870*. This document states that the Metropolitan Museum was founded for the purpose "of encouraging and developing the study of the fine arts—of advancing the general knowledge of kindred subjects, and, to that end, of furnishing popular instruction."

Following this dictate, the Museum has published many significant volumes in the course of its long history, but none more so than during the directorship of Philippe de Montebello, beginning in 1977 and ending in 2008. In this period, all of the Museum's curatorial departments were encouraged to publish their collections and to plan exhibitions and accompanying catalogues that would contribute to scholarship and increase knowledge of the Museum's holdings.

The Department of European Paintings, under the leadership of John Pope-Hennessy and then Everett Fahy, led the way by producing a number of retrospective exhibitions, principally of great Dutch, French, and Italian artists. Catalogues for some of these major exhibitions include *Manet 1832–1883*, edited by Françoise Cachin, Charles S. Moffet, et al. (1983); *Van Gogh in Arles*, by Ronald Pickvance (1984); *The Age of Caravaggio*, by Mina Gregori et al. (1985); *François Boucher, 1703–1770*, by Alastair Laing et al. (1986); *Van Gogh in Saint-Rémy and Auvers*, by Ronald Pickvance (1986); *Degas*, by Jean Sutherland Boggs et al. (1988) (fig. 171); *Velázquez*, by Antonio Domínguez Ortíz et al. (1989); *Canaletto*, by Katharine Baetjer and J. G. Links (1989); *Georges Seurat, 1859–1891*, by Robert L. Herbert et al. (1991); *Andrea Mantegna*, edited by Jane Martineau (1992); *Portraits by Ingres: Image of an Epoch*, edited by Gary Tinterow, Philip Conisbee, et al. (1999); *Vermeer and the Delft School*, by Walter Liedtke et al. (2001); and *Poussin and Nature: Arcadian Visions*, edited by Pierre Rosenberg and Keith Christiansen (2008) (fig. 175).

Opposite: 170. Some of the books published by the Metropolitan Museum, as exhibited in "The Philippe de Montebello Years: Curators Celebrate Three Decades of Acquisitions," 2008

The Department of Medieval Art also published significant volumes during Philippe's directorship. These notably included *Age of Spirituality: Late Antique and Early Christian Art, Third to Seventh Century*, edited by Helen C. Evans and William D. Wixom (1979), and *The Glory of Byzantium: Art and Culture of the Middle Byzantine Era, A.D. 843–1261* (1997) and *Byzantium: Faith and Power (1261–1557)* (2004) (fig. 174), both edited by Helen C. Evans.

All the other curatorial departments contributed to the cornucopia of distinguished volumes published during Philippe's tenure. The Department of Asian Art, for example, brought out *The Great Bronze Age of China: An Exhibition from the People's Republic of China*, edited by Wen Fong (1980); *Beyond Representation: Chinese Painting and Calligraphy, 8th–14th Century*, by Wen C. Fong (1992) (fig. 172); *Possessing the Past: Treasures from the National Palace Museum, Taipei*, by Wen C. Fong, James C. Y. Watt, et al. (1996); and *China: Dawn of a Golden Age, 200–750 A.D.*, by James Watt et al. (2004).

Some of the other notable publications issued by the many curatorial departments of the Museum are enumerated in the list below.

During Philippe's directorship, the Museum's publications became truly professional in that great care and attention were lavished not only on shaping their content but also on the editing of texts, on design, and on the accurate reproduction of illustrations. Color illustrations throughout the text became the norm, and great skill was employed in separating and proofing these images to exacting standards. All the Museum's publications were graced with thorough indexes, while bibliographies were carefully researched and included in all important publications.

The principal reason the Museum was able to enlarge and enrich its publishing program during Philippe's directorship was his conviction that scholarly publications are a main endeavor of the institution and that exhibition catalogues become the permanent record after the exhibitions have closed.

Philippe made every effort to persuade the trustees of the importance of funding these publications, and he endeavored to

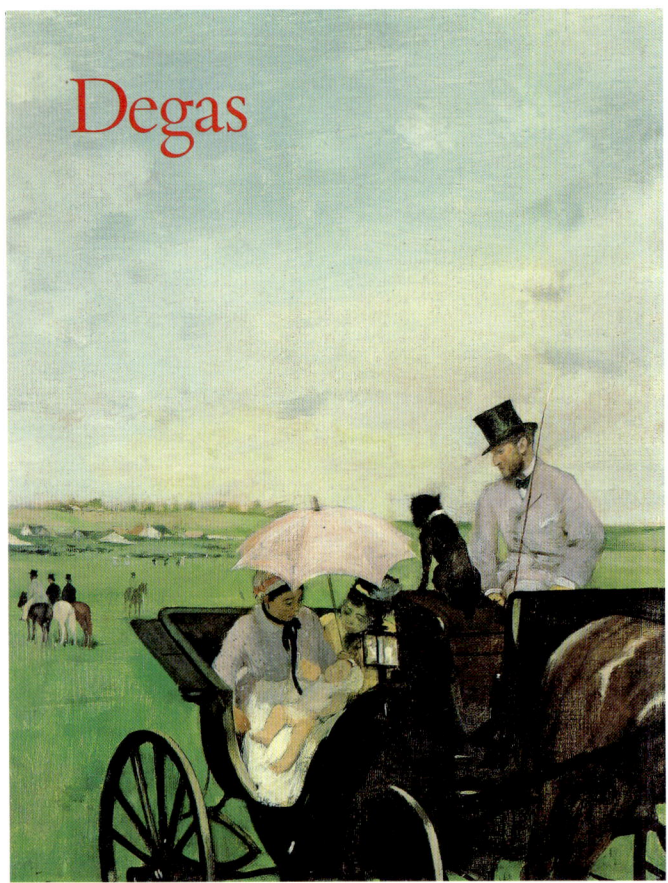

171. *Degas*, 1988

build publication funds to help support their costs. Patrons were found who shared his vision about the value of the Museum's publishing effort.

It can truly be said of Philippe that on his arrival as director he found the Museum publications a Model T Ford and on his departure he left them a Rolls-Royce.

The following list gives an overview of some of the most outstanding of the one thousand or so publications the Museum issued during Philippe's grand directorship.

1978–2008   *Recent Acquisitions*. Fall issues of *The Metropolitan Museum of Art Bulletin*

1980   *European Paintings in The Metropolitan Museum of Art by Artists Born in or before 1865: A Summary Catalogue*, 3 vols., by Katharine Baetjer

1982   *The Vatican Collections: The Papacy and Art*, by curators at the Vatican Museums and The Metropolitan Museum of Art

1983, 1994, 2005   *The Metropolitan Museum of Art Guide*, edited by Kathleen Howard

1984   *Flemish Paintings in The Metropolitan Museum of Art*, by Walter A. Liedtke

1984   *The Jack and Belle Linsky Collection in The Metropolitan Museum of Art*, by curators in the Departments of European Paintings, European Sculpture and Decorative Arts, and Medieval Art

1985   *American Furniture in The Metropolitan Museum of Art: Late Colonial Period: The Queen Anne and Chippendale Styles*, by Morrison H. Heckscher

1985   *European Post-Medieval Tapestries and Related Hangings in The Metropolitan Museum of Art*, 2 vols., by Edith Appleton Standen

1985   *India: Art and Culture, 1300–1900*, by Stuart Cary Welch

1985   *Liechtenstein: The Princely Collections*

1986   *The Age of Correggio and the Carracci: Emilian Painting of the Sixteenth and Seventeenth Centuries*

1986   *Treasures of the Holy Land: Ancient Art from the Israel Museum*, by curators of the Israel Museum

1987   *The Robert Lehman Collection, I: Italian Paintings*, by John Pope-Hennessy with Laurence B. Kanter

1987–97   The Metropolitan Museum of Art at Home series, 12 vols.

1988   *Fragonard*, by Pierre Rosenberg

1988   *Painting in Renaissance Siena, 1420–1500*, by Keith Christiansen et al.

1989   *The New Vision: Photography Between the Wars. Ford Motor Company Collection at The Metropolitan Museum of Art*, by Maria Morris Hambourg and Christopher Phillips

1989   *Twentieth-Century Modern Masters: The Jacques and Natasha Gelman Collection*, by Sabine Rewald et al., edited by William S. Lieberman

1990   *Mexico: Splendors of Thirty Centuries*, introduction by Octavio Paz

1992   *Al-Andalus: The Art of Islamic Spain*, edited by Jerrilynn D. Dodds

1993   *The Art of Medieval Spain*, A.D. 500–1200

1993   *Medieval Tapestries in The Metropolitan Museum of Art*, by Adolfo Salvatore Cavallo

1993   *Splendid Legacy: The Havemeyer Collection*, by Alice Cooney Frelinghuysen et al.

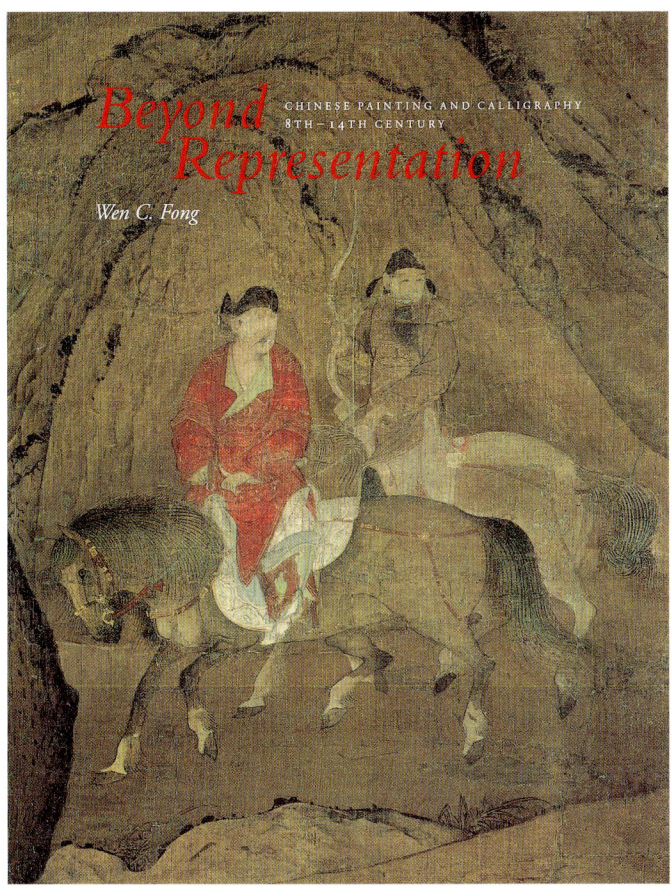

172. *Beyond Representation: Chinese Painting and Calligraphy, 8th–14th Century*, 1992

1993 *The Waking Dream: Photography's First Century. Selections from the Gilman Paper Company Collection*, by Maria Morris Hambourg et al.
1994 *Origins of Impressionism*, by Gary Tinterow and Henri Loyrette
1996 *Corot*, by Gary Tinterow et al.
1997 *The Drawings of Filippino Lippi and His Circle*, by George R. Goldner and Carmen C. Bambach
1998 *From Van Eyck to Breughel: Early Netherlandish Painting in The Metropolitan Museum of Art*, edited by Maryan W. Ainsworth and Keith Christiansen
1999 *Egyptian Art in the Age of the Pyramids*, edited by Dorothea Arnold
1999 *The Gubbio Studiolo and Its Conservation*, 2 vols., by Olga Raggio and Antoine M. Wilmering
2000 *Walker Evans*, by Maria Morris Hambourg, Jeff L. Rosenheim, et al.

2001 *Pieter Bruegel the Elder: Drawings and Prints*, edited by Nadine M. Orenstein (fig. 173)
2001 *Tapestry in the Renaissance: Art and Magnificence*, by Thomas P. Campbell et al.
2003 *Art of the First Cities: The Third Millennium B.C. from the Mediterranean to the Indus*, edited by Joan Aruz
2003 *Goddess: The Classsical Mode*, by Harold Koda
2003 *Leonardo da Vinci, Master Draftsman*, edited by Carmen C. Bambach
2003 *Manet/Velázquez: The French Taste for Spanish Painting*, by Gary Tinterow, Geneviève Lacambre, et al.
2004 *Childe Hassam, American Impressionist*, by H. Barbara Weinberg et al.
2005 *Hatshepsut: From Queen to Pharaoh*, edited by Catharine H. Roehrig et al.
2005 *Prague, The Crown of Bohemia, 1347–1437*, edited by Barbara Drake Boehm and Jiří Fajt

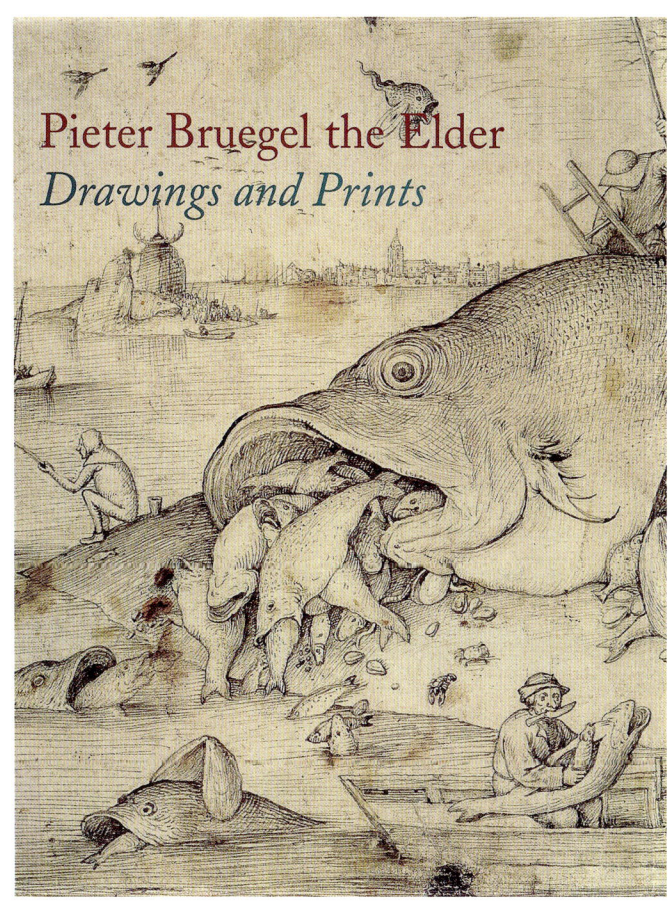

173. *Pieter Bruegel the Elder: Drawings and Prints*, 2001

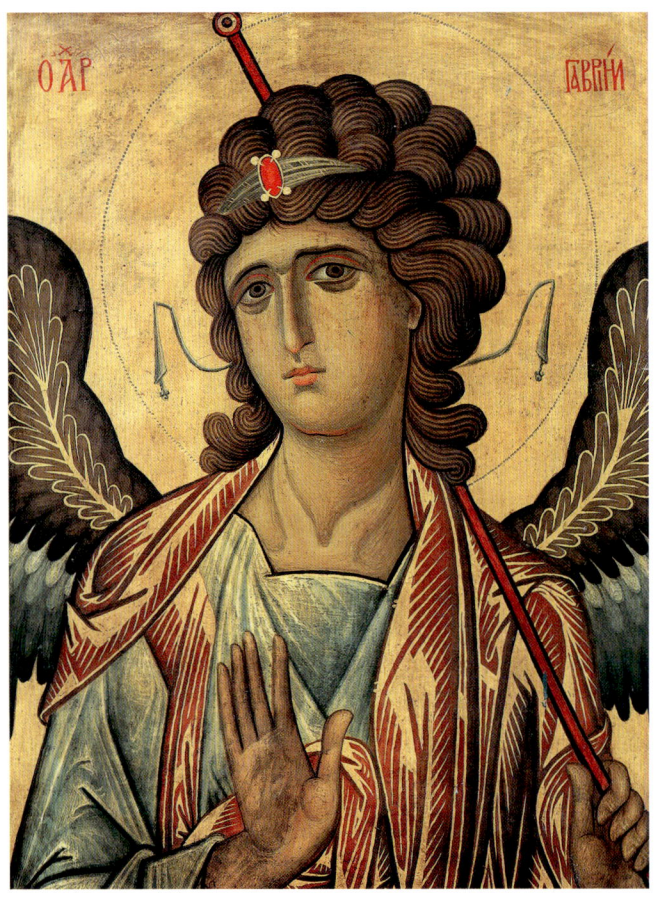

174. *Byzantium: Faith and Power (1261–1557)*, 2004

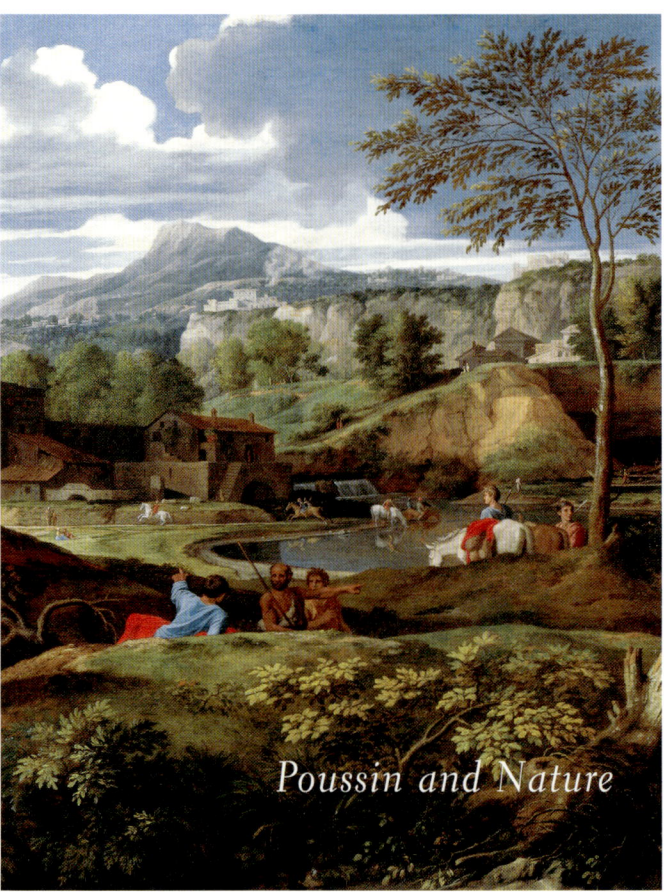

175. *Poussin and Nature: Arcadian Visions*, 2008

2005 *Vincent van Gogh: The Drawings*, by Colta Ives, Susan Alyson Stein, et al.

2006 *Glitter and Doom: German Portraits from the 1920s*, by Sabine Rewald et al.

2006 *Warriors of the Himalayas: Rediscovering the Arms and Armor of Tibet*, by Donald J. La Rocca et al.

2007 *American Furniture in The Metropolitan Museum of Art: I. Early Colonial Period: The Seventeenth-Century and William and Mary Styles*, by Frances Gruber Safford

2007 *American Quilts & Coverlets in The Metropolitan Museum of Art*, by Amelia Peck

2007 *Art of the Classical World in The Metropolitan Museum of Art: Greece, Cyprus, Etruria, Rome*, by Carlos A. Picón et al.

2007 *Dutch Paintings in The Metropolitan Museum of Art*, 2 vols., by Walter Liedtke

2007 *Eternal Ancestors: The Art of the Central African Reliquary*, edited by Alisa LaGamma

2007 *Impressed by Light: British Photographs from Paper Negatives, 1840–1860*, by Roger Taylor

2007 *Oceania: Art of the Pacific Islands in The Metropolitan Museum of Art*, by Eric Kjellgren

2007 *Poiret*, by Harold Koda and Andrew Bolton

2007 *The Wrightsman Pictures*, edited by Everett Fahy

2008 *Beyond Babylon: Art, Trade, and Diplomacy in the Second Millennium B.C.*, edited by Joan Aruz et al.

John P. O'Neill

INDEX

Numbers in *italics* refer to pages on which illustrations appear.

Abbott, Berenice, 136
Abemeyor, Michael, 106
Abemeyor, Nelly, Violet, and Elie, 106
"Abstract Expressionism and Other Modern Works: The Muriel Kallis Steinberg Newman Collection in The Metropolitan Museum of Art" (exhibition), 130, *130*; fig. 148
Acconci, Vito, 136
Adamson, Robert, 137
Adelson, Warren and Jan, 70, 73
Adlin, Jane, 133
Aesthetic movement, 69, 70
Africa, Oceania, and the Americas, Department of, 113–25
    African art, 115–18
    Jan Mitchell Treasury, *112*, 113–14; fig. 126
    Melanesian art, gallery for, 120–21, *120*; fig. 135
    Michael C. Rockefeller Memorial Collection, 115–17
    Michael C. Rockefeller Wing, 113, 122, 123, 127
    Oceanic art, 119–21
    P. de M.'s influence on, 114, 119, 121, 122, 124, 125
    Photograph Study Collection, 122–25
Agee, James, *Let Us Now Praise Famous Men* (with photographs by Walker Evans), 140
"Age of Caravaggio, The," exhibition, 38; catalogue, 151
"Age of Napoleon, The: Costume from Revolution to Empire, 1789–1815" (exhibition), 144, *144*; fig. 162
"Age of Rembrandt, The" (exhibition), 41
"Age of Spirituality: Late Antique and Early Christian Art, Third to Seventh Century," exhibition, xi, 25; catalogue, 151
Aguado, Onésipe, *Woman Seen from the Back*, *139*, 140; fig. 159
Ahhotep burial, Thebes, 14, *14*; fig. 18
A. Hyatt Mayor: Selected Writings and a Bibliography, 42
Ainsworth, Maryan W., 38, 41, 67

Aitken, Annie Laurie, Galleries of English Decorative Arts, 50
Akbar period painting, *Lion at Rest*, 107
Akhenaten, king of Egypt, 7, 8
Alabastron (perfume bottle; Hellenistic), 17, *18*; fig. 23
"Al-Andalus: The Art of Islamic Spain" (exhibition), 108
Alexander the Great, 8
"All That Glitters Is Not Gold" (exhibition), 53
"Along the Ancient Silk Routes: Central Asian Art from the West Berlin State Museums" (exhibition), 99
Al-Sabah Collection, Kuwait, 108
Altman bequest, 41
Amati, Andrea, violin, 76–77, *76*, *77*; figs. 90, 91
Amati Group, 77, 79
"American Art Poster of the 1890s, The: Gift of Leonard A. Lauder" (exhibition), 42
American Decorative Arts, Department of, 69; *see also* The American Wing
American Drawings and Watercolors (collection catalogue), 66–67
"American Furniture and the Art of Connoisseurship" (exhibition), 70
American Impressionism and Realism (exhibition catalogue), 70
American Paintings and Sculpture, Department of, 69, 128; *see also* The American Wing
American Paradise (exhibition catalogue), 70
American Rococo (exhibition catalogue), 70
Americans in Paris (exhibition catalogue), 70
"American Tonalism: Paintings, Drawings, Prints, and Photographs" (exhibition), 69–70
American Wing, The, x, xii, 69–73
    endowed curatorial positions in, 73
    evolution of, 69, 71, 72–73
    exhibitions, 69–70
    Friends of the American Wing, 70
    gifts and acquisitions, 71–72, 73
    opening of, 69
    P. de M., involvement in, 69, 70, 71, 72–73
    publications, 70–71
    William Cullen Bryant Fellows, 70

Amory, Dita, 61–64
Anatolia
    cuneiform tablet, 12–13, *13*; fig. 15
    furniture supports, 11, *11*; fig. 13
"Anatomy of a Building, The: Multiple Architecture of The Metropolitan Museum of Art" (P. de M. lecture), 83
Anavian, Habib, 107
Ancient Near Eastern Art, Department of
    "Art of the First Cities" (exhibition), 10, 11, 15
    "Beyond Babylon" (exhibition), 11–14, *14*, 15, *15*; figs. 18, 19, 20
    "Contact and Exchange" (conference), 10–11, 14
    and "universal museum," 10–15
Andrea Mantegna (exhibition catalogue), 151
Andrew, Thomas, *Safuni Lake, Savaii*, 123, *123*; fig. 138
"AngloMania: Tradition and Transgression in British Fashion" (exhibition), 53
Annenberg, Walter H. and Leonore, xii, 60, 103
Annenberg, Walter H. and Leonore, Collection Galleries, *127*, 130–31; fig. 143
Annenberg Foundation, 50, 54, 140
Anshutz, Thomas, *A Rose*, 71
Apollo Belvedere (Roman), 52
Apraxine, Pierre, 42, 139
Arbus, Diane, 140–41
    Blind couple in their bedroom, Queens, N.Y., 140
    Masked boy with friends, Coney Island, N.Y., 140
    Russian midget friends in a living room on 100th Street, N.Y.C., 140
    Woman with a veil on Fifth Avenue, N.Y.C., 140
Argerich, Martha, 84
armbands with tritoness and triton holding Erotes (Hellenistic), *20*, 21; fig. 27
armband with Herakles knot (Hellenistic), 21, *21*; fig. 32
Arms and Armor, Department of, 89–95
    acquisitions, 89–92
    exhibitions, 92–95

P. de M.'s influence on, 89, 92, 95
Sulzberger, Arthur Ochs, Gallery, 89, 94
Arnold, Dorothea, 3–9, 15
Arrau, Claudio, 84
"Art and Love in Renaissance Italy" (exhibition), 38
Art and the Empire City (exhibition catalogue), 70
Artists and Anatomists (publication), 42
"Art Museums, the Internet, and the New Technology" (P. de M. lecture), 83
"Art of Collecting, The" (P. de M. lecture), 83
Art of Illumination, The: The Limbourg Brothers and the Belles Heures of Jean de France, Duc de Berry (exhibition catalogue), 28
Art of Medieval Spain, The: A.D. 500–1200 (exhibition catalogue), 28
"Art of Precolumbian Gold, The: Jan Mitchell Collection" (exhibition), *112*, 113; fig. 126
"Art of the First Cities: The Third Millennium B.C. from the Mediterranean to the Indus" (exhibition), 10, 11, 15
"Art of the Royal Court: Splendors of Pietre Dure from the Palaces of Europe" (exhibition), 53
"Art of Time, The: Clocks and Watches from the Collection" (exhibition), 53
Arts and Crafts movement, 69
Aruz, Joan, 10–15
Ashkenazy, Vladimir, 84
Asian Art, Department of, xii, 97–103
  acquisitions, 97, 99, 100
  Arts of Japan galleries, 99, *100*; fig. 113
  Bishop, Heber R., jade collection, 103
  Dillon Galleries, 98, 103
  evolution of, 97–100, 103
  exhibitions, 97, 98, 99, 100
  Irving, Florence and Herbert, Asian Wing, xiii, 101–3
  Ming Room, 98, *98*; fig. 110
  Pan-Asian Collection, 99
  P. de M.'s involvement in, xii, 97, 99–100, *100*, 101, *101*, 103
  publications, 151
  Sackler Galleries, The, 99
Assyrian reliefs, xii
Astor, Brooke Russell, 98
Astor, Vincent, Foundation, 98
Astor Court, The, xii, 97–98

Atget, Eugène, 140
Attarouthi Treasury, 25
Augustus, Caesar, 17
Avedon, Richard, 138, 141
  Andy Warhol and the Members of The Factory, New York City, 138
  The Chicago Seven, 138
  The Mission Council, 138

Bache, Alice, 113
Bache bequest, 41
Bacot, Edmond, 135
Baetjer, Katharine, x–xiii, 151
Baldung Grien, Hans, *Saint John on Patmos,* 36
Baldus, Édouard, 135, 141
Ballard, James, 107
Balthus, *The Mountain, 129,* 130; fig. 146
Bambach, Carmen C., 46
Bard Graduate Center, 27, 53–54
Barenboim, Daniel, 84
Barnard, George Grey, 23
Barnet, Peter, 23–29
Barry, Michael, 111
Bastis, Christos G., 21
Battle, Kathleen, 83
Bayer, Andrea, 38
Bean, Jacob, 43–44, 45
Bearman, Kay, 130
Beatus of Liébana, manuscript leaf, *The First Angel Sounds the Trumpet; Fire, Hailstones, and Blood Are Cast upon the Earth,* 23, *24;* fig. 34
Beautiful Style, 24
Beaux Arts Trio, 83
Becher, Bernd and Hilla, 136
"Before Cortes" (exhibition), x
Belau female figure, 121
Bell, Louis V., Fund, 111
Bell, William, 140
Bellange, Jacques, 42, 45
Belles Heures of Jean, Duc de Berry, 23, 28
Bellini, Giovanni, altarpiece, 136, *137*; fig. 157
Bentley, Jerry H., 10–11
Berggruen, Heinz, 130
Berio, Luciano, 81
Berkman, Lillian Rojtman, 55
Bernini, Gianlorenzo, 44, 55
Bernstein, Aline, 143
Berry, Max and Heidi, 73

"Beyond Babylon: Art, Trade, and Diplomacy in the Second Millennium B.C." (exhibition), 11–14, *14,* 15, *15*; figs. 18, 19, 20
Beyond Representation: Chinese Painting and Calligraphy, 8th–14th Century (exhibition catalogue), 151, *153*; fig. 172
Biddulph, Peter, 75
bidri water-pipe base, 107
Binney, Edwin, 3rd, 106
Birch, Everett B., 110
Birch, Patti Cadby, 110
Bishop, Heber R., jade collection, 103
Black, Leon and Debra, 46
Blake, William, 46
Bloom, Claire, 83
"Blue Qur'an" (Fatimid period), *104,* 111; fig. 119
Blumenthal, George, 107
Blumka, Ruth, 107
Boardman, Elijah, 71
Boehm, Barbara Drake, 26, 27, 28, 56
Boggs, Jean Sutherland, 151
Bolet, Jorge, 84
Bonna, Jean, 46
Bonnard, Pierre, 42
Boorsch, Suzanne, 42
Booth, John Wilkes, 139
Bothmer, Bernard V., 5
Boucher, François, 44
Boulogne, Valentin de, *The Lute Player,* 34, *35*; fig. 46
Bourhis, Katell le, 144
Bourke-White, Margaret, 136
Brady, Mathew, 139
Brandely, Jean, 54
Brandt, Bill, 135
Brant, Peter, 129
Braque, Georges, 131
Brassaï, 136, 140
Braun, Adolphe, 135
Bream, Julian, 83
Brendel, Alfred, 83
Brettell, Richard, 67
Bronzino, Agnolo, 45
brooch, pediment-shaped (Greek), *20,* 21; fig. 31
Brooklyn Museum, 148–49
Brown, Jonathan, 65, 67
Brown, Katharine R., 28
Brown, Mary Elizabeth (Mrs. John Crosby Brown), 81

Brown, Ambassador and Mrs. W. L. Lyons, 73
Brueggen, Franz, 85
Bryant, William Cullen, Fellows, 70
Budapest String Quartet, 83–84
Buddha, standing (Gupta period), *96, 97*; fig. 109
Bull, Ole, 75
Bulletin (MMA publication), 42, 44, 46, 70–71
Burke, James and Diane, 111
Bustamante, Jean-Marc, *Lumière,* 136
Byrne, Janet S., 42
Byzantine art, 25–26, 28
"Byzantium: Faith and Power (1261–1557)," exhibition, 26; catalogue, 151, *154*; fig. 174

Cabirol, Barthélemy, 51
Cachin, Françoise, 151
Callot, Jacques, 45
"Cameo Appearances" (exhibition), 53
cameo glass fragment of large platter or tabletop (Roman), 18–19, *19*; fig. 26
cameo orant, 25
Camera Work (periodical), 135
Cameron, Julia Margaret, 137, 139
Campbell, Thomas P., xiii, 50, 52, 56–60
Canadian Broadcasting Corporation (CBC), 84
"Canaletto," exhibition, xii; catalogue, 151
Canova, Antonio, 55
Cantor, B. Gerald, Collection, 51
Cantor, Iris and B. Gerald, Exhibition Hall, xii, 146
Cantor, Iris and B. Gerald, Galleries, 48
Cantor, Iris and B. Gerald, Roof Garden, xii
Caravaggio (Michelangelo Merisi), 34, 38
   The Denial of Saint Peter, 36, 37; fig. 48
   Musicians, 36
Carboni, Stefano, 105–11
Caroline Islands, weather charm and seated figure, 121
Carpaccio, Vittore, 45
Carracci, Annibale, *Two Children Teasing a Cat,* 37
Carracci, Ludovico, 37
Carracci, the, 44
Carroll, Jane and Robert E., 130
Carroll, Lewis, *Alice Liddell as "The Beggar Maid,"* 139
Carson, Judith and Russell, 6
Cartier-Bresson, Henri, 136, 140

Castelnuovo-Tedesco, Lisbeth, 28
"Cast in Bronze: French Sculpture from Renaissance to Revolution" (exhibition), 53
Cavallo, Adolph, 28
"Celebrating Saint Petersburg" (exhibition), 53
Cézanne, Paul, 128, 131
Chambi, Martin, *Tiaguanaco, 125*; fig. 142
Champaigne, Philippe de, *Annunciation,* 34
Chapuis, Julien, 27
Charles IV, Holy Roman Emperor, 26
Charvet, Jules, 17
Chase, William Merritt, 70
Chassériau, Théodore, 132
Chilton, Richard L., Jr., 73
China: Dawn of a Golden Age (exhibition catalogue), 151
"Chocolate, Coffee, Tea" (exhibition), 53
Choiselat and Ratel, *Pavillon de Flore and the Tuileries Gardens,* 139
Christiansen, Keith, 34–37, 38, 151
Christus, Petrus, 38
Church, Frederic E., *Heart of the Andes,* 71
Cicéri, Pierre-Luc-Charles, 135
Clark, Carol, 67
Clark, Stephen C., 130
Clercq, Louis de, 139
Cloisters, The, 23–28, 41
   Early Gothic Hall, *27*, 28; fig. 38
   Saint Guilhem Cloister, 28
   Treasury, 23–25, 28
Cloisters, The: Studies in Honor of the Fiftieth Anniversary (MMA publication), 28
"Closed Circuit" (exhibition), 141
"Clouet to Seurat: French Drawings from the British Museum" (exhibition), 46
"Coaxing the Spirits to Dance: The Art of the Papuan Gulf" (exhibition), 124–25
Cochran, Alexander Smith, 107
Coecke van Aelst, Pieter, 60
Cohen, Joseph M., 140
Cohen, Karen B., 42, 44, 132
"Collection of Alfred Stieglitz, The: Pioneers of Modern Photography" (exhibition), 42
Colombian/Ecuadorian standing figure, 114, *114*; fig. 128
"Colonial Andes, The: Tapestries and Silverwork, 1530–1830" (exhibition), 52
Colt, Samuel, 89

Company painting, *Giant Indian Fruit Bat,* 110
Concerts & Lectures program, 83–87
   P. de M.'s appearances in, *82, 83, 85, 86, 87*; figs. 95, 96, 97
   P. de M.'s interest in and support for, 83, 84, 85, 86, *87*; fig. 98
Confucius, 77
Conisbee, Philip, 151
Constable, John, 137
"Contact and Exchange in the Ancient World" (conference), 10–11, 14
Cooper, Beatrice T., 7
Copley, John Singleton, 70
   self-portrait miniature, 71, *72*; fig. 86
Cordier, Charles
   La Capresse des colonies, 55
   La Juive d'Alger, 55
Corning Museum of Glass, 108
"Correggio and Parmigianino: Master Draftsmen of the Renaissance" (exhibition), 46
"Costume and Character in the Age of Ingres" (exhibition), 145
Costume Institute, The, 143–49
   acquisitions, 147–48
   exhibitions, 53, 99, 144–47
   "generation gap" in, 146
   interdepartmental loans, 145
   partnership with Brooklyn Museum, 148–49
   P. de M.'s involvement in, 143, 144–46, 147, 148–49
   textiles in, 57
"Counterparts: Form and Emotion in Photographs" (exhibition), 42
Cousin, Jean, the Elder, x, 58
Cowin, Joyce Berger, 73
Crawford, John M., Jr., 98, 100
Creti, Donato, 38
Crowley, Alice Lewisohn, 143
Crucifixion with Symbols of the Evangelists, The, 24, *25*; fig. 35
cuneiform tablets (Anatolia), 12–13, *13*; fig. 15
Cunniffe, Jane and Maurice, 73
cup with gilded-silver mounts (Bohemia), 24, *25*; fig. 36
Curzon, Clifford, 84
Cuvelier, Eugène, 135, 141
Cuyp, Aelbert, 46

cylinder seals and modern impressions
 bull-vaulting scene, lion and bull, weather
  god and worshiper, 13, *13*; fig. 17
 pharaoh and kneeling figures below vultures and Egyptian symbols, 13, *13*;
  fig. 16

daguerreotypy, 140
Daly, Jeff, 6
D'Ancona, Mirella Levi, 67
Dandridge, Pete, 27
"Dangerous Liaisons: Fashion and Furniture
 in the Eighteenth Century" (exhibition),
 50, 53, *142*, 145–46, *147*; figs. 161, 165
Daniel, Malcolm, 135–41
Dark, Philip J. C., *Nataptavo Masqueraders at
 Cape Gloucester, New Britain*, *122*, 123;
 fig. 137
"Daumier Drawings" (exhibition), 44
David, Jacques-Louis, *Death of Socrates*, 131
David, Sir Percival, 97
David-Weill, Michel, 24, 28
Davis, Alexander Jackson, 70
Davis, Peter G., 87
Degas, Hilaire-Germain-Edgar, 42, 46, 141
 Factory Smoke, 42, *43*; fig. 55
"Degas," exhibition, xii; catalogue, 151, *152*;
 fig. 171
Degas galleries, *132*; fig. 151
de Groot, Adelaide Milton, 9
de Groot family, 9
Delacroix, Eugène, x, 42, 44
 Abduction of Rebecca, 131
 Madame Henri François Riesener, 33, *33*; fig. 45
 The Natchez, 132
 Sunset, 44, *44*; fig. 56
de la Renta, Annette, 4, 7
Deller, Alfred, 84
Demidoff family, 50
Design in America: The Cranbrook Vision (exhi-
 bition catalogue), 70
Dick, Harris Brisbane, Fund, 111
Diehl, Charles-Guillaume, 54
Dillon, Douglas, x, xi–xii, 97, 100, *100*, *106*;
 fig. 120
Dillon, Douglas, Galleries for Chinese Paint-
 ings, xii, 98, 103
Dillon Fund, The, 97, 98
Dilworth, J. Richardson, xii

Dinesen, Isak, 138
Dior, Christian, 145
Doge's Palace, Venice, 108
Dogon lifesize standing male figure, 115
Dogon terracotta figure, 115
Domenichino, 37, 45
Domingo, Plácido, 84
Domínguez Ortiz, Antonio, 151
Donatello, circle of, *Winged Boy*, 55
Dosso Dossi, 38
Doubleday, Mrs. Nelson, 107
Draper, Dorothy, 16
Draper, James David, 48, 50, 53
Drawings, Department of, 43–44
Drawings and Prints, Department of, 45–47
"Drawings from the J. Paul Getty Museum"
 (exhibition), 44
"Drawings of Filippino Lippi and His Circle"
 (exhibition), 46
Dresser, Christopher, 54
Drexel, Joseph, 81
Druesedow, Jean, 144
Du Camp, Maxime, 139
Duccio di Buoninsegna, *Madonna and Child*,
 36, *36*; fig. 47
Dufy, Raoul, 148
Duke, Jennifer and Joseph, 138, 140
du Pré, Jacqueline, 83, 84
Dürer, Albrecht, 26, 46
"Düsseldorf School," 136
*Dutch Paintings in The Metropolitan Museum of
 Art* (collection catalogue), 41
Dyck, Anthony van, 32, 46

Eakins, Thomas, 70
Earl, Ralph, 71
Edo plaque with warrior and attendants, 116,
 116; fig. 131
Egyptian art, Department of, 3–9
 acquisitions, 7–8
 Amarna Period, 5, 7–8
 "black style" installations, 5
 Dahshur excavations, *8*, 9; fig. 10
 Deir el-Bahri excavations, 5, 6
 evolution of, x, 3
 exhibitions, 9
 Hatshepsut gallery, *2*, 3, *4*, 6, 7; figs. 3, 4
 installations, 3, 5–7
 P. de M.'s influence on, 3, 6, 7, 9

 pyramid of King Senwosret III, *8*, 9, *9*;
  figs. 10, 11
 Speos Artemidos temple, 9
 Temple of Dendur, 3, 5
 tomb of chancellor Meketra, 3, 5
 tomb of Perneb, *4*, 6, 7; fig. 5
 tombs of Hyksos elite, 6
Egyptian Atef crown, 21
"Eighteenth-Century French Drawings in
 New York Collections" (exhibition), 46
*18th Century Italian Drawings in The Metropol-
 itan Museum of Art* (collection catalogue),
 44
Eilenberg, Samuel, 100
Elizabeth II, queen of England, xii, 46
Elliott, John B., 119
Ellsworth, Robert H., 100
Emerson String Quartet, 84
"Enamels of Limoges: 1100–1350" (exhibition),
 27
"Enduring Rhythms: African Musical Instru-
 ments and the Americas" (exhibition),
 79–80
Engelhard, Charles, Court, xii, *68*, 69, 73; fig. 83
*English and French Medieval Stained Glass in
 the Collection of The Metropolitan
 Museum of Art* (collection catalogue), 28
English Concert, 85
"English Embroidery from The Metropolitan
 Museum of Art, 1580–1700: 'Twixt Art
 and Nature" (exhibition), 54
English statuette of Virgin and Child, 23
"Engravings of Giorgio Ghisi, The" (exhibi-
 tion), 42
Epstein, Sir Jacob, 117, 118
Erickson, Ernest, Foundation, 100
Ettinghausen, Elizabeth, 106
Ettinghausen, Richard, *106*, 105–6, 111; fig. 120
*Eugène Delacroix (1798–1863): Paintings,
 Drawings, and Prints from North
 American Collections* (exhibition
 catalogue), 44
Euphronios Krater, xi
*European Furniture in The Metropolitan
 Museum of Art: Highlights of the Collec-
 tion* (collection catalogue), 50
European Paintings, Department of, 31–33
 building the collection, 34–37, 132
 in-house exhibitions, 38–41, 145

P. de M.'s career in, x, xiii, 31
and P. de M.'s leadership, 32–33, 34, 37
publications, 151
European Sculpture and Decorative Arts (ESDA), Department of, 48–55
  acquisitions, 54–55
  evolution of, 48, *49*, 50, 54–55; fig. 61
  exhibitions, 51–53, 65
  partnerships of, 53–54
  P. de M.'s influence on, 48, 51, 53, 54, 55
  publications, 50
  textiles and tapestries, 56–60
European Textiles (collection catalogue), 67
Evans, Sir Arthur, 10
Evans, Helen C., 23, 26, 151
Evans, Walker, 123–24, 136, 140, 141
  Double Mask, *124*; fig. 139
  Kitchen Corner, Tenant Farmhouse, Hale County, Alabama, *134*, 140; fig. 155

Fahy, Everett, 31–33, 34, 35, 131
Fairchild, Sherman, Foundation, 28, 141
Fait, Jiří, 26
Fales, Martha Gandy, 71
Fang peoples
  female figure from reliquary ensemble, *116*, 117; fig. 130
  freestanding head, 116
Fashion Institute of Technology, 144
Fath, Jacques, 146
Favrile glass, 72
Fenton, Roger, 137, 139, 141
"Festival of International Piano Competition Winners, A ," (concert series), 86
15th and 16th Century Italian Drawings in The Metropolitan Museum of Art (collection catalogue), 44
15th–18th Century French Drawings in The Metropolitan Museum of Art (catalogue), 44
Fifteenth- to Eighteenth-Century European Drawings: Central Europe, The Netherlands, France, England (collection catalogue), 67
Fifteenth- to Eighteenth-Century European Paintings: France, Central Europe, The Netherlands, Spain, and Great Britain (collection catalogue), 67
"Fine Art of Acquisition, The" (P. de M. lecture), 83

Fiorino-Iannace, Giovanna, 57
First Emperor of Qin, 97
Fischer, Henry George, 3
Fisher, Annie, 84
"5,000 years of Korean Art" (exhibition), 99
"Flame and the Lotus, The: Indian and Southeast Asian Art from The Kronos Collections" (exhibition), 100
Fleischman, Larry and Barbara G., 70, 73
Fleischman, Martha J., 69, 73
Flemish tapestry, *The Triumph of Fame*, *59*, 60; fig. 70
"Flowers under Foot: Indian Carpets of the Mughal Era" (exhibition), 108
flutist, celestial (Gandharva), *103*, *103*; fig. 118
Foggini, Giovanni Battista, *Grand Prince Ferdinando de' Medici*, 50, *50*; fig. 62
Fong, Wen C., 97, 99, 151
Forbes, John W., silver plateau, 71
Ford, Barbara, 99
Ford, Tom, 146
Ford Motor Company Collection, xii, 42, 43, 136
Forster-Hahn, Françoise, 67
Fragonard, Jean-Honoré, *A Gathering at Woods' Edge*, 45, *47*; fig. 59
Frames (collection catalogue), 66
François Boucher, 1703–1770 (exhibition catalogue), 151
Frank, Robert, 135
"Frank Hurley in New Guinea" (exhibition), 122
Frazer, Margaret, 25
Freedberg, Sydney, 65
Frémiet, Emmanuel, 54
"French Architectural and Ornament Drawings of the Eighteenth Century" (exhibition), 42
French bookstand, ebony and ivory, 54
French flintlock gun, *88*, 89–92; *99*; detail, *90*, *91*–*92*; figs. 100, 101, 102
Freud, Lucien, *Naked Man, Back View*, *131*; fig. 150
Frick, Henry Clay, 63
Friede, John A., 119
Friedman, Tom, 136
Friedrich, Caspar David, 46
  Two Men Contemplating the Moon, 132
Friedsam bequest, 41
Friends of the American Wing, 70
Friends of the Department of Photographs, 140

Friends of Islamic Art, 110, 111
Froehner, Wilhelm, 17
From Attila to Charlemagne (collection catalogue), 28
"From the Lands of the Scythians: Ancient Art from the Museums of the U.S.S.R." (exhibition), xi
"From Poussin to Matisse: The Russian Taste for French Painting" (exhibition), xii
"From Queen to Empress: Victorian Dress, 1837–1877" (exhibition), 144
"From Van Eyck to Bruegel" (exhibition), 41
Fuller, Buckminster, 138
Fuseli, Henry, 46

Gabriel de Algora, flintlock gun (Spanish), 89, 92; detail, *91*
Galitz, Kathryn, 133
Gallagher, Michael, 34
Ganek, David and Danielle, 140
Ganymede group, earrings, 19, *20*, 21; fig. 30
Gardner, Alexander, 139
garland bowl (Roman), 18, *18*; fig. 24
Garuda Seated in Royal Ease, 99
Gauguin, Paul, 131
  Tahitian Faces, 45, *47*; fig. 60
Gebauer, Paul, 123
Geldzahler, Henry, 128–30
Gelman, Jacques and Natasha, xii, 130
Genet, Jean, 138
Georges Seurat, 1859–1891 (exhibition catalogue), 151
Gérard, Baron François-Pascal-Simon, 33, 132
Gergiev, Valery, 84
Gericault, Théodore, 45
  Evening: Landscape with an Aqueduct, *126*, 132; fig. 144
Germanisches Nationalmuseum, Nuremberg, 26
German Rococo silver, 55
Gérôme, Jean-Léon, *Bashi-Bazouk,* 33
Gerry, Peggy N. and Roger G., Charitable Trust, 73
Gevers, Johann Valentin, and Johann Andreas Thelot, mirror, *53*, 54; fig. 65
Gheyn, Jacques de, II, 46
Ghisi, Giorgio, 42
Giambruni, Helen, 42
Gieseking, Walter, 83

[159]

Gifford, Sanford R., 70
Gilman, Howard, 138
Gilman, Howard, Foundation, 43, 140
Gilman, Howard, Gallery, 141
Gilman Paper Company Collection, 42, 138–40
Giovanni di Balduccio, marble relief, 24
Giovanni di Paolo di Grazia, *The Creation of the World and the Expulsion from Paradise*, *63*, 64; fig. 76
Glass (collection catalogue), 67
"Glass of the Sultans" (exhibition), 108, 110
"Glenn Gould: An Homage" (Concerts & Lectures program), 84
Glenn Gould: A Portrait (documentary), 84
Glimcher, Arnold and Milly, 130
"Glory of Byzantium, The: Art and Culture of the Middle Byzantine Era, A.D. 843–1261," exhibition, 26; catalogue, 151
"Gods of War, The: Sacred Imagery and the Decoration of Arms and Armor" (exhibition), 93–94
Goethe, Johann Wolfgang von, 10
Gogh, Vincent van, 46
    exhibitions and catalogues, xii, 46, 151
    Shoes, 131
    Wheat Field with Cypresses, *128*, 131; fig. 145
Goldner, George R., 34, 45–47
Goldsmith, Horace W., Foundation, 140
Goldthorpe, Caroline, 144
Goldwater, Robert, 115, 117, 118
Gole, Pierre, 54
Goltzius, Hendrick, 46
Gonzalez-Torres, Felix, 136
gospel, fifteenth-century illuminated, 117–18
Goss, Jared, 133
"Gothic and Renaissance Art in Nuremberg, 1300–1500" (exhibition), 26
Gothic ivory carvings, 24
Gothic Revival library, 69
Gould, Florence, Galleries, 48, 50
Gould, Glenn, 84
Goya y Lucientes, Francisco de, 64
    Not This Time Either (Tampoco), *42*, 42; fig. 53
Graf, Urs, 46
Graham, Rodney, 136
"Great Bronze Age of China, The," exhibition, xii, 97; catalogue, 151
Gréau, Julien, 17

Greco, El, 32
    Saint Jerome as Scholar, *64*, 64; fig. 79
    View of Toledo, 36
Greek and Roman Art, Department of, 16–21
    acquisitions, 16–21
    evolution of, 16–17
    glass collection, 16–19
    "Greek Gold," 19–21
    Hellenistic Treasury, 17, 19
    Leon Levy and Shelby White Court, xiii, 16
    Roman Court (1926), 16, *16*; fig. 21
Greek and Roman Galleries, xiii
"Greek Gold: Jewelry of the Classical World" (exhibition), 19–21
Greek Revival parlor, 69
Greene, John Beasley, 139
Gregory, Alexis, 50, 86
Grès, Madame (Alix Barton), evening dress, *145*; fig. 163
Griswold, William, 44
Grunwald, Mrs. Henry A., 9
Guarneri del Gesù, violins by, 75–76, 84
Guarneri String Quartet, 84
Guercino, *Samson Captured by the Philistines*, 32, 36
Gurewitsch, Matthew, 84
Gursky, Andreas, 141
    Schiphol, 136

Habsburg dynasty, 61
Hale, Robert Beverly, 128, 129, 130
Hall, Evelyn A. J., 119
Hall, Gemma and Lewis, 111
Hals, Frans, 41
Hambourg, Maria Morris, 42, 43, 135, 137
Hamilton, Ann, *abc*, 141
Han Gan, *Night-Shining White*, 97, *99*; fig. 111
Hansen, Anne and John V., 4, 7
Harkness, Edward S., 4
Harnett, William M., 70
Harrison, Mary L., 36
Hart, Samuel, house, 73
Hassam, Childe, 70
    Celia Thaxter's Garden, Isles of Shoals, 71
Hatshepsut gallery, 2, 3, 4, 6, 7; figs. 3, 4
Hauser, Hermann, guitar, 80–81, *81*; fig. 94
Havemeyer, Louisine and Henry Osborne, xii, 40–41, 61, 72, 130
Haverkamp-Begemann, Egbert, 65, 67

Hawley family, 9
Hayes, John, 67
Hayes, William C., 3
    The Scepter of Egypt, 3
Hayward, Jane, 28
Hazen, Joseph, 129
head, commemorative, for altar of an oba, 116
Hearn, Maxwell K., 97–100
Hearst Foundation, 106
Heathcote, Josephine Mercy, Gallery, 50
Hecht, Johanna, 52
Heckscher, Morrison H., 69–73
Heemskerck, Maarten van, 46
Heeramaneck, Alice and Nasli M., 99, 107
Heifetz, Jascha, 75, 84
Heintz, Joseph, the Elder, 46
Heinz, Henry J., Galleries, 127, 132–33
Hellenistic Treasury, 17, 19
"Hendrick Goltzius, Dutch Master (1558–1617) Drawings, Prints, and Paintings" (exhibition), 46
Herbert, Robert L., 151
"Heroic Armor of the Italian Renaissance: Filippo Negroli and His Contemporaries" (exhibition), 92–93
Herter Brothers, 70, 72
Hess, Thomas, 130
"Highlights of the Irwin Untermyer Collection" (exhibition), 51
Hill, David Octavius, 137
Hillman, William Talbot, Foundation, 140
Hindman, Sandra, 67
Hirst, Damien, *The Physical Impossibility of Death in the Mind of Someone Living*, 133, *133*; fig. 154
Hoffmann, Hans, *A Hedgehog*, 46, *46*; fig. 58
Holcomb, Melanie, 27–28
Holmes, Mary Tavener, 46, 67
Holmgren, Robert J., 119
Holzer, Harold, 56
Holzer, Philip and Ann, 72
Homer, Winslow, 70
    Boys in a Dory, *72*; fig. 87
Hooch, Pieter de, 38
Horne, Marilyn, 83
Horowitz, Raymond J. and Margaret, 70, 73
Houghton, Arthur, x, 63
Houghton, James R., xiii
Hours of Jeanne d'Évreux, 23, 28

House of Bijapur, The (Deccani), 107
Hoving, Thomas, x, xi, 61, 63, 128
Howat, John K., 69, 70
Huebler, Douglas, 136
Hughes, Robert, 87
Hugo, Charles, 135
Hugo, Victor, 135
Hunt, Richard Morris, 70
Huntington bequest, 41
Hunt of the Unicorn tapestries, 23, 28
Hurley, Frank, 122
Husband, Timothy, 27, 28
Hvorostovsky, Dmitri, 83
Hyksos elite, tombs of, 6

Illuminations (collection catalogue), 67
"Impressionist Epoch, The" (exhibition), xi
"In Castel Durante" Painter (attrib.), majolica dish, 62, *62*; fig. 74
"Incisive Images: Ivories and Boxwoods from the Collection" (exhibition), 53
"India! Art and Culture: 1300–1900" (exhibition), 108
Ingres, Jean-Auguste-Dominique, 45
  portraits of Monsieur and Madame Leblanc, 131
  Princesse de Broglie, 61, *61*; fig. 72
Inness, George, 70
In Pursuit of Beauty: Americans and the Aesthetic Movement (exhibition catalogue), 70
Institut du Monde Arabe, Paris, 108
Institute for Bioarchaeology, 9
"In Style: Celebrating 50 Years of The Costume Institute" (exhibition), 144
Irving, Florence and Herbert, 101, *101*, 103; fig. 114
Irving, Florence and Herbert, Galleries for Chinese Decorative Arts, xiii, 101, 103
Irving, Florence and Herbert, Asian Wing, xiii, 101–3
Islamic Art, Department of, 105–11
  acquisitions, 106, 107, 111
  exhibitions, *106*, 108, 110; fig. 120
  Friends of Islamic Art, 110, 111
  Islamic Galleries, 111
  P. de M.'s donations to, 111
  P. de M.'s influence on, 105, 106, *106*, 107, 108, 110, 111; fig. 120

Islamic textile fragments, 111
Ismaʿil, Shah, at war, depiction on box, 106, *108*; fig. 123
Isthmian gold eagle pendant, 114, *114*; fig. 127
Italian Baroque painting, 36–37, 55
Italian Eighteenth-Century Drawings (collection catalogue), 65
Italian Fifteenth- to Seventeenth-Century Drawings (collection catalogue), 66
Italian Majolica (collection catalogue), 65
Italian Paintings (collection catalogue), 65
Italian Renaissance bronze gallery, 50
"Italian Renaissance Frames" (exhibition), 66
Ives, Colta, 42–44, 46, 135
Ivins, William, 135

"Jacqueline Kennedy: The White House Years" (exhibition), 146
Jaharis, Mary and Michael, 23, 25
  Galleries for Byzantine Art, xiii, *26*, 28; fig. 37
Jaharis Byzantine Lectionary, *22*, 25; fig. 33
Jaley, Louis, 90
Jaspers, Karl, 10
Jenkins, Speight, 84
Jenkins-Madina, Marilyn, 111
Jingyi Zhuren, 79
Joachim, Joseph, 75
Johns, Jasper, 129
  White Flag, 130, *133*; fig. 153
Johnson, Robert Wood, Jr., Gallery, 47, 141
Jones, Julie, 113–14
Josephson, Jack, 7
Juan de Flandes, *Marriage Feast at Cana*, 36
Juilliard String Quartet, 84

Kahsnitz, Rainer, 26
Kajitani, Nobuko, 56
Kalichstein, Joseph, 84
Kanter, Laurence B., 61, 65–67
Kapp, Richard, 84
Kawara, On, 136
Kelekian, Beatrice, 107
Kelekian, Nanette R., 107, 111
Kellen, Anna-Maria and Stephen, Foundation, 55
Kensett, John F., 70
Kerr, Justin, 123
Kertész, André, 135

Kevin Roche John Dinkeloo and Associates, x, 5, 6, 64, 73, 99
Kevorkian, Hagop, Fund Special Exhibitions Gallery, 108
Khalili, Nasser David, 107
Khuner, George and Marianne, 42
Kidd, Dafydd, 28
Kiefer, Anselm, *Bohemia Lies by the Sea*, 130, *131*; fig. 149
Kiehl, David W., 42
Kimmelman, Michael, 38, 83
"King of the World: A Mughal Manuscript from the Royal Library, Windsor Castle" (exhibition), 108
Kirchner, Johann Gottlieb, 52, 54
Kirstein, Lincoln, 130
Kisluk-Grosheide, Daniëlle, 50
Kissinger, Henry A., 98
Kjellgren, Eric, 119–21
Klee, Paul, 130
Klein, William, 135
Knox, George, 65
Koch, Ed, 98
Koda, Harold, 143–49
Koeppe, Wolfram, 50, 53
Komaroff, Linda, 108
Königliche Porzellan-Manufactur, Berlin, 54
Koopman, Ton, 85
Koreny, Fritz, 67
Kossak, Steven M., 100
koto, 79, *79*; fig. 93
Kramer, Mr. and Mrs. Charles, 43
Kravis, Henry R., Wing, xii, 48
Kravis, Mr. and Mrs. Henry R., 140
Kreisler, Fritz, 75
Kremer, Gidon, 83
Krishna's Foster Mother, Yashoda, with the Infant Krishna, 99, *100*, 103; fig. 112
Kronos Collections, 107–8
Ktisis mosaic fragment, 25, 29
Kutubiyya Mosque, Marrakesh, *minbar* (pulpit), *109*, 110
Kuyu peoples, three-headed figure, 117, *117*; fig. 132

La Fosse, Charles de, 44
LaGamma, Alisa, 115–18
Lambayeque gold, 114
Landowska, Wanda, 83

Lanmon, Dwight P., 67
Lannuier, Honoré, 70
	card tables, 71
Lanvin, Jeanne, evening ensemble, *149*; fig. 169
Laredo, Ruth, 84
La Rocca, Donald J., 92–95
Larrocha, Alicia de, 84
La Tour, Georges de, *The Penitent Magdalen,* 32, *33,* 34; fig. 44
La Tour, Maurice Quentin de, *Jean Charles Garnier d'Isle, xiii*; fig. 2
Lauder, Leonard A. and Evelyn, 42, 43
Lawler, Louise, 136
Le Brun, Charles, 34
LeCorbeiller, Clare, 48
Lee, Natalie, 67
Lee, Sherman E. and Ruth, 7
Lee, Thomas H., 140
"Legacy of Genghis Khan, The: Art and Culture in Western Asia, 1256–1353" (exhibition), 108
Le Gray, Gustave, 139, 141
	Tree Study, Forest of Fontainebleau, 135, *138*; fig. 158
Lehman, Arnold, 148–49
Lehman, Philip and Carrie, 61, 65
Lehman, Robert, x, 61, 63, 130
Lehman, Robert, Collection, x, xi, 41, 61–64
	bequest of, 63–64
	P. de M.'s support of and commitment to, 63, 65, 67
	publication of, 65–67
Lehman, Robert, Foundation, x, 65, 67
Lehman, Robert, Wing, 61, *62*, 64; fig. 75
Lehman family town house, 61, 62, *62*, 63, 64, 65; fig. 73
Leochares, 19
Leonardo da Vinci, 45
"Leonardo da Vinci: Anatomical Drawings from the Royal Library, Windsor Castle" (exhibition), 44
"Leonardo da Vinci: Master Draftsman" (exhibition), 46
"Leonardo da Vinci: Nature Studies from the Royal Library at Windsor Castle" (exhibition), 44
Lerner, Martin, 99
Le Roy, Victor Martin, 23
Les Arts Florissants, 85

Le Secq, Henri, 135
"Lesley and Emma Schaefer Collection, The: A Selective Presentation" (exhibition), 51
Le Sueur, Eustache, *Rape of Tamar,* 34
"Letters in Gold: Ottoman Calligraphy from the Sakıp Sabancı Collection, Istanbul" (exhibition), 108
Levine, Harriette and Noel, 140
Levine, James, 84
Levitt, Helen, 135, 141
Levy, Leon, xiii, 16
Levy, Leon, and Shelby White Court, xiii, 16
Lewis, A. B., *Interior of an Elema Men's House with Spirit Boards (Hohao),* 124, 125; fig. 140
Lewis, Michal, 42
Lewis, R. E., 42
Lewisohn, Irene, 143
Lewisohn family, 130
Leyden, Lucas van, *The Archangel Gabriel Announcing the Birth of Christ,* 45, 46; fig. 57
Libin, Laurence, 75
Lieberman, William S., 130
"Liechtenstein: The Princely Collections" (exhibition), 38, 52
Liedtke, Walter, 38–41, *39*, 151
Lilyquist, Christine, 3
Limoges enamels, 24, 27
Limondjian, Hilde, xiii, 83–87
Lincoln, Abraham, 139
Lindsay, Rebecca and Richard, 111
Links, J. G., 151
Linsky, Jack and Belle, xii, 48
Linsky, Jack and Belle, Collection, xii, 41, 48
"Lions, Dragons and Other Beasts: Aquamanilia of the Middle Ages, Vessels for Church and Table" (exhibition), 24, 27
Lippi, Filippino, 46
Lissitzky, El, 140
Little, Charles T., 28
Llober, Miguel, 80
Lorenzetti, Pietro, *Crucifixion,* 36
Lorrain, Claude, 45
	View of La Crescenza, 34
Los Angeles County Museum of Art, 108
Lotto, Lorenzo, *Venus and Cupid,* 32, *33,* 36; fig. 43

"Louis Comfort Tiffany and Laurelton Hall" (exhibition), 69
Louis-Philippe, king of France, 54
Luce, Henry R., Center for the Study of American Art, 69, 73
Luce, Henry R., Foundation, 73
Ludwig, Christa, 83
Ludwig I, king of Bavaria, 61
Luers, William H., xii, xiii, *100*
"Luminous Image, The: Painted Glass Roundels in the Lowlands, 1480–1560" (exhibition), 27
Lundberg, W. Bruce and Delaney H., 140
Luxor Museum, Egypt, 5
Lysippos, 21
Lythgoe, Albert M., 3

Mace, Arthur C., 3
MacGregor, Neil, 10
Machiavelli, Niccolò, *Il Principe,* 105, 106, 108, 110, 111
Mackay, Ernst, 10
Macomber, William B., xi–xii
Madagascar Couple, 118, *118*; fig. 133
Maiano, Benedetto da, *Saint Jerome in the Wilderness,* 55
Mailey, Jean, 99
Maisky, Mischa, 83
majolica, in the Lehman Collection, 62, *62*, 65, *65*; figs. 74, 80
"Making Music: Two Centuries of Musical Instrument Making in New York" (exhibition), 80
"Making of an Exhibition, The" (P. de M. lecture), 83
Malbin, Lydia Winston, 130
"Manchu Dragon, The: Costumes of China— The Ch'ing Dynasty" (exhibition), 99
mandala, cosmological, with Mount Meru, Yuan dynasty, *102*, 103; fig. 116
Mander, Karel van, the Elder, 55
Manet, Édouard, 42, 131
"Manet," exhibition, *xi*, xii; fig. 1; catalogue, 151
Mangareva figure, 121
Manney, Richard and Gloria, 69, 71
Manning, Robert L. and Bertina Suida, 42
Man Ray, 136
	Rayograph, 140
Manship, Paul, 70

[162]

Mantegna, Andrea, 151
  Bacchanal with a Wine Vat, 42, *43*; fig. 54
Maria Christina, Archduchess of Austria, 54
Maria Feodorovna, Czarina, 54
Maria Pavolvna, Grand Duchess, 54
Markus, Frits and Rita, 41, 46
Marlborough Gallery, New York, 138
Marquand, Henry G., 16, 17, 41
Marshall, Sir John, 10
Martin, Richard, 144–45
Martineau, Jane, 151
Martini, Simone, *Madonna and Child*, 64, 65, *66*; fig. 81
Marville, Charles, 135
"Master Drawings from the Woodner Collection" (exhibition), 44
Master of the Playing Cards, 46
"Masterpieces of Fifty Centuries" (exhibition), x
"Masterpieces of Tapestry" (exhibition), x–xi
Masur, Kurt, 84
Mathurian standing Buddha, Gupta period, *96*, 97; fig. 109
Matisse, Henri, 131
  The Young Sailor II, *129*, 130; fig. 147
Matisse, Pierre and Maria-Gaetana, collection of, 130
Matta-Clark, Gordon, 136
Mayor, A. Hyatt, 42, 135
Mazarin, Cardinal Jules, 34
McBey, Marguerite, 107
McHenry, Barnabas, 130
McHenry, John, 135
McKim, Mead and White, 16, 19, 69
McKinney, David E., xiii
Meckenem, Israhel van, 46
"Medieval and Renaissance Treasures from the Victoria and Albert" (exhibition), 53
Medieval Art, Department of, 23–29
  acquisitions, 23, 24, 25
  Attarouthi Treasure, 25
  Belles Heures of Jean, Duc de Berry, 23, 28
  The Cloisters, 23–28, *27*; fig. 38
  exhibitions, 24–27, 65
  Hours of Jeanne d'Évreux, 23, 28
  Hunt of the Unicorn tapestries, 23, 28
  Jaharis, Mary and Michael, Galleries for Byzantine Art, *26*, 28; fig. 37
  Jaharis Byzantine Lectionary, *22*, 25; fig. 33
  Medieval Europe Gallery, 28–29, *29*; fig. 40
  P. de M.'s influence on, 23, 25, 29
  publications, 28, 151
Medieval Tapestries in The Metropolitan Museum of Art (collection catalogue), 28
Meech-Pekarik, Julia, 99
Meissen porcelain lions, *52*, 54; fig. 64
Meketra, tomb of, 3, 5
Melanesian art, gallery for, 120–21, *120*; fig. 135
Mellon, Andrew W., Foundation, 141
Memling, Hans, *Portrait of a Young Man*, 67, *67*; fig. 82
Menschel, Joyce and Robert, 43, 140
  Hall for Modern Photography, 141
Menshikov, Alexander, 55
Menuhin, Yehudi, 83
Menzel, Adolph, 46
Messinger, Lisa, 133
Metropolitan Museum of Art, The
  blockbuster exhibitions in, x, 38
  centennial of, x
  Charter, Constitution, and By-Laws of 1870, 151
  growth and expansion of, x, xii, xiii
  internal reorganization of, xi
  Merchants and Masterpieces (publication), 33
  partnership of president and director in, xii
  P. de M.'s career in, x, xiii, 31
"Mexico: Splendors of Thirty Centuries" (exhibition), xii
Meyer, André, Galleries, 127
Meyerson, Marlene Nathan, Family Foundation, 140
Michener, Charles, 86
Middle Kingdom (Egypt), royal heads, 6
Miller, Elizabeth and Richard, 73
Milles, Carl, 16
Mills, Ezra, 69
Minasian, Ralph, 108
Minassian, Adrienne, 106, 111
Mininberg, Anne W. and David T., 7
"Mirror of the Medieval World" (exhibition), 24
Mitchell, Jan, 113
  Treasury of Precolumbian Gold, *112*, 113–14; fig. 126
Mitsuhiro, Karasumaru, 79
MMArtists, 85
Mobil Foundation, Inc., 108
Moffet, Charles S., 151
Moholy-Nagy, László, 140
  Photogram, 136, *136*; fig. 156

Moldavian silver-gilt ewer and basin, 54
Monastery of Saint Catherine, Mount Sinai, 26
Monet, Claude, 131
  Garden at Sainte-Adresse, xi
Monroe, Marilyn, 138
Montebello, Edith de, *87*, 111; fig. 98
Montebello, Georges de, 83
Montebello, Philippe de
  awards and honors to, xiii
  birth and early years of, x
  and blockbuster exhibitions, x, 38
  and exhibitions, 38, *39*
  influence and legacy of, *see specific departments*
  leadership talents of, xiii, 56, 58, 69
  Metropolitan Museum career of, x, xi, xii, xiii
  retirement announced, 60
  and the universal museum, 10, 12, 15, 101
  vision of, 41
Montefeltro, Federico da, 50
Montespan, Madame de, 48
Monzini, Carlo, 118
Moore, Edward C., 17, 106
Moore, J. Kenneth, 75–81
Moreau, Jean-Michel, 145
Morgan, J. Pierpont, 17, 24, 29, 41, 61, 63, 107
Morgan Library, New York, 132
mosaic glass jar (Hellenistic), 17, *17*; fig. 22
Mughal bridle or belt ornaments, 108
Mughal dagger and sheath, 107, *107*; fig. 122
Mughal marble *jali* screen and basin, 107
Muhammad, Sultan, *Allegory of Worldly and Otherworldly Drunkenness*, 110
Munger, Jeffrey, 50
Musées de France, x
Museo del Prado, Madrid, xii
Museum of Fine Arts, Houston, x
Museum of Modern Art, New York, 128
Museum of the City of New York, 69
"Museums: Why Should We Care?" (P. de M. lecture), 83
Mushekian, Margaret, 107
Musica Antiqua Köln, 85
Musical Instruments, Department of, 75–81
  Amati Group, 77, 79
  Amati violin, 76–77, *76*, *77*; figs. 90, 91
  exhibitions, 75–76, 79–80
  Guarneri del Gesù violins, 75–76, 84
  Hauser guitar, 80–81, *81*; fig. 94

[163]

koto, 79, *79*; fig. 93
organology in, 75
P. de M.'s involvement in, 75, 80, *81*; fig. 94
qin, 77–79; Prince Lu *qin*, 78–79
Tielke cittern, *74*, 80; fig. 89
Myers, Mary L., 42

Nadar, 135, 139, 141
Naef, Weston J., 42, 135
Nage people, ancestral couple, *119*; fig. 134
Namath, Hans, photograph by, *49*; fig. 61
Nash, Ogden, 86, 87
Nectanebo I and II, pharaohs, 8
Nefertiti, queen of Egypt, 14
Nègre, Charles, 135
Negroli, Filippo, 92–93
Neighborhood Playhouse, New York, 143
Newbery, Timothy, 66
New Britain bark-cloth effigy, 120
Newman, Muriel Kallis Steinberg, Collection, xii, 130, *130*; fig. 148
Newman, Sasha M., 42
Newton, Douglas, 119
"New Vision, The: Photography Between the World Wars, Ford Motor Company Collection at The Metropolitan Museum of Art" (exhibition), xii, 42, 136
New York, City of, xii, 28, 73
"New York Collects" (annual exhibition), 31
"New York Painting and Sculpture: 1940–1970" (exhibition), x, 129
New York University, Institute of Fine Arts, x, 65, 67
Nilsson, Birgit, 83
Nine Heroes tapestries, 28
Nineteenth- and Twentieth-Century European Drawings (collection catalogue), 67
Nineteenth- and Twentieth-Century European Paintings (collection catalogue), 67
Nineteenth-Century, Modern, and Contemporary Art, Department of, 127–33
acquisitions, 129–32
Annenberg, Walter H. and Leonore, Collection Galleries, *127*, 130–31; fig. 143
growth and development of, 127, 129–30, 132–33
Heinz, Henry J., II, Galleries, 127, 132–33
P. de M.'s influence on, 127, 130, 131, 132, *132*, 133; fig. 151

"19th-Century America" (exhibition), x
N'kondi power figure, 117
"Nurse's" Qu'ran, 111

Oceanic art, 119–21
Oceanic Heritage Foundation, 73
Oettingen-Wallerstein collection, 24
Offin, Charles Z., 42
oinochoe (jug; Roman), 18, *19*; fig. 25
Oistrakh, David, 83
O'Keeffe, Georgia, 137–38
O'Keeffe, Georgia, Foundation, 138
Old Kingdom (Egypt), lion sculpture, 7
Oliveira, Elmar, 75
Olivier, Ferdinand, 46
O'Neill, John P., xiii, 151–54
Oppenheim, Adela, 9
Oppenheim, Dennis, 136
Oppenordt, Alexandre-Jean, 54
Orange, His Royal Highness The Prince of, 39
Orpheus Chamber Orchestra, *82*, 83, 87; fig. 95
Osservanza Master, 64
O'Sullivan, Timothy, 140
Geographical and Geological Explorations and Surveys West of the 100th Meridian. Season of 1871, 135
Ottoman "animal" carpet, 111
Ottoman short sword (*yatagan*), 89

Packard, Harry G. C., Collection of Asian Art, 97, 99
Paganini, Niccolò, 75
"Pages of Perfection: Islamic Paintings and Calligraphy from the Russian Academy of Sciences, St. Petersburg" (exhibition), 108
Pahlavi, Farah, Empress of Iran, *106*; fig. 120
"Painterly Print, The: Monotypes from the Seventeenth to the Twentieth Century" (exhibition), 42
Pajou, Augustin, *Bearded Elder*, 55
palanquin finials, 110
Palladino, Pia, 67
Palma di Cesnola, Luigi, 16
Pan-Asian Collection, 99
panel with hunting scenes, 24, *27*; fig. 39
Parker, James, 48
Parmigianino, 46
Pasqualini, Marcantonio, 37

Patronato de la Alhambra y Generalife, Granada, 108
Pavarotti, Luciano, 84
Payson, Joan Whitney, Galleries, 69
Pelletan, Eugène, 135
Peluso, Ignazio, 55
"Pen and Parchment: Drawing in the Middle Ages" (exhibition), 28
pendant mask of queen mother Idia (Iyoba), 115–16, *115*; fig. 129
Penn, Irving, 138, 141
Perahia, Murray, 83, 84
Percier, Charles, 50
"Perfect Documents: Walker Evans and African Art" (exhibition), 123–24
Perino del Vaga, 44
Perkins, Richard S., xi
Perlman, Itzhak, 75, 83, 84
Perlman, Toby, 84
Perls, Mr. and Mrs. Klaus G., 116, 130
Permoser, Balthasar, 55
Marsyas, 55, *55*; fig. 67
Perneb, tomb of, *4*, 6, *7*; fig. 5
Perugino, 45
Peter of Sassoferrato, chalice, 23
Petrie, Carroll and Milton, European Sculpture Court, xii, 48, *49*; fig. 61
Petrie, William Flinders, 7
Pfeiffer Fund, 111
Phifer, Jean Parker, 73
"Philippe de Montebello Years, The: Curators Celebrate Three Decades of Acquisitions" (exhibition), vii, *150*, 151; fig. 170
Phillips, Christopher, 42
Phipps, Elena, 52, 56
Photographs, Department of, xii, 135–41
acquisitions, 135–40
establishment of, 43
exhibitions, 139, 140, 141
Friends group of, 140
Menschel Hall for Modern Photography, 141
and new media, 141
P. de M.'s influence on, xii, 135, 138, 140, 141
preservation, analysis, and conservation lab, 141
Photograph Study Collection, 122–25
PianoForte series, 86–87

[164]

Picasso, Pablo, 43, 131
Pickvance, Ronald, 151
Picón, Carlos A., 16–21
"Pictures Generation," 136
"Picturing Paradise: Colonial Photography of Samoa 1875–1925" (exhibition), 123
Pierce, Mrs. Hayford, 107
"Pierre Bonnard: The Graphic Art" (exhibition), 42
Pietà (limestone), 24
Pieter Bruegel the Elder: Drawings and Prints (exhibition catalogue), *153*; fig. 173
Piranesi, Giovanni Battista, 45
Pistrucci, Benedetto, *Head of the Medusa,* 55
plaque, brass, depicting an oba, 116
Pletnev, Mikhail, 84, 86
Plotnick, Harvey B., 110
Poel, Egbert van der, 38
Pogorelich, Ivo, 87
Poiret, Denise, 147–48, 149
Poiret, Paul, 147–48
  "Irudrée" evening gown, *149*; fig. 168
  "La Perse" coat, *148*; fig. 166
  "Manteau d'Auto" coat, *149*; fig. 167
"Poiret: King of Fashion" (exhibition), 148, *148*, *149*; figs. 166, 167, 168
Poitiers, Diane de, 58
Polke, Sigmar, 136
Pollens, Stewart, 75
Pollock, Jackson, 130
  Autumn Rhythm, 128
Polsky, Cynthia Hazen, 110, 130, 140
Pontormo, 45
Pope-Hennessy, Sir John, 35, 38, 65, 127
"Portraits by Ingres: Image of an Epoch," exhibition, 145; catalogue, 151
Posnansky, Arthur, *Sun Door, Tiahuanaco, 125*; fig. 141
Posner, Donald, 65, 67
Possessing the Past: Treasures from the National Palace Museum, Taipei (exhibition catalogue), 151
Posthorn, Stanley, 130
Pound, Ezra, 138
Poussin, Nicolas, 45
  The Companions of Rinaldo, 32
"Poussin: Works on Paper. Drawings from the Collection of Her Majesty Queen Elizabeth II" (exhibition), 46

Poussin and Nature: Arcadian Visions (exhibition catalogue), 151, 154; fig. 175
"Prague, The Crown of Bohemia, 1347–1437" (exhibition), 24, 26
Prendergast, Eugénie, Exhibitions of American Art, 70
Pressler, Menahem, 84
Preti, Mattia, *Pilate Washing His Hands,* 37
Price, Jessie and Charles, 46
Price, Leontyne, 84
Primordial Couple, 115
Prince, Richard, 136
Prince Lu *qin,* 78–79
"Princely Splendor: The Dresden Court, 1580–1620" (exhibition), 52–53
"Print in the North, The: Age of Albrecht Dürer and Lucas van Leyden" (exhibition), 46
Prints, Photographs, and Drawings, Department of, 42–44
  acquisitions, 42–43, 44
  and Department of Drawings, 43–44
  evolution of, 42, 43, 45
  exhibitions, 42
  P. de M.'s influence on, 42, 47
  photography collection in, 43; *see also* Photographs, Department of
  publications, 42, 44
"Prints of Vija Celmins, The" (exhibition), 46
Prud'hon, Pierre-Paul, 33, 132
publications, *150*, 151–54
  P. de M.'s influence on, xii, 38, 65, 70, 151–52
  representative listing, 152–54
  see also specific departments
Pulak, Cemal, 14
Pulitzer, Joseph, Bequest, 111
Purcell, Henry, 84
Pyhrr, Stuart W., 38, 89–92, 93

Rabinow, Rebecca A., 133
Rafferty, Emily K., xiii, 56
Raggio, Olga, 38, 48, *49*, 50, 51, 58, 60, 111
Ramesses II, king of Egypt, 15
Ramírez, Manuel, guitar, 80
Rampal, Jean-Pierre, 84
Rapa Nui (Easter Island), male figure, 119, *121*; fig. 136

Raphael, 38, 45
  The Miraculous Draft of Fishes, 52
Rasmussen, Jörg, 65
Ratti, Antonio, 56
Ratti, Antonio, Textile Center, 50, 56–57, *56*; fig. 68
Rauschenberg, Robert, 129
  Winter Pool, 132; fig. 152
Ray, Charles, 136
Recent Acquisitions (MMA publication), 32, 42
Redlin, Michel, Baroque casket, 54
Rekhmire, tomb of, facsimile painting from, 11, *11*; fig. 12
"Rembrandt/Not Rembrandt in The Metropolitan Museum of Art" (exhibition), 38, *39*, 40; fig. 50
Rembrandt van Rijn, 41, 46, 64
  Aristotle with a Bust of Homer, 36, *39*; fig. 50
  follower of: *Portrait of a Man ("The Auctioneer"), 39*; fig. 50
"Renaissance Ornament Prints and Drawings" (exhibition), 42
Renaissance Revival parlor, 69
Reni, Guido, 44
  Charity, 37
  Immaculate Conception, 36
Renoir, Pierre-Auguste, 128, 131
"Resplendence of the Spanish Monarchy: Renaissance Tapestries and Armor" (exhibition), 52
Revere, Paul, Jr., silver tea urn, 71
Rewald, Sabine, 133
rhyton (Turkmenistan), 11, *12*; fig. 14
Ribera, Jusepe de, 34
Richardson, Frank R., 54
Richman, Fred and Rita, 119
Richter, Gisela M. A., 16
Richter, Sviatoslav, 84
Rieder, William, 50
Riemenschneider, Tilman, 27
ring (Hellenistic), *20*, 21; fig. 28
ring with intaglio portrait of Tiberius (Roman), *20*, 21; fig. 29
Rippner, Samantha, 46
ritual figure (4th century B.C.–early Ptolemaic Period), *6*, 8; fig. 8
Riza-i 'Abbasi, Study of a bird, 107, *107*; fig. 121

[165]

Robinson, Duncan, 67
Robinson, Edward, 16
Robinson, Theodore, *Low Tide, Riverside Yacht Club,* 71
Roche, Kevin, 6, 73, 99
Rockefeller, John D., Jr., 23, 61
Rockefeller, John D., Sr., 69
Rockefeller, Michael C., 120
Rockefeller, Michael C., Memorial Collection of Primitive Art, x, xi, 115–17
Rockefeller, Michael C., Wing, x, xii, 113, 122, 123, 127
Rockefeller, Nelson A., 113, 115–18
Rococo Revival room, 69
Rococo wall lights, 54
Rodchenko, Alexander, 140
"Rodin: The B. Gerald Cantor Collection" (exhibition), 51
Rogers, Jacob S., 140
Rogers Fund, 111
Roman amphora, 17
Rorimer, James R., 3
Rosa, Salvator
    Bandits on a Rocky Coast, 36
    Dream of Aeneas, 37
    Self-Portrait, 36
Rosen, Mr. and Mrs. Jonathan P., 7, 8
Rosenberg, Pierre, 151
Rosenheim, Jeff, 140
Rosenkranz, Robert, 140
Rosenthal, Nan, 133
Ross, Alex, 85, 86
Rossellini, Isabella, 83, 87
Rossini, Gioacchino, 135
Rothko, Mark, 130
Rothstein, Edward, 84
Rousseau, Theodore, Jr., x, 61, 63
Rubel Collection, 136–37
Rubens, Peter Paul, 46, 52, 138
    A Forest at Dawn with a Deer Hunt, 35–36, *40*; fig. 51
    Rubens, His Wife Helena Fourment, and Their Daughter Clara Joanna, *30, 32, 35*; fig. 42
Ruff, Thomas, 136
Ruisdael, Jacob van, 41, 46
Russell, Jennifer, 56
Russell, John, 108
Ruttenberg, Janet, 42

Sabah, Shaykh Nasser al-, 106
Sacchi, Andrea, 37
Sachsen-Teschen, Albert Casimir, Duke of, 54
Sackler, Arthur M., Museum, Harvard University, 110
Sackler Galleries for Asian Art, The, 99
Sackler Wing, The, x, xii, 3
saddle (Tibet or China), 95, *95*; fig. 108
Safavid glazed ceramic water-pipe, 110
Saffiotti, Maria Francesca, 67
Saint-Aubin, Gabriel Jacques, 32, 42
Saint-Gaudens, Augustus, 70
    Diana, 71
Saint-Saëns, Camille, *Carnival of the Animals,* 82, 86, 87; figs. 95, 97
Saleh, Magda, 7
Salz, Sam, Foundation, 140
Salzmann, Auguste, 139
Sander, August, 136, 140, 141
Sanders, Samuel, 84
Sansai, Hosokawa, 79
Sargent, John Singer, 70, 71
    Mrs. Hugh Hammersley, 71
Saul, Mr. and Mrs. Andrew M., 140
Savall, Jordi, 85
Say, Fazil, 86
Schaefer, Lesley and Emma, Collection, 51
Schenk von Stauffenberg family, 55
Schiff, András, 83, 86–87
Schiff, David, 44
Schimmel, Norbert, 8, 106
Schinkel, Karl Friedrich, 50
Schliemann, Heinrich, 10
Schoenborn, Florene M., 130
Schoenborn-Buchheim, Edith Macy, 107
School of Paris, 130
Schuster, Peter-Klaus, 10
Schwartz, Barbara, 130
Scull, Robert and Ethel, 129
Sculpture and Decorative Arts (collection catalogue), 67
"Search for Alexander, The" (exhibition), 38
Sears, Adeline Harris, autograph quilt, *70*, 71; fig. 84
Seeley, George, *Winter Landscape,* 140
Segovia, Andrés, 80–81, *81*, 83, *85*; figs. 94, 96
Segovia, Emilita, Marquesa of Salobreña, 80, *85*; fig. 96

Selden, Mrs. Carl, 44
"Selections from the Permanent Collection of Indian and Southeast Asian Art" (exhibition), 99
Seley, Louis E., Theresa S., Hervey, and Eliot Jay, 106
Seley, Louis E. and Theresa S., Purchase Fund for Islamic Art, 111
Seley Carpet, 106
Senwosret III, king of Egypt, pyramid of, *8*, 9, *9*; figs. 10, 11
Serkin, Peter, 83, 84
Serkin, Rudolf, 84
Seurat, Georges-Pierre, 131
    Study for "Les Poseuses," *63*, 64; fig. 77
17th Century Italian Drawings in The Metropolitan Museum of Art (collection catalogue), 44
Shackleton, Ernest, 122
Shaker retiring room, 69
Sharp, Peter J., Foundation, 73
Shaw, James Byam, 65
Sheeler, Charles, 141
    Upper Deck, 140
Shepherd, Mary B., 28
Sherman, Cindy, 136
Siegel, Jeffrey, 84
Sills, Beverly, 84
Simmons, Laurie, 136
Simonson, Lee, 143
Simpson, Prof. William Kelly, 9
Sims, Lowery, 129
Sinauer, Barbara, 71
Singer, Dr. Joseph I., 43
Siskind, Aaron, 135
Sithathoryunet, Princess, 6
Smith, Steve, 85
Smithson, Robert, 136
Soldani, Massimiliano, 52
Sonnabend, Martin, 44
Sonnenburg, Hubert von, 40
Soulier, Charles, 135
Soultanian, Jack, 28
Spanish flintlock gun, 89, 92; detail, *91*; figs. 103, 104
"Spanish Guitar, The/La Guitarra Española" (exhibition), 81
Spear, Nathaniel, 107
Specht, James, 122

Sperling, Harry G., Fund, 44
Spertus, Anita E., 119
Spielvogel, Barbaralee Diamonstein, 130
Spiering, Frans, workshop of, *Liberation of Oriane,* 55
"Splendid Legacy: The Havemeyer Collection" (exhibition), 40–41
"Splendor of Dresden, The: Five Centuries of Art Collecting" (exhibition), 51–52
Spranger, Bartholomeus, 46
Staatliche Kunstsammlungen, Dresden, 52–53
Staatliche Museen zu Berlin, 10, 27
Stade, Frederica von, 83
Standen, Edith, 57–58
Starker, Janos, 83
Starn, Doug and Mike, *Horses,* 136
stationery box, Joseon dynasty (Korea), 101, *102;* fig. 117
Steichen, Edward, *Rodin—The Thinker,* 140
Steiger, Heidi S., 140
Stein, Perrin, 46
Stein, Susan Alyson, 46, 133
Steiner, Alice F., 44
Stella, Frank, 129
Sterling, Charles, 67
Stern, Isaac, 75, 83
Stieglitz, Alfred, 42, 135, 137–38, 141
Stieglitz, Alfred, Society, 140
Stieglitz Collection, 135, 136
Still, Clyfford, 130
Stone, George Cameron, 94
Storer, Ebenezer and Elizabeth Green, 71
Strand, Paul, 140, 141
Abstraction, Twin Lakes, Connecticut, 136
Strasbourg Cathedral, choir screen, 24
Strauss, Anne L., 133
Stravinsky, Igor, 138
Struth, Thomas, 141
San Zaccaria, Venice, 136, *137;* fig. 157
Stuart, Gilbert, 70
Captain John Gell, 71
Stuffmann, Margret, 44
Sugimoto, Hiroshi, 141
Süleyman the Magnificent, 89
Sully, Thomas, 71
Sulzberger, Arthur Ochs, xii, xiii
Sulzberger, Arthur Ochs, Gallery, 89, 94
Sutherland, Joan, 83
Sweerts, Michiel, *Clothing the Naked,* 36

sword (Tibet or China), 92, *94;* fig. 106
Szabo, George, 63, 65

Taburet-Delahaye, Elisabeth, 27
Tafelmusik, 85
talatats (relief blocks; Amarna Period), 5, 8; figs. 6, 7
Talbot, Charles, 67
Talbot, William Henry Fox, 137, 139, 141
Talleyrand-Périgord, Charles-Maurice de, 33
Talyarkhan, Shamina, 111
Tananbaum, Doris and Stanley, 73
Tang, Frances Young, Gallery, 103
"Tapestry in the Baroque: Threads of Splendor" (exhibition), 52, 58, *60;* fig. 71
"Tapestry in the Renaissance: Art and Magnificence" (exhibition), 52, *57,* 58; fig. 69
Tarnopol, Alexander and Grégoire, 44
Taylor, Billy, 84
Taylor, Francis Henry, 16, 128
Teijo, Gotō (attrib.), koto and accessories, *78, 79;* fig. 92
Tempesti, Anna Forlani, 66
temple attendants (China), *102,* 103; fig. 115
Temple of Dendur, x, xii, 3, 5
Tenenbaum, Ann, 140
Teo Kheng Chong, 78
Terian, Juliana and Peter, 73
textiles and tapestries, 56–60
  acquisitions, 60
  Antonio Ratti Textile Center, 50, 56–57, *56;* fig. 68
  Conservation Department, 52, 56, 57
  exhibitions, 58, 60
  Islamic fragments, 111
  P. de M.'s influence on, 56, 58, 60
  Textile Study Room, 57
Teynard, Félix, 139
Thaw, Eugene V., 132
Thayer, Scofield, 43
Thelot, Johann Andreas, 53, 54
Thorvaldsen, Bertel, *Nessus Abducting Deianaira,* 55
Three Women at the Tomb (ivory panel), 23
Thurman, Christa C. Mayer, 67
Thutmose III, wives of, jewelry, 14–15, *15;* fig. 19
Tiberius, Roman emperor, 19, *20,* 21; fig. 29

Tibetan arms and armor, 89, 92–95, *93, 94, 95;* figs. 105, 106, 107, 108
Tielke, Joachim, cittern, *74,* 80; fig. 89
Tiepolo, Giambattista, 64, 65
Tiepolo, Giovanni Domenico, xii
  A Dance in the Country, 32
  frescoed ceiling, Residenz, Würzburg, 36
  The Rest on the Flight into Egypt, 64, *64;* fig. 78
Tiffany, Louis Comfort, 69, 70, 72
"Tilman Riemenschneider: Master Sculptor of the Late Middle Ages" (exhibition), 27
Tinterow, Gary, 127–33, *132,* 151; fig. 151
Tisch Galleries, xii
Titian, 45, 138
Tobey, David and Julie, 46
Tokyo String Quartet, 84
Tomatsu, Shomei, 135, 141
Tomkins, Calvin, *Merchants and Masterpieces: The Story of the Metropolitan Museum of Art,* 33
Tomlinson, Janis A., 67
Tommasini, Anthony, 85
torso of a general (Egyptian, Late Period), *7,* 8; fig. 9
Tournachon, Adrien, *Self-Portrait,* 139
Townsend, John, 70
  dining table, 71
Townsend, Thomas, Newport chest-on-chest, 71, *71;* fig. 85
Tracy, Berry B., 69
"Treasures from the Kremlin: An Exhibition from the State Museums of the Moscow Kremlin" (exhibition), 52
"Treasures of Tutankhamun" (exhibition), xii, 3, 9
"Treasures of the World: Jeweled Art of India in the Age of the Mughals" (exhibition), 108
Troy, Jean François de
  The Declaration of Love, 31, 32; fig. 41
  The Garter, 31, 32; fig. 41
Tucker, Paul, 67
Tula, center table, 54, *54;* fig. 66
Tully, Alice, Foundation, 28
Turčić, Lawrence, 44
Tureck, Rosalyn, 84
Turkish Iznik plate, 111, *111;* fig. 125
Turkoman jewelry, 111

Turner, J. M. W., 137
Twentieth-Century Art, Department of, 129
"Twentieth-Century Modern Masters: The Jacques and Natasha Gelman Collection" (exhibition), xii
"Two Worlds of Andrew Wyeth: Kuerners and Olsons" (exhibition), xi
Tyler, Kenneth, 130

Uchida, Mitsuko, 83, 84
Ugolino da Siena, 64
Ukawa, Hidetoshi, *100*
Uluburun shipwreck, objects from, 13–14, *15*; fig. 20
Unicorn tapestries, 23, 28
Universal Limited Art Editions (ULAE), 43
"universal museum," 10–15, 101
Untermyer, Irwin, 48, 50, 51

Vallou de Villeneuve, Julien, 135
Vanderbilt family, 72
Vanderlyn, John, *Panoramic View of the Palace and Gardens of Versailles*, 6, 71
"Van Gogh in Arles," exhibition, xii; catalogue, 151
Van Gogh in Saint-Rémy and Auvers (exhibition catalogue), 151
Vanuatu slit gong, 121
Vasaro, Giovanni Maria, workshop of, majolica bowl, 65, *65*; fig. 80
"Vasemania: Neoclassical Form and Ornament in Europe, Selections from The Metropolitan Museum of Art" (exhibition), 53–54
"Vatican Collections: The Papacy and Art" (exhibition), xii, 52
Vaughn, Mr. and Mrs. James M., Jr., 9
Vaux, Calvert, 29
Velázquez, Diego Rodriguez de Silva y, 34
Juan de Pareja, xi, 33, 36
"Velázquez," exhibition, xii; catalogue, 151
Veneziano, Jacometto, 65
Vengerov, Maxim, 84
"Venice and the Islamic World, 828–1797" (exhibition), 108
Verité, Pierre, 117
Vermeer, Johannes, *Study of a Young Woman*, 31, 32, 36, 41, *41*; fig. 52

"Vermeer and the Delft School," exhibition, 38, *39*; 49; catalogue, 151
Victoria, queen of England, 71
video art, 141
Villazón, Rolando, 83
"Vincent van Gogh: The Drawings" (exhibition), 46
"Violin Masterpieces of Guarneri del Gesù" (exhibition), 75–76
Voronikhin, Andrei Nikiforovich, 54
Vouet, Simon, 34
Vreeland, Diana, 99, 143, 144, 145
Vries, Adriaen de, 52

Waddell, John C., 130, 136
"Waking Dream, The: Photography's First Century. Selections from the Gilman Paper Company Collection" (exhibition), 42, 139, 140
Walker, Daniel, 108, 110
Walker, Dr. Roxie, 9
"Walker Evans" (exhibition), 140
Wall, Jeff, 136, 141
Wallace, Lila Acheson, x, xii, 3, 130
Wallace, Lila Acheson, Gift, 111
Wallace, Lila Acheson, Wing, xii, 127, 130, 133
Wallace Funds, xii
Wallraf, Paul, 65
Walter, Paul W., 42
Wang, C. C., Family Collection, 97
Wang, Lulu C. and Anthony W., 73
Wang Hui, *The Kangxi Emperor's Southern Inspection Tour*, 97
Ward, John Quincy Adams, 70
Wardropper, Ian, 48–55, 60
Warhol, Andy, 129, 138
war mask (Mongolia or Tibet), 94, *95*; fig. 107
Warner Communications, Inc., 43
"Warriors of the Himalayas: Rediscovering the Arms and Armor of Tibet" (exhibition), 92, *93*, 95; fig. 105
Watkins, Carleton, 135, 140, 141
Watt, James C. Y., 97, 100, 101–3, 151
Watts, André, 84
Waverly Consort, 85
Webb, Virginia-Lee, 122–25
Weber, John, 25
Weindling, Liana, 7

Weir, J. Alden, 70
Weitzmann, Kurt, 25
Welch, Edith, 108
Welch, Stuart Cary, 106–8, 110
Wheeler, Candace, 70
Whistler, James McNeill, 42
White, Shelby, xiii, 16
Whitehouse, David B., 67, 108
Whitney, Wheelock, 132
Whitney Museum of American Art, New York, 128
Wiener, Malcolm H., 9
Wigmore, Barrie, 73
Wigmore, Deedee, 69, 73
Wilkinson, Charles K. and Irma, 106
"William Blake" (exhibition), 46
Williams, Dave and Reba, 130
Wilmering, Antoine, 50
Winlock, Herbert E., 3, 5
Witte, Emanuel de, 38
Wixom, William D., 23, 26, 151
Wolf, Erving and Joyce, Gallery, 69, 70, 73
Wolf, Marilyn and Marshall, 111
Wolfe, Catharine Lorillard, 128
Wolfe Fund, 131
Wolff, Martha, 67
Woodner Collection, 44
Woolley, Sir Leonard, 10
Worth, Irene, 83
Wright, Faith-dorian and Martin, 119
Wright, Frank Lloyd, 69, 70
Francis Little house, 73
Wrightsman, Charles, xii, 31–32, 48, 54
Wrightsman, Jayne, xii, 24, 31–33, 36, 48, 50, 53, 54, 132
Wrightsman Fund, 33
Wrightsman Galleries, 48, 50, *51*, 53, 145; fig. 63
Wunderman, Lester, 115, 123
Würth, Ignaz Josef, wine coolers, 54–55

Yasukawa, Takeshi, *100*
"Year 1200, The" (exhibition), x
Ysaÿe, Eugène, 75
Yūsai, Hosokawa, 79

Zaharia, Florica, 57
Zhang Biaorong, 98
Zuckerberg, Roy J., 73

PHOTOGRAPH CREDITS

Unless otherwise specified, all photographs were supplied by the owners of the works of art, who hold the copyright thereto, and are reproduced with permission. We have made every effort to obtain permissions for all copyright-protected images. If you have copyright-protected work in this publication and you have not given us permission, please contact the Metropolitan Museum's Editorial Department. Photographs of works in the Metropolitan Museum's collection are by The Photograph Studio, The Metropolitan Museum of Art. Additional photograph credits appear here.

Dieter Arnold: fig. 10

Photograph courtesy of BP: fig. 49

Courtesy Center for Creative Photography, University of Arizona, © 1991 Hans Namuth Estate: fig. 61

© Walker Evans Archive, The Metropolitan Museum of Art: fig. 155

© Jasper Johns/Licensed by VAGA, New York, NY: fig. 153

Sara Krulwich, NYT Pictures: fig. 1

Evan Lee: fig. 160

Photograph © 1986 Richard Lombard: fig. 94

© The New York Times: cover, frontispiece

Photograph by Don Pollard: figs. 95, 97, 114

Stan Ries: fig. 120

Star Black Photography: fig. 113

© Thomas Struth: fig. 157

© 2003 Succession H. Matisse, Paris/Artists Rights Society (ARS), New York: fig. 147

SANTIAGO CALATRAVA
SCULPTURE INTO ARCHITECTURE